Casebook in Abnormal Psychology

List of Related Titles

Abnormal Psychology

Abnormal Psychology: An Integrative Approach, 2nd ed.,
   by Barlow/Durand
Abnormal Psychology: An Introduction, 2nd ed.,
   by Durand/Barlow
Looking into Abnormal Psychology: Contemporary Readings,
   by Lilienfeld
Seeing Both Sides: Classic Controversies in Abnormal Psychology,
   by Lilienfeld

Psychopathology

Seeing Both Sides: Classic Controversies in Abnormal Psychology,
   by Lilienfeld

Clinical Behavior Disorders/Child Psychopathology

Abnormal Child Psychology,
   by Mash/Wolfe
Casebook in Child Behavior Disorders,
   by Kearney

Clinical Psychology

Clinical Psychology: Concepts, Methods, and Profession, 6th ed.,
   by Trull/Phares

Personality

Personality, 5th ed.,
   by Jerry Burger
Personality: Strategies and Issues, 8th ed.,
   by Liebert/Spiegler, as revised by Liebert/Liebert
Theories of Personality, 7th ed.,
   by Ryckman
Theories of Personality, 7th ed.,
   by Schultz/Schultz

This text may be ordered with our titles in Abnormal Psychology at a special discount. Please consult our website for the name of your local sales rep: http://www.psychology.wadsworth.com

Casebook in Abnormal Psychology

Timothy A. Brown
Boston University

David H. Barlow
Boston University

WADSWORTH

✳

™

THOMSON LEARNING

Australia • Canada • Mexico • Singapore • Spain • United Kingdom • United States

WADSWORTH

THOMSON LEARNING™

Sponsoring Editor: *Marianne Taflinger*	Interior Design: *Graphic World Publishing Services*
Marketing Manager: *Mark Linsenman*	
Editorial Assistant: *Stacy Green*	Cover Design: *Laurie Albrecht*
Production Editor: *Kirk Bomont*	Cover Photo: *Photodisc*
Production Service: *Graphic World Publishing Services*	Print Buyer: *Kris Waller*
	Typesetting: *Graphic World Inc.*
Permissions Editor: *Sue Ewing*	Printing and Binding: *Webcom*

For more information about this or any other Wadsworth products, contact:
WADSWORTH
511 Forest Lodge Road
Pacific Grove, CA 93950
USA
www.wadsworth.com
1-800-423-0563 (Thomson Learning Academic Resource Center)

Printed in Canada

10   9   8   7   6

Library of Congress Cataloging-in-Publication Data

Brown, Timothy A., [date]
    Casebook in abnormal psychology / Timothy A. Brown, David H. Barlow.
        p. cm.
    Includes bibliographical references and indexes.
    ISBN 0-534-36316-4
        1. Psychology, Pathological—Case studies.   2. Psychiatry—Case studies.
    I. Barlow, David H.   II. Title.

RC465 .B76 2001
616.89—dc21   00-049402

For Bonnie, Mom, and Grandma F.
(peas in a pod)

T. A. B.

To my students, present and past,
whose questions have helped
advance our science and practice

D. H. B.

About the Authors

Timothy A. Brown is Director of Research and Associate Director of the Center for Anxiety and Related Disorders and Research Professor at Boston University. He has published numerous scientific articles and chapters in the area of anxiety disorders. He has been a consultant to the National Institute of Mental Health on the evaluation of psychosocial and pharmacological treatments of anxiety disorders, and he has served as a consultant in large-scale projects focusing on the assessment and diagnosis of the anxiety disorders and using DSM-IV. In addition, he was a member of the DSM-IV Anxiety Disorders Advisory Committee for generalized anxiety disorder and mixed anxiety depression and the DSM-IV Text Revision. Recently, his research has focused on the classification of anxiety and mood disorders, methodological advances in the evaluation of short- and long-term outcome of treatments for anxiety disorders, and the causes, nature, and course of anxiety and mood disorders.

David H. Barlow is a world-renowned psychologist recognized as a leader and pioneer in the field of clinical psychology. He is Professor of Psychology and Director of Clinical Training Programs, as well as Director of the Center for Anxiety and Related Disorders at Boston University. He received his B.A. from the University of Notre Dame, his M.A. from Boston College, and his Ph.D. from the University of Vermont.

In honor of his excellence in scholarship, he was awarded the National Institute of Mental Health Merit Award. In 1988 he received an Award for Excellence in Research from the State University of New York. In 1989 he was awarded the Distinguished Scientist Award from the Society for a Science of Clinical Psychology of the American Psychological Association. He has published more than 300 scholarly articles and books in his career to date.

Brief Contents

Contents

Preface

Real Patients, Real Cases—In Rich Clinical Detail

All of the cases presented in this book are based on actual clinical histories and treatment outcomes, although patient names and identifying characteristics (e.g., demographics such as age, occupation, and marital/family history) have been changed to ensure confidentiality. The wide range of DSM-IV disorders discussed in the book is presented using an integrative approach that emphasizes how multidimensional influences that are interrelated and interacting (e.g., genetic, biological, social learning) combine into unified models of the causes and maintenance of the disorder and its treatment.

To keep the chapters at a readable length, we exclude the details of life history that do not affect onset, maintenance, or treatment outcome of the patient's disorder. However, we offer rich detail and explanations on the conceptualization, process, and outcome of treatment—far beyond what is typically seen in casebooks of this type.

A variety of treatments, both pharmacological and psychosocial, exist for most of the disorders discussed in this book. However, in most cases, the treatments presented here represent the most effective interventions developed to date for each particular disorder, as documented by the scientific literature. Nevertheless, in accord with the reality of clinical practice, the reader will note considerable variation in the extent to which patients improve.

Appreciating the Complexity of Diagnosis

Because many teachers of abnormal psychology frequently use cases in their quizzes, tests, midterms, and final exams, the final two cases provide only the clinical histories, not the diagnoses and treatment conceptualizations. These cases, Cases 18 and 19, are intended to be used as teaching tools to give students an opportunity to consider differential diagnosis and treatment planning of the cases described. The purpose of these "unsolved cases" is to stimulate class discussion on the complexities and vagaries in emotional disorders and to give an *appreciation of the complexity of diagnosis*. Case 18 is written as an "easier" case, perhaps similar to case snippets that are used in testing situations, whereas Case 19 is a more difficult differential diagnosis that may be used for extra credit or for more advanced students (the solutions to these two cases are available to the instructor on our website in the instructor area).

Changes in the Second Edition: A New Case and New Critical Thinking Questions

Based on the response to the first edition, we have dropped a less viable diagnosis and substituted a requested case on domestic violence (Case 6). Although domestic violence is not an official DSM-IV category, it is a designated area of study at the Centers for Disease Control and a troubling social problem. Because clinical psychologists can offer some useful treatments for this problem, we are pleased to present this case in this edition, and we welcome your comments about it.

Likewise, you will notice that we have added critical thinking questions at the end of every case to stimulate the student's thinking about the complexity and rich detail of these real cases and about what they may mean.

InfoTrac for Extended Research

As a part of the publisher's services, InfoTrac College Edition is available free of charge to students who purchase this casebook. InfoTrac is a fully searchable online university library that contains complete articles and images from over 700 scholarly and popular publications. Such access can help students with their independent research on topics relevant to abnormal psychology. Journals relevant to abnormal psychology include (among others): *Behavioral Health Treatment, Behavioral Medicine, Harvard Mental Health Letter, Annual Review of Psychology, British Journal of Psychology,* and the *Journal of Abnormal Child Psychology,* as well as related psychiatric journals.

Acknowledgments

The authors wish to thank the following individuals for providing clinical information that served as a basis for many of the case histories included in this book: Martin Antony, Denise Berotti, Karen Calhoun, Bruce Chorpita, Russ Denea, Patty DiBartolo, Maryrose Gerardi, Constance Kehrer, Shari Feldbau-Kohn, Lenna Knox, Patricia Miller, Laura Mufson, K. Daniel O'Leary, Tracy O'Leary, Patricia Resick, David Sakheim, Risa Weisberg, and Myrna Weissman. Thanks also to Guilford Press for permission to adapt work appearing in an earlier publication (*Clinical Handbook of Psychological Disorders,* 2nd ed., D. H. Barlow, Ed., 1993, Guilford Press) for use in Cases 4 and 14 of this book.

We would also like to thank the reviewers for their constructive comments on earlier versions of these case presentations. They include: Bruce Levine, Nassau Community College; Benjamin Harris, University of Wisconsin–Parkside; Pamela Brouillard, Texas A&M–Corpus Christi; Eric Cooley, Western Oregon State University; and Louis R. Franzini, San Diego State University. Reviewers for the previous edition were: Montie A. Campbell, Oklahoma Baptist University; Ronald G. Evans, Washburn University; William Fremouw, West Virginia State University; Frank Goodkin, Castleton State University; Elizabeth A. Klonoff, California State University–San Bernardino; Carol Thompson, Muskegon Community College; and Raymond M. Zurawski, St. Norbert College.

Timothy A. Brown
David H. Barlow

Generalized Anxiety Disorder

Adrian Holdsworth was a 39-year-old Caucasian woman with two children (a son, age 12, and a daughter, age 7). Since obtaining her bachelor's degree in business administration 8 years ago, Adrian had worked as a bank manager. Adrian had become increasingly worried about her ability to concentrate and remember things at work. Therefore, she went to see her family doctor for an evaluation. Finding no physical basis for her concentration and memory difficulties, Adrian's doctor referred her to a neuropsychologist for a more detailed assessment of her cognitive functioning. The neuropsychologist deemed Adrian's complaints to be anxiety related, and thus he encouraged her to seek out the services of an anxiety disorders clinic.

During her initial visit to the clinic, Adrian again expressed her concerns about her lapses in concentration and memory. She stated that, due to these lapses, she had made some "financially disastrous" errors at work. Consequently, she was advised by her supervisor to take some vacation time to relax and "get her head together." Feeling devastated by her supervisor's remark, Adrian became convinced that her concentration and memory problems were serious and perhaps the result of her brief experimentation with marijuana in college. In addition to her problems with concentration and memory and worries that her job was in jeopardy, Adrian claimed that she was unable to relax outside the office. She also reported low self-esteem and difficulties in making decisions. With regard to the latter complaint, Adrian indicated that she frequently ruminated prior to making a decision (e.g., "Is this the right decision, or should I do that?"); as a result, she often avoided making decisions altogether.

Adrian's concentration and memory problems usually occurred when she was anxious and worried about some life matter. Indeed, Adrian stated that she was in a state of anxiety and worry about 75% of her waking hours during an average day. Adrian reported that she worried a great deal about her job performance, her children's well-being, and her relationships with men. In addition, Adrian worried about a variety of minor matters such as getting to appointments on time, keeping her house clean, and maintaining regular contact with family and friends. For example, with regard to worry about her children's well-being, Adrian often became very anxious that her kids may have been hurt or killed if they were out in the neighborhood playing and she had not heard from them in a couple of hours. (The nature and content of Adrian's other worries are discussed later in this chapter.)

In addition to being *excessive* (e.g., failure to hear from one's children in 2 hours is not sufficient grounds to conclude that they may have been killed), Adrian experienced her worries as *uncontrollable*. Adrian's worry was uncontrollable in the sense that, when a worry came into her mind, she felt incapable of dismissing the thoughts and getting her mind focused back on the task at hand. For instance, Adrian would become more anxious and worried at work when her supervisor was around (due to her concern that he would evaluate her job performance negatively). Because Adrian was so preoccupied with her worries about being negatively evaluated, she would be less attentive to her work and thus was more apt to make mistakes. During these periods of increased worry, Adrian would be more forgetful because her mind had not been focused on her work (e.g., she would often forget what her supervisor had told her because she was focused more on her worries about job performance than on what he was saying to her). In addition to concentration and memory difficulties, Adrian's anxiety and worry were accompanied by the following symptoms: irritability, problems in getting and staying asleep, frequent muscle tension and headaches, and a feeling of being keyed up or on edge.

Adrian was very distressed about her excessive worry and anxiety: "I hate feeling this way all day. I just want to feel normal and in control of what's going on in my life!" In addition to the distress they caused, Adrian's symptoms interfered a great deal with her life. For example, she spent many extra hours at work and arrived at the office 30 minutes early every day to "make sure that I have my day all planned out as much as possible" (to decrease the likelihood of committing errors in her work). It took Adrian much longer than necessary to accomplish tasks or to make decisions because she would question and worry about the accuracy of every step in the process. In addition, Adrian reported that her symptoms had a negative impact on her social and family life. She claimed that her children often complained to her that she was always in a bad mood. Adrian indicated that she was spending less time with her friends and had noticed that the few men she had dated never seemed to call her back after the first or second date: "They can sense that I'm not a fun person." Moreover, Adrian's worry and anxiety had affected her physically. She reported having "borderline hypertension" (moderately elevated blood pressure), which her family doctor had attributed to stress. Adrian also had a history of migraine headaches that were fairly well controlled with prescription medication but seemed more likely to occur after she worried excessively.

In addition to her worry and anxiety over various life matters (e.g., job performance, children's well-being), Adrian reported some discomfort in social situations in which she might be observed or evaluated by others. Specifically, Adrian said that dating, being assertive, participating in meetings, and public speaking were situations that she tended to endure with moderately high levels of anxiety and distress. Despite her fear of being evaluated negatively by others, however, Adrian stated that she rarely avoided these social situations. She noted that some of her apprehension of these social situations was related to her concern that she would lose her train of thought during the interaction and be embarrassed.

Clinical History

Adrian reported a fairly typical middle-class upbringing. She got along quite well with her two younger brothers and her parents. Although she regarded her parents as "uptight and serious," she did not believe that either of them had a history of an emotional disorder (e.g., anxiety, depression). In fact, the only family member that Adrian could recall who had such difficulties was her paternal grandfather, who had alcoholism. Adrian thought of herself as being shy throughout childhood; nevertheless, she reported several enduring friendships and hobbies. She had been an A student until high school (age 14), when she and her family moved to another city and Adrian started attending a new school where she did not know anyone. On the basis of her past grades and test scores, Adrian was advised to take honors classes at her new school. At this time Adrian began to worry excessively. Specifically, she worried that she would fail these classes. She began to have trouble sleeping

before an exam and noticed some trouble concentrating in her more challenging classes. Her fear of failure emerged at this time, and Adrian began to
procrastinate on homework assignments and complete them at the last
minute. She also recalled that her shyness increased during this period; she
felt more anxious around boys and more hesitant to speak up in class.

Adrian's parents and friends tried to reassure her that everything was fine
and not to worry. Adrian's teachers also tried to help her relax, and some
offered to read rough drafts of her papers to provide reassurance that she
would ultimately receive a passing grade for her work. However, Adrian's
worries and insomnia increased even more when she started getting B's in a
few of her classes. She feared that, because she was no longer a straight-A
student, she might not be able to get into college. Her increasing sleep problems contributed to her worries as well—Adrian was concerned that if she did
not get enough sleep, her schoolwork would suffer all the more.

Adrian's symptoms tended to wax and wane throughout her high school
and college years. She noticed that she slept better and had fewer concentration and memory problems during summer vacations and holidays. However,
she experienced increased anxiety and tension when returning to school and
during exam periods. Dating often increased Adrian's anxiety as well, based
on her worries that her date would not like her or would evaluate her negatively. As a result, and because Adrian's parents, whom she regarded as strict,
had not permitted her to date until she was 17, Adrian dated infrequently.
Nevertheless, during her senior year of college, she met the man she eventually married at age 22.

During the first few years of her marriage, Adrian noticed that she felt
less anxious. Yet, problems arose in her marriage after the birth of her two
children. Her husband, who was a biochemist and a native of Hungary,
wanted to move the family back to his homeland so that he could take an academic position in Budapest. Adrian wanted her children to be raised in the
United States and had no desire to live outside the country herself. This conflict eventually led to divorce, and her husband moved back to Budapest
alone. At first, he visited the children over the holidays and during summers.
However, as the children got older, they began to travel during vacations to
visit their father in Hungary. During these visits, Adrian began to worry
excessively about her children's safety and well-being. This worry, along with
her concerns about job performance, minor matters, and her relationships
with men, spiraled to higher and higher levels of frequency and intensity.

As noted earlier, Adrian also worried about her brief experimentation
with marijuana during college. Although she had tried marijuana on only a
handful of occasions when she was 22, Adrian was concerned that these experiences had killed some of her brain cells, causing her persistent problems
with her memory and concentration. Adrian's family doctor had reassured her
that it was highly unlikely her past marijuana use had permanently altered her

memory and concentration. Adrian was able to accept this reassurance, but her confidence in her doctor's words usually eroded over the course of a few days, or as soon as she perceived that she was having trouble concentrating or remembering.

DSM-IV Diagnosis

Based on this information, Adrian was assigned the following DSM-IV diagnosis:

Axis I	300.02	Generalized anxiety disorder (principal diagnosis)
	300.23	Social phobia
Axis II	V71.09	No diagnosis on Axis II
Axis III	Borderline hypertension, migraine headaches	
Axis IV	Single parent, stressful work environment	
Axis V	Global assessment of functioning = 70 (current)	

At the beginning of treatment, Adrian displayed all of the symptoms of DSM-IV generalized anxiety disorder (GAD; American Psychiatric Association, 1994). In DSM-IV, GAD is defined by the following features: (a) excessive anxiety and worry, occurring more days than not for at least 6 months, about a number of events or activities (such as work or school performance); (b) the person finds it difficult to control the worry; and (c) the anxiety and worry are associated with three (or more) of the following six symptoms: restlessness or feeling keyed up or on edge, being easily fatigued, difficulty concentrating or mind going blank, irritability, muscle tension, and sleep disturbance (difficulty in falling or staying asleep, or restless, unsatisfying sleep). To warrant a DSM-IV diagnosis, these symptoms must cause the person considerable distress or lifestyle interference. Moreover, a diagnosis of GAD is ruled out when the symptoms of worry and generalized anxiety are better accounted for by another emotional disorder (e.g., worry about having unexpected panic attacks, as in panic disorder, should not be considered as contributing to a GAD diagnosis), the physical effects of a substance (e.g., drugs of abuse, medications), or a general medical condition.

Note that GAD should not be the diagnosis when its symptoms (i.e., chronic anxiety and worry) occur exclusively during the course of a mood disorder such as major depression or bipolar disorder. Although not part of the formal criteria for these diagnoses, generalized anxiety and worry are quite common associated features of mood disorders. Thus, if generalized anxiety and worry occur only during a mood disorder, according to DSM-IV these symptoms are best subsumed under the mood disorder diagnosis rather than considered to be a manifestation of a separate disorder.

The nature and treatment of generalized anxiety disorder are discussed in more detail throughout the remainder of this case. A full discussion on social phobia is presented in Case 3.

CASE FORMULATION USING THE INTEGRATIVE MODEL

Similar to the other anxiety disorders discussed in this book (e.g., panic disorder, social phobia), the integrative model of GAD highlights the role of both biological and psychological factors in the origins and maintenance of this condition (Barlow & Durand, 1999). Biological factors are viewed as contributing to vulnerability to GAD. As noted in other chapters in this book on anxiety disorders, investigations of anxiety as a human trait show a clear heritable factor. Likewise, studies have indicated that there may be a genetic contribution to GAD. For example, GAD tends to run in families, as reflected by findings showing a higher frequency of GAD among first-order relatives (i.e., parents, siblings) of patients with GAD than among persons with no anxiety disorders or persons with panic disorder (Noyes, Clarkson, Crowe, Yates, & McChesney, 1987; Noyes et al., 1992). These findings have been strengthened by a twin study (Kendler, Neale, Kessler, Heath, & Eaves, 1992) in which the researchers found that the risk of GAD was somewhat greater in monozygotic (identical) female twins than in dizygotic (fraternal) female twins when one twin already had GAD. Because monozygotic twins have exactly the same genes whereas dizygotic twins share only about 50% of each other's genes (the same amount shared with first-order relatives), the higher rate of GAD in monozygotic twin pairs suggests that genetic factors contribute to the development of this disorder. However, this finding requires replication because earlier studies failed to demonstrate conclusively the role of genetic factors in GAD (Andrews, Stewart, Allen, & Henderson, 1990; Torgersen, 1990).

Preliminary evidence suggests that patients with GAD may possess a distinguishing feature that is important in understanding the causes and maintenance of this disorder. Unlike persons without anxiety disorders, persons with GAD show *diminished responsiveness* on many physiological measures such as heart rate, blood pressure, skin conductance, and respiration when undergoing a stressful laboratory task (e.g., detection of predetermined target numbers on a computer screen that displays a rapidly scrolling series of numbers) (Hoehn-Saric, McLeod, & Zimmerli, 1989). Compared to patients with other anxiety disorders, such as those with panic disorder, research has found that patients with GAD report a predominance of symptoms of tension (e.g., muscle tension, irritability) as opposed to symptoms of autonomic arousal (e.g., accelerated heart rate, shortness of breath) (Brown, Marten, & Barlow, 1995).

This was true for Adrian, who reported that her chronic worry was accompanied mainly by symptoms of irritability, problems in getting and staying asleep, muscle tension and headaches, and feelings of being keyed up and on edge. Findings such as these have led researchers to consider persons with GAD to be *autonomic restrictors* because symptoms of tension have been observed to predominate over symptoms of autonomic arousal in these individuals.

What might account for these findings, which, if borne out in future research, would demonstrate a clear distinction between persons with GAD and persons with some other anxiety disorder? The answer may be related to certain cognitive characteristics of these persons. Specifically, persons with GAD are highly hypervigilant or sensitive to potential threat in general, particularly if the threat has some personal relevance. This feature is also seen in the other anxiety disorders; however, the attentional focus on the threat cues is more specific to the particular disorder (e.g., in the case on panic disorder, John Donahue was very hypervigilant for physical sensations that might signify an imminent panic attack). Unlike other anxiety disorders such as panic disorder, the attentional focus on potential threat is more "generalized" on the events of everyday life. Indeed, a cardinal feature of GAD is the general tendency to overestimate the risk or threat (worry) of everyday events and activities. This was clearly evident in Adrian, who worried excessively about her job performance, her children's well-being, her relationships with men, and a number of minor matters (e.g., getting to appointments on time, keeping her house clean, maintaining regular contact with family and friends).

Research has shown that worry is more strongly related to symptoms of tension than to symptoms of autonomic arousal (Brown, Antony, & Barlow, 1992; Brown et al., 1995). So why is worry associated with a predominance of tension symptoms and autonomic restriction? In a possible explanation for this association, Borkovec and colleagues found that although persons with GAD show restrictions in autonomic arousal, they evidence elevations in EEG beta activity, reflecting intense cognitive processing in the frontal lobes of the brain, particularly in the left hemisphere (Carter, Johnson, & Borkovec, 1986). Thus, it has been hypothesized that people with GAD engage in intense worry without accompanying images of the topic that is of concern to them (imagery would be reflected by activity in the right hemisphere of the brain). Accordingly, worry may cause autonomic restriction (Borkovec, 1994). Worriers may be so preoccupied in *thinking* about potential problems or threats that they do not have the attentional capacity to create *images* of these issues in their minds. In other words, worriers may avoid these images because the images of threat are associated with higher levels of negative emotions and autonomic activity. As you will note from your reading of this and other chapters in this book on anxiety disorders, imaginal exposure to threatening material (e.g., prolonged visualization in one's mind of flying on an airplane as an initial step in the treatment of fear of flying) is an important technique of treatment. Although imaginal exposure is associated with increased distress initially, continued exposure to these threatening images typically results in enduring anxiety reduction (see Case 4, "Posttraumatic Stress Disorder," for more details on this process). However, because persons with GAD do not naturally engage in this process, they may avoid much of the unpleasantness associated with the negative affect and imagery, but they are never able to "work through" the problems they face and arrive at solutions. Therefore, they become chronic worriers with accompanying autonomic inflexibility and persistent symptoms of tension (e.g., muscle aches and tension, irritability). The connections between worry, avoidance, and ineffective problem solving are illustrated by Adrian's performance in high school. Excessively worrying that she might fail in her honors classes, Adrian had trouble sleeping before exams and had trouble concentrating in her more challenging classes. Adrian's concerns about failure in these classes became so aversive that she began to procrastinate and leave homework assignments uncompleted until the last minute (this avoidance reinforced the idea in Adrian's mind that she was prone to failure).

Treatment Goals and Planning

Adrian was offered a program at the anxiety disorders clinic called "worry control treatment" (Craske, Barlow, & O'Leary, 1992). This treatment approach includes the following elements: cognitive therapy, worry exposure, and worry behavior prevention. In cognitive therapy, the content of the patient's worrisome thoughts and predictions is identified. Once these thoughts are identified, the patient is taught methods to critically evaluate the validity of his or her predictions, with the ultimate goal of replacing these misperceptions with more accurate interpretations. For example, as illustrated in the next section of this case, Adrian was guided by her therapist to realize that she had misinterpreted events at work (e.g., suggestions by her supervisor to take a vacation as signs that she was going to be fired). Based on the conceptual model discussed previously, worry exposure involves techniques where the patient is asked to directly confront anxiety-provoking images of their worrisome predictions (e.g., based on her worries when she hadn't heard from her children in a few hours, Adrian would be asked to hold, for several minutes, an image in her mind of her children being involved in an accident). Used in conjunction with cognitive therapy, these techniques would allow Adrian to confront and work through anxious predictions and images that she had avoided through worry. Finally, the technique of worry behavior prevention involves identifying and eliminating activities in which patients engage in response to their worry. This is done because these behaviors can maintain or strengthen worrisome thoughts. For instance, Adrian always arrived at work early because she felt that if she did not get organized beforehand, she would make many errors during the workday and would ultimately be fired. Thus, her habit of arriving to work early could be viewed as maintaining her belief that she was prone to errors that would result in her dismissal (e.g., "the only reason I have not committed 'fatal' errors is because I have decreased their likelihood by getting to work early"). In one application of worry behavior prevention, Adrian would be asked to arrive at work at the regular time and compare the actual outcome of this behavior change (e.g., no effects on her job performance or on her supervisor's appraisal of her performance) to her feared prediction of what would occur (e.g., marked increase in mistakes on the job leading to a negative evaluation by her supervisor). Thus, worry behavior prevention can be another powerful technique for assisting patients to challenge and refute their feared predictions (worries) about day-to-day events.

COURSE OF TREATMENT AND TREATMENT OUTCOME

During the first few sessions of treatment, Adrian received a psychoeducational (teaching) component in which the nature of anxiety and worry was explained and a rationale for treatment was provided. At this time, Adrian was asked to begin keeping daily records of her thoughts and her anxiety symptoms (self-monitoring). The types of information that she monitored included daily levels of anxiety, depression, and pleasantness; percentage of the day spent worrying; triggers of episodes of worry; and the content of her thoughts and nature of her behaviors associated with her worry. In addition to providing an indicator of the extent of her improvement across therapy, these self-monitoring records were very important to the application of the various treatment techniques (e.g., identification of the thoughts to be evaluated in session with cognitive therapy).

As treatment progressed, it became apparent that Adrian had two areas of worry that occurred most frequently and intensely and that were the most difficult for her to control: job performance (and related problems with concentration and memory) and her children's well-being. Thus, a good portion of treatment focused on these areas. For example, in the cognitive therapy component of treatment, Adrian learned about two basic types of anxiety-producing thoughts: *probability overestimation,* that is, overestimating the likelihood of negative or harmful events ("I'm going to be fired at work"), and *catastrophic thinking,* which involves the perception that if a negative event were to occur, it would be "catastrophic" or beyond the person's ability to cope (e.g., "If I'm fired, I'll wind up desolate and penniless because I won't be able to get another job") (see Case 2 for further descriptions and examples of these thoughts). After Adrian and her therapist identified these thoughts, they began the process of examining the validity of these perceptions with the goal of replacing them with more accurate interpretations.

For instance, on one of her self-monitoring records, Adrian wrote down her prediction that she would be fired for making her supervisor angry at work (see Figure 1.1; Tom is Adrian's supervisor). This was clearly a probability overestimation because Adrian was a very good employee and had never been even close to being fired in her life (even in past instances when she had disagreements with her supervisor). During this process, Adrian was asked to evaluate the accuracy of her perception that her supervisor's remark to take some vacation time was reflective of his inclination to have her fired. Adrian had avoided asking her supervisor to clarify this remark, based on her concern that it would confirm her fears that he wanted to terminate her. After being helped by her therapist to see many different possible reasons why her supervisor might have made this comment, Adrian approached him to find out why he had said this to her. Much to her surprise (and directly challenging her feared prediction), Adrian's supervisor replied that he regarded her as a valued employee, that he definitely did not want her to leave the bank, and that he had made the remark based on his observation that she was long overdue for a vacation.

The technique of worry exposure also assisted Adrian in examining the validity of her worrisome thoughts and in gaining control over her worry. Adrian was instructed to set aside a specific time each day (usually an hour in the evening) to devote to attending to her worries. Starting with her strongest worries (job performance, children's well-being), she was told to identify her worst feared outcome related to the worry (e.g., her children being killed in an automobile accident). Then, Adrian was asked to hold, for 20 to 30 minutes at a time, an image in her mind of the feared outcome. Following this "imaginal exposure," she was instructed to use cognitive therapy techniques to challenge the accuracy of this prediction (e.g., list alternatives, other than a fatal accident, for why her children did not telephone her at an expected time). In addition to providing Adrian the opportunity to work through the worries that she typically avoided, the worry exposure technique also assisted her in feeling more in control of her worries that intruded into her mind throughout the day. Because worry exposure provided her "free rein" to worry for a full hour each day, Adrian was better able to dismiss the worries as they occurred naturally because she knew she would give them her full attention later in the day.

This technique was very important in addressing Adrian's worries about the well-being of her children. For example, when her children were away in Hungary for the summer (as was the case during the first half of Adrian's treatment), Adrian consistently worried that they had been killed in a car accident because "Hungarian drivers are the worst, except for Basque Spaniards."

DAILY RECORD OF WORRY CONTROL

Date _____ 6/12 _____   Time began _____ 5:30 _____ am/(pm)
                                   End _____ 6:15 _____ am/(pm)

Anxiety   0 . . . . 1 . . . . 2 . . . . 3 . . .(4). . . 5 . . . . 6 . . . .7 8
(circle)   None   Mild   Moderate   Severe   Extreme

Symptoms During Hour:			
Trembling/Twitching/Shaky	_____	Nausea/Diarrhea	_____
Muscle tension/Aches/Sore	_____	Hot flashes/Chills	_____
Restlessness	3	Frequent urination	_____
Fatigue	_____	Trouble swallowing	_____
Shortness of breath	_____	Keyed up/On edge	4
Pounding/Racing heart	_____	Easily startled/Jumpy	_____
Sweating/Clammy hands	_____	Difficulty concentrating	_____
Dry mouth	_____	Trouble sleeping	_____
Dizzy/Lightheadedness	_____	Irritability	3

Worry content: *I didn't do what my boss, Tom, asked me to do. He asked me to call Frank*
                 about a problem at work, but I thought it was better to go through Mary.
                 I heard that Tom ran into Frank, who told him I hadn't called.

Worst possible
feared outcome: *Tom will be angry that I didn't do what he asked me to do. He'll fire me.*

Anxiety (0–8):   5

Possible
alternatives: *He's not angry. When I explain what I did he'll understand. Maybe I*
                 won't ever have to explain. People make mistakes—I made a mistake. Tom's
                 not the hothead I sometimes think he is. He's just a bit gruff on the outside.
                 In the end, it won't matter. It will be settled one way or the other.

Belief in worry
(0–100):   60   *(This one really*
                     set me back!)

Anxiety (0–8):   2

Figure 1.1   Daily record of worry control.

Additionally, when the kids did not call her back within 30 minutes after she had telephoned to say hello and check up on them, Adrian worried that perhaps they had been kidnapped or killed (probability overestimations). She frequently stated how upsetting it was for her to have these thoughts, that she hated to even think them, much less write them down or hold images of these predictions in her mind for up to 30 minutes at a time. Adrian added, "I'd never be able to handle it if something happened to my kids" (catastrophic thinking).

In fact, Adrian was initially somewhat noncompliant with regularly completing her daily worry exposures at home, stating that "they take up too much time." However, another reason for her occasional noncompliance seemed to be the high levels of anxiety that these exercises evoked when they focused on Adrian's worries about the safety of her children. The therapist addressed this reason by reminding Adrian of the rationale for worry exposure and by pointing out to her that the high levels of distress these exercises produced emphasized her need to work through her worries in order to feel more comfortable and less worried in her day-to-day life. In addition, the therapist assisted Adrian to generate alternatives to her worst-feared outcome that her kids must have been injured or killed if she had not heard from them. At first, Adrian had considerable difficulty coming up with other reasons for why time might pass without her hearing from the children. However, through her work in the therapy sessions and in her daily worry exposures, Adrian began to see how unlikely her children were to be harmed, in comparison to more plausible alternatives (see Figure 1.2).

Over time, Adrian discovered that she worried less and less about her children as the time approached for them to return home. Instead of being worried about them, she began to feel excited at the prospect of seeing them again. Additionally, Adrian found that when she spoke with them on the phone, the less frequently she called, the more positive their conversations (her frequent telephone calls to check on them was a worry behavior). Adrian said, "Now I look forward to our calls and I don't get so worked up about talking to my kids." For virtually all of her worries that she addressed (e.g., children's well-being, job performance, possible brain damage from marijuana experimentation), Adrian ultimately found the worry exposure hours to be quite helpful. In them she learned to systematically confront her fears and to think of more realistic, less catastrophic possible outcomes and solutions.

Worry behavior prevention was the other major technique used in Adrian's treatment. First, she and her therapist identified the behaviors that Adrian was engaging in that served to maintain or strengthen her worries. In Adrian's case, these behaviors included arriving at work early and staying late, frequent calls to her children in Hungary (at the start of treatment,

DAILY RECORD OF WORRY CONTROL

Date _____7/3_____   Time began _____6:30_____ am/pm

End _____7:30_____ am/pm

Anxiety   0 . . . . 1 . . . . 2 . . . . 3 . . . . 4 . . . . ⑤ . . . 6 . . . .7 8
(circle)   None   Mild   Moderate   Severe   Extreme

Symptoms During Hour:			
Trembling/Twitching/Shaky	____	Nausea/Diarrhea	____
Muscle tension/Aches/Sore	3	Hot flashes/Chills	____
Restlessness	4	Frequent urination	____
Fatigue	5	Trouble swallowing	____
Shortness of breath	____	Keyed up/On edge	4
Pounding/Racing heart	____	Easily startled/Jumpy	____
Sweating/Clammy hands	____	Difficulty concentrating	____
Dry mouth	1	Trouble sleeping	____
Dizzy/Lightheadedness	____	Irritability	3

Worry content: *The children haven't called me back yet.*

It's been over 2 hours since I called.

Worst possible feared outcome: *They've been hurt or killed in a car accident.*

Anxiety (0–8): _____8_____

Possible alternatives: *They're OK—They're out playing. They forgot. Maybe they're*

preoccupied with something or maybe their grandmother forgot to

let them know that I called. They could be just reading or drawing or

playing games with each other. A friend might have stopped by.

Belief in worry (0–100): _____65_____

Anxiety (0–8): _____4_____

Figure 1.2   Daily record of worry control.

Adrian called them several times per day!), excessive housecleaning (due to her concern that a friend might drop by and conclude that she was a slob), and sleeping only 6 hours per night ("There's so much to do, and I get worried that I'm not accomplishing the things I need to if I go to bed early"). As noted before, one of the goals of worry behavior prevention is to have the patient discontinue the behavior and compare the actual outcome of this behavior change to their feared prediction (worry) of what will occur following this change. The application of this technique to Adrian's habit of arriving at work early was discussed earlier in this chapter (she learned that arriving at work and leaving at normal hours did not result in an increase in mistakes on the job and negative evaluations by her supervisor). Over the course of treatment, similar practices were completed for Adrian's other worry behaviors (e.g., go to bed earlier and earlier to the point of getting 8 hours of sleep per night; gradually decrease the frequency of telephone calls to children to calling them once every other day; gradually relax the schedule for housecleaning). In fact, the seemingly minor intervention of moving up Adrian's bedtime had a substantial impact on her anxiety symptoms. Not only did this activity refute her prediction that she would not be able to accomplish necessary tasks if she slept more than 6 hours, but also Adrian began to sleep better and, over time, reported fewer concentration problems and less irritability.

In total, Adrian received 15 sessions of treatment. At the end of treatment, Adrian reported decreased levels of worry and anxiety. She still evidenced a tendency to worry about her children, work, minor matters, and her health (i.e., her concentration and memory) but reported that her worries occupied only 5% to 10% of her day, in contrast to 75% of the day at pretreatment. Although Adrian continued to worry excessively on occasion, she said that she felt more in control of her worry. Her children also noticed that she was "less moody" and "more fun to be around." Her sleep improved, and she began attending an exercise class that she enjoyed.

Adrian observed some improvements in her concentration and memory, and hence she reported higher self-esteem and self-confidence at work. Remaining concentration problems occurred intermittently and did not seem to be triggered by any particular situation; however, Adrian noted that her concentration difficulties were largely confined to her working hours. The therapist hypothesized that these symptoms may have been best accounted for by Adrian's remaining social phobia concerns (her social phobia was not directly addressed in treatment). Specifically, they accounted for her apprehension of dealing with authority figures, being assertive, and interacting with customers and employees. Indeed, although she continued to report some fear of being negatively evaluated by others, Adrian did report some improvement in this area. For example, Adrian began to go on more social outings with friends, and she stated that she was beginning to feel less anxious about dating. Thus, while Adrian continued to show some apprehension of certain social situations, she rarely avoided them and did not feel that these symptoms interfered with her life to any measurable degree.

DISCUSSION

Adrian had a diagnosis that is one of the most common among the anxiety disorders. Studies have provided estimates of the lifetime prevalence for GAD in the general population ranging from 1.9% to 5.4% ("lifetime prevalence" refers to percentage of persons who meet criteria for GAD at some point during their lives). The most recent prevalence data for GAD have come from the National Comorbidity Survey, where more than 8,000 persons in the community were evaluated with structured interviews. This study obtained prevalence estimates of 1.6% and 5.1% for current and lifetime GAD, respectively (Wittchen, Zhao, Kessler, & Eaton, 1994). A consistent finding in these community surveys is a 2:1 female-to-male preponderance of GAD (e.g., Blazer, George, & Hughes, 1991; Wittchen et al., 1994).

Anxiety in its various forms is very prevalent in the elderly. For example, Himmelfarb and Murrell (1984) found that 17% of elderly men and 21.5% of elderly women had sufficiently severe anxiety symptoms to warrant treatment, although it is not clear how many of these individuals actually met criteria for GAD. Another indicator of the potential prevalence of GAD symptoms in the elderly comes from more recent data showing that the use of minor tranquilizers is very high (ranging from 17% to 50%) in this population (Salzman, 1991).

Although GAD was once thought to be associated with less distress and impairment often found in other anxiety disorders (such as panic disorder and obsessive-compulsive disorder), recent data indicate otherwise. In the large National Comorbidity Survey, it was found that 82% of persons with GAD reported that their problem was associated with significant impairment, as indexed by past treatment-seeking behavior (either drugs or psychotherapy) or substantial life-style interference (Wittchen et al., 1994). In addition, research has routinely shown that GAD rarely presents in isolation. Community surveys indicate that 90.4% of persons with GAD have a history of some other mental disorder at some point in their lives (Wittchen et al., 1994). Studies of patient samples have found that more than 80% of patients with a current diagnosis of GAD have additional anxiety or mood disorders at the time of their assessment (Brown & Barlow, 1992). In this study of patients with GAD, the most commonly occurring additional diagnoses were found to be panic disorder, social phobia, and mood disorders (major depression, dysthymia). In addition, this study found that among patients with other anxiety disorder diagnoses that were deemed to be more significant and in need of treatment, 23% also had GAD (making it the most common additional diagnosis found in patients with anxiety disorders).

Like Adrian, some people with GAD report an onset in early adulthood or late adolescence, usually in response to some form of life stress (Hoehn-Saric, Hazlett, & McLeod, 1993). However, the majority of studies find that GAD is associated with an earlier and more gradual onset than most other anxiety disorders (Brown, Barlow, & Liebowitz, 1994). Indeed, many patients with GAD report feeling anxious, tense, and worried all their lives (Noyes et al., 1992; Sanderson & Barlow, 1990).

Although persons with GAD who seek treatment are perhaps most likely to receive medications (because a large portion seek treatment in primary care settings), the available evidence indicates that any positive effects of drugs are relatively weak and short-lived (Schweizer & Rickels, 1991). The most frequently used drug for the treatment of GAD has been the benzodiazepines (i.e., minor tranquilizers such as diazepam [Valium]). In addition to finding that any beneficial effects these medications have are modest and transient, researchers have observed certain risks associated with this form of treatment. For instance, benzodiazepines appear to create problems with both cognitive and motor functioning (e.g., O'Hanlon, Haak, Blaauw, & Riemersma, 1982; Tyrer & Owen, 1984). Specifically, people do not seem to be as "alert" cognitively on the job or at school when they are taking benzodiazepines. Moreover, these drugs may impair a person's ability to drive a car, and they seem to be associated with a higher frequency of falls that result in hip fractures in the elderly (Ray, Gurwitz, Decker, & Kennedy, 1992). More important, research has indicated that benzodiazepines may produce both psychological and physical dependence, making it quite difficult for people to stop taking the drug (Noyes, Garvey, Cook, & Suelzer, 1991; Rickels, Schweizer, Case, & Greenblatt, 1990). Based on these considerations, most researchers agree that the optimal use of benzodiazepines is for short-term relief of anxiety associated with a temporary crisis or stressful event (e.g., a family crisis) and that these medications should not be used for long-term anxiety management.

Interestingly, psychological treatments also have not fared very well in producing lasting benefits for patients with GAD. For example, many studies examining the effectiveness of psychosocial treatments have observed that these interventions are not more powerful than placebo psychotherapies (e.g., a "placebo" treatment might involve providing general reassurance to patients without directly delivering components that are believed to be effective in reducing the symptoms of GAD) (for a review, see Brown, O'Leary, & Barlow, 1993). One possible reason for the modest outcomes observed in these studies is that many of the treatments examined were somewhat nonspecific (e.g., relaxation training to reduce general anxiety symptoms) and did not contain components that were tailored to address the key aspects of GAD, namely, excessive and uncontrollable worry (Brown et al., 1994). This lack of specificity was due in part to the fact that the diagnostic definition of GAD has changed radically over the past 15 years, evolving from a residual category to describe general symptoms of anxiety that could not be accounted for by another diagnosis (DSM-III; American Psychiatric Association, 1980) to a full-fledged Axis I diagnosis with its own unique and defining key feature (excessive and uncontrollable worry about a number of events and activities; DSM-IV).

More recently, investigators have developed and evaluated psychosocial treatments that directly target excessive worry. These treatments are very similar to the form of therapy Adrian received. Specifically, these interventions include components of cognitive therapy and direct exposure to worry-related images. For example, Borkovec and colleagues constructed such a treatment and found it to be significantly better than a "placebo" psychological treatment, both at posttreatment and 1-year follow-up (Borkovec & Costello, 1993). Although their treatment was superior to placebo therapy (and, to a certain extent, superior to relaxation training), only 58% of patients met criteria for high endstate functioning at 1-year follow-up (high endstate is a term used in treatment outcome research to reflect a therapeutic response in which no or minimal symptoms of the disorder remain). Thus, although these findings are quite encouraging in reference to prior studies, where therapy was found to be no more effective than placebo, the fact that just over half of patients show durable and substantial improvement points to the need for the development of more powerful treatments for GAD.

THINKING CRITICALLY

1. Worry is the key diagnostic feature of generalized anxiety disorder (GAD) as defined by DSM-IV. Because everyone tends to worry on occasion, what do you think differentiates normal worry from the worry found in GAD?
2. While in treatment, some persons with GAD are reluctant to relinquish their worrying and worry behaviors because they believe these features are helpful to them (e.g., Adrian arrived at work 30 minutes early each morning to plan out her day and to decrease the likelihood of making mistakes or overlooking important tasks). Do you believe worry can have adaptive qualities? If so, what are they? What do you believe are the negative consequences of worry, especially when the worry is at the level found in GAD?
3. Unlike most anxiety disorders (e.g., panic disorder, obsessive-compulsive disorder), research indicates that GAD has a gradual onset that frequently dates back to childhood; many adults with GAD recall being tense, anx-

ious, and worried all of their lives. Why do you think this is the case? Do you believe that the tendency to worry excessively is more like an enduring personality characteristic than a symptom that occurs acutely from time to time?

4. In addition to the strategies discussed in Adrian's treatment, what other methods do you think would be helpful in treating persons with GAD?

Panic Disorder with Agoraphobia

John Donahue was a 45-year-old married Caucasian man with three sons. Although well-educated and successful (he was a high school principal), John had been experiencing difficulties with panic attacks for the past 15 years. Despite a number of consultations with mental health professionals throughout the prior several years, John's panic attacks had not decreased substantially. In fact, John experienced an increase in the frequency of his panic attacks when he and his family moved to upstate New York so that he could begin work at a new school. Certain that he could overcome his panic attacks, John searched the phone book for sources of possible help. John was excited to see an advertisement for a clinic specializing in the treatment of anxiety disorders. After showing the ad to his wife, John quickly set up an appointment at the clinic.

During his first visit to the clinic, John told his therapist that he was experiencing two to five panic attacks per month. John's therapist asked him to describe a typical recent panic attack. John recalled a panic attack that had occurred the previous week. The panic attack happened while John was driving with his family to a computer store. John had not been aware of feeling anxious before the panic attack, although he recollected that he might have been "keyed up" over the kids making a lot of noise in the back seat. In fact, John remembered that the attack began right after he had quickly turned around to tell the kids to "settle down." Immediately after he turned back to look at the road, John felt dizzy. As soon as he noticed this sensation, John experienced a rapid and intense surge of other sensations, including sweating, accelerated heart rate, hot flushes, trembling, and the feeling of being detached from his body (depersonalization). In response to this intense surge, John began to move around in the driver's seat, shifting his posture and quickly taking his hands off the steering wheel, only to grab the wheel again more firmly. When his wife asked him if he was okay, John could not answer her because he felt so stricken by the sensations and was so focused on trying to gain control over them. Fearing that he was going to crash the car, John quickly pulled to the side of the road. He jumped out of the car and walked quickly around to the passenger's side. He lowered himself into a squatting position and tried to gain control over his breathing by using techniques he and his wife had learned in Lamaze classes. After 10 minutes had passed, John began to feel better. Because of a high level of anxiety that continued to linger after the panic attack and because he feared that he might experience another attack, however, John asked his wife to do the driving for the remainder of the day. John told his therapist that he had been even more hesitant about driving since then, particularly on the road where he experienced the attack.

Although the majority of his panic attacks had now become associated with specific situations (i.e., they tended to occur more in some situations than others or, in DSM-IV terms, the panics were "situationally predisposed"), John reported that he still occasionally had panic attacks that came totally out of the blue. John stated that, while he was having only a few panic attacks per month on average, he was experiencing a high level of anxiety every day, focused on the possibility that he might have another panic attack at any time. Indeed, John had developed extensive apprehension or avoidance regarding a variety of situations. These situations included driving (particularly long distances or interstate driving), air travel, elevators, wide open spaces (e.g., empty parking lots), taking long walks alone, movie theaters, church, and being out of town. Knowing that it would be very important in treatment, John's therapist tried to determine exactly what John was afraid of regarding what might happen if a panic attack were to occur in these situations. John recalled that when his panic attacks were most severe (i.e., a period of several years after his panic attacks first emerged), he thought that they had a physical cause. Specifically, John feared that the panic attacks were symptoms of a heart disease that his doctors had failed to identify. However, John told his therapist that, at the present time, he was not concerned about dying or having a physical disease because his doctors had persuaded him that he was okay. Rather, John was now most afraid of losing control by either passing out or by losing control of his arms and legs and falling over. In fact, John reported that during some of his more intense panic attacks, such as the one he had just described, his arms and legs *had* jerked around in an involuntary and uncontrollable fashion. John's fear of passing out, falling over, or losing control of limbs appeared to occur in most situations in which he experienced apprehension and avoidance; for example, driving (losing control of the car and crashing), church, elevators, and wide open spaces (falling over and drawing attention to himself).

In gathering more information that might later be useful in treatment, John's therapist asked him if he carried specific things with him or did things in response to a panic attack that either (a) helped him feel more comfortable in difficult situations or (b) seemed to decrease the likelihood that a feared consequence (e.g., fainting) would occur. Through this questioning, John's therapist was able to identify the following "safety behaviors" and "safety signals": 24-hour access to anti-anxiety medication, driving to the side of the road, holding on to stationary objects, and remaining near walls. Safety behaviors and signals are defined and discussed in more detail later in the chapter.

Clinical History

During the initial appointment, John told his therapist about his long history of panic attacks. John recalled that his first panic attack had occurred 15 years ago. It had happened at 4:30 in the morning in his living room. John had fallen asleep on the sofa at around 1:00 a.m. after returning from a night of drinking with some of his friends. Just after awakening at 4:30, John suddenly felt stomach pains and a pulsating sensation in the back of his neck. All of a sudden, John noticed that his heart was racing, too. He immediately leaped off the sofa. As soon as he got up, John felt dizzy and feared that his head was "about to pop." John recalled that he "staggered" out the door to get some fresh air. Once outside, he began pacing and scratching the back of his neck and head in an effort to reduce his sensations. Although he did not know what he was suffering from, John was certain that he was dying. Despite this belief and the high intensity of the sensations, the attack only lasted about 5 to 7 minutes. When he began feeling better, he went back inside and awakened his wife to tell her what had happened.

The morning after this panic attack, John called his family doctor, who agreed to see him on the same day. John's doctor told him that he was in good health. The physician speculated that John's nerves were just "letting off steam," perhaps due to the recent arrival of John's first child and the fact that it was nearing the end of the school year, which was always an extremely busy time for John. To help him relax, John's doctor gave him a prescription for Valium. John did not fill the prescription because the attacks did not return immediately. However, John remembered having a second panic attack about a month later. From then on, the panic attacks began to occur more regularly. When the panic attacks became recurrent, John started to avoid situations in which the panic attacks had occurred, as well as situations in which he feared a panic attack was more likely to occur. On three occasions during the first few years of his panic attacks, John went to the emergency room of his local hospital because he was sure that his symptoms were a sign of a heart attack. It was during one of these emergency room visits that John first heard the term *panic attack* as a descriptor of his symptoms. The 7-year period after John's panic attacks first emerged was a particularly rough time for him because, as a method of trying to cope with panic attacks of increasing frequency and intensity, he relied on alcohol. In fact, John said he was drinking a case of beer per day during that time. Fortunately, with the assistance of therapists at a local community mental health center and a brief hospital stay, John's alcohol dependence ended quite abruptly after 7 years of heavy drinking (this occurred 6 years prior to his first visit to the anxiety disorders clinic). However, around that time a psychiatrist prescribed John a high dosage of Xanax (the brand name for alprazolam, a high-potency benzodiazepine), which he still used. In addition to the Xanax, John had been treated on a regular basis with psychotherapy by a clinical social worker for several years. He regarded his work with this social worker to be somewhat helpful because he was able to learn more about the nature of panic attacks, as well as some ways of coping with the attacks, such as telling himself calming statements like "This will pass." In the interim, he had relied on self-help books that he read regularly. Unfortunately, he found these books of limited value in furthering his recovery.

John's therapist inquired about his family background and asked if there was any history of emotional disorders in the family. John reported an extensive family history of psychological problems, which occurred almost exclusively on his mother's side of the family. In addition to a long and continuing bout with alcoholism, John's mother had also suffered from panic disorder with agoraphobia. Although John had always considered his mother to be an anxious woman who was constantly worried and excessively concerned about her and her children's physical symptoms, John did not realize his mother had suffered from panic disorder until he had been diagnosed as having the same condition. In addition to his mother, John noted that his maternal grandfather and two of his mother's sisters had alcoholism or had abused alcohol. His maternal grandmother and another aunt on his mother's side had suffered from panic disorder; in fact, his aunt's agoraphobia was so severe that she had been housebound with the condition for 7 years. Of his three siblings, John stated that his older brother abused alcohol. He noted that both his sister and younger brother did not have a history of any emotional or substance use disorders.

After gathering this information, John's therapist administered a brief, semistructured clinical interview that evaluated for the presence of other DSM-IV anxiety disorders, mood disorders, somatoform disorders, and substance use disorders and screened for the presence of other syndromes (e.g., psychotic disorders). Beyond his past diagnosis of alcohol dependence, John did not have any other diagnoses with the exception of some symptoms of recurrent worry about several areas (e.g., job performance, children's well-being), which are indicative of a generalized anxiety disorder. However, John's therapist did not assign generalized anxiety disorder as an additional diagnosis because he regarded these symptoms as both "subclinical" (i.e., they were not severe or frequent enough to warrant a DSM-IV diagnosis) and, to some degree, better accounted for by the symptoms associated with John's panic attacks (e.g., most of John's chronic anxiety was due to his worry about having additional panic attacks).

DSM-IV Diagnosis

Therefore, based on the preceding information, John's five-axis DSM-IV diagnosis was as follows:

Axis I	300.21	Panic disorder with agoraphobia
Axis II	V71.09	No diagnosis on Axis II
Axis III	None	
Axis IV	Relocation to new state, job change, stressful work schedule	
Axis V	Global assessment of functioning = 58 (current)	

In many respects, John's symptoms and history reflected the typical case of panic disorder with agoraphobia. For instance, his symptoms were quite consistent with the DSM-IV definition of panic disorder (American Psychiatric Association, 1994). In DSM-IV, the key criteria for panic disorder are (a) recurrent unexpected panic attacks and (b) at least one of the attacks has been followed by 1 month (or more) of one (or more) of the following: (1) persistent concern about having additional attacks, (2) worry about the implications of the attack or its consequences (e.g., losing control, having a heart attack, "going crazy"), or (3) a significant change in behavior related to the attacks. John's experience was also consistent with the DSM-IV definition of agoraphobia: (a) anxiety about being in places or situations from which escape might be difficult (or embarrassing) or in which help may not be available in the event of having an unexpected or situationally predisposed panic attack and (b) the situations are avoided (e.g., travel is restricted) or else endured with marked distress or with anxiety about having a panic attack or paniclike symptoms or require the presence of a companion.

Note that John's past diagnosis of alcohol dependence was not listed in his five-axis DSM-IV diagnosis. John's therapist could have listed on Axis I the diagnosis "alcohol dependence" with the specifier "with sustained full remission." This specifier is appropriate when the person has not displayed any symptoms of alcohol dependence or abuse for a period of 12 months or longer. However, DSM-IV notes that clinical judgment should be exercised to decide between listing the diagnosis with the "sustained full remission" specifier or not listing the diagnosis at all (which, in a sense, denotes full recovery). Guidelines that the clinician might use for making this decision include the length of time that has elapsed since the last symptoms were present, the total duration of the problem, and the potential need for continued evaluation. Because John had displayed no symptoms of alcohol abuse or dependence for over 6 years (despite the fact that his panic attacks continued), his therapist decided not to list alcohol dependence on the five-axis diagnosis (see Case 13 for a fuller discussion of alcohol dependence and abuse).

CASE FORMULATION USING THE INTEGRATIVE MODEL

John's therapist attempted to do much of the case formulation and treatment planning during the initial assessment session. In addition to obtaining the information necessary for making a DSM-IV diagnosis, the therapist collected as much information as possible on what he believed to be the maintaining factors of John's panic disorder. Such information included panic attack symptoms, agoraphobic situations, cognitions associated with panic attacks and anticipatory anxiety, and safety behaviors and safety signals. The importance of obtaining this type of information is based on the integrative model on the causes and maintenance of panic disorder (Barlow, 1988; Barlow & Durand, 1999). This model acknowledges the evidence attesting to the fact that we all inherit some vulnerability to experiencing stress (Eysenck, 1967; Tellegen et al., 1988). Specifically, this vulnerability is the tendency to be neurobiologically overreactive to the stress of common life events. Based on a number of factors such as genetics, some individuals are more likely than others to experience an emergency alarm reaction (unexpected panic attack or "false alarm"). Thus, according to the integrative model, panic attacks are the normal emotion of *fear* (i.e., the fight or flight response) experienced at inappropriate or unexpected times. John's background would be highly consistent with this aspect of the model and research evidence indicating that genetic factors are influential in the transmission of panic attacks (Kendler, Neale, Kessler, Heath, & Eaves, 1992; Torgersen, 1983). Given the extensive history of panic disorder and alcoholism in his biological relatives, it would be quite reasonable to assume that, compared to others who do not have this familial background, John inherited a higher level of vulnerability to experience a false alarm. Moreover, John experienced his first panic attack (false alarm) during a period of time that many would regard as stressful (i.e., birth of first child, hectic work schedule). This would also be consistent with the model that asserts that the first panic attack usually arises in the context of life stress because the stress activates or "triggers" the pre-existing vulnerability (the diathesis-stress model). Indeed, many researchers have found that the majority of patients with panic disorder (more than 70%) report that their first panic attack occurred during a stressful period of their lives (Craske & Barlow, 1993).

However, vulnerability alone does not determine whether the person will develop a panic disorder. Instead, vulnerability may set the stage for the development of a panic disorder if the right psychological and social factors line up. A central factor of this nature in panic disorder is the emergence of *anxiety* over the possibility of additional attacks. This anxiety, which is also focused on the specific physical sensations that might signal the next attack, is characterized by a strong sense of uncontrollability and cognitive distortions regarding the consequences or meaning of the attack and its associated symptoms. These cognition distortions are usually related to unrealistic inferences that the panic attack may be a sign of, or result in, physical harm (e.g., heart attack, stroke) or to fears of going crazy or losing control (e.g., a sign of schizophrenia or nervous breakdown; extreme embarrassment due to screaming, fleeing, and the like). The tendency to think that the worst is going to happen when panic attack symptoms are encountered was clearly evident in John. As discussed earlier, during the initial stages of his panic disorder, John feared that his panic attacks were a sign of serious physical illness (e.g., heart disease). In later stages of his disorder, John's primary fears related to his belief that a panic attack would cause him to pass out or lose control of his arms and legs. Clinical experience has shown that the content of patients' thoughts regarding the feared consequences of their panic attacks may change over the course of their disorder. What would cause John to interpret these sensations in such a catastrophic manner? One reason specified by the integrative model as to why persons acquire the tendency to interpret normal physical sensations as threatening is through learning experiences early in life. For example, John may have learned in childhood to regard physical sensations as potentially dangerous by watching his mother respond to symptoms in this manner (modeling).

As noted by the integrative model, false alarms quickly become associated in the person's mind with some external and internal cues that were present during the panic attack. In the instance of external cues, if a person has a panic attack in a certain situation, they may be apprehensive of or avoid this situation in the future because the situation becomes a cue for future panic attacks. For instance, John quickly began to fear and avoid driving after he experienced a few bad panic attacks behind the wheel of the car. This is consistent with a large amount of research evidence that indicates that agoraphobia (situational avoidance) is an associated feature of unexpected panic attacks; it always arises *after* the attacks (only a small proportion of patients with panic disorder never develop any symptoms of agoraphobia; Barlow, 1988). In the instance of internal cues, the person who experiences unexpected panic attacks may quickly begin to associate the physical sensations that occur during their attacks with the panic attack itself. The specific term for this process is *interoceptive conditioning,* which means that if certain physical sensations (e.g., rapid heart rate) are repeatedly associated with fear (as would occur in a panic attack), then the sensation itself may acquire the ability to produce anxiety or fear (e.g., vigorous exercise produces an increase in heart rate, which, in turn, produces anxiety or panic due to interoceptive conditioning). In a later treatment session, John reported that since his panic disorder had begun, he had avoided consumption of caffeinated beverages and vigorous exercise due to the fear that these activities might provoke a panic attack. Because these initial false alarms become associated with a variety of external and internal cues through a learning process (conditioning), they are referred to in the integrative model as "learned alarms" (i.e., learned, phobic alarm responses to physical sensations).

Treatment Goals and Planning

John's therapist was a licensed clinical psychologist who specialized in the treatment of anxiety disorders from a cognitive-behavioral perspective. A central goal in the cognitive-behavioral treatment of panic disorder is to assist the patient in gaining a sense of control over their panic attacks and to teach them to be totally nonfearful over the possibility of having additional panic attacks. To a large degree, treatment is not focused on the panic attack itself. Rather, treatment addresses the patient's anxiety over experiencing additional panics, which is conceptualized in the integrative model to be the primary reason why the panic attacks continue over time (i.e., anxiety about future panic attacks is a *maintaining factor*). Adhering to this model, John's therapist found it important to obtain information regarding John's feared consequences of panic (e.g., passing out, falling over), the types of situations he avoided, and the reasons why he avoided these situations. This information would be important for two aspects of John's treatment: (a) cognitive therapy and (b) situational exposure. Using principles and techniques developed by Aaron Beck (Beck & Emery, 1985) and David Clark (1986, 1988), cognitive therapy would be used to help John identify and modify his thoughts and attitudes concerning the danger of the sensations and situations associated with his panic attacks.

Because John had a panic disorder that was accompanied with agoraphobia (as is true for most patients with panic disorder), John's therapist planned to incorporate situational exposure in John's treatment to reduce his avoidance of situations such as driving, church, and movie theaters. Situational exposure would entail (a) preparing a list of the situations John feared and avoided; (b) arranging John's list in a hierarchical fashion, starting with the least difficult situations and ending with the most difficult situations (referred to as a fear and avoidance hierarchy); and (c), beginning with the least difficult situations (i.e., the situations that John feared the least), assigning John to enter these situations at predetermined times and durations. Situational exposure (sometimes called *in vivo exposure*) can be delivered in many formats, such as *graduated* (which John's therapist elected to use) and *massed* (also referred to as *flooding,* whereby the therapist arranges for the patient to immediately encounter her or his most feared and avoided situations, usually for long durations). Although John's therapist was planning to employ situational exposure in a *self-assisted* format (whereby the patient performs most of the exposure practices alone), this technique can also be (a) *therapist-assisted,* in which the therapist accompanies patients in their exposure practices, and (b) *spouse-assisted,* in which the spouse (or a close friend) of the patient serves as a coach or aide for the exposure practices. One advantage of the therapist-assisted format is the assurance that the patient is being exposed to feared situations in the most beneficial manner possible. A patient assigned to perform exposure tasks on his or her own may not always complete the practices in a therapeutic way. For example, one principle of situational exposure is that, in order for the exposure to be of therapeutic value, the patient must remain in the feared situation long enough to see a decrease in anxiety. Occasionally, patients who are assigned to independently carry out exposure practices flee the situation as soon as they experience a high level of anxiety. Besides preventing them from becoming less fearful of the situation, fleeing may make confronting the situation even more difficult in the future because patients had previously fled the situation with extreme anxiety. In addition to increasing the likelihood that the patient's exposures are completed in a therapeutic fashion, exposure assisted by the spouse may have certain advantages. Using this format, the spouse learns all about the nature of panic disorder and the methods that are useful in its treatment. In addition to the potential for positive interpersonal change (e.g., less conflict resulting from increased understanding of the disorder), having the spouse learn to be a coach in the patient's treatment may increase the number of exposures completed between therapy sessions (because some patients put off exposure assignments due to their fear of encountering the situation; Barlow, O'Brien, & Last, 1984). Moreover, this approach can eliminate things the spouse may normally do in response to the patient's symptoms that actually help to *maintain* the disorder. Examples of spouse behaviors that might contribute to the maintenance of the patient's panic disorder include (a) validating the patient's cognitions associated with the panic attacks (e.g., "You're right, honey. These doctors don't know what they're doing if they can't give you a straight answer about what's wrong with your heart") and (b) reinforcing the patient's tendency to escape or avoid situations (e.g., "Damn it, pull over before you crash and kill all of us!"). Both the spouse- and therapist-assisted formats have the potential disadvantage of fostering a sense of dependency on the spouse or therapist in order to confront feared situations successfully; this problem, which occurs rarely, can usually be prevented by requiring the patient to perform a certain number of the exposure practices independently.

As is commonly done in cognitive-behavioral treatment, John's therapist planned to integrate situational exposure with the techniques of cognitive therapy. Relating to this issue, John's therapist inquired about the things John did to try to prevent or cope with a panic attack (i.e., his safety behaviors and signals, such as having constant access to medication and remaining close to walls or stationary objects to prevent him from falling in the event of a panic attack). As is the case with situational avoidance, the reliance on these safety behaviors, which the patient does to reduce anxiety, may actually *increase or at least maintain* anxiety and panic in the long run because these actions prevent him from invalidating his feared predictions regarding the consequences of panic.

For example, each time John experienced a bad panic attack while alone, he would fall to the ground, which he felt was a *consequence* of the panic attack. However, John's therapist was struck by the fact that this never occurred outside a situation in which falling to the ground would be acceptable to John; that is, even though he had experienced many severe panic attacks in public places, he was able to prevent himself from falling to the ground or from moving his arms and legs in an "uncontrollable" fashion (although if he could not escape the situation, he often found somewhere to sit down or something to lean against). Almost every panic attack that had been associated with falling had occurred at home! Therefore, John's therapist viewed these actions (falling to the ground, sitting down, leaning against something) as safety behaviors that were John's attempts to cope with the attack by preventing the feared consequence of passing out or collapsing physically. Although John used them to reduce his anxiety, these behaviors were causing his anxiety to persist over time because they prevented him from disproving his prediction that he would faint. That is, because John had never remained standing throughout a really bad panic attack, he had not learned that falling or fainting was a highly improbable consequence of his panic attacks. In fact, because John felt that his panic attacks were causing him to fall to the floor, his safety behaviors supported his belief that a panic attack could result in fainting or falling.

A central component of panic control treatment is interoceptive exposure (Barlow & Craske, 1994; Craske & Barlow, 1993). As noted earlier, after experiencing unexpected panic attacks, a person quickly begins to associate the physical sensations that occur during attacks with the panic attack itself (interoceptive conditioning). Consequently, the person begins to fear and avoid activities that produce these sensations (e.g., exercise, drinking caffeine or alcoholic beverages, saunas) because these sensations have developed into internal cues for a panic attack. This phenomenon can be addressed in treatment with interoceptive exposure. Much in the fashion of situational exposure, this procedure entails repeated, systematic exposure to the physical sensations that the patient is known to fear (e.g., dizziness, rapid heart rate). As discussed later, John's therapist often found it very useful to combine the technique of interoceptive exposure with cognitive therapy, especially when the interoceptive exposures were successful at producing high levels of anxiety or panic.

COURSE OF TREATMENT AND TREATMENT OUTCOME

After the initial assessment session, John and his therapist scheduled the first treatment session. During this session, the therapist obtained more information about John's symptoms, such as the types of activities John avoided as the result of interoceptive conditioning (e.g., caffeine, vigorous exercise). The therapist spent a good portion of the first treatment session providing John with information on the nature of anxiety and panic, including a discussion of the integrative model of panic disorder and an overview and rationale of the treatment program, which would involve cognitive restructuring, situational exposure, and interoceptive exposure. At the end of the first session, John was given self-monitoring forms to record his daily levels of anxiety, depression, and fear of panic, as well as his panic attacks.

In the next session, John and the therapist developed two fear and avoidance hierarchies (FAH): one for agoraphobic situations and a preliminary one for interoceptive activities (more activities were added when this component of the treatment program was reached). Each item on these FAHs was very specific with regard to the situation or activity, the duration, and other relevant information (e.g., alone versus accompanied, time of day). For example, one item on John's situational FAH was "Drive up the interstate to Exit #10, alone, after dark." As noted earlier, the items on both FAHs were arranged in a hierarchical fashion (from least to most difficult) based on his fear and avoidance ratings for each item. To measure his progress, the therapist asked John to provide new fear and avoidance ratings on both FAHs at the beginning of all of their subsequent sessions. At the end of this session, John selected one item toward the bottom of his situational FAH to practice two or three times before the next meeting.

In the third session, the therapist discussed the principles and techniques of situational exposure and informed John that, at the end of each session from here on out, they would select an item off his FAH for him to perform a few times as between-session practice. Also starting in this session, the therapist began to focus on the cognitive therapy component of the treatment program. After discussing the nature of automatic thoughts, John and his therapist talked about the best way to identify cognitions that contributed to anxiety and panic. The therapist told John that patients often have difficulty identifying the feared predictions that are *most responsible* for their anxiety in a particular situation, partly because these thoughts can occur outside the person's awareness. Also, the therapist told John that patients may focus on cognitions that are too general because of either insufficient self-questioning or the tendency to avoid thinking about their feared predictions (because focusing on these thoughts may increase anxiety). For instance, a patient may identify and attempt to counter the prediction that "if I panic in a situation that is unsafe, the panic attack will persist for hours or maybe days" rather than go a step or two further by asking, "What do I fear will occur if I experience a panic attack that does not subside in this situation?" As a guideline in this process, John was told that he could be sure that he had identified an important cognition if another person would experience a similar level of anxiety if they were to have this same thought about a given situation or sensation. After rehearsing methods of identifying automatic thoughts, the therapist described two basic forms of anxiety-producing cognitions: *probability overestimation,* or overestimating the likelihood of a negative outcome of panic (e.g., John's prediction that a panic attack may result in losing control of the car and crashing); and *catastrophic thinking,* the perception that a negative outcome would be catastrophic or beyond the person's ability to cope (e.g., if John were to collapse due to a panic attack in church, he perceived the social consequences to be insufferable because of others' harsh judgments of him as weak or sick).

In this and subsequent sessions, the therapist guided John on the most effective manner of challenging his feared predictions. Like many other patients, John tended to be too global in countering his anxiety cognitions; for example, he would counter his fear of passing out by simply telling himself, "I have never passed out before." In challenging feared predictions, John was told that it was important to gather as much factual evidence as possible that would disprove the thought, for example: "A panic attack is physically the same thing as a fight-or-flight response. I wouldn't be concerned about fainting if I had this response after almost getting in a car crash—why should I be concerned about fainting due to a false alarm?" In addition, John was instructed to cite all evidence he could think of that *supported* the accuracy of his feared prediction. Thus, as part of cognitive therapy, John's therapist found it important not only to assist him in countering the cognition but also to assist him in challenging the evidence that John believed supported his feared prediction. This procedure afforded a very thorough processing of John's feared predictions and also reduced his tendency to "counter his counterarguments," for example, "Well, it's true that I never passed out behind the wheel of my car. However, I might have fainted if I hadn't pulled over and gotten some fresh air in time!" As part of the cognitive therapy component of the program, John used self-monitoring forms to record his anxiety-producing cognitions and his attempts at challenging these beliefs, as they occurred between sessions. In addition to a routine check of his other self-monitoring forms, the review of these materials became an indispensable part of each session (usually right at the beginning of each meeting). The review guided the discussion of what had occurred in the preceding week and the ways in which John could "fine-tune" his skills to become increasingly effective.

After introducing prediction testing as part of cognitive therapy (discussed later), John's therapist initiated the interoceptive exposure component of the program. After explaining the rationale of this component, the therapist asked John to do a number of sensation-producing activities during the session as a way of identifying potential exercises. These activities included things like breathing through a small straw for 2 minutes, running in place for a minute, and hyperventilating for a minute. As they went through 10 or 12 activities, John and his therapist identified several that would be useful as future interoceptive exposures (based on John's report of moderate to high anxiety and their similarity to natural panic).

Particularly similar for John was the exercise of spinning in a chair for 1 minute. Indeed, roughly 20 seconds into the exercise, John stopped abruptly in a full-blown panic attack. Though noting that John was too shaken to speak, the therapist could see that John was about to fall from his chair to the floor. John's therapist viewed this as an important opportunity in treatment, so in a firm voice, he instructed John to stand up quickly. John seemed to respond without thinking but the next thing he knew, he was standing in front of his therapist, with blinking eyes and a face beaded in sweat. Because the therapist noticed that John had spread his feet far apart (to stabilize himself), he instructed John to place his feet together. Much to John's amazement, John informed his therapist that the panic attack had subsided.

Ultimately, this turned out to be one of the most important moments in John's treatment for the following reasons: (a) it provided him with strong disconfirming evidence that a panic attack would cause him to fall to the floor; (b) it suggested to him that when he had fallen to the floor during panic, he had basically *chosen* to fall as a way of coping with the panic, that is, "beaten the panic to the punch" by falling to the floor in a more controlled way before the panic caused him to fall in a way that could be harmful, such as hitting his head on the floor; and (c) it demonstrated how the use of safety behaviors, which John used to cope with or reduce anxiety, may actually increase or prolong his anxiety. In the case of falling to the floor, this behavior prevented John from learning that a panic attack would never result in his passing out or falling over; in fact, this behavior usually increased his anxiety because he misinterpreted his voluntary drop to the floor as a consequence of some of his panic attacks.

Because several of the interoceptive activities produced high levels of anxiety, the therapist incorporated *prediction testing* into John's in- and between-session exposure exercises. Prediction testing is a technique of cognitive therapy in which the therapist and patient design a behavioral experiment to test the validity of the patient's predictions concerning the consequences of panic or the elimination of a safety behavior or the patient's predictions about what might occur during exposure to a difficult situation. For example, in a later session, John and the therapist planned to do several exposure trials of chair spinning in order to decrease John's anxiety over the sensation of dizziness, which was a frequent symptom of John's panic attacks and the sensation he feared the most because he thought it could lead to fainting or falling. Prior to the first trial, the therapist obtained John's predictions regarding the consequences of spinning as well as his rating of the accuracy of his prediction. John predicted a 50% chance that the first trial of chair spinning would cause him to fall to the floor and cause his limbs to jerk uncontrollably. The therapist recorded these predictions and instructed John to begin the first trial. Once again, John stopped the trial prematurely because the spinning elicited a panic attack, of stronger intensity than the first one. As before, the therapist noticed that John was beginning to head for the floor, so he instructed John to do what he had been told to do several weeks back when they had first began interoceptive exposure (chair spinning was at the top of John's hierarchy of interoceptive activities, so it had taken them several sessions to arrive at this exercise). Again, John complied with his therapist by standing with his feet close together. Like the first time, his panic attack subsided quickly. They compared John's predictions about the first trial to the actual consequences of the trial. After providing his predictions of the outcome of the second trial (his perceived chance of falling had dropped to 15%), John spun himself in the chair again.

Because the next several trials also produced high levels of anxiety, the therapist continued to have John test his concern about falling by performing actions that would seriously challenge this prediction. Set up as a prediction test, the therapist asked John do things after each chair-spinning trial that he predicted would *increase* the likelihood of falling (e.g., standing with feet together and arms spread apart, standing on one leg, standing while bending forward). Each time, John's feared prediction was disconfirmed by the outcome of the trial. By the end of this session, his anxiety had dropped from an 8+ on the first trial (using a 0 to 8 scale) to a 2. As with other interoceptive exercises, John was assigned chair spinning as between-session practice, to be performed in a graduated manner (with regard to duration, alone versus having wife in house). Later in the stages of interoceptive exposure, John completed practices involving more "naturalistic" activities (such as drinking caffeinated beverages). These types of exercises were also helpful in John's treatment because they exposed him to sensations that were less predictable in their intensity and duration, and hence these sensations were more similar to naturally occurring anxiety.

Although the therapist regarded cognitive countering as an important part of John's treatment, he relied heavily on prediction testing as a method of challenging John's anxiety-producing cognitions. This was done not only in tandem with interoceptive exposure but as a way to challenge thoughts associated with anxiety due to the anticipation of scheduled situational exposure practices and events that came up naturally (e.g., attending his wife's office party). This technique also was a helpful adjunct in the later stages of situational exposure when John was asked to enter these difficult situations without access to his safety behaviors (e.g., take elevator 20 floors while standing in the center of the elevator; drive up 10 exits of the interstate, alone, while leaving Xanax bottle at home). In addition, the therapist incorporated prediction testing in John's practices where situational and interoceptive exposure were combined (e.g., drink two cans of Mountain Dew before interstate driving).

When John was engaging in these combined exposures regularly without difficulty and with negligible anticipatory anxiety, his therapist was confident that John could independently apply the techniques of treatment to eliminate or reduce the symptoms that remained (e.g., air travel continued to be feared moderately, given that he did not have the opportunity to practice this item). After the 15th session, John met with his therapist on a monthly basis for five more sessions. By the final session, the therapist felt that John's panic disorder was "in partial remission"; at this point, John had some lingering apprehension of one or two activities, and, on an infrequent basis, he experienced a limited symptom attack that was usually associated with life stress. Of note, during the course of the monthly sessions, John had decreased his Xanax use to 1 mg per day, with the assistance of his prescribing physician. Six months after the final session, John telephoned his therapist to inform him that he was both panic-free and Xanax-free.

DISCUSSION

John's first panic attack occurred when he was 30, which is concordant with the research evidence that, for the roughly 3.5% to 5.3% of the population who develop panic disorder or agoraphobia during their lives (Kessler et al., 1994), the onset of the condition most often occurs in early adulthood, usually between the ages of 25 and 29 (Öst, 1987). Like most individuals who have panic disorder, John developed the complication of agoraphobia. In fact, John's agoraphobia was fairly substantial (i.e., he avoided a wide number of situations), which was somewhat at odds with the average case because most patients who suffer from extensive agoraphobia are women (Barlow, 1988). Whereas women outnumber men in the prevalence of agoraphobia, research has found that men are much more likely than women to develop substance abuse or dependence (usually alcohol; cf. Kushner, Sher, & Beitman, 1990). Although John drank a lot prior to the onset of his panic disorder, his drinking increased substantially when he began to have panic attacks regularly. This "self-medicating" only complicated his condition. As with most patients who successfully overcome their alcohol dependence, John's anxiety disorder was just as or even more severe than it was before he began drinking excessively (Chambless, Cherney, Caputo, & Rheinstein, 1987).

Despite his history of alcohol dependence, John was fortunate not to have any additional disorders at the time of his treatment. John's lack of comorbidity (presence of more than one diagnosis in the same person) is of note because most research studies have found that anxiety disorders rarely present in isolation. For example, a study (Moras, Di Nardo, Brown, & Barlow, 1995) examining the rates and patterns of comorbidity among the anxiety and mood disorders found that, of patients with a principal DSM-III-R diagnosis of panic disorder with agoraphobia, the percentage receiving at least one additional diagnosis at the time of the assessment ranged from 51% to 72% (patients with more extensive agoraphobia were more likely to have comorbid diagnoses). In this study, the most common additional diagnoses in patients with panic disorder with agoraphobia were generalized anxiety disorder, mood disorders (major depression or dysthymia), and social phobia. In addition, several studies have found that anywhere from 27% to 65% of patients with panic disorder with agoraphobia have a coexisting personality disorder. However, these figures are likely to be overestimates because most of these studies evaluated personality disorders with questionnaires rather than structured diagnostic interviews (Brown & Barlow, 1992a).

John had suffered from panic disorder for more than 15 years before he obtained specialized treatment for the condition. Unfortunately, this is also consistent with most patients' experience. Indeed, although panic disorder is one of the most prevalent psychological disorders, most patients have the problem for many years before securing appropriate treatment. This is due in part to the fact that not until 1980 was panic disorder recognized by the DSM system as a specific anxiety disorder (before then, panic attacks were viewed as a form of free-floating, generalized anxiety). Consequently, effective treatments for panic disorder have not been in existence for very long. Despite the current availability of both psychological and pharmacological treatments, many people who suffer from panic disorder still have difficulty finding appropriate treatment (or appropriate assessment). The major (yet very recent) strides in understanding the nature and treatment of panic disorder have yet to be disseminated adequately to all health care professionals. Recognizing this problem, our government's National Institute of Mental Health has sponsored a nationwide program to increase public and professional awareness of panic disorder (e.g., methods to enhance early detection) and the services available for the assessment and treatment of the condition.

Although psychosocial treatments that target panic attacks directly are relatively new, many research studies now attest to their effectiveness. These studies indicate that psychosocial treatments, such as the one described in this chapter, may even be more effective than the most common drug treatments, such as alprazolam (Xanax) (Brown & Barlow, 1992b). The potential advantage of psychosocial treatments over drug treatments is most evident in long-term outcome (i.e., the level of patient functioning several months after treatment has ended) because drug treatments are often associated with relapse when the medication is discontinued (cf. Brown & Barlow, 1992b). In contrast, patients treated with cognitive-behavioral approaches may enjoy more durable treatment gains because they have *learned* a variety of skills to respond to physical sensations or difficult situations in a nonanxious manner.

For example, in a major outcome study comparing the effectiveness of cognitive therapy, imipramine, and applied relaxation, David Clark and his colleagues (1994) found that a significantly greater percentage of patients who received cognitive therapy were classified as panic-free (85%) at the 15-month follow-up than patients in the other two treatment conditions (60% and 47% for imipramine and applied relaxation, respectively). Similarly, the percentage of patients who met "high endstate functioning criteria" at 15-month follow-up was significantly higher in the cognitive therapy condition (70%) than for imipramine (45%) and applied relaxation (32%) (high endstate was defined as no panic attacks in the month before the assessment plus a clinical severity rating of 2 or less on a 0 to 8 scale of distress and impairment). These findings are quite similar to those obtained by Craske, Brown, and Barlow (1991), who examined the long-term efficacy of a cognitive-behavioral treatment similar to that used by Clark and colleagues. Specifically, 86.7% of patients completing treatment were classified as panic-free at the 24-month follow-up; 53.3% met criteria for high endstate functioning. In this study, the discrepancy in the rates of panic-free status and high endstate status seemed to be due in part to several patients who were panic-free but still had other significant symptoms such as agoraphobic avoidance. It is interesting to note that, for research purposes, both the Clark et al. (1994) and Craske et al. (1991) studies used versions of cognitive-behavioral therapy that did not contain situational exposure. The findings from Craske et al. (1991) support the long-held clinical belief that when agoraphobia accompanies panic disorder, situational exposure should almost always be part of the treatment program. These results suggest that the elimination of panic attacks via cognitive therapy and interoceptive exposure does not ensure the elimination of agoraphobia. ~~situation~~ ~~exposure~~

THINKING CRITICALLY

1. Many persons with panic disorder with agoraphobia (PDA) state that they had never heard of "panic attacks" at the time they experienced their first attack. Some researchers believe that the general public's unfamiliarity with the nature and causes of panic attacks makes people more prone to develop PDA after an initial "out of the blue" attack; this lack of knowledge makes people more apt to misinterpret the first attack and become highly fearful of having additional attacks. Do you think this is true, and if so, why? If you did not know what a panic attack was and you experienced one, how do you think you would interpret and react to the unexpected, intense rush of fear and physical symptoms? Do you think you would be apprehensive of going back to the place where the panic attack occurred? Why? Do you believe that PDA could often be prevented if people were provided factual information about panic attacks before they ever experienced them? Why or why not?

2. As in the case of John, men are more likely than women to cope with their panic attacks by using alcohol or other drugs; women are more likely than men to develop extensive agoraphobic avoidance in response to panic attacks. Why do you think this is the case?

3. As noted in this case, panic disorder is quite prevalent in the general population. If you had a friend or family member who had begun to experience occasional panic attacks, how would you respond to them? Consider how the social and familial environment of a person with PDA might foster or maintain that person's apprehension or avoidance of daily activities (e.g., going to the store, driving, running errands).

4. Although not really an issue in John's treatment, some research has shown that persons who are taking medications (e.g., Xanax, an antidepressant) do not respond as well to cognitive-behavioral treatment as do persons who are not taking medications during therapy. What factors might contribute to this finding?

Case

3

Adolescent Social Phobia

Bonnie LaRue's parents heard about a treatment program for adolescents with social anxiety from the parents of a boy who had recently completed the program successfully. The information about the program was very timely because Bonnie had lately been asking her parents for help with her fear and anxiety. Accordingly, after hearing about the program, Mrs. LaRue contacted the clinic and arranged an initial evaluation appointment for the family.

At the time of her first appointment, Bonnie was a 15-year-old Caucasian girl in the 9th grade. As part of the evaluation, Bonnie and her parents were interviewed separately by a clinical psychologist who specialized in the treatment of childhood anxiety disorders. At the outset of the interview, Bonnie stated that her problem was that she would get nervous about everything, particularly things at school and doing anything new. When asked to give an example, Bonnie told the interviewer that her father wanted her to go to camp this summer, but that she did not want to because of her "nerves." During the course of the interview, it became clear that Bonnie's anxiety stemmed from a persistent fear of social situations where she might be the focus of other people's attention. For example, Bonnie reported that she felt very self-

37

conscious in the mall and constantly worried about what others might think of her.

The interviewer asked Bonnie about a variety of situations that are frequently feared or avoided by teenagers with social anxiety. For almost every situation, Bonnie reported at least some level of fear and avoidance. Bonnie stated that she was very fearful of such situations as eating in public, using public restrooms, being in crowded places, and meeting new people. She claimed that she would almost always try to avoid these situations. At school, Bonnie reported fear and avoidance of such activities as speaking up in class, writing on the blackboard, and talking to her teachers or school principal. Although she was very good at playing the flute, Bonnie said that she had dropped out of the school band because of her anxiety over participating in band performances. In addition to anxiety about talking to teachers, she reported that she feared talking to unfamiliar adults (such as store clerks). In fact, Bonnie stated that she would never answer the telephone in her home. She claimed that she was also very hesitant to use the phone when she would have to interact with strangers to do such things as ask for information or order pizza.

In most of these situations, Bonnie said that her fear and avoidance related to her worry about possibly saying the wrong thing or not knowing what to say or do, which would lead others to think badly of her. Quite often, her fear of these situations would be so intense that she would experience a full-blown panic attack. When Bonnie had a panic attack, the following symptoms would usually accompany her intense fear: accelerated heart rate, chest discomfort, shortness of breath, hot flashes, sweating, trembling, dizziness, and difficulty swallowing. Bonnie also reported that she would often get headaches and stomachaches when she was anticipating a situation that she found difficult. Although Bonnie often had panic attacks, the interviewer determined that her attacks always occurred during, or in anticipation of, difficult social situations.

To ascertain a thorough picture of the nature of Bonnie's difficulties, the psychologist conducted a separate interview with Bonnie's parents. While confirming what Bonnie had said, Mr. and Mrs. LaRue conveyed that their child's social anxiety was even more severe than what she had indicated. They stated that even though it was May, Bonnie was already worried and had stomachaches about beginning the 10th grade in the fall. Her parents related that Bonnie was "terrified" in public. She would not order or pay for herself in fast-food restaurants but, instead, would have her younger sister do everything for her. Although Bonnie had stated that she was not hesitant to go to parties and her parents noted that she had gone to parties during junior high school, they said Bonnie had not gone to any high school parties due to anxiety about dressing up and how she might appear to others. Although Bonnie was good-looking, they noted that she was usually quite concerned about her physical appearance. Moreover, Bonnie's parents said that when she went to parties, Bonnie would insist on going with a "safe" person—one of her best friends. Her parents reported that Bonnie would never initiate any activities, join clubs, invite friends over, or even call friends on the telephone. They said that the "last straw" had occurred 2 weeks before when they had a family gathering at their home with a number of relatives and friends attending. Because of the large number of people in the house, Bonnie had experienced a panic attack and locked herself in her bedroom for the entire day until the last guests had left.

Clinical History

Bonnie was the first of two children with a sister 2 years younger. Bonnie grew up in a happy, middle-class home. Bonnie's father was a building contractor; her mother worked as a bank teller. Her parents were happily married and had always been quite supportive of her. In response to Bonnie's social anxiety, they had pushed her to socialize more, which seemed to have the opposite effect in that Bonnie would become even more avoidant. Bonnie's parents reported no history of anxiety problems among the immediate relatives of the family. Except for typical sibling conflicts, Bonnie got along quite well with her sister. Despite her problems with social anxiety, Bonnie had two or three close friends and a number of "acquaintance" friends. Indeed, her parents told the interviewer that Bonnie could always make friends; she just would never make the first move. However, Bonnie preferred to spend time with her close friends with whom she felt safe because they were also extremely shy and had the same evaluation concerns that Bonnie did. Each day at school, the group ate lunch together and stayed together apart from the other students between classes.

Bonnie's grades at school were usually B's and a few C's. Her parents said that Bonnie achieved these grades with little effort. Interestingly, while Bonnie was often quite fearful of school, she had not missed many days over the past several school years (in fact, not a single day of the current school year). Her parents noted that Bonnie always had stomachaches before school, but she had never asked to stay home.

Although she had always been somewhat shy, Bonnie's social anxiety increased dramatically a year before her first contact with the clinic. This increase seemed to be related to two factors: (1) confrontation with all of the changes associated with entering high school (e.g., new environment, new classmates, dances, greater demands to speak up in class) and (2) a breakup with her boyfriend. After breaking up with her boyfriend the previous summer, Bonnie did not feel like doing anything or going anywhere. Particularly for 2 months during the past year (after learning that her ex-boyfriend was dating another girl), Bonnie felt very depressed. During this time, she did not sleep well, felt very fatigued, had problems concentrating, and felt worthless. Bonnie recalled that, during this time, she frequently thought and dreamed about her ex-boyfriend. A month or so before her initial evaluation, Bonnie's depression began to lift. Bonnie told the interviewer that she was beginning to return to her normal mood, in part because she had started dating another boy. However, her new boyfriend was just as shy as she was. Her parents expressed some concern that spending a lot of time with a shy boy would prevent Bonnie from coming out of her shell.

DSM-IV Diagnosis

On the basis of the information collected from the interviews of her and her parents, Bonnie was assigned the following DSM-IV diagnosis:

Axis I	300.23	Social phobia (generalized)
	296.21	Major depressive disorder, single episode, mild (in partial remission)
Axis II	V71.09	No diagnosis on Axis II
Axis III	None	
Axis IV	Breakup with boyfriend, new school	
Axis V	Global assessment of functioning = 62 (current)	

Bonnie's presentation before treatment met the DSM-IV definition of social phobia (American Psychiatric Association, 1994). In DSM-IV, the key criteria for the disorder are: (a) a marked and persistent fear of one or more social or performance situations in which the person is exposed to unfamiliar people or to possible scrutiny by others; the individual fears acting in a way (or showing anxiety symptoms) that will be humiliating or embarrassing; (b) exposure to the feared situation almost invariably provokes anxiety, which may take the form of a panic attack; (c) the person recognizes that the fear is excessive or unreasonable (in children, this feature may be absent); and (d) the feared social or performance situations are avoided or endured with intense anxiety and distress. With regard to criterion b, as discussed in some detail in the next section, some people develop social phobia after experiencing unexpected panic attacks in social situations (which would seem to be more characteristic of panic disorder). For example, it might be appropriate to assign a diagnosis of social phobia for a teacher whose difficulty began with unexpected panic attacks in front of the classroom (prior to the panic attacks, the teacher had been quite comfortable giving lectures). Using DSM-IV, the diagnostician would consider this to be social phobia rather than panic disorder so long as the person's panic attacks occurred *only* in the social situation; if the person was having panic attacks in other situations (e.g., while at home alone), panic disorder would be considered to be the appropriate DSM-IV diagnosis. Often, the focus of the patient's concern can be helpful in distinguishing social phobia from panic disorder. For example, the panic attacks of many persons with social phobia are *triggered* by an extreme concern about being negatively evaluated by others. With regard to Bonnie's case, her panic attacks are best conceptualized as features of social phobia because they (a) occur only in social situations and (b) are triggered by her intense fear of negative social evaluation. However, if Bonnie had experienced panic attacks that occurred outside social situations or for no apparent reason and if anxiety stemmed mainly from her concern about having additional panic attacks (as opposed to her concern about how she will appear to others), then a diagnosis of panic disorder would likely be appropriate.

When Bonnie was diagnosed as having social phobia, her diagnosis was assigned with the specifier "generalized." In DSM-IV, this specifier is included with the diagnosis when the person is fearful of most social situations. This was certainly true for Bonnie, who reported being fearful and avoidant of almost all situations the psychologist inquired about during the intake evaluation interview.

More information on the nature and treatment of social phobia is presented in the remaining sections of this chapter. For information on Bonnie's additional diagnosis (major depressive disorder), see Case 8.

CASE FORMULATION USING THE INTEGRATIVE MODEL

Many facets of the integrative model of social phobia are similar to the model of panic disorder discussed earlier in this book. As with panic disorder and other emotional disorders, the conceptualization of social phobia is based on a "diathesis-stress" model (Barlow & Durand, 1999). One important dimension of this diathesis (or vulnerability) is biological. This biological vulnerability relates to an inherited tendency to develop anxiety (or to experience a false alarm under stress; see Case 2) or a tendency to be very socially inhibited. The research of Kagan and colleagues (e.g., Kagan, Reznick, & Snidman, 1988; Kagan & Snidman, 1991) has demonstrated that some infants are born with a temperamental profile or trait of inhibition or shyness. While these dimensions are viewed as operating on a continuum in the general population (i.e., people vary in the amount of characteristics possessed), infants with high levels of this trait become more agitated and cry more frequently than infants low on this trait when presented with toys or other normal stimuli. Researchers have also found that social phobia runs in families. These studies indicate that relatives of people with social phobia have a significantly higher risk of developing the disorder than those whose relatives are without social phobia (e.g., 16% versus 5% in Fyer, Mannuzza, Chapman, Liebowitz, & Klein, 1993). Although Bonnie did not have a history of anxiety disorders in her family, some evidence of biological vulnerability was present from her parents' report that she had been a shy child since birth (i.e., before she ever had a chance to learn to be shy by watching other individuals behave in this manner).

However, as with other emotional disorders, a biological vulnerability is not sufficient to produce a social phobia based on the integrative model. Here is where psychological factors (or the "stress" component of the diathesis-stress model) are operative. As with panic disorder, when under stress, a biologically vulnerable person might have an unexpected panic attack (a false alarm). In the case of social phobia, this alarm occurs in a social situation, and the person develops anxiety about having additional false alarms (panic attacks) in the same or similar social situations. Subsequently, the person avoids these situations due to the fear of having more false alarms. (As noted in the previous section of this chapter, although recurrent panic attacks may suggest the presence of panic disorder, social phobia is indeed the correct diagnosis if the person's panic attacks are confined to certain social situations.) In addition to false alarms, some social phobias begin with the person experiencing a "true alarm" in a social situation. For example, some adults and adolescents with social phobia recall that their problem began after being traumatized in a social situation (e.g., ridiculed or extremely embarrassed) during childhood or early adolescence. For example, one adult male with social phobia recalled that his problem began after being derided and harshly criticized in front of his peers by a high school instructor during a class presentation. This taunting produced high levels of anxiety or even panic that he began to associate with the same and similar social situations.

In addition to the contribution of genetics in the development of the disorder (Fyer et al., 1993), psychological aspects of the person's family may be associated with the vulnerability for social phobia. For example, one study found that the parents of people with social phobia are significantly more socially fearful and concerned with others' evaluative opinions than the parents of persons who have panic disorder (Bruch, Heimberg, Berger, & Collins, 1989). It seems that these parents may pass these social concerns onto their children (e.g., the child may learn to be apprehensive of social situations by observing their parents respond in this manner).

Through one or more of these pathways, the person with social phobia develops a variety of distorted thoughts (cognitions) concerning what might happen in social situations ("I hope I don't make a fool of myself") and regarding their self-evaluation of how they performed in the situation ("They could see I didn't know what I was talking about"). The cognitive aspect of social phobia frequently involves fear of negative evaluation by others, selective attention to negative aspects of how one responded in a social situation (e.g., in recollecting a social interaction, remembering only the one instance of stuttering and not how well the rest of the conversation went), and very high standards for how one should behave and appear in these contexts (Arkowitz, 1977; Heimberg, Dodge, & Becker, 1987). This last characteristic was evident in Bonnie in that she was extremely concerned about her physical appearance (even though she was an attractive girl, she frequently berated her looks). As with most people with social phobia, Bonnie was highly fearful of being evaluated negatively by others. In the majority of situations in which she was fearful, Bonnie worried that others would think badly of her because she would not know what to say or she would say or do the wrong thing. Consequently, she avoided these situations or had someone else (such as her younger sister) do things for her. This avoidance is viewed as a key maintaining feature of social phobia. Like other anxiety disorders such as panic disorder with agoraphobia, the avoidance prevents the person from learning to be nonfearful of the difficult situations (e.g., confronting the situation helps the person disconfirm negative predictions of what might happen).

Treatment Goals and Planning

After the initial interview, the psychologist recommended that Bonnie participate in a treatment program at the clinic. This program involved a cognitive-behavioral treatment package that was developed specifically for adolescents with social phobia (Heimberg, Liebowitz, Hope, & Schneier, 1995). The therapy was delivered in a 16-session group format (usually four to six adolescents). The program was intentionally designed to be delivered in a small-group format for several reasons, one being that this format would help with a key aspect of treatment: exposure to social situations. As in the treatment of other anxiety disorders, exposure involves arranging for the person to confront feared or avoided situations (to reduce avoidance and assist the person in learning to be nonfearful of the situation). Because a person with social phobia is apprehensive of certain types of social interaction, the members of the treatment group could be used as a part of the initial exposure exercises (e.g., have the patient deliver a speech or play a musical instrument in front of the group). In addition to therapeutic exposure, a key element of Bonnie's treatment would be cognitive therapy. Cognitive therapy would identify the types of things Bonnie said or thought to herself that contributed to her fear and avoidance of social situations. Usually, these thoughts concerned predictions of all of the terrible things that would happen. Next, she would be taught methods of challenging these fearful predictions in a very thorough way. Bonnie's therapists would also utilize the situational exposure exercises to assist her in challenging her anxious predictions (e.g., comparing what actually happened in a social interaction to what Bonnie had predicted). Finally, Bonnie's treatment would include social skills training. Partly because they are so avoidant of many situations, some persons with social phobia never learn to behave in a socially effective manner. Social skills training is an educational approach of identifying skills deficits (e.g., inappropriate ways of interacting with people), introducing appropriate behaviors (often modeled by the therapist), and then giving the patient the opportunity to repeatedly rehearse the behavior (with feedback from the therapist and group members) until the patient can respond in a smooth and natural fashion (Heimberg & Barlow, 1988).

COURSE OF TREATMENT AND TREATMENT OUTCOME

With considerable trepidation, Bonnie attended her first group treatment session. In addition to Bonnie, five teenagers were assigned to this group: two boys and three girls. The group was led by a licensed clinical psychologist and a senior graduate student who was training to become a clinical psychologist. The primary goals of this first meeting were to have each of the group members introduce themselves, establish the ground rules for the group (e.g., importance of attendance, participation, and completion of between-sessions homework), and provide a rationale for the techniques to be covered over the next 15 sessions. Bonnie was extremely anxious when called on to introduce herself to the group and describe some of her problem areas. However, she did offer a few areas and noted that eating in front of others was a particularly difficult situation for her. This was the only time in this session that Bonnie spoke up in group.

During this session, the therapists assisted each of the group members in developing a fear and avoidance hierarchy (FAH). The FAH contained 10 situations, arranged from least to most difficult, that the person currently feared and avoided. Later, these situations would serve as targets for the situational exposure practices. Items on Bonnie's FAH included eating in front of others, ordering pizza over the phone, talking in front of the class, playing the flute in front of others, and buying things in a store. At the beginning of every session, the therapists had each member of the group rate each item on the FAH for current level of fear and avoidance, as a method of evaluating progress. In addition, the group was provided self-monitoring forms to record their daily anxiety levels. They were asked to do this self-monitoring throughout treatment. In later sessions, after the topics were introduced, this self-monitoring also required group members to record difficult social situations they had encountered and to write down how they acted and what they thought in anticipation of, and during, these situations.

In the second session, Bonnie was a bit more talkative. However, she spoke only when called on. Nevertheless, she did a very thorough job with her between-session homework, which was to specify her goals for the treatment program. Some of the goals Bonnie listed were (a) giving an oral report in school without being so nervous, (b) ordering a pizza over the phone without worrying about messing up, and (c) not feeling anxious when going to places where she didn't know everyone. The therapists spent a considerable portion of this session providing the group with an explanation of the nature of anxiety. For example, a three-systems model was reviewed in which anxiety was explained as consisting of three components (or systems): physiological (sensations such as racing heart or trembling), cognitive (thoughts such as "I'm going to make a fool of myself"), and behavioral (actions such as avoiding a situation or not making eye contact). Each person in the group was asked to do a "three-systems analysis" of a recent episode of anxiety (i.e., break down the episode into its three components). They were told that doing so was important for future anxiety episodes because the information would be very useful when applying the treatment techniques they would learn.

In the next three sessions, the cognitive component of the three-systems model of anxiety was addressed. During these sessions, Bonnie continued to be very hesitant to speak in group and would often nod her head instead of speaking to answer questions. Nevertheless, she was very motivated for treatment and compliant with the group exercises and between-sessions homework. She was quite attentive to the therapists' instructions on how to identify thoughts that trigger anxiety (referred to as *automatic thoughts*). Bonnie and the rest of the group were given a list of the types of automatic thoughts that produce anxiety (e.g., "all or none thinking," that is, thinking in black or white or either-or terms: "If I stutter one time when I'm presenting an oral report, that shows that I'm a poor speaker"). After each type of automatic thought was defined, each member of the group was asked to provide a specific example based on personal experience. Next, the therapists instructed the group on how to challenge these thoughts by treating the thought as a guess rather than a fact and then generating all the evidence they can to support or disprove the thought (referred to as *brainstorming*). In the early phases of this component of treatment, the therapists assisted Bonnie in challenging her belief that she was *unable* to accomplish certain social activities. For example, Bonnie initially maintained the idea that she could not order pizza over the phone as she would be too anxious to complete the call effectively.

After she had "brainstormed" this prediction a few times, Bonnie began to consider the notion that she could order pizza over the phone; it would just be very difficult the first several times, and at present she was not prepared to attempt it.

By the sixth session, Bonnie was beginning to feel more comfortable in the group. For example, she was starting to participate when the group would brainstorm a member's automatic thought. In this session, the therapists introduced the social skills training component of the treatment program. To begin this component, the therapists role played a conversation between socially skilled and unskilled teenagers. The group members were asked to identify instances of good and poor social skills, both verbal and nonverbal. The group was also asked to identify social behaviors that would improve the quality of a social interaction. During this discussion, Bonnie spoke up and listed "facing the person you're talking to" as an example of good social skills. The therapists discussed the steps to be taken to improve social skill deficits (e.g., identify the deficit, imagine practicing the skill, anticipate difficulties that may arise while trying to change the behavior, actually practice the skill, self-praise after completing the practice). A couple of examples that Bonnie identified as targets for social skills training were to cease playing with her hair during social interactions and to increase her eye contact with the people she spoke to. Assertiveness training was covered in this session as well.

In the next session, Bonnie was more verbal than she had ever been. In fact, she volunteered to participate in a role play to illustrate good social skills. Bonnie role played an interaction that typically produced considerable anxiety: asking a teacher for assistance with a class assignment. With another group member acting as the teacher, Bonnie role played this interaction for 5 minutes. After the role play, the group and the therapists critiqued Bonnie's performance (e.g., one group member said, "It was good that when you noticed that you were playing with your hair, you stopped and looked at the teacher").

Bonnie was also beginning to show improvement in another aspect of group: snack time. At the halfway point of most sessions, there was a 15-minute period when refreshments were served. This period was not really a break because the therapists used the time to assist the group in shaping their social skills and to target other aspects of social anxiety in a graduated manner. For example, in addition to fostering the group members' comfort when they were interacting informally with each other, this period would often be used to rehearse a new skill (e.g., to shape public speaking skills, members would take turns reading a passage from a book to the group). Because refreshments were served (sodas, light snacks), this portion of the session was very difficult for Bonnie at first because it required her to eat in front of others. However, at this session her therapists noticed that Bonnie was eating with little difficulty.

Despite the gains she was achieving, Bonnie became very anxious when the therapists introduced the next phase of the group. The next seven sessions would involve therapeutic exposure: In a graduated way, each member of the group would begin to confront the situations listed on her or his FAH. At this time Bonnie's parents called the therapists to provide them with an update on her progress. Her parents told the therapists that they were encouraged with certain aspects of Bonnie's response to treatment. For example, they noted that Bonnie was now doing things she had once avoided, such as answering the telephone and ordering in restaurants; in fact, Bonnie was ordering for her boyfriend, who was shyer than she was! However, her parents said that Bonnie and her boyfriend still would not eat in front of each other's parents. More troublesome, they reported that Bonnie had refused an audition to play the flute for the school band, even though she had no problems playing the piece she would have performed in the audition. The therapists responded that these two areas, eating in public and playing the flute, would be given thorough attention in the upcoming situational exposures.

In the next meeting, the group was informed about the procedures and purposes of situational exposure. After an item from the FAH was selected by the adolescent, the situation was simulated in the group by using the other members. Prior to initiating the exposure, the patient was asked to identify his or her worst fears of what could happen. These fears were incorporated into the exposure. The patient's anxiety was monitored before and during the exposure, and anxiety-producing cognitions were identified and challenged after the exercise. The exposure was then assigned to be practiced between sessions.

Because her parents had urged her to bring her flute to the session, Bonnie selected "playing the flute in front of others" as her first exposure. The therapists asked Bonnie what was the worst thing she feared might happen while she played the flute in front of others. Bonnie replied that she most feared that her audience would whisper, giggle, and not pay attention to her playing. Bonnie elected to play the piece she would have been asked to perform at the audition for the school band. For the first several minutes, Bonnie played the piece in front of the other group members and the two therapists. At the end of each minute of the exposure, Bonnie was asked to rate her level of anxiety on a 0 (none) to 8 (as much as you could imagine) scale. Initially, Bonnie's ratings were 7s and 8s; by the sixth minute of the exposure, she rated her anxiety as a 5. At this point the therapists brought several strangers—graduate students who worked in the clinic—into the room. For the first few minutes, Bonnie's anxiety increased to 6 or 7 again, particularly when the "strangers" began to whisper and giggle. However, Bonnie continued to play, and by the end of the 10-minute exposure trial, she rated her anxiety as a 4 (moderate). She acknowledged the group's praise for her meeting her goals of completing the entire exposure, playing loud enough, and facing the audience the whole time. For homework, Bonnie was assigned to play the flute for her family and her boyfriend's family.

In subsequent sessions, Bonnie and the other group members worked up their FAHs to confront situations that were more difficult for them. By the 14th session, Bonnie was prepared to confront her most difficult situation: eating in front of others. Unlike the "mini-exposures" that occurred at snack time, Bonnie was asked to eat in front of the group while everyone watched. Halfway through the exposure, a new set of unfamiliar people came into the room to watch Bonnie eat. Perhaps because she had become more comfortable with similar situations through previous exposure practices (e.g., eating alone in a crowded cafeteria), Bonnie's anxiety was not as high as it had been for playing the flute, which was a less difficult item on her FAH. Her anxiety ratings ranged from a 6 to a 2 by the end of the trial. Bonnie said that one reason why the practice had not been that difficult was because it was easier to eat the food used in the exposure trial (potato chips). She said that pizza would be much more difficult because it was harder to chew and because of the stringy cheese (she worried that others would think she was stupid when it came to eating pizza). Bonnie was asked to bring pizza to the next session for her next exposure practice.

In the next session, Bonnie ate pizza in front of the group and four new strangers. Although initially anxious, she met her goals of being able to chew and swallow and to make eye contact and conversation while she was eating. After the first exposure trial, Bonnie remarked that when she began to become anxious, she either stopped eating or slowed down her eating considerably. Accordingly, Bonnie was asked to complete another exposure trial, this time eating the pizza more quickly. For homework, Bonnie was assigned to eat with her boyfriend's family.

The final session was spent reviewing what had been covered in the program and planning how each of the group members could refine and continue to apply the skills they had learned for areas that still needed to be addressed. This meeting closed with an hour-long farewell party.

As part of the treatment program, Bonnie was contacted for evaluations immediately after treatment had ended and 6 and 12 months later. At the post-treatment evaluation, Bonnie was considered to still have signs of social phobia; however, these symptoms were rated as being not frequent or severe enough to meet the DSM-IV definition of social phobia. Notably, Bonnie's depression was in full remission (i.e., Bonnie had not displayed symptoms of this disorder for more than 6 months). At the 6- and 12-month follow-up interviews, Bonnie showed even further improvement, as she was continuing to apply the techniques she learned in group. At these assessments, Bonnie reported no fear or avoidance of eating in public, talking to teachers or other adults, or participating in meetings. In fact, between the two follow-up evaluations, Bonnie had auditioned for and joined the school band. Nevertheless, she still noted that she was apprehensive of some situations (e.g., using public bathrooms, writing on the blackboard, giving oral presentations in class). Bonnie's parents stated that "she has come a long way" and "Bonnie's a normal kid now." They reported that many things that used to be very hard had become easy for her, but that Bonnie was still uncomfortable with entering totally new situations (e.g., interacting with a new teacher at the beginning of the school year); despite some anticipatory anxiety, however, she would almost never avoid these situations.

DISCUSSION

Considering the general population (both children and adults), the 12-month prevalence of social phobia is roughly 8% (i.e., 8% of persons surveyed met criteria for social phobia at some time during the 12 months prior to being interviewed); roughly 13% of persons meet the criteria for social phobia sometime during their lives (Kessler et al., 1994). In these large community surveys, the sex ratio for the disorder is approximately 70% female and 30% male (Schneier, Johnson, Hornig, Liebowitz, & Weissman, 1992). These figures do not include the high proportion of people who consider themselves shy or who report feeling uncomfortable with certain social situations, such as dating or asserting themselves. As in Bonnie's case, whereas many people report a lifelong history of being shy, the full-blown disorder of social phobia most often begins in the teenage years with a peak age of onset at about $15\frac{1}{2}$ years. Studies indicate that social phobia tends to occur more in persons who are younger (ages 18 to 29), less educated, single, and of a lower socioeconomic class.

Like many other anxiety disorders, social phobia often does not present in isolation (Brown & Barlow, 1992a). Consistent with Bonnie's presentation, studies have indicated that persons with social phobia frequently (roughly 20% of cases) meet criteria for having a mood disorder (major depression, dysthymia) as well. Social phobia is often present in patients who seek treatment for another disorder that is more interfering or distressing. For example, one study (Moras, Di Nardo, Brown, & Barlow, 1995) found social phobia to be the second most frequently assigned additional diagnosis (behind generalized anxiety disorder) in patients with other anxiety or mood disorders.

All evidence for the effectiveness of psychosocial treatments for social phobia comes from studies of adult patients; controlled investigations of these treatments for children and adolescents are ongoing. The first studies to evaluate treatments for social phobia involved social skills training only.

However, researchers later concluded that an intervention relying on social skills training alone is inadequate in the treatment of social phobia for several reasons, including (a) many patients with social phobia do not have social skills deficits and (b) social skills training does not target many of the maintaining features of the disorder (e.g., situational avoidance, cognitive distortions relating to the overestimation of risk in social situations; see Heimberg et al., 1987, for a review). Thus, studies began to examine treatment approaches that targeted the specific features of social phobia. Findings from these investigations revealed that these approaches can be very effective in the treatment of this disorder.

Research has suggested that the most effective interventions for social phobia are those that include both cognitive techniques and situational exposure, similar to the treatment program that Bonnie completed. For instance, Mattick and Peters (1988) compared the effectiveness of exposure alone to exposure plus cognitive restructuring in 51 patients with social phobia. Although both conditions showed considerable improvement, patients treated in the exposure plus cognitive restructuring condition showed more improvement than patients treated with exposure alone on many of the treatment outcome variables that were examined. At a 3-month follow-up evaluation, patients in the exposure plus cognitive restructuring group showed continued improvement whereas patients treated with exposure alone showed no change. In a similar study with a different set of patients, these findings were supported overall (Mattick, Peters, & Clarke, 1989).

The treatment program that Bonnie completed was modeled after a protocol developed for adults by Heimberg and his colleagues (Heimberg et al., 1990, 1995). In the first controlled study of this treatment package, Heimberg et al. (1990) compared their cognitive-behavioral group treatment to a credible placebo treatment (educational-supportive therapy). This latter condition was designed to be an approach that patients would view as an effective treatment for social phobia but contained no elements that researchers believed were helpful to treat this disorder. These types of conditions are sometimes useful in therapy outcome research because they assist the investigators in learning whether their treatment package is effective for reasons other than nonspecific factors such as attention, treatment credibility, patient expectations, and the "pressure" patients may feel at the end of treatment to report that the intervention has been helpful to them. Interestingly, Heimberg et al. (1990) found that both groups showed significant improvement, suggesting that "nonspecific" effects may account for some of the change in the patients. However, patients in the cognitive-behavioral group showed significantly more improvement than the placebo group at each of the assessments (posttreatment, 3- and 6-month follow-ups). In fact, whereas many of the gains noted in the placebo group at posttreatment were no longer evident at 6-

month follow-up, patients treated with cognitive-behavioral therapy continued to show improvement. Moreover, a recently published study of these patients indicated that those treated with cognitive-behavioral therapy maintained their treatment gains 5 years after the program had ended (Heimberg, Salzman, Holt, & Blendell, 1995).

Because certain drugs have been effective in the treatment of social phobia (e.g., the tricyclic antidepressants and the monoamine oxidase inhibitors; see Liebowitz et al., 1992), research is now beginning to compare psychosocial treatments to drug treatments. One such study is comparing the effectiveness of the cognitive-behavioral treatment developed by Heimberg and colleagues to the monoamine oxidase inhibitor, phenelzine. Preliminary results show that both treatments are roughly equal in their effectiveness in the short term (Heimberg, 1993, cited in Barlow, 1994). However, there is some evidence that the cognitive-behavioral treatment may be more effective than phenelzine in the long term because some patients treated with phenelzine show a return of symptoms after the drug has been discontinued. This is similar to the findings of several studies examining the long-term outcome of drug treatments of panic disorder (see Brown & Barlow, 1992b, for a review). These results suggest that an advantage of cognitive-behavioral treatments over drug treatments might be that, when treated with these programs, patients learn things that they can continue to apply long after treatment has ended.

However, another goal of the study examining the effectiveness of cognitive-behavioral therapy and phenelzine is to see whether certain subgroups of patients with social phobia respond better to one form of treatment or the other. It has been suggested that cognitive-behavioral therapy is most effective for patients who fear only a certain set of social situations (e.g., public speaking); some researchers speculate that drug treatment may be more effective than nondrug treatments for patients with generalized social phobia. Fortunately, this was not the case for Bonnie, whose generalized social phobia responded quite well to cognitive-behavioral group treatment.

THINKING CRITICALLY

1. As in the case of Bonnie, many persons experience mood disorders (e.g., major depression) during the course of their social phobia. Why do you think this is the case? What features of social phobia are similar to the features and possible risk factors of depression?
2. Like panic disorder, social phobia is very prevalent in the general population. Why do you think this is the case? What factors do you believe are the most important causes of social phobia?

3. Some degree of shyness or social anxiety is found in most individuals (e.g., feeling anxious when giving a class presentation, trying to be assertive, or asking someone on a date). What do you think separates normal social anxiety from a DSM-IV diagnosis of social phobia?
4. Bonnie received group treatment for her social anxiety. What are the advantages and disadvantages of group treatment (versus individual treatment) as an intervention for social phobia?

4

Posttraumatic Stress Disorder

C indy Oakley responded to a community advertisement for a university-based research clinic that was evaluating treatments for victims of sexual assault. At the time of her first contact with the clinic, Cindy was a 26-year-old Caucasian woman with two children. She was not employed outside her home, although she had recently been hired to do some freelance work that was scheduled to start in a few weeks.

During her first interview at the clinic, Cindy reported that she had been depressed for the last 3 months. The depression had started shortly after Cindy had ended a 5-week extramarital affair. During the affair, Cindy began to have flashbacks of events from 10 years in the past. These events centered around a series of repeated rapes that occurred when she was 16 years old. In addition to distressing images of these events that seemed to come into her mind out of nowhere, these flashbacks included times when Cindy would momentarily feel as if the past were occurring all over again. When Cindy realized that this affair coincided with the exact time of year that she had been raped, she broke off the affair. Nevertheless, Cindy became increasingly depressed and agitated as more memories surfaced.

It was only now, a decade later, that Cindy began to label what had occurred then as rape. At the initial interview, Cindy stated that she had been raped repeatedly over a 5-week period by a close friend of the family. This boy, who was the same age as Cindy (16 years old) lived across the street. Because the boy came from an abusive family, Cindy's family "adopted" him. He was best friends with her brother, and so he spent a lot of time at their home. Cindy's parents were also quite fond of him. Prior to the rape, Cindy said that she had had a "brother-sister" relationship with the boy, whose name was Mark.

Cindy gave only a sketchy account of these incidents during the first interview and made very little eye contact with the interviewer. The interviewer did not press for details during this session but rather focused on standardized questions from a structured clinical interview that was part of the research program. During the interview, Cindy reported that she had been a virgin prior to the rape and had trusted Mark quite a bit before the assault. She was verbally threatened by him, although no weapons or physical injuries were involved. Cindy was subjected to a range of sex acts, including oral, vaginal, and anal intercourse. During the assaults, her most prominent reactions were feeling detached and numb, guilty, and embarrassed. The incidents were not reported to the police, and she never received medical care.

During the initial interview, Cindy stated that she often smoked marijuana. She was defensive about her use of it and said that she did not want to quit. In addition, Cindy stated that one of her previous therapists had made a big deal over her marijuana use. When Cindy had told this therapist that she felt that she was using marijuana as a crutch, he informed her that marijuana was her main problem. She disagreed, told the therapist that she did not want to make marijuana the focus of her treatment, and quit therapy. In fact, besides the single session with this therapist, Cindy had sought therapy two previous times; however, each of these contacts had lasted only one session.

Clinical History

Cindy described her childhood as a happy one. She characterized her house as the safe house in the neighborhood, where all the kids could come to play and where some found refuge from problems in their own homes. Cindy's father had been a Vietnam veteran who continued to have posttraumatic stress disorder from events he had experienced during the war. She described her father as emotionally shut off, yet spoke very fondly of him. She described her mother as a self-help fanatic who kept the house filled with self-help books. Cindy also stated that she had a close and supportive relationship with her mother. As noted earlier, Cindy had one older brother who was best friends with the boy who had raped her. Cindy claimed that she was close to her brother until the rape; since the rape, they rarely interacted with each other.

After describing her childhood before the rape, Cindy told the therapist about how drastically things had changed since these incidents. Cindy said that she had told her mother what had happened and that her mother stopped the abuse. After the therapist questioned her a bit further, however, Cindy recalled that she had told her mother that Mark had been "coming on" to her, that it had gotten out of control, and that she needed help getting out of the situation. The abuse ended after Cindy's mother told Mark to leave Cindy alone. Cindy never told her mother that she had been raped. Therefore, her family did not understand why she had changed. After the rape, Cindy withdrew from her normal high school activities and began to hang out with troubled kids. Over the year following the assaults, Cindy lied often and began drinking. She described herself as floating in and out of reality. She and her mother fought frequently. A year after the rape, a friend of hers was driving recklessly and crashed the car in which Cindy was a passenger. Cindy was out of school for 2 months with a broken back. She recalled that over the next few years she became a "total rebel" and dated a "wild guy who was totally bad news." She became pregnant by him and, not knowing what to do, consulted her father. Her father took over and arranged for an abortion. Although Cindy said that she might have ultimately made the same decision, she now regretted that she had relinquished her right to decide. Cindy did not have the self-confidence to go to college. Her mother talked her into taking classes at a business school for secretarial training. She had worked as an executive secretary until the current year. At the time of this initial interview, Cindy had been unemployed for 6 months.

Cindy stated that fortunately she had had the "good sense" 5 years ago to marry a fine man with whom she had two children. Cindy said that her husband was very supportive of her and did not give up on her after the affair. Cindy's husband was also very supportive of her efforts to receive therapy. Other than her husband, however, Cindy claimed that her social support was rather poor. In fact, Cindy reported receiving negative reactions to her disclosure about the assault from others who were closest to her. For example, Cindy recalled that she had once told one of her best friends that she was having a difficult week because the memories of the rape were surfacing. Her friend, a woman she had known since high school, responded by saying, "Get over it."

DSM-IV Diagnosis

On the basis of the information collected during the initial interview, Cindy was assigned the following DSM-IV diagnosis:

Axis I	309.81	Posttraumatic stress disorder, chronic (principal diagnosis)
	296.21	Major depressive disorder, single episode, mild
	305.20	Cannabis abuse
Axis II	V71.09	No diagnosis on Axis II
Axis III	None	
Axis IV	Unemployment	
Axis V	Global assessment of functioning = 55 (current)	

Although she received additional diagnoses of major depression and cannabis abuse at pretreatment, Cindy was assigned a principal DSM-IV diagnosis of posttraumatic stress disorder (PTSD; American Psychiatric Association, 1994). If an individual presents with more than one diagnosis, the term *principal* is used to denote the diagnosis that is associated with the greatest amount of distress or life-style interference (i.e., the diagnosis most in need of treatment at the time).

Posttraumatic stress disorder (PTSD) is a type of anxiety disorder. In DSM-IV, the key criteria for PTSD are (a) the person has been exposed to a traumatic event in which both of the following were present: (1) the person experienced, witnessed, or was confronted with an event that involved actual or threatened death or serious injury, or a threat to the physical integrity of self or others, and (2) the person's response involved intense fear, helplessness, or horror; (b) the traumatic event is persistently reexperienced in one (or more) ways (e.g., distressing dreams or intrusive recollections of the event, acting or feeling as if the event were recurring, intense distress and physical reactivity at exposure to cues that symbolize or resemble the event); (c) persistent avoidance of stimuli associated with the trauma (e.g., avoidance of activities, places, or people that arouse recollection of the trauma, inability to recall an important aspect of the trauma) and numbing of general responsiveness (feeling detached or estranged from others, restricted range of emotions); and (d) persistent symptoms of increased arousal (e.g., sleep difficulties, irritability or anger outbursts, exaggerated startle response).

As seen in her five-axis diagnosis, the diagnosis of PTSD was assigned along with the specifier "chronic." In DSM-IV, "chronic" is assigned when the duration of symptoms is 3 months or more; when the duration is under 3 months, the clinician should use the specifier "acute." In addition to the "chronic" or "acute" specifier, DSM-IV uses the specifier "with delayed onset" for cases when the onset of PTSD symptoms is at least 6 months after the trauma. Although Cindy experienced a substantial increase in her symptoms following her extramarital affair, she had evidenced a wide array of PTSD symptoms since the trauma (e.g., distress upon exposure to cues of the rape, inability to recall aspects of the rape, irritability, feelings of detachment). Hence, the "with delayed onset" specifier was not used in her case.

A fuller discussion of the nature and treatment of PTSD is provided in the remaining sections of this chapter. For a discussion of the major depressive and substance use disorders, see Cases 8 and 13.

CASE FORMULATION USING THE INTEGRATIVE MODEL

As is the case with most of the other disorders discussed in this book, the integrative model of PTSD is very useful in guiding how psychological difficulties stemming from exposure to extreme stress should be evaluated and treated (Barlow & Durand, 1999). Although exposure to stressful life events may often contribute to the development of a wide variety of emotional disorders (e.g., panic disorder, major depression), the experience of a traumatic stress is a *necessary* causal factor in the development of PTSD. However, exposure to extreme stress (e.g., sexual assault, combat, natural disasters, severe automobile accidents) alone is not *sufficient* to produce PTSD. Several studies have indicated that, even under conditions of intense or prolonged exposure to traumatic events (e.g., being held as a prisoner of war), many individuals do not develop PTSD (Foy, Sipprelle, Rueger, & Carroll, 1984; Kulka et al., 1990). Thus, whereas exposure to extreme stress is necessary to the development of PTSD, whether a person develops PTSD after experiencing a traumatic event is also related to a number of other biological, psychological, and social factors.

Like other emotional disorders (anxiety disorders, mood disorders), biological factors appear to contribute to the vulnerability to develop PTSD. Although specific biological markers (e.g., genes) have not been identified, research has shown that persons who have a family history of anxiety disorders are more likely to develop PTSD (Davidson, Swartz, Storck, Krishnan, & Hammett, 1985; Foy, Carroll, & Donahoe, 1987). As in panic disorder, this vulnerability may be the tendency to be neurobiologically overreactive to stress (Jones & Barlow, 1990). Recent evidence providing further support for the role of biological factors comes from a twin study. In this study, if one twin had PTSD, a monozygotic (identical) twin experiencing the same amount of combat exposure was more likely to develop PTSD than a dizygotic (fraternal) twin (True et al., 1993). Because monozygotic twins have exactly the same genes whereas dizygotic twins share only about 50% of each other's genes, the higher rate of PTSD in monozygotic twin pairs suggests that genetic factors contribute to the development of PTSD.

Both the integrative model and recent studies (e.g., Mellman & Davis, 1985; Rainey, Manov, Aleem, & Toth, 1990; Southwick, Krystal, Johnson, & Charney, 1992) attest to the similarity of PTSD and panic disorder. In the integrative model, it is assumed that the alarm reaction is much the same in both panic disorder and PTSD (see Case 2). However, while the alarm in panic disorder is false, in PTSD the initial alarm is true because a real danger is present. Nevertheless, if the true alarm is severe enough, a person may develop a conditioned or learned alarm reaction to cues that resemble or remind them of the trauma. For instance, the combat veteran who witnessed his buddies perish during intense firefights in Vietnam may relive some of these memories when confronted with stimuli that remind him of these events (e.g., gunfights in movies, a car backfiring, being near a wooded area). The most common ways that traumatic events are "relived" in PTSD are distressing dreams of the event, flashbacks (acting or feeling as if the event were recurring; in addition to vivid memories, they may take the form of hallucinations or the sense that one was actually experiencing the trauma again), physical and emotional distress when exposed to cues that symbolize or resemble the event, and distressing images or thoughts.

Similar to the model of panic disorder, a central factor in the development of PTSD is the emergence of intense anxiety about the possibility of having additional reliving experiences. The extent to which this anxiety develops depends in part on the level of a person's preexisting vulnerability, particularly if the severity of the traumatic event is rather low. For example, Foy et al. (1987) found that at very high levels of trauma, these vulnerabilities matter less because most people who experience very extreme stress develop PTSD (e.g., most persons would experience symptoms of PTSD if exposed to very extreme events such as being held prisoner of war and witnessing many friends being brutally tortured and killed). This finding has been replicated in other studies that have found a strong correlation between the extent of exposure to extreme stress and the amount of PTSD symptomatology (e.g., Kulka et al., 1990). Conversely, at lower levels of stress, vulnerability (e.g., level of psychological functioning prior to the event) is more strongly predictive of posttrauma adjustment.

Factors besides preexisting vulnerability have been shown to contribute to psychological functioning after experiencing traumatic events. In addition, the style by which a person copes with stress (Fairbank, Hansen, & Fitterling, 1991) and social and cultural factors play a major role in the development of PTSD. These studies have indicated that those who have a strong and supportive group of people around them (i.e., social support) are much less likely to develop PTSD after experiencing a trauma (Carroll, Rueger, Foy, &

Donahoe, 1985). For example, Frye and Stockton (1982) found the highest levels of PTSD in Vietnam veterans whose families expected them to adjust quickly to civilian life and who did not acknowledge the traumatic nature of the veteran's experiences. Indeed, it has been speculated that an important factor contributing to the high rate of PTSD in Vietnam veterans was the negative social and political context of the war. This environment discouraged many veterans from discussing their experiences, which, as will be seen later in the discussion of direct therapeutic exposure, is an important factor in determining whether a person will continue to have adjustment difficulties.

Indeed, all psychosocial theories of PTSD assert that a key factor in the maintenance of the disorder is escape from and avoidance of the distressing cues that symbolize or resemble the traumatic event (Foa, Steketee, & Rothbaum, 1989; Keane, Fairbank, Caddell, Zimering, & Bender, 1985). That is, because people persistently avoid thoughts, images, memories, and activities that are associated with the event, their anxiety and fear (i.e., learned alarms) do not diminish over time. Information-processing models of PTSD (e.g., Chemtob, Roitblat, Hamada, Carlson, & Twentyman; 1988; Foa et al., 1989) underscore the notion that exposure to extreme stress may be associated with drastic alterations in the way people view themselves and the world (e.g., "The world is an unsafe place," "People cannot be trusted," "I am responsible for what has happened"). Accordingly, their avoidance of the trauma may prevent them from examining and challenging these cognitions, which would also contribute to the maintenance of their adjustment difficulties.

Many aspects of Cindy's history are consistent with the integrative model. Although Cindy did not report an extensive family history of emotional disorders that would be suggestive of biological vulnerability, her father suffered from PTSD due to his experiences in Vietnam. As noted earlier, it appears that biological vulnerability is less important in the development of PTSD in instances where a person is exposed to severe trauma, such as repeated and violent sexual assault or extensive exposure to combat. Concordant with the integrative model and the nature of PTSD, Cindy experienced an exacerbation in PTSD symptoms when she was confronted with cues that reminded her of the rapes that had occurred 10 years ago; that is, she began to have flashbacks of the rapes during the time she was having an extramarital affair. Her avoidance of the event and low level of social support were factors that seemed to contribute strongly to why Cindy continued to have difficulties 10 years after the trauma. For instance, partly due to her embarrassment over what had happened to her, Cindy never reported the assaults. In fact, the rare instances Cindy had attempted to discuss her experiences with others were usually met with negative reactions, which reinforced her tendency to keep this information to herself. Much evidence from Cindy's report indicated that she had attempted to avoid thinking about her negative experiences. Evidence of this avoidance included a history of treatment contacts that lasted only one session, use of alcohol and marijuana, and distancing herself from her brother, who had been best friends with her assailant. Further evidence of Cindy's avoidance was observed in the initial interview session, in which she offered only a sketchy account of what had happened to her. As guided by the integrative model of PTSD, a major focus of treatment would be Cindy's avoidance because this factor is viewed to be key in the maintenance of the disorder.

Treatment Goals and Planning

After the intake interview, Cindy was assigned a licensed clinical psychologist who had extensive experience in the development and delivery of cognitive-behavioral treatments for victims of sexual assault. Specifically, Cindy's treatment would involve *cognitive processing therapy,* an intervention designed to treat the specific symptoms of PTSD in victims of sexual assault (Resick & Schnicke, 1993). As with other cognitive-behavioral treatments of PTSD, an important component of Cindy's therapy would be systematic exposure to the memories and cues surrounding her sexual assaults. The goal of exposure is to have the patient recall the assault in detail and to process the memory until it is no longer painful or distressing. This does not occur naturally over time because of the person's efforts to avoid this upsetting material. Unlike other forms of therapeutic exposure (e.g., exposure to live spiders for a person with a specific phobia of them), it is usually not practical to arrange for the patient with PTSD to be exposed to real-life fear cues (e.g., automobile accidents, physical assaults, combat). Hence, therapeutic exposure in the treatment of PTSD is typically done by having the patient fully imagine and recall all of the events, plus their thoughts and feelings connected to the traumatic event (referred to as "imaginal exposure" versus "situational" or "in vivo" exposure when real life cues are used).

Cognitive processing therapy differs from imaginal exposure in a number of ways. Because this form of treatment is based on an information-processing model of PTSD (discussed earlier), the victim's thoughts and feelings concerning the traumatic event represent a principal focus of treatment. Specifically, imaginal exposure alone is not considered to be sufficient in reducing PTSD symptoms because it does not directly address the patient's faulty cognitions that have developed as the result of the trauma. For instance, after exposure treatment, sexual assault victims may continue to blame themselves and feel shame, distrust, or anger to an extent that would contribute to the maintenance of intrusive memories, arousal, and avoidance (Calhoun & Resick, 1993). Accordingly, cognitive processing therapy contains a cognitive restructuring component to address these thinking patterns.

COURSE OF TREATMENT AND
TREATMENT OUTCOME

Cindy arrived 45 minutes late for her first treatment session. Her therapist considered Cindy's behavior to be avoidant and told her that this behavior is a symptom of PTSD. Cindy's therapist talked about how avoidance had prevented her from recovering from the rape and that Cindy was going to need to confront her fears head-on in order to deal with them in therapy. Cindy admitted that she had been afraid to come to the session and said that she could see the storm coming (distressing emotions and memories). Nevertheless, Cindy expressed hopefulness about the outcome of treatment, and another session was scheduled.

Although Cindy arrived on time for the next session, she admitted that she had smoked marijuana before the session to calm her nerves. Because Cindy had prematurely terminated treatment with a previous therapist who had made a "big deal" of her marijuana use, Cindy's therapist downplayed it in this session. However, the therapist did label her marijuana use as another form of avoidance and asked Cindy not to use marijuana before sessions or while completing homework assignments. Cindy agreed.

Some of the major goals on the agenda of this session were to (a) describe the symptoms of PTSD and inform Cindy how these symptoms developed and why they had not disappeared, (b) present an overview and rationale of treatment and have Cindy understand why homework completion and session attendance are so important, and (c) establish rapport and allow Cindy some time to talk about the rapes or any other issues. Toward the end of this session, Cindy's therapist explained three major goals of treatment: (a) to remember and accept the rapes, (b) to allow Cindy to feel her emotions and let them run their course so the memories could be put away without such strong feelings still attached, and (c) to get Cindy's beliefs (e.g., relating to trust, safety) that had been disrupted and distorted by the assaults back in balance. During the entire session, Cindy remained wrapped and huddled in her jacket, yet she was quite attentive and agreed to complete the first homework assignment. In this assignment, Cindy was asked to write at least one page about the meaning of her rapes, including the effects on her beliefs about herself, others, and the world. In addition to beginning the therapeutic exposure aspect of treatment, the purpose of this assignment was to gather information on how Cindy interpreted her sexual assault. This information would be very useful in the cognitive restructuring component of treatment.

The purposes of the next session were to discuss how Cindy interpreted the event and to begin to help her identify and label emotions and thoughts associated with the experience. Cindy arrived at the session with obvious emotion and cried periodically throughout the meeting. During the session, the therapist asked Cindy to read her homework assignment aloud. In cognitive processing therapy, patients are always asked to read their assignments aloud to help them confront their thoughts, feelings, and reactions to the material. Based on what Cindy had written and other comments she made during the meeting, it was clear that she believed that she had allowed the rapes to happen. She also expressed considerable distrust and anger with society, particularly politicians and people with money and power. It became evident to the therapist that this anger and distrust stemmed from the fact that Cindy's rapist had gone on to a military academy and was now enjoying an illustrious career. Cindy felt unsupported by her family, even though she had chosen not to tell them what had happened. Although the therapist did not directly challenge these interpretations, she did point out to Cindy that traumatic experiences can cause people to view themselves, others, and the world inaccurately. The therapist also noted that some interpretations and reactions that follow naturally from rape and do not need to be altered. For example, the therapist stated that she would not challenge Cindy's belief that her rights had been violated and that she feels angry. Instead, the therapist encouraged Cindy to feel the anger so that this emotion could run its course.

For homework, Cindy was provided with self-monitoring forms to assist her in further identifying her thoughts and feelings and the strong connection between them. Each time Cindy experienced a negative emotion or a symptom of PTSD (e.g., intrusive recollection of the rape), she was asked to record the situation, where it occurred, the thoughts she was having at the time, and the types of feelings she was experiencing (e.g., ashamed, sense of loss). In the next session, Cindy and her therapist continued to identify thoughts and feelings connected to Cindy's sexual assault. At the end of this session, Cindy's therapist introduced the therapeutic exposure component of treatment. Specifically, Cindy was asked, for homework, to write a detailed account of the most traumatic rape she had experienced (of the several assaults that Cindy had undergone, she considered the first assault to be the most traumatic). She was instructed to include as many sensory details as possible, including her thoughts and feelings during the rape (based on the evidence that exposure therapy is most effective when all possible cues are incorporated in the exposure). Cindy was told that if there were parts of the rape that she did not remember, she should mark this on the paper and continue on at the point she remembered next. In addition, she was instructed to read the account to herself every day until her next session. The therapist told Cindy that the purposes of the assignment were to help her regain the full memory of the assaults and to allow her to feel her emotions about it so that they could run their course. Cindy was also reassured that though this week might be difficult for her, it would not continue to be so intense, and that she would soon be over the most difficult part of therapy.

At the start of the next session, Cindy was asked to read her account of the rape out loud. Cindy quietly read the 10 pages she had written, crying most of the time. She read about how Mark and she were alone at her house dancing together as part of practice to win a contest. After the song was over, Mark began to kiss her and touch her breast. Cindy tried to push him away, but he tightened his arms around her and whispered that he could tell that she liked it. He wrestled Cindy down to the hall to her own bedroom and pinned her on her bed. In considerable detail, Cindy read about how she was raped. It ended with Mark kissing her on the cheek and leaving her room quietly. After noticing the semen on her stomach and blood on her inner thighs, Cindy recalled that she spent the next 30 minutes huddled in the shower sobbing uncontrollably (even for 10 minutes after the hot water ran out). Even though it was only 4:30 p.m., Cindy put on her pajamas after the shower and went to bed in her parents' room. When her mother got home, she told her that she was sick. Cindy spent a sleepless night in the room, her thoughts racing over such things as how could she possibly explain to her parents and her boyfriend what had happened, her mixed-up feelings about Mark ("I had been proud of him but now I was disgusted"), and her loss of virginity. Cindy described why she had elected not to tell anyone about the incident: "I chose not to tell to save a lot of people from being hurt." She also wrote of her encounter with Mark the next day. Mark said that he wanted to talk with her after school. Thinking that he maybe wanted to apologize, Cindy agreed to meet him at her house. She planned to "rip him up" with her words, but ultimately forgive him; "After all," she thought, "even though it had been violent, Mark had been gentle." Cindy then wrote how their meeting did not turn out that way. Although Mark began by saying he was sorry, he said that he knew that she liked it because she didn't scream or fight and didn't tell anyone afterwards. Mark told her that she was strong enough to stop it and she didn't. He then led Cindy to her bedroom and raped her again. Cindy wrote that she let Mark put her on her own bed and have sex. She felt it didn't matter anymore; if anyone knew, it would destroy her. She also recalled how Mark began threatening her: What if her parents or her boyfriend knew? There was no way that Cindy could get away from him! Cindy also wrote about how she began to feel that her own home was not safe anymore.

After reading her account, Cindy and her therapist discussed how much anger Cindy had and how she had turned her anger against society. Cindy also described how difficult things had been the past week with her husband. They had gotten into several fights, and Cindy was angry at her husband for no longer being supportive. The therapist talked about other people's reactions to rape, and she told Cindy that sometimes people's strong emotions interfere with their ability to be supportive. An important aspect of this session was that in writing and talking about the rape in detail, Cindy began to realize that she was not personally responsible for what had happened to her. Specifically, she and her therapist talked about the fact that while Cindy had not told others about the rape to avoid hurting them, Mark had used it against her by forcing her to believe that she had remained silent because she had liked it. The therapist told Cindy that she had done the best she could in an impossible situation. She praised Cindy for doing a great job on the writing assignment and told her that it was important not to quit now. Cindy replied by saying she was more determined than ever. For homework, the therapist asked Cindy to write the entire account of the rape again and to add any details she might have left out the first time. In addition, Cindy was instructed to record any thoughts or feelings she was having now in parentheses along with her thoughts and feelings at the time of the assaults.

Cindy was quite cheerful and animated at the next session. She reported that she had felt a great deal of energy and had accomplished much of her housework over the past week. She also stated that she and her husband had talked. He had apologized and had since been very sensitive, loving, and supportive. The therapist asked Cindy how the writing had gone. Cindy responded that this time there were no tears—she was a little shaky but not as emotional. New to her written account of the assaults and their aftermath was her description of how Mark had asked Cindy's brother if he could come to her wedding. Mark went to her wedding in his academy uniform. He had asked her to dance. Cindy recalled dancing with him in her wedding dress as everyone else was so cheerful and happy looking at the bride. She remembered all the girls at the wedding asking who that gorgeous guy in the uniform was. Because her husband had passed out from drinking too much at the reception, Cindy sat up all night alone, feeling sad and angry and wondering why Mark had wanted to go to her wedding. She wrote about how she had had bad feelings about her wedding for the next 2 years.

After Cindy read this account, the therapist helped her recognize that she didn't have to be afraid of her emotions anymore and that she was learning to tolerate her feelings, even intense feelings. Cindy talked some more about her reactions to other people. She focused on her brother and described how she thought that her brother had let her down because he did not see the truth about Mark. The therapist asked if Cindy had ever tried to talk to her brother about this matter. She replied that "it would be like talking to a brick wall"; besides, her brother was still friends with Mark and wrapped up in his own life. The therapist also addressed Cindy's distrust of society and successful people, stemming from her experiences with Mark. She suggested to Cindy that the fact that Mark went on to the academy was perhaps not relevant to the rape or to whether she could trust people. Instead, what may have been more relevant is the fact that Mark was from a troubled, abusive home and perhaps he was lashing out. Cindy began to accept that she may have made a faulty connection between the person who had raped her and went on to be successful and everyone else who is successful.

During the next several sessions, Cindy and her therapist more thoroughly addressed the cognitive component of Cindy's problem with cognitive restructuring. Specifically, the therapist helped Cindy to identify and challenge her negative beliefs that had developed in response to the rape. To assist in this process, the therapist introduced a faulty thinking patterns list, which included seven types of cognitive errors that may be associated with the aftermath of sexual assault. For example, one type of faulty thinking pattern is called "overgeneralization," which refers to drawing a broad conclusion on the basis of a single event. As noted earlier, Cindy overgeneralized a great deal of distrust and anger from Mark, who had gone on to a successful military career, to all successful or powerful people. By the sixth treatment session, Cindy started a new job and was working more than 40 hours per week. Although she was excited by the job and the people she was meeting, Cindy expressed concern about how much she was changing. She told the therapist that she wanted to figure out what things she did not want to change. After some questioning, her therapist got the impression that Cindy was still ambivalent about what it meant to be successful; in other words, Cindy feared that if she changed too much, she would become one of those people she had always despised. As in the treatment of other disorders (e.g., see Case 2), the therapist challenged these cognitive errors by helping Cindy examine all of the factual evidence that would support or refute a belief such as "no successful people can be trusted." Over time, Cindy told her therapist that she had noticed her views were beginning to change. When she saw somebody with a nice car or saw an authority figure on television, Cindy was starting to tell herself, "Just because someone accomplishes something, that doesn't mean they walked over bodies to get there. Maybe they worked hard."

Similarly, the rape had affected Cindy's beliefs about the safety of the world. Her belief that the world was an unsafe place was reinforced by the news on television. Cindy said that she almost never watched the news because it showed how violent the world had become and how bad everyone was. Using the faulty thinking patterns list, the therapist helped Cindy realize that this conclusion was an example of "disregarding important aspects of a situation." Specifically, Cindy started to realize that she was not considering the fact that this was the "news," that events on the news are announced because they are unusual, bad, or important. Newscasters do not talk about how many millions of people were not crime victims or did not do something illegal that day.

Cindy's distant relationship with her brother was addressed as well. Cindy had expressed her desire to never tell her brother about the rape, not because she worried that he might side with Mark (whom her brother was still friendly with), but because she did not want to hurt him. The therapist pointed out that while Cindy had stopped Mark from destroying her life, he was still interfering with her relationship with her brother. The therapist told Cindy that her brother was probably old enough now to handle what Cindy would tell him. She suggested that Cindy might approach the subject with her brother by telling him something like: "There's something that happened a long time ago that I never told you about because I was afraid that it would hurt you. However, I can see what it's doing to our relationship to keep this big secret between us." After Cindy and her therapist had discussed this, Cindy arrived at the next session stating that she had written a letter to her brother that she would most likely not send. She read the letter aloud. In it, Cindy expressed her concerns that her brother would be hurt and that he might not believe what had happened. This was also true for her father, whom Cindy was protecting because he had PTSD from Vietnam. Nevertheless, Cindy conveyed a sense of relief over the realization that she was not responsible for how her brother and father would react. With the guidance of her therapist, Cindy realized that she was not giving them the opportunity to grow closer to her and thus she was cutting herself off from important sources of social support.

In later sessions, Cindy and her therapist discussed issues relating to self-esteem. Cindy said that, although it was not a big problem now, she once had a negative view of herself because she felt that she was responsible for what had happened to her. In addition to assisting Cindy in identifying and challenging her cognitions that had lowered her self-esteem, the therapist assigned homework activities to help Cindy with her views of herself and others. For instance, Cindy was asked to practice giving and receiving compliments every day and to do one thing nice for herself each day. When she first began these exercises, Cindy found it awkward to reach out and compliment others. However, the results were positive. One time at a family gathering, Cindy found that she was able to disarm a usually critical in-law by complimenting her. She also got better at receiving compliments. When her husband complimented her, Cindy did not downplay the comment but rather listened and thanked him.

As an assignment for the last therapy session, Cindy was asked to rewrite what the rape meant to her. At the beginning of this session, the therapist asked Cindy to read aloud what she had written. Cindy read about how much she and her views had changed as the result of the work that she and her therapist had accomplished. She spoke of how she was not responsible for what had happened and that she had nothing to be ashamed about:

> A part of this is the girl who was raped, abused, and manipulated. I will never forget, but I will not let it destroy me. That girl survived and did a damn good job. . . . To pull my deepest, darkest inner secret up has been very hard. It was poisoning me though. With genuine help, I pulled that secret demon out and faced him head on. Thank you [the therapist]. I couldn't do it alone. You helped me because you were let in. You were the first one I trusted. You helped me break the ice.

In reviewing Cindy's progress, the therapist read what Cindy had written the first time at the beginning of treatment. Cindy laughed at the line she had written about most people being greedy, self-righteous scum. Cindy ended the session by acknowledging what she had accomplished and her goals for the future. One of these goals was to improve her relationships with her brother and with her father.

A week after this session, Cindy met with another clinician for a post-treatment evaluation. The results of this assessment indicated that Cindy no longer met diagnostic criteria for PTSD, major depression, and marijuana abuse. All of her scores on questionnaire measures of PTSD, depression, and overall functioning were quite positive and well within the normal range. Evaluations conducted 3 and 6 months after therapy revealed that Cindy continued to do well and score in the nonsymptomatic range on all questionnaire measures.

Two weeks after treatment, Cindy telephoned the therapist to tell her that she had told her brother about the rapes. As expected, her brother had a hard time comprehending that a good friend of his had raped his sister. Cindy was pleased that she told him because he would now understand why she had distanced herself from him. Three months later, she told her therapist that her relationship with her brother was still a bit strained, partly due to the fact that he was pushing her to confront Mark. Cindy did not succumb to this and asserted that she would not consider confronting Mark until she felt confident that she could handle whatever reactions Mark had. Otherwise, Cindy reported great strides in her other personal relationships. Her job was going well, and she had made several close friends at work. Her relationship with her father was improving. Although they did not talk about the rape, they were spending more time together and talked about Cindy's work and other family news.

DISCUSSION

In the population at large, the lifetime prevalence of PTSD ranges from 1% to 2.6%, depending on the survey (Helzer, Robins, & McEvoy, 1987). However, prevalence rates of PTSD are much higher in people who have been exposed to extreme stress (e.g., rape victims, combat veterans). Estimates of the prevalence of rape have varied widely across studies due in part to differences in the methodological approach used in these investigations (cf. Brown, Abueg, & Fairbank, 1992). In one recent study (Kilpatrick, Edmunds, & Seymour, 1992), 13% of women reported that they had been victims of completed, forcible rape; of these women, 39% had been raped more than once. These figures are much higher when other forms of sexual assault are included in the prevalence estimate, such as attempted rape (e.g., 14.5% to 24%; cf. Kilpatrick et al., 1985; Koss, 1983; Russell, 1984). In addition, several studies of female college students have revealed a startlingly high prevalence (as high as 77.6%) of some form of sexual aggression in dating situations (e.g., Koss, Gidycz, & Wisniewski, 1987; Muehlenhard & Linton, 1987). These studies indicate that, as was the case with Cindy, the rapist is frequently an acquaintance or friend of the victim. This finding is significant in light of evidence that acquaintance rape often leads to adjustment difficulties that are more severe than those associated with stranger rape, perhaps because of a greater disruption in the victim's perceptions of trust and safety (McCahill, Meyer, & Fischman, 1979; Resick, 1983).

Evidence from a national survey (Kilpatrick et al., 1992) found that 31% of rape victims develop PTSD at some time after the assault. A large national survey that examined the prevalence of PTSD in Vietnam veterans (Kulka et al., 1990) indicated that 15% of male and 9% of female veterans who served in the Vietnam theater (i.e., Vietnam, Cambodia, or Laos) met diagnostic criteria for PTSD, either currently or within the past 6 months from the time they were evaluated (i.e., 6-month prevalence). An additional 1.1% of male and 7.8% of female Vietnam theater veterans met study criteria for "partial PTSD" (presence of clinically significant symptoms that did not meet the diagnostic threshold for PTSD).

As was true for Cindy, the symptoms of PTSD are often not the only problem that stems from sexual assault. Just like Cindy, who was assigned an additional diagnosis of major depression at the start of treatment, symptoms of depression are quite common in rape victims. Compared to a rate of 2.2% in nonvictims, Kilpatrick et al. (1985) found that 19.2% of rape victims had attempted suicide at some point following the assault; another 44% reported suicidal thoughts but no attempts. Findings from one study suggest that depressive symptoms may persist for several years after the assault, if left untreated (Ellis, Atkeson, & Calhoun, 1981). In addition to depression, substance use problems (e.g., Burnam et al., 1988) and sexual dysfunctions (e.g., Becker, Skinner, Abel, & Cichon, 1986) are frequent sequelae to sexual assault. Similarly, a high rate of diagnostic comorbidity (especially depression, substance abuse, and other anxiety disorders) has been found in Vietnam veterans with PTSD (Kulka et al., 1990).

Because PTSD is a relatively new diagnosis (it first appeared in the DSM in 1980), firm evidence for the effectiveness of psychosocial treatments for the disorder has become available only over the last several years. As discussed earlier in this chapter, almost all of these treatments have incorporated some form of therapeutic exposure to the cues resembling or symbolizing the traumatic event (Fairbank & Brown, 1987); another frequently used form of treatment involves cognitive and stress management and coping interventions. One type of stress management intervention is stress inoculation training, which includes relaxation training, diaphragmatic breathing, role playing, and techniques to stop or cope with intrusive thoughts about the traumatic event (Veronen & Kilpatrick, 1983). In one of the few large, controlled studies that have directly compared these two forms of treatment in rape victims, Foa, Rothbaum, Riggs, & Murdock (1991) found that the coping skills–based treatment, stress inoculation training (SIT), was more effective than prolonged exposure (imaginal exposure to trauma memories) immediately after the end of treatment. Both treatments were more effective than a waiting list and supportive therapy. However, prolonged exposure was found to be more effective than SIT when patients were reevaluated 3.5 months after treatment. The authors of this study speculated that the long-term superiority of prolonged exposure may be due to the fact that direct exposure techniques result in permanent changes in PTSD symptomatology; in contrast, the techniques introduced in SIT (e.g., coping skills, relaxation) may require continued application to maintain their effectiveness. In the studies of Vietnam combat veterans with PTSD, prolonged, imaginal exposure has been found to be more effective than either a waiting list (Keane, Fairbank, Caddell, & Zimering, 1989) or the standard outpatient program delivered by the Veterans Administration (Boudewyns & Hyer, 1990; Cooper & Clum, 1989).

As is often found in the treatment of other emotional disorders, it is likely that researchers will eventually demonstrate that some combination of exposure and cognitive or coping skills therapy will be the most effective in the treatment of patients with PTSD (Calhoun & Resick, 1993). Cindy responded quite well to such a treatment—cognitive processing therapy (Resick & Schnicke, 1993). It is interesting to note that this treatment contains an exposure component that is quite different from the typical exposure-based treatments such as the one used by Foa et al. (1991), in which patients are repeatedly exposed to trauma cues in a prolonged manner. In cognitive processing therapy, patients write about the traumatic event in detail and are asked to read their account aloud during the session. Despite the fact that this treatment contains less therapeutic exposure than other exposure-based treatments, early results attest to the efficacy of this approach (Resick & Schnicke, 1993). For example, in a study of rape victims with PTSD, 88% of women treated with cognitive processing therapy no longer had the disorder at posttreatment; at 6-month follow-up, this rate increased to 92%. As was true for Cindy, patients participating in this study showed marked improvements in their accompanying depression as the result of cognitive processing therapy.

THINKING CRITICALLY

1. In designing the diagnostic criteria for posttraumatic stress disorder (PTSD) in DSM-IV, considerable effort was devoted to wording these criteria so that the diagnosis would only apply to individuals who develop symptoms (e.g., nightmares, intrusive recollections) after experiencing *extreme stress or trauma* (see "DSM-IV Diagnosis" in this case). When these events involve stressors such as sexual assault or combat, it is clear that the "traumatic event" criterion for PTSD has been met. However, for

some stressors this judgment is not straightforward (e.g., running over the beloved family pet with the car or viewing graphic news footage of a brutal war, crime, or murder). Based on the diagnostic criteria listed in the "DSM-IV Diagnosis" section of this case, what types of stressful events do you believe qualify and do not qualify for the PTSD diagnosis? Do you think these criteria should be revised to allow persons who suffered less extreme stressors to be given the PTSD diagnosis if they are experiencing all the other symptoms? What would the ramifications (e.g., legal, insurance) be if the criteria were relaxed to include less severe stressors?

2. In cognitive-behavioral treatments for PTSD, some form of repeated, prolonged exposure to the traumatic memories (e.g., imaginal exposure, writing a detailed account of the trauma) is emphasized as a key therapeutic component. Do you believe this is true, or do you think that PTSD can be treated successfully with other methods that do not involve confrontation of these painful and highly distressing recollections?

3. Although the effects of her sexual assault had been manifested in other ways (e.g., substance abuse, reckless behavior), Cindy did not experience the first clear-cut symptoms of PTSD until 10 years after these events occurred. What factors do you think can contribute to such a delayed onset of PTSD symptoms? Do you believe that memories of past physical or sexual abuse can be fully repressed and later remembered? Why or why not?

4. Much research has been conducted on persons with PTSD, whereas scientists have often neglected the fact that many people who were exposed to severe trauma never develop the symptoms of this disorder. What personal characteristics and aspects of the social environment do you think would help a person adjust well to extreme stress?

Case

5

Obsessive-Compulsive Disorder

at Montgomery was referred by her psychiatrist to a clinic specializing in psychological treatments for anxiety disorders. In the 3 years preceding her referral to the clinic, Pat had participated in two studies examining the effectiveness of medications in the treatment of obsessive-compulsive disorder (OCD). In the first of these projects, Pat had taken a tricyclic antidepressant called Anafranil (clomipramine). In the second study, Pat was prescribed a different type of antidepressant medication, Prozac (fluoxetine). Although both drugs were antidepressants, research had shown that these medications can be effective for OCD. However, Pat's symptoms had not responded to either drug. Given that Pat had not benefited from two of the leading drug treatments for OCD, her psychiatrist recommended that she try a psychosocial approach for her problem.

At the time of her referral to the anxiety disorders clinic, Pat was a 40-year-old Caucasian woman with two daughters (ages 20 and 22). Pat reported that, for the past 6 years, she was intensely fearful of becoming contaminated by germs that would cause her to come down with some deadly disease. As a result, she would wash her hands several times a day. At the time of her first visit to the clinic, Pat claimed that she washed her hands more than

71

40 times per day. In fact, the psychologist noticed that Pat's hands were very red and the skin around her fingernails had receded; each time Pat "cleaned" her hands, she would scour them with a rough pad and detergent. In addition to her handwashing, Pat repeatedly and excessively cleaned other things she came in contact with, including dishes, clothes, furniture, and doorknobs. On a typical day, Pat spent 4 hours washing her hands and cleaning these other objects. Although she usually took one shower a day, Pat would spend 60 to 90 minutes in the shower. When Pat washed her hair, she would keep the soap in her hair until she had counted to 100 to ensure that her head and hair were clean enough and free of contaminants such as germs.

Pat also feared that she could be contaminated by her food. In addition, she worried that her husband and children could contaminate her food. As a result, Pat kept her food separate from her family's food and would not allow them to come in contact with her food (nor would she touch her family's food). For several food products, Pat kept separate containers for herself and for her family. For example, there were always two milk cartons in her refrigerator: one for her and one for the rest of the family. After completing meals, Pat washed her own dishes before washing the dishes of her family. After washing the dishes excessively (dishwashing often took 45 minutes), Pat spent a great deal of time cleaning her hands.

Pat reported that a principal source of contamination by germs related to funerals, funeral homes, and dead bodies. For example, Pat felt contaminated if she happened to drive by a funeral home or a funeral procession. Pat feared or avoided many objects because she worried that someone who had been to a funeral and may have indirectly come in contact with the dead body, may have come into contact with those objects. There were dozens of objects in Pat's environment that she feared had been in contact with a funeral (e.g., clothes, shoes, doorknobs, toys, foods, rooms). One reason why Pat considered so many things to be contaminated was that she believed that something could become contaminated if it came in contact with something else that was already contaminated. For example, Pat owned a purse that she feared was contaminated by a friend of hers who had visited their home. Because this friend had mistaken Pat's purse for her own, she had picked it up briefly. When Pat later learned that her friend had recently attended a funeral, she insisted that her husband take the purse out of the house. In fact, Pat demanded that her husband take the purse out of the house by going through the window because it was the shortest path out of their home. Her husband complied and put her purse in the storage shed. Although it had been 4 years since this occurred, Pat had not gone near the shed or the purse, despite the fact that the purse contained two hundred dollars and her credit cards. Subsequent to her friend's visit, Pat rarely visited other people because she feared that they had attended a funeral.

Before Pat would begin washing, she always experienced strong urges to rid herself of germs and contamination. Whereas Pat had attempted to resist her urges to wash in the initial stages of her problem, she noted that she rarely resisted these urges now. In fact, now her attempts to resist the urges often triggered a panic attack. In addition to her fears of contamination, Pat worried that these panic attacks would cause her to go crazy or "flip out" until she gave in to the urges. Once she initiated her cleaning rituals, her panic attack usually subsided quickly.

Unlike some individuals with OCD (see the discussion section of this chapter), throughout the course of her problem Pat was able to recognize that her obsessions and compulsions were excessive and unreasonable. Although Pat could sometimes hold an objective view that her chances of being contaminated were very low, her intense fear of contamination overrode this realization (similar in nature to the person who fears and avoids air travel but who can concede that the realistic chances of crashing are remote).

Clinical History

Pat reported that she began to notice the first signs of her problem during her high school years (e.g., she was more concerned with cleanliness than her peers appeared to be). However, not until 6 years before her first visit to the anxiety disorders clinic were Pat's symptoms severe enough to warrant a diagnosis of OCD. Pat could not recall any factors (e.g., stressful life events, death or illness in the family, attendance at a funeral) that were connected to her increase in symptoms 6 years ago. Pat also could not recall if any of her family or relatives had a history of OCD-related difficulties. However, Pat did report that both her sister and her father had suffered from, and sought treatment for, anxiety problems that appeared to meet the definition of panic disorder.

Since her problem had intensified 6 years ago, Pat said that her life had been pretty rough. As noted earlier, Pat had sought treatment on two occasions, both involving drug interventions, with little success. Until 2 years before her first visit to the anxiety disorders clinic, Pat had worked as a vocational counselor at a state-run employment agency. Despite excellent job security and benefits, Pat had quit this position due to her fear of coming into contact with persons who had been to a funeral (or who had been in contact with another person who had been to a funeral). She had been unemployed since then. Pat reported that her family was very supportive of her problem. While her husband would occasionally become frustrated over her compulsions (i.e., washing) and her inability to do certain things or work outside the home, usually he would be cooperative with Pat's cleaning rituals (e.g., he would take "contaminated" things out of the house and permit her to buy separate foods for herself).

As part of her first visit to the anxiety disorders clinic, Pat underwent a structured clinical interview that was designed to comprehensively evaluate the anxiety and mood disorders and associated conditions such as the substance use and somatoform disorders. In addition to establishing the nature of Pat's OCD symptoms, this interview revealed a few other problem areas. Although it was not a major area of concern, Pat reported a strong fear of snakes. More important, Pat reported ongoing difficulties with depression that had begun around the time that she completed the first medication program for her OCD and noticed that she was not getting any better. In addition to feeling down most of the time over the last few years, Pat reported moderate symptoms of poor appetite, trouble sleeping, and decreased interest in activities she usually found pleasurable (all symptoms of depression). More recently, Pat reported an intensification in her depression. At the time of the interview, Pat stated that in addition to the symptoms that had been present for the past few years (e.g., poor appetite, insomnia), her depression had been accompanied by loss of energy, fatigability, feelings of guilt, concentration difficulties, and mild thoughts about the possibility that life may not be worth living. With regard to this last symptom, Pat denied thoughts or intent of suicide. She related her depression to her increasing doubts and sense of hopelessness about ever recovering from her symptoms of OCD.

DSM-IV Diagnosis

On the basis of this information, Pat was assigned the following DSM-IV diagnosis:

Axis I	300.30	Obsessive-compulsive disorder (principal diagnosis)
	296.22	Major depressive disorder, single episode, moderate
	300.40	Dysthymic disorder, late onset
	300.29	Specific phobia, animal type (snakes)
Axis II	V71.09	No diagnosis on Axis II
Axis III	None	
Axis IV	Unemployment	
Axis V	Global assessment of functioning = 50 (current)	

In accord with the impression of her therapist, the symptoms that Pat reported during her first visit to the anxiety disorders clinic were quite consistent with the DSM-IV definition of OCD (American Psychiatric Association, 1994). Obsessive-compulsive disorder is a form of anxiety disorder. In DSM-IV, the essential features of the disorder are recurrent obsessions or compulsions that are severe enough to be time-consuming (i.e., they take up more than 1 hour a day) or cause marked distress or significant life-style impairment (i.e., interfere with the person's normal routine, occupational or academic functioning, or usual social activities or relationships).

Obsessions are defined by DSM-IV as possessing all of the following features: (a) recurrent and persistent thoughts, impulses, or images that are experienced as intrusive and inappropriate and that cause marked anxiety or distress; (b) the person attempts to ignore or suppress such thoughts, impulses, or images or tries to neutralize them with some other thought or action; and (c) the person recognizes that the obsessions are a product of his or her own mind. This latter specification is important in the differentiation of OCD from psychotic disorders (such as schizophrenia), wherein intrusive and distressing thoughts or images are often perceived by the individual as being inserted into their mind from an outside source. Nevertheless, when clinicians assign the diagnosis of OCD, they have the option of including the DSM-IV specifier "with poor insight." This specifier is appropriate when the patient with OCD does not recognize that the obsessions (and compulsions) are excessive or unreasonable. As with the specifiers for other DSM-IV disorders (e.g., "generalized" type in social phobia), this specifier is included because it conveys more about the nature of the patient's OCD, including its treatment prognosis. Indeed, there is some evidence that patients who have OCD with poor insight do not fare as well in exposure and response prevention treatment (Foa & Kozak, 1989). Pat's diagnosis had not been assigned with this specifier because she had perceived her fears of contamination as somewhat irrational.

Pat suffered from one of the most common types of obsession: thoughts of contamination (e.g., contracting germs from doorknobs, money, toilets, and so on). In addition to fears of contamination, other types of obsessions include excessive doubting (e.g., uncertainty if one has locked the door or turned off appliances; concerns that tasks such as managing personal finances were not completed or were completed inaccurately), fear that one has caused accidental harm to oneself or others (e.g., accidentally poisoning someone, unknowingly hitting a pedestrian while driving), nonsensical or aggressive impulses (e.g., undressing in public, hurting self or others intentionally), horrific or sexual images or impulses (e.g., images of mutilated bodies, images of having sex with one's parents or a religious figure), and nonsensical thoughts or images (e.g., numbers, letters, songs, jingles, or phrases). Note from this list of examples and the DSM-IV criteria that obsessions may take the form of thoughts, images, or urges and impulses.

Compulsions are defined by DSM-IV as having the following features: (a) repetitive behaviors or mental acts that the person feels driven to perform in response to an obsession or according to rules that must be applied rigidly, and (b) the behaviors or mental acts are aimed at preventing or reducing distress or preventing some dreaded event or situation; however, these behaviors or mental acts either are not connected in a realistic way with what they are designed to neutralize or prevent or are clearly excessive. Pat experienced one of the most prevalent forms of compulsions: washing and cleaning. Note that the DSM-IV criteria state that compulsions can take the form of either overt behaviors (such as Pat's washing and cleaning) or mental acts. Other types of behavioral compulsions include *checking* (e.g., assuring that doors are locked or appliances are turned off, retracing a driving route to make sure that one has not struck a pedestrian, reexamining waste baskets to ensure that important material has not been discarded), *hoarding* (e.g., collecting things such as newspapers, garbage, or trivial items due to the belief that the material will be needed at some time in the future), and *adhering to certain rules and sequences* (e.g., maintaining symmetry such as touching an object with one's left hand if the object had been previously touched with the right hand; adhering to specific routine or order in daily activities such as putting on clothes in the same order). Types of mental compulsions include counting (e.g., certain letters or numbers, objects in the environment), and internal repetition of material (e.g., phrases, words, prayers) in order to "neutralize" one's obsessions.

The DSM-IV diagnostic criteria for OCD do not require that the person experience both obsessions and compulsions in order to be assigned the disorder. For example, studies have indicated that roughly 25% of patients with OCD do not evidence compulsive behavior (e.g., Brown, Moras, Zinbarg, & Barlow, 1993; Mavissakalian, Turner, & Michelson, 1985). However, these studies were conducted when previous editions of the DSM were in place. Not until DSM-IV were mental acts such as internal repetition considered as a type of compulsion. Thus, it is likely that there is a much smaller proportion of patients with OCD who do not evidence any form of compulsions whatsoever (as low as 2%; see Foa & Kozak, 1995).

A full discussion of the nature and treatment of OCD is presented in the remaining sections of this chapter. Note that Pat was assigned three additional diagnoses, including major depressive disorder and dysthymic disorder. These conditions are discussed in detail in Case 8.

CASE FORMULATION USING THE INTEGRATIVE MODEL

As with the other disorders discussed in this book, the integrative model of OCD is a diathesis-stress model emphasizing both biological and psychological factors (Barlow & Durand, 1999). Part of the diathesis component of this model is the biological vulnerability to experience anxiety. Indeed, findings of studies examining twins or the rates of disorders among family members have provided some evidence that OCD tends to run in families (e.g., Black, Noyes, Goldstein, & Blum, 1992). This dimension was somewhat evident in Pat, who did not recall a family history of OCD but did indicate a history of panic disorder in her first-order relatives. This provided some evidence that Pat may have possessed a biological tendency to experience anxiety.

Although Pat could not recall any life events that contributed to the onset or increase in her OCD symptoms, the integrative model underscores the importance of stress in the origins of this disorder. For example, in addition to triggering unexpected panic attacks (see Case 2), research has shown that the frequency of both intrusive, unpleasant thoughts and ritualistic behavior (e.g., washing, checking) increases when we are in the midst of some stressful situation (Parkinson & Rachman, 1981a, 1981b). Whereas stress may trigger these symptoms, it is not sufficient in producing full-blown OCD. In other words, while many people experience intrusive thoughts or ritualistic behavior after being exposed to stressful life events, most do not go on to develop OCD.

So what factors determine whether these initial symptoms develop into OCD? As in the other anxiety disorders (such as panic disorder), the integrative model asserts that anxiety focused on the possibility of experiencing additional symptoms is a central factor in the cause of OCD. Specifically, a person who has some intrusive thoughts in response to life stress may be anxious over the possibility of having more of these thoughts because they perceive these thoughts as dangerous or unacceptable. Consequently, the person attempts to suppress these thoughts. However, suppression has the opposite effect of increasing the frequency and intensity of the thoughts, a phenomenon that has been supported by recent research evidence (e.g., Salkovskis & Campbell, 1994). These points are consistent with recently developed cognitive models of OCD that underscore the position that people who believe some thoughts are unacceptable or dangerous are at greater risk for developing OCD (Salkovskis, 1985, 1989).

The integrative model addresses why some people may develop anxiety over experiencing additional OCD symptoms such as intrusive thoughts. Consistent with ideas expressed in cognitive conceptualizations of OCD (e.g., Salkovskis, 1989), the model specifies that these individuals may have had previous experiences that have taught them to perceive some thoughts as dangerous or unacceptable. This would represent a psychological diathesis or vulnerability to develop OCD. For example, a person who was raised in a devoutly religious family may hold strong beliefs about the appropriateness and acceptability of thoughts relating to such areas as sex and abortion. These individuals may respond with considerable distress to having thoughts of this nature. The negative perceptions of obsessive thoughts may often take the form of exaggerated assumptions about whether actual harm can result from the intrusive thoughts themselves (e.g., a thought about something can cause it to happen) and about the degree of personal responsibility for preventing harm to oneself or others (e.g., failure to prevent harm relating to the thought is just as bad as causing the harm directly). These features were evident in Pat, who equated the idea of contamination with the distinct risk of contracting germs which could be passed between herself and her family.

Although compulsions (e.g., washing, checking) and other attempts at neutralizing obsessional material (e.g., repeating phrases, words, or prayers) are features that contribute to the DSM-IV definition of OCD, they are also considered to be the phenomena that maintain the disorder over time. For example, although Pat's excessive handwashing would often result in short-term relief (e.g., her panic attacks would subside after she washed), it maintained her problem over the long term by preventing her from disconfirming her predictions regarding the risk and anticipated harm of being contaminated (e.g., she never learned that washing was not necessary to prevent contamination). The patient's social environment can also contribute to the maintenance of OCD. Pat's family often acquiesced to her compulsive symptoms. Examples include her husband's compliance with her demands to take her "contaminated" purse out of the house and her family's agreement to allow Pat to keep separate food and dishes.

Treatment Goals and Planning

The anxiety disorders clinic that Pat was referred to offered a treatment program that was developed specifically for OCD. Pat was fortunate in the fact that she lived in close proximity to a clinic that offered this type of treatment; very few clinics in the United States have expertise in the type of program that Pat would undergo. This treatment approach is referred to as *exposure and response prevention* (ERP), a highly structured treatment whereby the patient's rituals (compulsive behavior) are actively prevented while the patient is systematically and gradually exposed to the feared thoughts (obsessions) and situations (e.g., cues that trigger the fear of becoming contaminated, such as shaking hands with a stranger). By arranging for the patient to confront these fear cues (obsessions, situations) while at the same time preventing them from engaging in their ritual or neutralizing behavior, the treatment approach is directly addressing the key maintaining features of OCD (e.g., avoidance of feared stimuli, engaging in compulsive behavior to neutralize obsessional thoughts). In addition, cognitive restructuring often represents an important adjunct to ERP to address the patient's beliefs regarding the acceptability or significance of their intrusive thoughts or images

(Salkovskis, 1989). However, ERP itself is important in changing the patient's cognitions surrounding the OCD symptoms. For instance, the procedures aimed at preventing compulsive behavior seem to foster "reality testing" in that the patient learns—at both a rational level and an emotional level—that no harmful consequences will occur, irrespective of whether the rituals are carried out.

Finally, as is often the case of the treatment of other emotional disorders (e.g., panic disorder; cf. Barlow, O'Brien, & Last, 1984), the effectiveness of interventions for OCD can often be enhanced by involving the patient's social network. Consistent with Pat's presentation, patients' family or friends may respond to their symptoms in a manner that helps to maintain the disorder. In addition to helping patients' significant others in better understanding the problem, this approach can be effective in eliminating behaviors that contribute to the maintenance of OCD.

COURSE OF TREATMENT AND TREATMENT OUTCOME

Shortly after her initial evaluation, Pat and her husband met the therapist for the first treatment session. The therapist had requested that Pat's husband attend the first several sessions to increase his understanding of the disorder and to assist Pat in applying the techniques of treatment in the most effective way possible. In addition to establishing rapport, the therapist's primary objectives of this session were to (a) obtain additional information that would be relevant to treatment planning, (b) provide the patient with an explanation of the causes of OCD and a rationale and explanation for the treatment approach, (c) define what targets (symptoms) the treatment would address, and (d) instruct the patient in the methods of self-monitoring. During this session, Pat and her therapist agreed that the primary targets of treatment would be to decrease her fear of objects associated with funerals, to eliminate her compulsive rituals, and to decrease her levels of generalized anxiety and tension. In fact, this latter target (i.e., high generalized anxiety) had not been discussed during Pat's intake evaluation. Thus, at this time Pat's therapist considered incorporating progressive muscle relaxation training as an additional treatment component. Other than this issue, the therapist regarded Pat's problem to be a relatively straightforward example of OCD.

During the first session, the therapist solicited from Pat a long list of fear triggers (e.g., objects that elicited panic attacks, thoughts of contamination, and compulsive behavior) and rituals. This information would be very important in the development of ERP exercises. The therapist provided Pat with the integrative model of OCD, emphasizing the factors that had maintained her difficulty over time (e.g., her avoidance of fear triggers, her washing and cleaning rituals). She was provided with self-monitoring forms to generate daily records of the frequency and intensity of symptoms such as anxiety, depression, pleasant feelings, obsessions, and compulsive behavior. Pat was told to continue daily self-monitoring throughout treatment because this information would be very useful in tracking her response to the program. Finally, Pat was informed about the techniques and rationale of ERP. She was told that, for the most part, the ERP would be carried out in a graduated format. For example, the feared objects and situations that were identified in this session were listed in order of least to most anxiety provoking. The ERP would be delivered in a graduated way by using less feared objects and situations in the initial exposures or by addressing intensely feared triggers by starting with imaginal exposure before confronting the trigger in real life. Imaginal exposure involves having patients confront feared objects and situations by using their imagination (e.g., picturing oneself coming in contact with a contaminated object). To begin this process, the therapist asked Pat to, over the next few days, gradually increase the length of time between when she had the urge to wash or clean and when she actually engaged in this ritual.

Pat made significant progress as early as the second session, which occurred 3 days later. Given that Pat was extremely motivated and compliant with treatment initiatives (e.g., she had been very good about delaying the onset of her rituals between sessions), she and her therapist decided to accelerate the process of ERP. Pat's husband had brought to the session a pair of his shoes that Pat believed were contaminated because he had worn them to a funeral several years ago. Even though Pat was extremely fearful of these shoes because they were directly connected with a funeral, she asked that they be used in her first ERP practice. After some discussion, they designed the following ERP practice: Pat would touch the top of the shoes with a piece of food and then eat the food. The reason why eating the "contaminated" food was part of this exposure was because it made Pat's usual ritual of washing less relevant (i.e., there would be little use for washing if she had swallowed the food). Pretzels were selected as the food to be used in the ERP because they were readily available from the vending machine at the clinic. During this session (which lasted 2½ hours), Pat ate an entire small bag of pretzels that she had touched to the shoes. When eating the first several pretzels, Pat reported a very high level of anxiety, but she never experienced a panic attack. However, this anxiety soon turned to joy because Pat was extremely surprised and pleased by her ability to perform such a feat. Due to the considerable gains that were achieved in this session, the therapist directed Pat to do several things that he had thought he would not have assigned until later in her treatment. First, Pat was instructed not to engage in any more compulsive rituals (e.g., refrain from handwashing after coming in contact with a "contaminated" object). Second, she was told to limit her daily shower to 10 minutes. Third, Pat was assigned to complete 3 hours of ERP per day. Two hours a day would be spent performing ERP practices using objects previously used in session (e.g., her husband's shoes) or objects that were similar to these objects in terms of their level of difficulty (rated by Pat as producing a similar level of anxiety). The final hour of ERP would involve imaginal exposure. This form of exposure required Pat to hold an image of being in contact with an object or being in a situation that was at the top of her list (e.g., the most feared objects and situations, such as touching a dead body). Pat's husband was instructed on how to serve as a coach in these between-sessions ERP exercises. He was also told to monitor Pat's compliance with the response-prevention aspect of treatment. For example, Pat's husband ensured that Pat was limiting her showers to 10 minutes per day. He also assisted her (by being supportive and reminding her of the importance of not completing the rituals) in not engaging in a washing-cleaning ritual after coming into contact with an object that evoked an intense urge to "decontaminate" herself.

Over the next several sessions, Pat and her therapist continued to apply ERP, including exposures to items at the top of her list. Pat's husband was assisted in identifying the types of things he and the family did that contributed to the maintenance of Pat's OCD. As a result, he no longer permitted her to keep separate food and dishes for herself. In addition, Pat was required to wash her dishes and clothes with her family's (and refrain from washing her hands after these tasks). Unlike many patients with OCD, Pat experienced little difficulty in applying ERP to most of the items on her hierarchy of feared items and situations. However, one of the most difficult ERP exercises that Pat encountered was to eat food that had been in contact with the purse that had been in the shed. Recall that, several years earlier, Pat had forced her husband to take the purse out of the house (through the window, for that matter) because a woman who had been to a funeral had touched the purse. Even though one might think that other tasks Pat had completed would have been more difficult (e.g., her husband's shoes had actually been at a funeral), the ERP practices involving this purse were among the hardest for Pat to accomplish. Indeed, after this exposure had been completed in the therapy session, Pat ran into a few problems when she was performing her daily ERP exercises. For instance, Pat experienced a panic attack a few times during these exposures. However, she prevented herself from washing, and her fear usually diminished by the second hour of the exposure. Moreover, she was rewarded by being now able to access the two hundred dollars that had been stowed in this purse for the last few years! Another difficult practice for Pat involved handling or eating food that was in contact with a business card from a nearby funeral home.

In addition, Pat evidenced a brief return to her compulsive rituals following a particularly difficult assignment. For this assignment, Pat was instructed to clean a cupboard in her pantry that contained several objects that had been "quarantined" over the past few years and therefore had not been opened. She was also instructed to handle the objects in the cupboard that she had regarded as contaminated. If handling these objects was not difficult enough, Pat realized halfway through the exposure that the "dirt" in the cupboard she was handling was actually rat droppings. This revelation produced a panic attack and a temporary increase in her unnecessary washing and cleaning rituals. However, Pat's therapist required her to continue the ERP exercise involving the cupboard, despite the presence of the rat droppings. Pat's cleaning rituals disappeared over the next 2 to 3 days.

Another minor complication in Pat's treatment was the fact that her levels of anxiety and depression increased somewhat during the middle of the program. After some questioning, the therapist concluded that Pat's negative emotions were related to her concerns that she would not be able to hold onto the considerable gains she had made. Consequently, the therapist utilized the procedures of cognitive therapy for a good part of the next two sessions. In addition to assisting Pat in identifying and challenging her thoughts that elicited these negative emotions, the therapist underscored the importance of continued application of ERP in maintaining her treatment gains.

Another issue that arose during Pat's treatment involved her fear of snakes. This issue became salient because spring arrived midway through the treatment program. Due to the warmer weather, Pat had encountered a snake in her backyard on a few occasions. At the time of her intake evaluation, Pat's fear was considered to be a typical case of snake phobia. However, in discussing her encounters with snakes, the therapist noted that these incidents had provoked intense fear and obsessional thoughts of contamination. In fact, Pat reported that on two occasions, she had washed herself after seeing the snake. Hence, the therapist considered exposure to snakes to be relevant to the treatment of Pat's OCD; her fear was not a straightforward instance of a specific phobia (persons with a specific phobia of snakes usually fear snakes for other reasons such as being bitten).

Fortunately (although it did not seem so fortunate to Pat at the time), the clinic housed a live snake for use in the treatment of patients with snake phobias. To address Pat's fear, she and her therapist developed a plan for graduated exposure to snakes. The initial ERP items included handling and viewing the following objects: (a) a book on snakes, (b) a rubber snake, and (c) a rubber snake that had been contaminated by the therapist who had previously handled the clinic's live snake. After she began to feel comfortable with these tasks, Pat progressed to watching her therapist handle the live snake. For homework, Pat was requested to perform daily ERP trials using the rubber snake and the book on snakes.

At the next session, Pat reported that while her funeral-related obsessions and compulsions had not returned, she had washed on two occasions after completing her ERP practices involving snakes. Thus, a good portion of the session was spent by having Pat watch her therapist handle the snake. For homework, Pat was instructed to continue her exposures to the rubber snake and the snake book. In addition, she was asked to visit pet stores and spend prolonged periods watching live snakes in their cages.

These exercises proved to be helpful because Pat reported at the next session to be minimally anxious over being in the presence of the rubber snake or the book about snakes. However, she still reported apprehension over live snakes and declined her therapist's suggestion that she handle the clinic's snake during this session. Instead, Pat was instructed to walk around and touch the area in her backyard where she had encountered snakes in the past. Also, because Pat denied any fear of funeral-related objects, she agreed with her therapist's suggestion that they spend their next session visiting a funeral home.

Indeed, Pat's assertion that she was no longer troubled by funeral-related objects was confirmed by the visit to the funeral home. She experienced no anxiety or urges to wash during the visit. Because of the possibility that Pat may have felt safer on this visit in the presence of the therapist, she was assigned to visit the funeral home with her husband during the week. Despite the significant strides she had achieved with her OCD symptoms, Pat reported that she continued to experience moderate levels of generalized anxiety and tension. Thus, she and her therapist decided to focus on progressive muscle relaxation as the final main component of treatment.

Pat responded very well to relaxation training. The initial exercises involved hour-long procedures during which she was guided in tensing and relaxing 16 different muscle areas throughout her body. The relaxing effects of these procedures were deepened by having Pat imagine pleasant and calming scenes (e.g., lying on a sunny and quiet beach). The therapist audiotaped this in-session relaxation induction so that Pat could practice with the tape at home. In later sessions, the relaxation exercises were modified to more "portable" (i.e., readily applied wherever Pat was, in the event she noticed an increase in anxiety or tension). This goal was achieved by first reducing the number of target muscle areas to eight and later to four. Finally, Pat was taught to deploy the technique of "cue-controlled relaxation," which is a very portable procedure for attaining a feeling of relaxation. Even though relaxation training was afforded considerable attention in these sessions, Pat was instructed to continue applying ERP throughout.

Once all of the procedures of relaxation training had been covered, Pat and her therapist met on a monthly basis for three more sessions. At the last session (of 14 sessions in all), Pat's therapist considered her to be virtually symptom-free. Her therapist regarded the following as factors that were instrumental in Pat's favorable response to treatment: (a) the nature of Pat's symptoms made it relatively straightforward to design ERP practices (e.g., her fear triggers such as funeral home business cards were readily defined and easily accessible) and (b) Pat's compulsive rituals were overt in nature (i.e., they were *behaviors* such as washing and cleaning) and thus were fairly easy to prevent (response prevention can be difficult if the patient's attempts at neutralizing obsessional material entails covert acts such as mentally repeating phrases or counting). In addition, the therapist considered Pat's high level of compliance and motivation as contributing to her positive outcome. Nevertheless, the therapist discovered that, because nearly all her symptoms had remitted, Pat was not currently completing ERP trials at the rate that had been suggested to ensure the maintenance of her gains. To conclude this session, the therapist emphasized the importance of continued practice and offered Pat the opportunity to contact the clinic in the future should any questions or problems arise.

A few days after this final session, an independently conducted interview by another clinician confirmed her therapist's impression that Pat had come a long way with her OCD. Pat showed no signs of obsessional or compulsive symptoms related to what used to be her most central fear: objects that had been in contact with funerals or funeral-related materials. Moreover, Pat reported very low levels of anxiety and tension in response to the relaxation component of treatment. She also remarked that her family life had improved (e.g., the frustration that her family had occasionally expressed as the result of her OCD symptoms was now gone). Indeed, the fact that Pat's husband was very supportive and made himself available for her treatment was another important factor in her success with the program. Despite these tremendous strides, which Pat had not been able to achieve with previous trials of antidepressant medication, a few symptom areas remained. First, Pat still evidenced a mild fear of contamination when she encountered a live snake in her neighborhood (she never got to the stage in therapy where she agreed to handle the clinic's snake). Second, many mood disorder symptoms (major depression, dysthymia) remained that had been noted prior to treatment. Although these symptoms had decreased significantly in response to her improvement with the OCD, some of Pat's depression seemed to be unrelated to her OCD. Rather, the interviewer noted that some of Pat's negative affect was related to her beliefs that she was not employable or worthy of holding a steady job. Pat was provided with a referral to a clinical psychologist in the area who specialized in the cognitive-behavioral treatment of depression.

Pat came back to the clinic 12 months later for a follow-up interview. The results of this interview indicated that Pat was still doing much better than she had been prior to entering the OCD program. However, she reported that, in the previous 2 months, her obsessional thoughts of being contaminated by funeral-related objects had increased somewhat; her mild fear of being contaminated by snakes had remained unchanged. It was apparent to the interviewer that this increase in symptoms was related to the fact that Pat was performing ERP exercises infrequently. Pat acknowledged that she knew what she had to do to overcome this recent exacerbation of symptoms; nevertheless, she stated that she found it difficult to push herself to initiate ERP practices on her own. Consequently, Pat was scheduled to meet with another therapist for two or three "booster" sessions to reestablish the exposure exercises. This strategy was very successful in resolving her partial relapse and reinitiating the regularity with which Pat completed ERP practices. However, at this point in time, some of Pat's symptoms of depression remained (Pat did not follow through on the referral for depression treatment), and she had not begun to look for work outside her home.

DISCUSSION

Recent findings from epidemiological studies indicate that the lifetime prevalence of OCD is 2.6% (Karno & Golding, 1991). However, this estimate pertains to the frequency with which people meet the diagnostic definition of OCD sometime during their lives. Additional evidence suggests that many people experience symptoms of OCD that, while not meeting the DSM definition of the disorder, are nonetheless associated with some degree of distress or lifestyle interference. For example, one study found that 10% to 15% of "normal" college undergraduates reported engaging in some form of checking behavior that was substantial enough to score within the range of patients with OCD (Frost, Sher, & Geen, 1986). As noted earlier, the OCD symptoms (e.g., intrusive thoughts, checking) of these nonclinical persons frequently are precipitated by some form of life stress (Parkinson & Rachman, 1981a, 1981b).

Patients with OCD are more likely to be female. Recent evidence from patient and epidemiological samples indicates that 55% to 60% of patients with OCD are female (Karno & Golding, 1991; Rasmussen & Tsuang, 1986). The average age of onset of the disorder ranges from early adolescence to the mid-20s. However, males have an earlier peak age of onset (i.e., 13 to 15) than do females (ages 20 to 24; Rasmussen & Eisen, 1990). If left untreated, the majority of persons with OCD experience a chronic "waxing and waning" course, with an increase in symptoms that is often related to life stress.

As was true for Pat, patients with OCD often have a history of a current or past mood disorder, such as major depression or dysthymic disorder. In fact, some researchers have suggested that the high rate of co-occurrence between OCD and the mood disorders, as well as the evidence that OCD may respond to antidepressant medication, points to the possibility that OCD is not an anxiety disorder but a variant of a mood disorder (e.g., Insel, Zahn, & Murphy, 1985). The association between OCD and depression may be relevant to treatment as well. One study found that patients with OCD who had a coexisting mood disorder did not respond as well and had a higher rate of relapse associated with cognitive-behavioral treatment of the disorder (Foa, Grayson, & Steketee, 1982). However, subsequent studies did not find depression to be related to treatment outcome (Basoglu, Lax, Kasvikis, & Marks, 1988; Foa, Steketee, Kozak, & McCarthy, 1990), suggesting that patients who are depressed are as responsive to treatments for OCD as non-depressed patients.

Interestingly, several studies have shown an association between OCD and the tic disorders such as Tourette's syndrome, which involves both motor tics (involuntary movements of the head or limbs) and vocal tics (involuntary utterances of words or sounds such as clicks, grunts, yelps, snorts, or coughs). Studies of patients with OCD indicate that 20% to 30% report a current or past history of tics (e.g., Pauls, 1989); 5% to 7% of patients with OCD have been found to suffer from the full-blown Tourette's syndrome (Rasmussen & Eisen, 1989). Studies of patients with Tourette's syndrome indicate that 36% to 52% meet criteria for OCD (Leckman & Chittenden, 1990; Pauls, Towbin, Leckman, Zahner, & Cohen, 1986).

Prior to undergoing the cognitive-behavioral treatment program, Pat had been prescribed two medications that have frequently been used in studies of the treatment of OCD (i.e., Anafranil [clomipramine], Prozac [fluoxetine]). Although Pat's problem did not respond to these medications at all, the results of recent outcome studies suggest that these drugs can be effective for some patients (see Riggs & Foa, 1993, for a review). The most effective drugs seem to inhibit the reuptake of serotonin (such as Prozac) and therefore belong to a class of drugs called serotonin-specific reuptake inhibitors (SSRIs). However, the average treatment gain is modest, and relapse frequently occurs when the medication is discontinued (e.g., Greist, 1990; Pato, Zohar-Kadouch, Zohar, & Murphy, 1988). For severe cases of OCD that do not respond to any other form of conventional treatment, neurosurgery (e.g., a surgical lesion to the cingulate bundle of the brain) represents another type of medical intervention (Jenike et al., 1991).

Although medications can be effective for some patients, cognitive-behavioral treatments appear to be the treatment of choice for OCD. Indeed, recent evidence indicates that 90% of patients treated with exposure and response prevention (ERP) show substantial improvement by the end of the treatment program; unlike the long-term results of medication treatments, 75% maintain their improvement over the long term (Riggs & Foa, 1993). Direct comparisons of ERP to drug treatments such as Anafranil have attested to the superiority of cognitive-behavioral treatment (e.g., Marks et al., 1988). However, whereas ERP is effective in the reduction of OCD symptoms, a substantial minority of patients either do not respond to the treatment (roughly 10%), do not maintain their gains (roughly 25%), or refuse this form of intervention altogether (roughly 25%). Thus, researchers continue to strive to develop more effective treatments and to identify predictors of treatment outcome. Recent reviews of the literature have concluded that patients with OCD who do not evidence overt compulsions are the least responsive to treatment (Christensen, Hadzi-Pavlovic, Andrews, & Mattick, 1987). Nevertheless, this poorer outcome might be related to clinicians' failure to identify and address mental compulsions, a problem that may have been lessened by the acknowledgment of this form of compulsion in DSM-IV (Salkovskis & Westbrook, 1989). More recently, researchers have begun to examine the effectiveness of interventions that combine medications and ERP to see whether this combination treatment is more effective than either treatment alone (Riggs & Foa, 1993). Large studies examining the combined and isolated effects of the SSRIs and ERP are in progress.

THINKING CRITICALLY

1. Research has indicated that in some persons, a strict, devoutly religious upbringing was a factor that contributed to the development of obsessive-compulsive disorder (OCD). Based on the information provided in the section "Case Formulation Using the Integrative Model" in this case, why might this be? What other social and developmental factors do you think might contribute to the origins of OCD?
2. As noted in this case, a person can meet the DSM-IV criteria for OCD without having overt, behavioral compulsions such as repetitive hand-washing or showering or repetitive checking of doorlocks, appliances, and so on. Do you think it would be harder to treat such cases using the intervention described in Pat's treatment? If so, what alterations in the intervention do you think would be helpful in the treatment of OCD when behavioral compulsions are not present?
3. How do obsessions differ from excessive worry as described in Case 1, "Generalized Anxiety Disorder"?

4. What are the different types of obsessions and compulsions? Does this diversity suggest to you that the different forms of obsessions and compulsions might differ in their modes of onset (i.e., they develop in response to different causal factors)? Do the various types of obsessions and compulsions require differing approaches to treatment? For example, would you treat a person with washing rituals differently from a person who has prominent hoarding rituals? How would these interventions differ?

Case

6

Physical Abuse of Adult (Domestic Violence)

At the insistence of his girlfriend, Scott Herring called the Domestic Violence Treatment Clinic to schedule an appointment with a therapist. At the time of this contact, Scott was a 32-year-old divorced Caucasian man with two children (a 7-year-old daughter and 5-year-old son) who was employed as a construction worker. He was dealing with a difficult divorce and the resulting loss of his children when his ex-wife received full custody of them. Scott was not granted visitation rights because, among other things, he was out of town during the divorce hearings and had a violation of an order of protection on his record. Moreover, Scott was having difficulties with his current girlfriend, who lived with him. Specifically, Scott had repeatedly been verbally and physically aggressive toward her. She threatened to leave him if he did not seek treatment for these difficulties.

During his first visit to the clinic, Scott admitted having problems with uncontrollable anger and rage. He reported "losing control" and verbally and physically abusing his girlfriend. He would kick and grab her several times a week, and would severely beat her one to two times a month. Scott explained that he felt as if he "blacked out" during these violent episodes. He explained that he felt that he was very impulsive—that he did not think through what was that he felt that he was very impulsive—that he did not think through what was going on, but instead jumped right in. He reported feeling awful afterward. However, Scott also explained that being aggressive was very helpful for him— that is, when he was aggressive, he usually got what he wanted. Scott also reported an inability to separate feelings of love and negativity. That is, he felt that everyone from whom he had ever received love (e.g., his parents) had hurt him in some way (e.g., he reported being verbally and physically abused by his parents). Consequently, he feared that he could not give or accept love if not accompanied by negative actions.

In addition, Scott described feelings of depression. He stated that he was not able to get out of bed in the morning, and felt like only "bad things" would ever happen to him. The stress of his divorce and his inability to see his children were also contributing to his depression.

Clinical History

Both of Scott's parents were alcoholics throughout his childhood. Although he claimed to remember little of his childhood, he had vivid memories of his parents beating him. He also remembered being beaten by his parents for not sticking up for his siblings in school, even if that meant getting into physical fights at school. Scott believed that his parents favored his siblings over him. In addition, his mother often threatened to leave the family, and actually did so on at least three occasions. An instance that Scott clearly recalled was on a Christmas Eve when his mother got drunk, verbally chastised Scott and his brother, and threatened to leave. When he woke up on Christmas Day, she was not there.

Scott was rarely able to predict when the punishments from his parents would come, or understand why they were coming. He did remember that some of these beatings were followed by apologies and promises never to do it again. After her departures from the household, Scott's mother would return and often explain that she left because she loved him, and that her absence was good for him. Because of these experiences—parental abandonment or beatings followed by apologies and expressions of love—Scott believed that he learned to equate love with feelings of hurt. As a result of his mother's abandonment in childhood, Scott feared that even as an adult others he cared about would leave him, especially his ex-wife and new girlfriend. When his ex-wife and new girlfriend threatened to leave him, Scott often lost control, which usually led to physical abuse.

Scott was 25 years old when he first exhibited physical and verbal domestic violence. At that time, Scott was a hardworking blue-collar worker who had been married to his first wife for two years. He did not have a lot of money saved, and thus worked long hours and was often away from home to provide his wife and soon-to-be family (his wife was pregnant with their first child) with a respectable home. His pregnant wife was bothered by his absence. Scott was also distressed by the fact that he had to be away so often, and he began to resent his wife for giving him a hard time about it. According to him, all of their interactions, both on the phone and in person, were marked by terrible screaming matches that typically culminated in Scott threatening his wife with physical violence and leaving.

In addition to long work hours and marital conflict, Scott recalled several other chronic stressors during this time. One stressor was Scott's estrangement from his parents and siblings. With a child on the way, he hoped to start a new life for himself with his new family. Each attempt to begin this life, in addition to frequent marital discord, reminded Scott of the stressors he experienced as a child, and he became increasingly frustrated. A second stressor, as mentioned earlier, was that Scott did not have any money saved and was working long hours and was often away from home, trying to make enough money to support his growing family. In addition to creating a rift in his marital relationship, the long hours of manual labor in his job were an enormous stress on him physically, causing him back and knee problems. At times, Scott was unable to walk and was often in severe pain. Due to his long working hours, Scott began taking over-the-counter medication to help him stay awake. In retrospect, Scott believed that these pills were affecting his personality, making him more sensitive to a number of issues and events.

During Scott's wife's pregnancy with their first child, the couple argued frequently. Late in the pregnancy, the couple had a terrible argument and his wife pulled a kitchen knife on Scott. Although Scott later realized that his wife pulled the knife because she thought she was in danger, at the time Scott thought her attack was offensive and he punched her in the face, giving her a black eye. This was the first time that Scott was physically aggressive toward his wife. He immediately felt terrible about hitting her, especially because she was pregnant. Scott also felt unaware of how it happened. He remembered getting very frustrated, then blacking out. The next thing he knew, he had punched her. Although Scott felt remorse and begged his wife for forgiveness, he noticed "positive" effects of his actions. He was aware that his wife stopped yelling at him and left him alone as a result of his physically aggressive act. According to him, she "obviously realized how much she was bothering me." Scott stated that he felt he could never get his point across, and was even uncomfortable trying to do so. After hitting his wife, Scott thought that she finally "got," or understood, what he was trying to get across—his point was finally made. Therefore, although he did not feel he could have controlled his aggressive act (he blacked out right before it occurred), Scott saw some positive consequences as a result of his aggression. However, regardless of the benefits he noticed, Scott swore to his wife and to himself he would never hit her again.

As his wife came nearer to her due date, Scott began to feel even more stressed. He felt that no matter how hard he worked, there was never enough money and his wife was never satisfied. He also wanted a relationship with his parents and siblings more and more, but the closer he tried to get, the worse things seemed to be between him and them. At this same time, Scott's brother, who had a drug addiction, was getting worse (i.e., he was taking stronger drugs at greater frequencies). Scott believed that his wife was complaining more than ever about his hours and their relationship. She often threatened to leave him, and to never let him see their newborn child. Scott was very much looking forward to starting over with a new family and could not bear the idea of being separated from his child. He believed his wife knew this was his weak spot; thus, she continually threatened him with it. Consequently, Scott's blackouts began to occur more often, always resulting in his punching, kicking, and slapping his pregnant wife. Although Scott always felt remorseful and promised to never do it again, these aggressive episodes nonetheless occurred at greater frequency.

For a period of time after his first child (a daughter) was born, Scott's acts of physical aggression ceased. However, after about a year passed, Scott became increasingly angry that his wife had not returned to work. He would barely talk to his wife, and appeared to be holding everything in. Scott began to express himself only through verbal and physical abuse. Much of Scott's physical abuse was triggered by his wife's continual verbal and sometimes physical aggression toward him. She often brought up the fact that he hit her while she was pregnant, and threatened to leave him if his current acts of physical abuse continued.

As time went by, Scott became physically aggressive more regularly, and verbally expressed his feelings and desires less and less. Things were tense at work (he was still working long hours, and was on the road often), and were even worse at home. Roughly two years after his daughter was born, Scott and his wife had a son. By this point, the couple rarely spoke. Scott was providing well for his family, but was never home to spend time with them. Scott had a feeling his wife was having an affair but he could not prove it. He searched for evidence of the affair, and, as he discovered more "signs," threatened her more often. The more aggressive he became, the more his wife retaliated. According to Scott, even when he was trying to get his violence under control (which he had managed to do for a brief time), she would provoke him. Scott believed that his wife was looking for a way to "get him out of the picture" so she could divorce him and leave him with nothing. Scott recalled that she told his family that he pushed her down the stairs, when in fact he had not.

After several more months of constant fighting and physical aggression, Scott's wife filed for a divorce. Scott moved out of their home and in with a friend. Over the next few weeks, Scott had little contact with his wife. When his wife was at work, Scott visited his children, whom he adored, and whom he swore never bonded with their mother. About a month later, Scott went to his house to pick up some things and was arrested. According to Scott, unbeknownst to him, his wife had "unfairly" gotten a restraining order against him. As a result, he was arrested in front of his children for going to the house. To make matters worse, his wife's new boyfriend, the man Scott had suspected she was having an affair with, had moved into his home.

After a short stay in jail, Scott moved into a tiny apartment, stopped working, and rarely communicated with anyone. He fell into a major depression. After a few weeks, he began communicating with a woman he met on the Internet. A few weeks later, Scott moved to another state to live with her, allowing his divorce to proceed without his input. This impulsive decision had devastating consequences for Scott because, in his absence, the court awarded full custody of the children to Scott's wife and he was not granted visitation rights.

At the time of his first presentation to the Domestic Violence Treatment Clinic, Scott was exhibiting a pattern of verbal and physical aggression with his current partner similar to that exhibited with his ex-wife. Scott's new girlfriend had a number of psychological disorders herself, which strongly contributed to their extremely chaotic relationship. Scott attributed his current aggression to a number of ongoing stressors. For instance, Scott's brother had recently passed away from a heart attack, which Scott believed was caused by his drug use. Scott still desired a closer relationship with his parents and other siblings, but did not know how to achieve one. He had very little social support.

In addition, Scott continued to have a very difficult work schedule, working nights and weekends, and was often on the road for days. He had a modest income and much of the money he made was given to his ex-wife for child support. Scott was also deeply bothered by the fact that he did not have custody of his children. Even though she was not legally bound to do so, Scott's ex-wife often allowed him to have his children on weekends. However, Scott usually was unable to see his children at this time because he often worked weekends.

Moreover, Scott believed that his ex-wife's new partner was violent toward his children, and he felt very helpless to protect them. At the time of Scott's first contact with the Clinic, there had been 11 reports filed to Child Protective Services (CPS) by either Scott or his ex-wife against the other. The most recent report was filed by his ex-wife against him, for neglect. The incident involved Scott beating his new girlfriend in front of his children. CPS declared the case unfounded, even though Scott admitted committing this aggressive act.

Based on the results of the structured diagnostic interview administered at intake to the Domestic Violence Clinic, Scott was found to have social phobia, bipolar II disorder, and borderline personality disorder (see Cases 3, 9, and 14, respectively, for a detailed description of these conditions). Consistent with his diagnosis of borderline personality disorder, Scott was very impulsive and rarely thought a decision through before reacting to it. His consistent automatic interpretation of others' behaviors was that they were trying to hurt him. That is, Scott often assumed that other people's behaviors (especially his ex-wife's) were done for negative reasons. As a result, he often felt on guard, and almost always believed that others' behavior was intended to hurt him. Thus, he would typically respond to other people's behaviors in a defensive, aggressive manner.

Consistent with the criteria for hypomania in bipolar II disorder, Scott would at times cycle into a phase where he felt very good about himself. He would go on and on about how smart he was, how powerful he was, how he was always right, and how nothing could hurt him. During these phases, Scott would act extremely impulsively, never thinking through the consequences of his actions. When asked why he thought nothing bad would come of his behaviors, Scott would answer "Because I am Scott, nothing can happen to me!" However, this attitude would often lead to impulsive behavior, including physical violence, that frequently left Scott depressed and remorseful, or led to other negative consequences (e.g., reports filed to CPS). As noted earlier in this case, at the time of his presentation to the Clinic, Scott was in a depressive phase of this disorder, exhibiting symptoms of depressed mood, loss of interest in his usual activities, hypersomnia, feelings of worthlessness, and agitation.

Scott also described many problems he had with acting assertively. He felt he did not know how to ask for what he needed, or how to explain his point of view to people. Therefore, he would wait until he was extremely angry, and then would be very aggressive to get what he wanted or he would use aggression and his physical size to intimidate others to try to get his point across. Because he was typically reinforced for this behavior (e.g., others often relented to Scott's wishes after he became aggressive), Scott became more and more likely to use it. Scott said that if he were not able to use his aggressive behaviors, he would not be able to get what he wanted. He believed that as a result of not getting what he wanted, he would go into a depression, which he often did, as reflected in his diagnosis of bipolar II disorder.

DSM-IV Diagnosis

Based on this information, Scott was assigned the following five-axis DSM-IV diagnosis:

Axis I	V61.1 Physical abuse of adult, (principal diagnosis)
	V61.1 Partner relational problem
	296.89 Bipolar II disorder, depressed
Axis II	301.83 Borderline personality disorder
Axis III	Severe shoulder problems
Axis IV	Estranged from family, hectic work schedule, divorce, death of brother, poor social support
Axis V	Global assessment of functioning 5 55 (current)

As seen in his five-axis diagnosis, Scott was assigned two V-Codes, V61.1 physical abuse of adult and partner relational problem, to convey his primary difficulties that prompted his request for treatment. V-Codes are found in a section of the DSM-IV called "Other Conditions That May Be a Focus of Clinical Attention." Other examples of V-Code conditions include academic or occupational problem, physical or sexual abuse of child, adult or child/adolescent antisocial behavior, and phase of life problem. These conditions are appropriately diagnosed in the following instances: (1) the problem is the focus of treatment and the person has no other Axis I or II mental disorder (e.g., a partner relational problem, such as marital conflict, in which neither partner has a mental disorder); (2) the person has a co-occurring mental disorder that is unrelated to the V-Code condition (e.g., using the previous example, one of the partners has a specific phobia of elevators that does not contribute to the marital conflict); or (3) the person has a mental disorder that is related to the V-Code condition, but the V-Code condition is sufficiently severe to warrant independent clinical attention (American Psychiatric Association, 1994a).

This third instance applied to Scott's diagnosis. Clearly, the symptoms of his co-occurring conditions, his borderline personality disorder in particular, were contributing to his acts of domestic violence. However, his physical and verbal aggression were quite marked and warranted clinical attention apart from these other conditions. Because the features of borderline personality disorder and unassertiveness contributed to Scott's domestic violence, they were targets in his treatment, as is discussed in the following sections.

CASE FORMULATION AND TREATMENT PLANNING

Because Scott was severely beating his girlfriend on a frequent basis, the primary goal of treatment was to stop the aggression before other treatment goals and plans were set. In the typical intervention used by the Domestic Violence Clinic, the first 3 to 4 sessions consist of assessment and treatment planning. However, in Scott's case, treatment for the aggression began in the second session. Although some assessment was done during that time, further assessment was not conducted until Scott's aggression was controlled. The conceptualization of Scott's domestic violence was as follows: Scott often interpreted others' behaviors as having negative intent. As a result, he immediately reacted defensively and engaged in behaviors that were harmful to him and others. These behaviors were almost always physical and verbal aggression. Therefore, after immediate initiatives to control Scott's physical aggression, treatment focused on methods to control his "hot thoughts" (e.g., misperceptions of others' actions) and to control his impulsive behaviors. Specifically, this phase of treatment taught Scott: (1) to control his negative interpretations of others' behaviors by thinking and reinterpreting others' motives as neutral or positive (cognitive restructuring); and (2) to control his impulsive behaviors and to think through the consequences of situations.

Scott's treatment also included assertiveness training. After these problematic behaviors were controlled, Scott needed a behavior to replace his impulsive and aggressive reactions. Therefore, assertiveness training was employed to teach Scott how to deal effectively and appropriately with everyday occurrences and stressful situations.

At the time of his initial consultation, Scott's girlfriend was also seeing a therapist at the Domestic Violence Treatment Clinic (i.e., the clinic treated both perpetrators and victims of domestic violence). Thus, Scott's therapist obtained written consent from Scott and his girlfriend to discuss the case with Scott's girlfriend's therapist. This allowed Scott's therapist to receive assessments and updates from Scott's girlfriend and her therapist on the status of Scott's aggression. This information was extremely helpful in providing additional information about the contributing and maintaining factors of Scott's aggression, and on his progress throughout treatment.

COURSE OF TREATMENT AND TREATMENT OUTCOME

As noted earlier, before work on other areas could proceed, it was important to first get Scott's aggressive outbursts under control. To address this goal, Scott's therapist followed a cognitive-behavioral treatment model for domestic anger control (Vivian & Heyman, 1996). Scott was first taught the techniques of "time-out." It is important for both members of the couple to understand and follow the rules of the time-out procedure. Because the therapist was not working with Scott's girlfriend, who was the primary target of his aggression, Scott was asked to explain the technique to her as well. Scott's girlfriend's therapist was also asked to go over the time-out procedure with her. Time-out consists of 6 steps: (1) monitor one's anger, (2) ask for a time-out, (3) have the partner acknowledge the request for time-out, (4) separate, (5) cool off and calm down, and (6) return later to finish the discussion (Neidig & Friedman, 1984). In other words, Scott was taught to monitor his emotions to detect when he was becoming angry during an interaction with his girlfriend. At that point, he was instructed to ask for a time-out, before his emotions escalated into an aggressive outburst. After his girlfriend acknowledged the request for a time-out, the couple would separate (go to different rooms) to allow their emotions to calm down. Scott was taught additional techniques to help his feelings of anger to run their course (e.g., cognitive restructuring) during the cool-off period. After this cool-off period, the couple would resume the discussion they were having before the time-out was called.

During this period of treatment, Scott's therapist also focused on making sure he was aware of his emotions before he got to the point at which he became aggressive (e.g., the monitoring component of time-out). Scott described his behavior before beginning treatment as immediately going from being calm to being intensely angry. The therapist explained to Scott that anger is not an on/off switch but instead occurs in gradations. The therapist had Scott focus on his physiological reaction (e.g., feeling hot, grinding teeth) and the thoughts leading to anger that occurred just before he became aggressive. This was difficult for Scott, but after a few sessions he was able to recognize the gradation between feeling completely calm and feeling intensely angry. Next, Scott and his therapist focused on the triggers that set him on the path to intense anger and physical aggression. His therapist discovered that the major trigger always resulting in aggression was Scott's girlfriend not making eye contact with him. After probing, Scott admitted that he interpreted this behavior as his girlfriend thinking she was better than him, and not caring enough to listen to what he had to say. His internal thoughts and interpretations would get him so irritated that he would inevitably become aggressive. Thus, therapy was focused on controlling these thoughts—that is, stopping the hot thoughts that led to physical aggression. When Scott recognized his hot thoughts, he took a time-out.

In the initial phase of therapy, Scott would often make very dramatic points. The therapist was sure that Scott's behaviors were examples of what he did outside the office, so she was very careful to provide the opportunity for corrective experiences based on her responses. For example, one evening Scott came into the therapy session in a rage. This was the fourth session, and although Scott had begun to employ techniques to control his aggressive behavior, these techniques had yet to come to him naturally. As Scott began explaining what had him so agitated, he began pacing the small office, often banging the walls. The therapist sat, completely calm, and asked him to sit down. Scott stared right at her and said through his teeth, "Why, am I scaring you?" The therapist looked right back at him and said, "No—you're making me dizzy." Scott found this very humorous, and the situation was immediately defused. His therapist later learned that although Scott typically acted in an intimidating manner, he was often hurt when others acknowledged their fear of him, and this caused him to react more aggressively. When Scott saw that his therapist was not intimidated or affected by his behavior, he immediately calmed down, and rarely came to therapy sessions in such a state again. It was also at this time that Scott's therapist learned the power of humor in a tense therapy session, and she often employed humor in later sessions with him.

After about two months, Scott was still experiencing some hot thoughts, but was able to control them, usually by taking a time-out when they appeared. After his physical aggression was controlled, therapy focused on his negative interpretations of other's behavior, and his own impulsive reactions and behaviors.

Scott had always been very mistrusting and believed that other people's motives were negative. Any actions that were taken by another toward him that were not blatantly positive (and even some that were) were interpreted by Scott as "That person is trying to hurt me or press my buttons," and so on. Furthermore, Scott was very impulsive. Consistent with his negative interpretations of others' motives, he typically reacted without thinking through the situation. For instance, if he had allowed himself a few minutes to think about his ex-wife's behaviors, Scott might have realized that her motive was to help him see the children more, not to try to hurt him. This was an example of Scott's automatic negative interpretation of others' behaviors that often led to his impulsive negative reactions. In other words, Scott reacted to what he believed was a negative situation and often created a negative situation that did not exist in the first place.

In an effort to control his negative interpretations of others' behaviors, Scott was taught to proceed through the following steps: (1) focus on a particular situation; (2) identify what his ultimate goals were for the situation; and (3) determine whether or not his goals were met. If his goals were not met, Scott was guided to examine his thoughts and behaviors during the situation—specifically, Scott's cognitive interpretations of others' behaviors and how these thoughts led to his own negative behaviors. For example, Scott was sure that his ex-wife was always "playing games" and her goal was to "destroy" him. Therefore, regardless of her actions toward him, Scott's immediate impression was that she was trying to "push his buttons," and he automatically reacted defensively. Because his goals were rarely met in these instances, the therapist had Scott focus on how his own behaviors may have been impeding his goals.

When Scott finally acknowledged that his behaviors might be contributing to the unsuccessful attainment of his goals, his therapy was focused on ways to change his behaviors in these situations. The goal was to help him learn to stop, think about his girlfriend's or ex-wife's (or anyone's) behavior, and come up with a positive or at least a neutral interpretation of the behavior. Thus, the therapist relied strongly on the techniques of cognitive therapy (Beck, 1976) during this treatment phase (see Case 2, "Panic Disorder with Agoraphobia," and Case 8, "Major Depression," for a detailed discussion of these techniques).

As noted earlier, Scott was able to control his aggressive behavior after 8 to 10 therapy sessions through the use of techniques such as time-out. However, working toward the goal of controlling Scott's negative thoughts and subsequent inappropriate and impulsive behaviors (e.g., verbal aggression, saying extremely inappropriate things, quitting his job) was a much more difficult task. After about 15 sessions of working on these goals, it became apparent that while Scott did an excellent job of thinking through his thoughts before acting on them in the therapy session, he was having a difficult time doing so with his girlfriend, ex-wife, and others he interacted with (e.g., his boss, parents, authorities at the courthouse). The therapist explored the possible reasons for this discrepancy in Scott's behaviors. After probing for some time, it became clear to Scott that he automatically interpreted his therapist's actions as being motivated by concern for him. As a result, no matter what the therapist did, Scott interpreted it as positive and was able to behave appropriately in the therapy sessions.

Coming to this realization was not easy for Scott. The therapist continually asked him what was different about her that made him capable of thinking through his actions and making appropriate decisions in her presence. During one session, after the therapist's continuous probing, Scott crawled up in his chair, covered himself with his jacket, and whispered, "Because you care about me." This was an incredible breakthrough for Scott. As mentioned earlier, Scott associated caring and love with underlying motives of hurt. Acknowledging that the therapist cared about him and only had his best interests in mind was a very important corrective experience. Scott was finally able to pair caring behaviors with positive motives. After that session, Scott was more capable of seeing positive or at least neutral intent in the behavior of his girlfriend, ex-wife, and boss. He was also more likely to stop and rethink others' motives, and was often able to correct his initial thoughts if they were negative. He became less prone to react defensively, and what would have become a negative situation was often avoided. In addition, Scott's new method of thinking through situations solidified the decline in his physically aggressive behaviors, and led to a decrease in his verbally aggressive behaviors, as well.

The strong therapeutic relationship between Scott and his therapist was very influential in several other aspects of his treatment. For example, after several months in treatment, Scott made a derogative comment about Jewish people in session. Specifically, Scott said that Jewish people think they are better than others are, and the motives of their behaviors are always to prove they are better than others. Although Scott was unaware of it, his therapist was Jewish and was irritated by his comment. Nevertheless, she decided to let the comment slide for the time being and possibly address it in a later session. In their next meeting, Scott made a negative comment about a person of a different race, who happened to be a good friend of his. When the therapist asked Scott how his friend would feel if he heard him making such a comment, Scott explained that his friend would not care because they "joke" about things like that all the time. When asked how he would feel if he unintentionally made a comment that hurt someone, Scott replied that he would not care. The therapist then asked Scott how he would feel if he made a comment that unintentionally hurt her. Scott suddenly got very quiet and said, "It would kill me if I ever hurt you—I would never want to do that." The therapist took that opportunity to explain to Scott that he needed to think through all of his comments, especially those concerning race, religion, and culture, because he might unintentionally hurt someone "like me." From that time on, Scott did not make any other derogatory comments, but explained that there were times when he almost said something derogatory, but remembered how he felt in session when he thought about accidentally hurting his therapist.

The next phase of treatment addressed Scott's difficulty in social interactions and problems with assertiveness. Scott explained that he had always had trouble expressing himself. For example, at home when he was child, Scott's parents would yell at him, regardless of what he said or did. As a result, he rarely spoke and would wait until he was really upset or really angry before expressing himself. This pattern continued into adulthood and typically culminated in Scott's expressing himself in an inappropriate manner. Scott explained that when he thought about expressing himself appropriately instead of aggressively, he could feel his stomach get queasy and his face get hot. This was because he would focus on the fact that he would not know what to say if the other person said something back to him. Scott believed that when a person is aggressive, other people do not answer back. If he could ensure that others did not answer back, his problem was solved.

To address these issues, Scott was taught the skills of assertiveness training. An important aspect of this intervention is behavioral rehearsal of situations calling for assertive behavior (Goldfried & Davison, 1994). First, Scott was taught how to stay task-focused and relaxed when discussing a topic that called for him to be assertive. By role-playing in session (e.g., his therapist would act the part of Scott's ex-wife, girlfriend, or boss), Scott practiced being assertive in situations that had actually occurred in which he acted aggressively instead of assertively, and he practiced for difficult situations that would occur in the future.

At the time this case was written, Scott had received 60 individual treatment sessions at the Domestic Violence Clinic. His treatment is still ongoing and is focused on secondary disorders (e.g., bipolar II disorder, borderline personality disorder) and his assertive behaviors. Scott has responded very well to treatment for his presenting problem of physical and verbal aggression. Scott has not been aggressive toward his girlfriend for over a year, and he is no longer aggressive in his daily interactions. In addition, he has generalized his anger control techniques into other areas including interactions with his ex-wife and with his boss at work. He has been more successful in controlling his impulsive thoughts and behaviors, and has often been rewarded for doing so. As a result of his successful anger control, Scott has been able to resume relationships with his family. Moreover, because he has been able to keep his anger controlled with his ex-wife, she has been more agreeable to his spending time with his children. She allows him to have the children every weekend. This has been very reinforcing for Scott.

Although Scott no longer acts out aggressively when he believes people are trying to hurt him, he still gets extremely agitated on occasion. If he is very angry, he has trouble reinterpreting others' behaviors, and immediately assumes they are trying to hurt him. In the past, after thoughts of this nature, Scott would immediately seek out that person and try to "hurt them back." Although he does not do that anymore, at times he still experiences anger and associated symptoms such as loss of sleep and poor eating habits. These episodes are often triggered by stressors that have remained in Scott's life, including the custody battle for his kids (Scott continues to believe that his children are not in appropriate hands), financial difficulties, the poor health of both his parents, and a brother with a serious drug problem (recall Scott lost another brother to the same problem before his treatment began).

DISCUSSION

A considerable amount of research is needed on the prevalence, nature, prediction, prevention, and treatment of domestic violence. Although specific estimates are lacking, the prevalence of marital violence alone (spousal abuse) is believed to be at epidemic proportions. For example, in national surveys conducted in the 1970s and 1980s, 12% to 16% of homes reported at least one act of violence by one spouse against another within the past year (Straus & Gelles, 1986; Straus, Gelles, & Steinmetz, 1980). The prevalence of spousal aggression appears to vary across stages of the marital relationship. For example, in a study by O'Leary and colleagues (1989), 272 community couples were evaluated longitudinally at pre-marriage (1 month before marriage), and 18 and 30 months after marriage. Results indicated that more women than men reported being physically aggressive against their partners at pre-marriage (44% versus 31%) and at 18 months into the marriage (36% versus 27%). However, at 30 months, the rates of marital aggression did not significantly differ between the sexes (32% for women, 25% for men). The majority of these aggressive acts involved pushing, grabbing, or shoving.

There appear to be minimal differences between sexes when considering any form of spousal aggression (cf., O'Leary et al., 1989; Straus & Gelles, 1986; Straus et al., 1980). However, research indicates that men are more likely to engage in more severe forms of aggression that result in physical damage (Berk, Berk, Loseke, & Rauma, 1983; Straus et al., 1980), although cultural factors may moderate this finding, as will be discussed later in this case. Moreover, some researchers believe that, in many cases, women's aggression in fact represents acts of self-defense (Browne, 1987; Walker, 1989). Research from a national survey (Straus & Gelles, 1990) indicated that more than 3 out of every 100 women were severely assaulted by their male partners in the prior year (i.e., they were punched, kicked, choked, beaten, or threatened or injured with a knife or gun). Estimates suggest that close to 2,000 women in the United States die each year as a direct result of spousal abuse (Strube, 1988), and that over half of all murders of adult females are due to homicide by their partners (Browne, 1993; Browne & Williams, 1989). Of course, acts of spousal aggression have many other possible serious consequences for the victim such as post-traumatic stress disorder (see Case 4) and other emotional problems (e.g., depression, substance abuse), physical disfigurement or disability, or miscarriage (Browne, 1993; Carden, 1994). Acts of marital violence also have the serious consequence of highly elevated risk that the abuse will extend to the victimization of children in the household (Ross, 1996). Exposure to domestic violence in childhood has also been strongly linked to aggressive behavior in adulthood (e.g., Beasley & Stoltenberg, 1992; Hastings & Hamberger, 1988). In a recent review of this literature, Feldman (1997) concluded that "perhaps the most consistent finding in family violence research is that domestically violent males are far more likely than nonviolent males to have been victims of abuse or witness to interparental aggression as children" (p. 308).

Research examining the demographic predictors of domestic violence suggests that acts of spousal aggression are more likely to occur in younger couples (O'Leary et al., 1989; Straus et al., 1980). O'Leary et al. (1989) attributed their high prevalence estimates of spousal aggression, which were 3 to 4 times greater than that found by Straus et al. (1980), to be due mainly to their use of a younger sample. Studies indicate that all forms of physical assault decrease with age (e.g., Arias, Samios, & O'Leary, 1987; Straus et al., 1980). Although spousal aggression exists in all socioeconomic classes (Hornung, McCullough, & Sugimoto, 1981), some findings indicate that marital violence is associated with unemployment, lower income, low educational attainment, and fewer social support resources (e.g., Magdol et al., 1997; Margolin & Burman, 1993; Straus et al., 1980).

A multitude of factors have been linked to the prediction of spousal abuse (cf. Holtzworth-Munroe & Stuart, 1994). However, evidence of the association between marital discord and marital violence has been somewhat inconclusive. For example, a study examining the characteristics of abusive couples found marital discord to be the strongest correlate of spousal aggression (Rosenbaum & O'Leary, 1981); however, a later study found no relationship between marital distress and the first-time use of physical aggression (Murphy & O'Leary, 1989). The findings of O'Leary et al. (1989), discussed earlier, indicate that premarital acts of aggression strongly predict subsequent aggression in the marriage (although factors contributing to premarital aggression are not well understood). In addition, *psychological aggressiveness* has been found to predict subsequent physical aggression (Cascardi, O'Leary, Lawrence, & Schlee, 1995; Margolin, John, & Gleberman, 1988; Murphy & O'Leary, 1989; O'Leary, Malone, & Tyree, 1994). Common manifestations of psychological aggressiveness include acting to deliberately spite or insult the partner and attempting to dominate or control their behavior.

Whereas many attempts have been made to associate spousal violence with co-occurring DSM-IV diagnoses such as antisocial personality disorder and alcohol or substance use disorders (e.g., Conner & Ackerley, 1994; O'Leary, 1988; Van Hasselt, Morrison, & Bellack, 1985), many researchers believe that spousal aggression can be more strongly predicted by preexisting traits or emotional characteristics of the abuser and by aspects of the abuser's interpersonal style. Emotional characteristics and traits that have commonly been linked to wife abuse include hostility and anger, high power or control needs, depression, and low self-esteem and unassertiveness (e.g., Carden, 1994; Dutton & Strachan, 1987; Flournoy & Wilson, 1991; Hastings & Hamberger, 1988; Maiuro, Cahn, Vitaliano, Wagner, & Zegree, 1988; see Dutton, 1995 and

Feldman, 1997, for reviews). Interpersonal behaviors of the male that have been found to be associated with spousal abuse include spouse-specific communication skills deficits, difficulty expressing affection and forming trusting relationships, and handling conflictual marital discussions in a belittling, hostile, and nonconstructive manner (e.g., Dutton, 1995; Dutton & Strachan, 1987; Holtzworth-Munroe & Anglin, 1991; Holtzworth-Munroe & Hutchinson, 1993; Margolin et al., 1988; Rosenbaum & O'Leary, 1981).

Initial evidence suggests that cultural factors are also important to consider in the cause and prediction of domestic violence. Although several studies have been unable to find strong sex differences, research indicates that in some cultures physical violence is more commonly perpetrated by women than men. For instance, in a community study of partner violence in young adults from New Zealand, acts of physical aggression by 37% of females and 22% of males were reported; severe physical violence by 19% and 6% of females and males was reported (Magdol et al., 1997). Studies have found, on the whole, few differences in the prevalence of domestic violence across racial and ethnic groups. For example, in the National Alcohol and Family Violence Survey of 1,970 families, Kantor, Jasinski, and Aldarondo (1994) found that the rates of wife assault did not differ strongly across three major Hispanic-American groups and an Anglo-American group when norms regarding violence approval, age, and economic stressors were held constant. However, these researchers found evidence of subgroups within these ethnicities, in which norms sanctioning or accepting wife assaults were prevalent. The existence of such norms was found to be a strong risk factor for wife abuse.

In a subsequent study of this sample, Jasinski, Asdigian, and Kantor (1997) found evidence of racial and ethnic differences in the relationship between work stress, alcohol abuse, and marital violence. These researchers noted that whereas previous research has established that work stress and alcohol abuse are associated with increased risks for wife assaults, studies had not addressed the possibility that these relationships vary by ethnicity (Anglo-American versus Hispanic-American). Their findings indicated that Anglo and Hispanic husbands each experienced different types of work stress, and that these men coped with those stressors differently. Among Hispanic husbands, work stressors were associated with increased levels of alcohol abuse and violence. In contrast, in Anglo husbands, work stressors were associated with elevated levels of drinking, but not marital violence.

Considerable work has been done in the development of interventions for the prevention and treatment of domestic violence (e.g., Caeser & Hamberger, 1989; Faulkner, Stoltenberg, Cogen, Nolder, & Shooter, 1992; O'Leary, Heyman, & Jongsma, 1998; Halford & Markman, 1997). However, controlled research on the short- and long-term effectiveness of these therapies is needed. The typical cognitive-behavioral approach to spousal abuse contains elements along the lines that Scott received in his treatment. Specifically, these treatments include (a) anger management (including time-out), (b) communication and social-skills training, (c) cognitive restructuring, (d) stress management and problem-solving training (i.e., to manage and reduce life stress that may be a contributing factor to anger and frustration leading to aggressive behavior); and (e) assertiveness training and modeling or role playing of new behaviors. As illustrated in the case description of Scott, each of these components was important in the successful treatment of his physical aggression.

THINKING CRITICALLY

1. Although it was once assumed that males were much more likely to perpetrate acts of marital violence than females, some research indicates this is not the case. The rates of such acts are roughly equivalent across sexes when any form of aggression is considered; in some cultures, women evidence a higher rate of aggression. What factors do you believe account for this finding? What variables do you think most strongly predict acts of domestic violence? Do you think these risk factors differ for males and females? Why or why not?

2. Some women who have been victims of domestic physical abuse remain in the household despite having suffered numerous severe attacks from their partners. What factors do you believe are most influential in accounting for why these women remain in the same household as their abusers? What do you think would be a victim's best response after an initial act of spousal abuse has been committed against her? Would your reply differ if the victim was male instead of female? Why or why not?

3. Most persons who are treated for domestic aggression have additional psychological disorders (e.g., at the time of Scott's treatment, he was diagnosed as having bipolar II disorder and borderline personality disorder). How might these co-occurring disorders complicate treatment of domestic violence? Do you think that certain disorders are causally linked to acts of domestic violence? If so, which ones? Do you think the approach to treating domestic violence should be modified when comorbid disorders are involved? How so?

4. Do you believe that the personality characteristics, behaviors, or psychological disorders in the partner can increase the likelihood or frequency of violent acts by the perpetrator? If so, what features of the victimized partner might contribute to the rate of domestic violence? Do you think that the victim should always be included in the treatment of domestically violent persons? In what instances should the victim be included in treatment, and when not (or always not)? Why?

Dissociative Identity Disorder

(Multiple Personality Disorder)

A t the time of her first visit for outpatient treatment with a clinical psychologist, Wendy Howe was a 35-year-old, unemployed, divorced Caucasian woman with two children (a son age 20 and a daughter age 15). During the preceding year, Wendy had been hospitalized in a number of inpatient psychiatric units. During these hospitalizations, Wendy's symptoms had been given a variety of diagnoses—depression, substance abuse, schizophrenia, borderline personality disorder—and Wendy had undergone many different psychological and drug treatments. She had been treated with antidepressants, neuroleptics, anti-anxiety drugs, lithium, seizure medications, and beta-blockers; at the time of her first visit with the psychologist, Wendy was being prescribed all of the above. None of these interventions had proved helpful; instead, Wendy's symptoms had gotten worse. Her hospital treatment team had felt that they could not discharge Wendy because she displayed strong suicidal impulses and engaged in some very severe self-injurious behaviors. In fact, at the time of the initial outpatient consult with the clinical psychologist, Wendy had been on one-on-one observation in the hospital for the past 2 months, and the hospital had recommended transferring her to a long-term inpatient program.

The clinical psychologist received a call from a case manager for Wendy's insurance carrier who was trying to find an outpatient therapist familiar with the treatment of dissociative disorders. The insurance company considered Wendy to be a "large loss case," given her frequent psychiatric and medical hospital admissions (many of Wendy's medical admissions were for self-inflicted injuries) and her poor prognosis. The hospital treatment team had decided that Wendy would show a long downhill course, should be put on long-term disability, and should be treated with neuroleptics (a class of medications used to treat psychotic symptoms characteristic of schizophrenia) to keep her sedated enough to be less likely to hurt herself. The case manager informed the psychologist that the insurance company was willing to "try anything if it could get and keep Wendy out of the hospital."

Clinical History

Wendy's psychological difficulties were clearly linked to a very tumultuous childhood. As a child, Wendy lived with her violent and abusive mother in a small urban area; her father had left the household when Wendy's mother was pregnant with her. Throughout Wendy's childhood, the family was very poor and lived in tenements. Wendy's mother was unemployed for much of Wendy's childhood and made money to support her addictions to alcohol and heroin by selling Wendy for childhood prostitution. Wendy had been physically and sexually abused as far back as she could remember. In fact, there were hospital records of a severe physical abuse incident that occurred before Wendy was 2 years old. Wendy's mother was extremely sadistic and had tortured her regularly with extreme and violent means. For example, without any provocation, Wendy's mother would burn and cut her on various parts of her body, would give her enemas (sometimes with very hot or very cold water), would insert objects into Wendy's vagina and anus, and would watch while other people sexually or physically abused her. Her mother also abused Wendy's siblings (two brothers, two sisters), often making them watch as each was tortured. Sometimes her mother would force one sibling to physically or sexually hurt another. Wendy's grandfather sexually and physically abused her as well, as did many of her mother's boyfriends.

These abuse incidents were very frequent and very severe. Many of these incidents resulted in trips to the emergency room, and occasionally Wendy received inpatient treatment for internal injuries. When Wendy was 15, she suffered an exceptionally violent rape by one of her mother's boyfriends. The rape resulted in hospitalization due to the severity of her physical injuries, and plastic surgery was necessary to reconstruct her face. This rape also resulted in a pregnancy and the subsequent birth of her son. Legal records documented the assault and rape by her mother's boyfriend; in fact, this individual was later convicted and jailed for the rapes of five other women. School, hospital, and legal records documented virtually all of the other abuse incidents that Wendy described. Wendy's victimization history extended into early adulthood: There were records indicating that she had been raped three times, had been sexually exploited by a doctor, and even had her home taken over by some drug dealers looking for a place to stay.

Wendy stated that she had tried to block her childhood abuse from her consciousness in order to be able to parent her children. She said that she had spent all of her adult life struggling to "put it behind her." Yet, the effects of her abuse had dominated her life. For example, because of her mother's terrorizing about bathroom functions, Wendy could not remember the last time she was able to use a toilet. Because she feared toilets a great deal, she would delay bathroom functions as long as she could, and then she gave herself enemas to void more quickly. Consequently, Wendy felt that she was unable to travel far from home in the event she needed privacy to give herself an enema. Wendy's enema use had been so extensive that she had permanent intestinal damage.

Until the year of her recurrent psychiatric hospitalizations (i.e., the year preceding Wendy's first visit with the clinical psychologist), Wendy had been somewhat successful at holding things together in a fragile fashion. Although she had dropped out of school during the 10th grade because of the birth of her son and her severe abuse at home, Wendy had obtained her high school equivalency diploma by taking a state exam. At age 17, she married in order to get out of her mother's house, a marriage that lasted 1 year. At the age of 20, Wendy had a second child (a daughter) from a brief relationship she was having with a married man. Although she had worked at many different jobs (e.g., waitressing, bartending, sales, secretarial work), until her hospitalizations Wendy had been working steadily for 5 years as a telephone operator.

However, two major events seemed to trigger Wendy's decompensation over the preceding year. First, Wendy learned that she would no longer be able to continue her job as a telephone operator because she had developed carpal tunnel syndrome in both arms from working with poorly designed work equipment. The telephone company wanted to place her on disability, provide corrective surgery, and then retrain her for another type of employment. Wendy had not complied with this plan, largely due to her fear that she would be molested by the doctor while she was under anesthesia (as had occurred to her several years before). Consequently, Wendy felt very afraid of her uncertain economic future and the possibility of two painful surgeries to correct her carpal tunnel syndrome.

Second, during this time Wendy's son entered an alcohol treatment program after getting in an alcohol-related automobile accident. The treatment program requested information on the family's substance abuse, psychiatric, and medical histories. In particular, the program was investigating the possibility that Wendy's son had bipolar disorder (see Case 9) and wanted to know about any family history of this disorder. Wendy had not had any contact with her son's father, who was in prison serving a 20-year sentence for the rapes of five women. However, in order to get the necessary medical history information for her son, Wendy went to the prison to interview him. Wendy was able to obtain the necessary information, but the visit evoked the memory of this man's violent rape of her at age 15. Wendy was overwhelmed by the flood of feelings and memories that she had previously tried so hard to block out of her mind.

Having this occur when she was already feeling vulnerable about her job status and possible surgery was too much for her. Seeing her son's father again had opened up the floodgates, and she could not stop the memories of her past abuses from pouring into her mind. Typical of the person with a severe posttraumatic stress disorder (PTSD; see Case 4), she began to have distressing flashbacks of her childhood abuse almost continuously. During a flashback, Wendy would reexperience the traumatic events so vividly—through visual images, sounds, and bodily sensations—that she would feel as if the abuse was happening to her all over again. She had regular nightmares about her abuse experiences. Being an avid drawer and painter, Wendy began to focus all of her artwork on traumatic material (described in more detail later). She had an exaggerated startle reflex (e.g., she became very upset from hearing a sudden noise such as a popping balloon), and she had great difficulty calming down after such a reaction. She showed significant problems with her memory and concentration. Also, Wendy had considerable sleep difficulties and could not sleep at all in a bed (much of her sexual abuse occurred in bed) or if other people (including her children) were nearby. Thus, Wendy usually slept on the floor or in a closet.

Wendy also experienced a major disruption in her spirituality; that is, she questioned the reality of God. This seemed to be due to the fact that Wendy's mother had been overtly highly religious but had used her beliefs as a justification for much of her abuse of Wendy: "I need to give you this enema with cleaning fluid to clean you out because you are such a dirty and evil sinner." Moreover, when Wendy was 16, she had produced a "stillborn" child. Her mother told her that this child could never go to heaven because he had not been baptized. Since that experience, Wendy had struggled with her view of God and religion and had constantly felt guilty and anxious about the status of this baby.

Roughly a month after her visit to the prison, Wendy's symptoms had become so severe, and she had become so distressed over them, that she committed a very serious suicide attempt. Consequently, Wendy was admitted to a psychiatric hospital for the first time, an admission lasting 2 weeks.

As she had done in childhood, Wendy tried very hard to distance herself from these memories and to calm herself. One method Wendy used to cast the intrusive memories out of her mind was injuring herself with self-inflicted cuts and burns. She was covered with bruises from hitting herself with heavy objects, and she had many scars, cuts, and burn marks on her arms, legs, and chest. In addition, Wendy had an open wound on her foot that she had not allowed to heal for 15 years. During one of her hospitalizations, this wound had become infected (as it had been on many occasions in the past), and the hospital staff was frustrated in their attempts to treat it because Wendy kept removing the bandages and re-opening the wound. Later, it was learned that Wendy had received medical attention for the wound many times in the past (sometimes surgery and stitches), but Wendy had always taken out the stitches and kept the wound from healing. For years, Wendy was in constant pain and had trouble walking and getting around easily. Although the staff did not know it at the time, Wendy cut herself vaginally on a regular basis during her hospital stays; the staff could not understand at the the time why Wendy had become so anemic.

In addition, Wendy had learned to rely on her hypnotic abilities to psychologically distance herself from her distressing memories and emotions. Specifically, Wendy learned to dissociate herself from the ongoing abuse she suffered throughout childhood. At first, this strategy helped Wendy to cope with the ongoing abuse by psychologically separating her from the trauma. However, her *dissociation* had become so extensive (in DSM-IV, the term *dissociation* refers to a disruption in a person's consciousness, memory, identity, or perception of the environment) that, since childhood, Wendy had developed more than 20 distinct personalities. Wendy often found herself in a trance, either reliving abusive experiences or so distanced from them that she felt unreal or inhuman (symptoms corresponding to the terms *derealization* and *depersonalization* in DSM-IV). By distancing herself from traumatic cues, Wendy came to have major problems with amnesia: She would often "lose" large sections of time (occasionally hours at once) when she could not recall what she had done or where he had been. For example, even subtle cues or reminders of abuse incidents could trigger a dissociative episode in which Wendy would switch to a different personality; once she had returned to her usual state, Wendy could not recall what had occurred during the episode.

Each of Wendy's personalities had its own distinct pattern of behaviors (e.g., speech, posture, mannerisms), perceived ages, sex, and appearance. Each personality had a unique store of information, memories, and access to feelings. Amazingly, each of Wendy's personalities possessed different physical reactions or different physical abilities, such as different responses to medications and different types of allergies or allergic reactions, and even different eyesight abilities (i.e., different personalities required different eyeglass prescriptions). Based on his initial sessions with her, Wendy's clinical psychologist reasoned that when Wendy experienced major incidents of abuse, she had frequently coped by "walling" off the part of herself that was taking the abuse so that the rest of her did not know about what was taking place. By dividing things up this way, Wendy was able to have parts of herself that could contain the feelings and knowledge about the tortures and abuse that were going on at home and thereby still be able to have other parts of herself that could handle going to school (and later, going to work). However, these parts of her began to take on lives of their own as they were repeatedly called upon to handle other abusive situations. For instance, one personality would always be present when her grandfather would orally rape her. Thus, this personality had developed with no sense of taste and a minimal gag reflex. Another personality handled being burned by her mother and was able to be insensitive to and tolerant of physical pain. Yet another personality was experienced as having no mouth, stemming from experiences where Wendy's mother burned her every time she screamed.

As is typical for most persons with dissociative identity disorder, Wendy possessed many child personalities. These personalities tended to be the parts of Wendy that had been walled off during childhood abuse incidents and therefore had been stopped in time. These personalities saw themselves as the age at which the abuse had occurred and often believed that it was still that year and that they were still living in the same place, going to the same school, and so forth. The voices, postures, drawings, penmanship, and vocabularies of these personalities were all age appropriate. Each personality had its own purpose, and many of the characteristics of each personality contributed to these functions. Personalities that handled torture were anesthetic (as were the ones present during episodes of self-injurious behavior, such as removing stitches from the foot wound). Personalities that had been forced to submit to her mother's bidding had internalized these rules and presented as little tyrants. Personalities that were left with the pain from the torture and abuse seemed autistic (e.g., socially detached and nonresponsive), whereas the personalities who handled school or work were quite charming and able to relate. In fact, Wendy had typically been quite functional in highly structured and consistent environments (where the switching of personalities would be less likely) and had been able to do well at most of her jobs. However, even after a good work day, Wendy would often come home and hide in her closet until morning because of her perceptions that her traumatic experiences were happening to her all over again.

Most of these personalities were very isolated from the others. Many did not know about each other, and some did not know about the abuse. One personality (named "Susan") had been developed to handle sex with the men to whom Wendy's mother had sold her for prostitution. Susan quickly learned that if she initiated the sexual interaction and found a way to experience sexual feelings, it would be far less painful. Thus, Susan had come to believe that she loved sex, and she would actively engage the men her mother brought around. This coping style was very helpful when Wendy was a child as a means of dealing with such a turbulent environment. However, after Wendy had left her mother's home for good, "Susan," by virtue of being cut off from the other personalities, did not know that anything had changed. For many years, Susan continued to seek out men for sexual encounters. (In her normal state, Wendy reported that she had abstained from sex for many years, with the exception of occasional prostitution to support herself and her children after she was placed on leave at the telephone company.) If the situation became violent or abusive, Susan would "leave," and another personality would handle that aspect of the encounter. Therefore, Susan did not know about the violence and would feel quite comfortable bringing home the same individual who had abused her a few weeks before.

Another childhood personality was perceived as being male. This personality had developed after Wendy had witnessed some men choose her and another girl for violent sex, leaving her brothers unharmed. Wendy felt that if only she could have been a boy, then she would have been safe. Consequently, a "boy" personality emerged so that Wendy could feel safe between episodes of abuse. When being that little boy, Wendy felt invulnerable and able to concentrate on other things.

Because Wendy's personalities were so distinct and separated from one another, their abrupt emergence often caused her considerable interpersonal difficulties. People always viewed Wendy as weird, inconsistent, and eccentric. Because they often witnessed Wendy change personalities without understanding what they were seeing, they would become confused as to why her preferences, memories, attitudes, and general demeanor would change in such dramatic and unpredictable ways. Wendy lost many relationships due to such behavior and, as noted earlier, was frequently taken advantage of by exploitive persons.

Initially, Wendy had tried hard to minimize and deny all of her dissociative symptoms, in part because acknowledging such problems would have meant becoming aware of aspects of her past that she was unwilling to tolerate. Because most of her dissociative symptoms had been present since childhood, to some degree Wendy felt quite accustomed to them and had come to believe that everyone lived the way she did; for example, later in treatment, Wendy was quite surprised to learn that not everyone lost large sections of time when they could not remember where they had been or what they had done. One of Wendy's personalities would often be activated in public, usually triggered by cues that reminded her of past abuse (e.g., watching a movie that contained scenes of rape with a group of people). The corresponding personality would emerge and be very confused about place and time (because the personality had been formed years ago in an abusive environment) and would act in ways that would confuse others around her (e.g., begin speaking in a childish manner, then run out of the house and hide under the porch). If this occurred when Wendy was alone, she would "forget" that she had just lost time. When this occurred in the presence of others, Wendy would be unaware of the episode and very confused about the reactions of those around her. If they forced her to face what had just happened, Wendy would usually try to "fake it" and pretend that she was fooling around, or else she would try to make excuses for her behavior. However, when people would not allow her to forget such behavior, Wendy would become quite upset and frightened.

Although Wendy's dissociative symptoms (e.g., trances), multiple personalities, and self-injurious behavior could be viewed as her way of effectively distancing herself from painful memories and feelings, Wendy experienced increasing feelings of self-hatred and blame for engaging in such protective maneuvers. Prior to treatment, Wendy had made no connection between her protective behaviors and her traumatic experiences, and thus she regarded these behaviors as a sign that she was crazy (an opinion others frequently voiced who happened to witness such behavior). For example, if Wendy began to experience a distressing recollection of a past abuse incident, she occasionally cut or burned herself during a dissociative state to make the memory stop. Although she often felt better momentarily, Wendy would then berate herself for being so "perverse" as to cut or burn herself. She did not understand that she had needed to do so to avoid becoming totally overwhelmed by the distressing memory.

DSM-IV Diagnosis

On the basis of this information, Wendy was assigned the following DSM-IV diagnosis:

Axis I	300.14	Dissociative identity disorder (principal diagnosis)
	309.81	Posttraumatic stress disorder, chronic
	296.33	Major depressive disorder, severe without psychotic features
Axis II	301.83	Borderline personality disorder (provisional diagnosis)
Axis III		Carpal tunnel syndrome, intestinal damage from laxative abuse
Axis IV		Unemployment, inadequate finances, severe family discord
Axis V		Global assessment of functioning = 25 (current)

Prior to beginning her outpatient treatment, Wendy exhibited all the symptoms of the DSM-IV diagnosis, dissociative identity disorder (DID; American Psychiatric Association, 1994). In DSM-IV, DID is defined by the following features: (a) the presence of two or more distinct identities or personality states, (b) at least two of these identities or personality states recurrently take control of the person's behavior, (c) inability to recall important personal information that is too extensive to be explained by ordinary forgetfulness, and (d) the disturbance is not due to the direct effects of a substance (e.g., blackouts during alcohol intoxication) or a general medical condition (e.g., complex partial seizures).

In DSM-IV, DID is included in a category referred to as the dissociative disorders, which are characterized by alterations in perceptions or a sense of detachment from one's own self, from one's world, or from memory processes. The most extreme form of dissociative disorder is DID, reflecting the fact that dissociation can be so extensive that whole new identities are formed. Other types of DSM-IV dissociative disorders include: *dissociative amnesia* (extensive inability to recall important personal information, usually traumatic or stressful in nature), *dissociative fugue* (sudden, unexpected travel away from home or work, accompanied by an inability to recall one's past and confusion about personal identity or the assumption of a new identity), and *depersonalization disorder* (persistent or recurrent feeling of being detached from one's mental processes or body that is accompanied by intact reality testing; i.e, the person is aware that it is only a feeling and that he or she is not really detached from the body or mental processes).

The nature and treatment of dissociative identity disorder (referred to as "multiple personality disorder" in the revised third edition of the DSM) are discussed in more detail in the next sections of the chapter. Posttraumatic stress disorder, major depression, and borderline personality disorder are discussed in Cases 4, 8, and 14, respectively. However, note that Wendy's borderline personality disorder was assigned with the qualifier "provisional diagnosis." This qualifier is used when the features of the disorder are present but there is uncertainty about whether the formal criteria for the disorder are met. In Wendy's case, the clinician wished to document the presence of symptoms characteristic of borderline personality disorder (e.g., self-mutilation, unstable self-image or sense of self) but was mindful of the fact that many of these features could possibly be subsumed under (or better accounted for by) her other diagnoses.

CASE FORMULATION USING
THE INTEGRATIVE MODEL

Although the causes of DID are not well understood (cf. Barlow & Durand, 1999), the research in this area has revealed some striking similarities in the histories and characteristics of patients with this disorder. Although not part of the formal DSM-IV definition of DID, research has shown that virtually every patient with this disorder has been exposed to extreme traumatic events, usually in the form of sexual or physical abuse. This was certainly true for Wendy, who suffered severe physical and sexual abuse throughout her childhood and adolescence. How common is trauma in the histories of patients with DID? In an investigation of 100 persons with DID, 97% had experienced significant trauma, usually sexual or physical abuse (Putnam, Guroff, Silberman, Barban, & Post, 1986). A history of incest was observed in 68% of this sample. In another study that reviewed 97 cases of DID, 95% of patients reported physical or sexual abuse (Ross et al., 1990). In many cases, this abuse was unspeakably severe and sadistic: Some patients reported that they had been buried alive; others reported being tortured with burns (e.g., from steam irons or matches) or with cuts (e.g., from razor blades or glass). In fact, researchers have discovered that the background for some patients with DID is a childhood filled with Satanism and ritual abuse that is part of satanic cults (Sakheim & Devine, 1992).

These observations have led researchers to believe that the origins of DID are a natural tendency to escape or "dissociate" from the persistent distress and suffering associated with severe abuse (Kluft, 1991). The tendency to try to psychologically "distance" oneself from painful or stressful events or memories is quite natural and is a feature present in everyone to some extent. For example, it is quite common for otherwise normal individuals who are undergoing unusual stress to attempt to escape or dissociate from the emotional or physical pain in some way (Spiegel & Cardena, 1991). Noyes and Kletti (1977) surveyed more than 100 persons who had experienced various life-threatening situations (e.g., severe accidents) and found that most had experienced some type of dissociation such as feelings of unreality (referred to as *derealization*), blunting of emotional or physical pain, and even a feeling of being detached from their bodies (referred to as *depersonalization*).

These features were quite evident in Wendy, who coped by psychologically walling herself off from the part that was taking the severe abuse. As noted earlier, this allowed Wendy to have parts of herself that could contain the feelings and knowledge about the abuse, while other parts of herself could handle the more normal aspects of her life (e.g., going to school or work). However, these parts began to have lives of their own because they were repeatedly called on to handle abusive situations. Consequently, these personalities were very isolated from the others; many did not know about the others, and some were not even aware of the abuse.

Obviously, not everyone who has been exposed to extreme stress or abuse develops multiple personalities or other dissociative symptoms (e.g., amnesia). Thus, the question arises as to what are the characteristics of persons who are more likely to develop these symptoms following exposure to traumatic events. Although no strong research exists in support of this notion, many researchers believe that people who are more hypnotizable (or "suggestible") are able to use dissociation as a survival skill against extreme trauma (Putnam, 1991). Being in a hypnotic trance is very similar to "dissociating" (Carlson & Putnam, 1989). In a hypnotic trance, people tend to become totally absorbed or focused on one aspect of their world (and become very vulnerable to suggestions by the hypnotist). Moreover, in the phenomenon of self-hypnosis, a person might be able to dissociate from most of the world around them and "suggest" to themselves that, for example, they won't feel any pain in their hands. Accordingly, development of DID may be linked to a person's ability to use self-hypnosis to dissociate parts of themselves from severe abuse or trauma; hence, the person's identity separates into multiple dissociative identities. As mentioned earlier, Wendy's clinical psychologist believed that she was very hypnotizable and felt that she had learned to rely on this ability to psychologically distance herself from her distressing memories and emotions.

Treatment Goals and Planning

Therapy for DID necessitates that the patient gently move toward dismantling the walls that have developed between the personalities, which psychologists often refer to as *alters,* the root word for "others." This process involves (a) recognizing the existence and gradually getting to know the different alters, (b) understanding the purposes that each alter has served, (c) learning new coping strategies and obtaining increased supports so that more awareness of traumatic memories is tolerable, (d) confronting and reliving the early traumas to understand the original need for the walls and to process the intense negative feelings and thoughts associated with these memories, and (e) coming to understand the ways in which the traumas affected many ways of coping and learning how the present differs from the past in ways that allow new and more adaptive (i.e., nondissociative) coping strategies to be used.

You might note that step (d) in the treatment of DID is similar to a therapeutic strategy used to treat PTSD (see Case 4). Specifically, the therapist must assist patients to gradually visualize and relive aspects of their traumatic experiences. In treating both DID and PTSD, a goal is to work through and reduce the negative emotions and thoughts that are linked to these distressing memories. However, unlike the treatment of PTSD, other goals in the treatment of DID are to uncover each of the patient's personalities formed as the result of these traumas and to understand the purposes that these alters served. Ultimately, after this information is uncovered and after new coping strategies are learned, the walls between these alters may become more permeable, allowing the patient to integrate these aspects of themselves into a single personality.

COURSE OF TREATMENT
AND TREATMENT OUTCOME

A crucial initial phase of treatment is to develop a sufficiently safe and trusting therapeutic relationship for the patient. Clearly, such a relationship was necessary for Wendy to concede to exploring the terrifying memories of her childhood. Frequently, establishing a strong therapeutic relationship is quite difficult because of these patients' extreme distrust, based on their negative childhood experiences with family or caretakers. However, one incident during this phase of Wendy's treatment proved to her that the therapist really cared about her. Several months after this incident, Wendy reported that this was the turning point in her treatment that led her to become more engaged in the therapeutic process. As noted in the beginning of the case, when Wendy began outpatient treatment with the psychologist, she was out of work because of an on-the-job injury. Over the first several months of her treatment, Wendy's disability payments had not started to come in. Yet, her rent was due, and her landlord made it clear that she would be evicted if she did not pay. Wendy also had no money left for food for herself or for her children, and she had no family or friends who were willing and able to lend her money. Therefore, the therapist lent Wendy five hundred dollars so she would not be homeless and so she could buy groceries. Wendy was "blown away" by this kindness and trust on his part, as she had never before really experienced caring from someone else. This is particularly noteworthy because most mental health professionals would not recommend such a practice as lending a patient money because of the conflicts and confusion that it can create in the therapeutic relationship. However, in this instance, Wendy felt that the loan was the first time someone had trusted her and had wanted to help with no strings attached. Ultimately, the therapeutic relationship was the most important factor in Wendy's treatment: The therapist had to honestly care about her and communicate his belief in her ability to get well (as well as display a genuine respect for and appreciation of her amazing survival skills). Moreover, the therapist had to possess a willingness to hang in there through some very scary and frustrating times when Wendy was confronting and working through her memories and emotions.

Until the loan, an ongoing problem in Wendy's treatment was her potential for harming herself. She was chronically suicidal and on the verge of injuring herself for most of the first year of treatment. However, these symptoms gradually decreased as Wendy became more engaged in the treatment process and as she began to understand the causes of these symptoms. One focus of Wendy's therapy was understanding the connection between her symptoms and the early events for which these symptoms provided protection. In the first step, Wendy was guided to see that the symptom or behavior in question served an important function and was thus not meaningless or crazy. Once she understood the function of this behavior, she was assisted in becoming aware of how current situations differed from those in the past when the behavior developed. Finally, the therapist helped Wendy to substitute more appropriate and adaptive methods of coping with the behavior.

For example, this process was used to address the open wound on Wendy's foot that she had not allowed to heal for 15 years. As a child, Wendy had incurred many injuries that resulted in stitches. However, once she got home from the hospital, her mother would use the stitched-up wound as a chance to be sadistic. The mother became enraged that someone had helped

Wendy and told her not to trust such help from anyone. To teach Wendy that "help is only going to cause more pain," her mother would pull on the stitches while pouring alcohol on the wound. Consequently, the sight of stitches terrified Wendy, as she knew what lay ahead, and she developed a personality who would take out stitches in order to avoid her mother's reaction to them. Thus, in this instance, Wendy's understanding of the purpose of her symptom led to her seeing that no one was going to behave in the manner her mother had. Wendy realized that she was now an adult who could protect herself from such attacks and that it was, in fact, safe to leave in stitches.

For this progress to occur, the alter that pulled stitches had to become known to the rest of her. Wendy initially viewed him (the alter personality was male) as a terrible tormentor and a part of her she would like to eliminate. However, once his role was understood, Wendy began to view him more accurately as a protector rather than a villain, and she ultimately embraced him for his true purpose, protecting her from these sadistic attacks. Once the alter knew more about the present and the rest of her knew more about this aspect of the past, Wendy was able to have her foot stitched and finally allowed it to heal. Of course, this change also meant dealing with the vast array of feelings that were evoked by remembering the severity of her mother's cruelty.

In another example of this therapeutic process, it became apparent to the therapist that Wendy's regular practice of burning or cutting herself served to help her get into a trance (self-hypnotic) state. Wendy hurt herself when she was feeling the intrusion of painful memories, and, once in this state, she could use her own hypnotic abilities to push away these feelings and be in a calmer, more peaceful place. Once this process was understood, it was relatively easy to assist Wendy to develop and use an alternative way of coping. This coping strategy involved the therapeutic application of hypnosis. When painful feelings began to intrude, Wendy learned to use self-hypnosis by inducing a trance with guided imagery. This technique worked just as well as self-injury had worked to elicit an altered state but allowed Wendy to avoid harm to her body. In addition to the use of hypnosis to teach Wendy to soothe herself when these memories intruded, during the treatment sessions the therapist relied on hypnosis a great deal to facilitate communication among Wendy's alters. Again, this aspect of treatment was very important because it helped Wendy integrate these aspects of herself into a single personality.

During the course of treatment, Wendy became able to remember and integrate the terrible experiences of her childhood. Thus, she had less need for the rigid walls between her various personalities. The artwork that Wendy was doing during this phase of treatment illustrated this process. As noted earlier in this chapter, Wendy had always been an avid painter and drawer; in fact, she harbored a secret desire of becoming a commercial artist. The therapist's view was that Wendy's art and the therapeutic work centered around it became the most significant aspect of her treatment. Early in treatment,

Wendy regularly drew pictures of babies who were crying (Figure 7.1). The pictures were two-dimensional but generally showed what Wendy referred to as the "mutant baby inside her." This was Wendy's sense of a personality that was walled off from her awareness but felt very "bad" and "evil"—part of her that she wanted to destroy. One day, after many discussions with her therapist, Wendy brought in a picture of this baby that no longer had the chaos inside the eyes but, rather, was a picture of a baby with the chaos *outside* her (Figure 7.2). The therapist felt that this was the turning point in her treatment. That night, Wendy went home and was flooded with memories of having been raped and beaten as a small child by her mother. That night Wendy also drew a very graphic picture of the abuse experience (Figure 7.3). This was an incredibly important event in her therapy because she changed her understanding of herself and her symptoms from being "I am crazy and have these awful parts of myself and weird symptoms" to "I am a normal person who was terribly abused and therefore understandably developed extreme kinds of coping mechanisms." At first, the "baby" part of her was finally able to sleep and be calm, but the rest of her was in turmoil from knowing about the traumas. However, as Wendy worked through her feelings about the abuse, she continued to draw pictures of the baby that showed a healthier development from that point forward (Figure 7.4). The baby was able to experience a variety of feelings and needs and then gradually begin to grow up and join the rest of Wendy's personality (Figure 7.5).

Another valuable aspect of treatment addressed Wendy's disrupted sense of spirituality. Recall that Wendy had continually struggled with her view of God and religion (and had experienced considerable guilt and anxiety) after being told at the age of 16 that her stillborn child would never go to heaven because he had not been baptized. At one point in therapy, a minister was invited to some of the sessions to discuss this issue. He ultimately offered to perform what he called a "baptism in spirit," in which he baptized her baby so the baby could move on to heaven. This ceremony created intense relief for Wendy and helped her to see that the church could be a loving and helpful institution.

At the time this chapter was written, Wendy was continuing to attend regular sessions with the clinical psychologist. Thus far, she has been in therapy for 4 years (more than 400 treatment sessions). Although Wendy had attended two sessions per week, she has recently decreased meetings to twice per month. Given the remarkable improvements she has achieved, Wendy is using these sessions in a more supportive capacity. Most notably, the walls between her personalities have gradually become more and more fluid, and Wendy now feels that all of the feelings, behaviors, and qualities are her. None of these personalities have gotten lost in the process (i.e., the abilities and memories of each personality remain intact); rather, out of the pieces a far more whole person has emerged who is able to utilize many lost strengths and abilities. She has dramatically decreased her use of dissociation as a protective maneuver and experiences lost time or other such symptoms only occasionally, when a new memory is emerging, and then it does not last long. Wendy still experiences flashbacks of new parts of various memories sometimes, but she is much more able to tolerate them and to deal with these experiences rapidly and effectively. In addition, she still exhibits an exaggerated startle response, which is characteristic of many trauma survivors who have completed treatment successfully. Nevertheless, Wendy's dissociative symptoms no longer interfere with her life, and her therapist considers her symptoms to no longer qualify for a DSM-IV diagnosis. Remarkably, Wendy is off all psychotropic medications, yet is no longer depressed or anxious, and she no longer experiences psychotic episodes. She has given up her self-injurious behaviors, which had included burning or cutting herself, inserting objects into herself, and giving herself enemas.

As the result of treatment, Wendy's interpersonal relationships have improved dramatically. She has been able to establish honest and supportive friendships and learned to deal in healthier ways with her children (e.g., to rely on them less for support and to set better boundaries with them). She removed herself from a number of abusive relationships and has become more assertive and direct in all of her social interactions. Wendy continues to have sexual problems, primarily a fear of being sexually involved, and has not yet explored this aspect of relating. However, she is just beginning to allow herself to get close to a man and is currently enjoying flirtation for the first time in her life.

One focus of treatment was to assist Wendy in attaining her degree in commercial art. Not only did Wendy obtain this credential, but she also found work and started making a good income. Financial security was totally new to her and proved to be an important facet in her healing process. She was able to purchase her own condominium, a kind of security that she had never imagined possible.

Currently, Wendy is working on a book using her artwork to illustrate the healing process so that other child abuse survivors will have a helpful guide. She wants to reach out to other "hopeless cases" to show that the process of healing is very difficult but can be navigated successfully. Wendy is also helping others more directly, such as volunteering with people with physical disabilities. She says that she has been fortunate in the ways that people have cared about and helped her, and she wants to be able to give help back to people who need it. Moreover, Wendy is helping to raise her granddaughter, an adorable little girl, of whom she is very proud and able to love. Although Wendy raised her own children, she was so removed from her feelings that she often experienced them as not really hers. Wendy's granddaughter is a very real person to her, and others note that their relationship is delightful to watch.

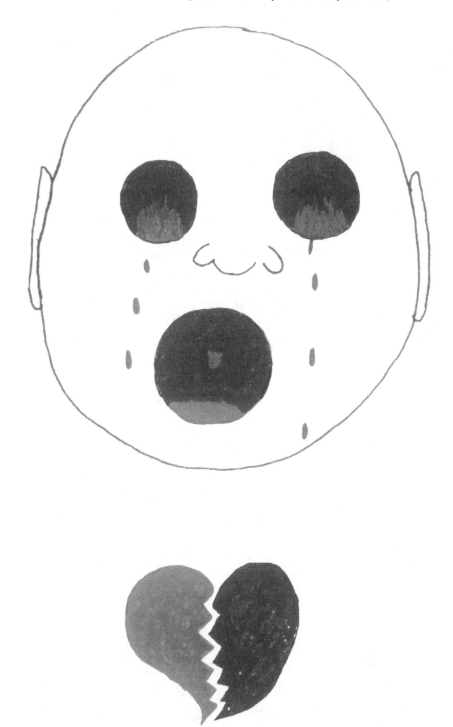

Figure 7.1

Figure 7.2

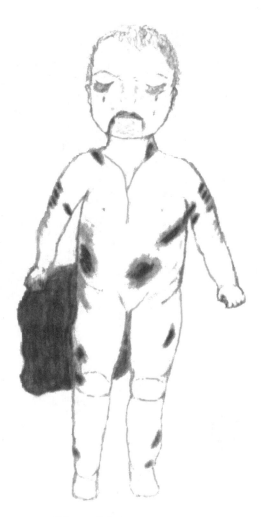

Figure 7.3

Figure 7.4

Figure 7.5

DISCUSSION

Recall that one of the criteria of the DSM-IV diagnosis of dissociative identity disorder (DID; American Psychiatric Association, 1994) is the requirement that the disturbance is not due to the direct effects of a substance (e.g., blackouts during alcohol intoxication) or a general medical condition (e.g., complex partial seizures). This criterion D is based in part on evidence that individuals with certain neurological disorders, particularly seizure disorders, may often experience dissociative symptoms (e.g., Cardena, Lewis-Fernandez, Bear, Pakianathan, & Spiegel, in press). For example, Devinsky, Feldman, Burrowes, and Bromfield (1989) reported that roughly 6% of patients with temporal lobe epilepsy reported "out of body" experiences (referred to in DSM-IV as "depersonalization"). In another study of patients with temporal lobe epilepsy, approximately 50% showed some kind of dissociative symptom, including development of alternate identities (Schenk & Bear, 1981).

Such findings suggest that dissociative symptoms may result from abnormal electrical activity in the brain. While more research is required, our existing scientific knowledge highlights some strong differences between persons with dissociative symptoms that are associated with diagnosed seizure disorders and persons with DID. For instance, patients with seizure disorders usually report that their dissociative symptoms began in adulthood and were not associated with a traumatic event. As discussed previously, virtually all patients with DID report a past history of exposure to trauma (usually physical or sexual abuse) and recall that their dissociative symptoms emerged shortly after these experiences.

If you have read Case 4 on posttraumatic stress disorder (PTSD), it may have occurred to you that the origins of DID and PTSD are similar—specifically, that both conditions reflect strong emotional reactions to a severe trauma, although exposure to a traumatic event is not a diagnostic criterion for DID. Moreover, dissociative symptoms are frequently present in PTSD (e.g., dissociative flashbacks, inability to recall significant aspects of the traumatic event). Based on this overlap, many researchers have concluded that DID could be a very extreme subtype of PTSD, with a greater emphasis on the process of dissociation than on symptoms of anxiety (although dissociation and anxiety are present in both DID and PTSD). However, given the paucity of research on DID, this observation is merely a speculation that needs to be verified (or refuted) in future investigations.

The prevalence of DID is still not known, although researchers now think that it is more common than we previously estimated (Kluft, 1991). Studies that have examined patients diagnosed with DID have found the ratio of females to males as high as 9 to 1. The onset of DID is almost always in childhood. The condition tends not to remit in the absence of treatment (Putnam et al., 1986), although the frequency of "switching" (shifts in personality states) may decrease with age (Sakheim & Devine, 1992). As with Wendy, several case studies of patients with DID suggest that different personalities may emerge over the years in response to different life events. It very rarely occurs in the absence of other clinical diagnoses. Consistent with Wendy's case, depression, PTSD, and borderline personality disorder (among other diagnoses) are frequently assigned as additional diagnoses to individuals with DID (Ross et al., 1990).

As with all other aspects of DID (e.g., prevalence, course, etiology), very little research has been conducted on the development and evaluation of treatments for this disorder. However, several case studies have reported success in reintegrating identities during long-term therapy (e.g., Putnam, 1989; Ross, 1989). Unfortunately, what little evidence that does exist suggests that the prognosis for most patients is poor. For example, Coon (1986) found that only 5 of 20 patients were successful in treatment (defined as full integration of one's identities). There is no evidence to date to indicate that medications add significantly to a favorable outcome. Thus, in light of the unquestionably severe levels of distress and life-style interference associated with DID (documented in the case of Wendy), the development of effective treatments for this disorder is strongly needed.

THINKING CRITICALLY

1. There continues to be controversy over whether dissociative identity disorder (DID) actually exists. Do you believe it is possible for some people to have several different personalities that may or may not be aware of each other? Why or why not?

2. DID has been used as a legal defense in murder trials (i.e., the person committed the murder under an "alter" personality and was arguably unaware of the crime, therefore not responsible for it). Do you think that DID can be a credible and viable defense in some legal cases? If someone, in fact, had DID at the time he or she committed a serious crime, should he or she be held accountable for those actions? Do you think it is possible for some defendants to convincingly fake the symptoms of DID?

3. What factors do you think account for the finding that DID is much more common in females than in males?

4. Most cases of DID begin in the same fashion as cases of posttraumatic stress disorder (PTSD)—exposure to extremely stressful or traumatic events such as sexual or physical abuse. What factors do you believe account for exposure to trauma manifesting as DID in some cases and PTSD in others?

Case

8

Major Depression

A t the time of her referral to the psychology clinic, Liona Barrueco was a 13-year-old Hispanic girl in the 7th grade. Liona had attended a private school over the past 2 years after completing a gifted and talented program for inner city children in the public schools. Shortly before her first visit to the clinic, Liona told one of her friends at school that she had thought about killing herself. This friend persuaded Liona to see the school's psychologist. After meeting briefly with her, the school psychologist called Liona's mother to recommend that she seek help for her daughter. Liona's mother promptly arranged the initial appointment at the psychology clinic.

During the intake evaluation session, Liona reported that she was feeling increasingly depressed and was having more suicidal thoughts that were scaring her. Liona said that she now felt that she needed help to feel better. Although Liona's mother stated that she had not realized that her daughter was depressed, she had noticed that Liona had become more irritable, oppositional, and difficult to manage at home. As the clinical interview progressed, it became clear that Liona had been experiencing depression for a long time. Liona said that she had felt down and depressed almost every day over the past year. More recently,

127

these feelings had intensified and had been accompanied by other symptoms. For example, over the past 6 months, Liona had experienced irritability, loss of energy, and fatigue. Indeed, Liona stated that these feelings and her increasing loss of interest in her normal activities (e.g., visiting with friends, participating in the school's swimming team) had led her to "just feel like sleeping all the time." She had also noticed that her appetite had decreased, although, while she had eaten a bit less than usual, Liona's change in appetite had not been associated with any weight loss. In addition, Liona said that, for the last several months, she had experienced some difficulty sleeping; specifically, most mornings she was waking up 1 or 2 hours earlier than she intended.

Since her depression began, Liona had experienced other symptoms, including frequent headaches and occasional episodes of feeling like she was in a dream or detached from her body (a symptom referred to as *depersonalization*). She stated that she had been constantly worried about such matters as her physical appearance and whether she had done something wrong (e.g., unknowingly upset one of her teachers or classmates). In fact, as the result of her increasing irritability, Liona had gotten into more conflicts with her peers and was having more arguments with her parents and two younger sisters (ages 6 and 9). Although Liona denied any problems concentrating in school, her grades had dropped over the 3 months preceding her initial session at the clinic.

Much of Liona's depression and suicidal thoughts seemed to be triggered by her conflicts with her peers and family. After these arguments, Liona usually isolated herself from others and would become preoccupied by her sense of insecurity and dislike of herself. At these times Liona was most likely to experience suicidal thoughts. Specifically, Liona said that she would feel like the world was coming down on her and would then think about suicide by letting herself drown in the pool at school. In fact, 3 months before her intake evaluation, Liona had made a suicidal gesture by superficially scratching her wrist with a razor blade. Liona had told no one about this incident, and no one had noticed the scratches on her wrist. Two months later, Liona had jumped into the school's pool during swimming practice. Although she had not thought about drowning herself before getting in the pool, while she was underwater, Liona found that she couldn't catch her breath. For a moment, Liona thought about just letting herself sink to the bottom to drown and wondered what that would be like. Later, a classmate she told about these feelings persuaded her to see the school psychologist. Although Liona had not decided to see the school psychologist on her own, she felt relieved by the opportunity to express the feelings she had been having.

Clinical History

Liona's symptoms of depression began when she was 11, although they had not intensified or become persistent until the year preceding her first visit to the psychology clinic. When the symptoms first emerged, Liona was living with her mother and two sisters. Her parents had been divorced since she was a toddler. However, over the years since the divorce, Liona's father continued to move in and out of the house and back and forth from Mexico. During this time, he fathered Liona's two younger sisters. Liona's mother was unemployed, and the family received public assistance and lived in a poor urban community.

Liona had been faced with several stressors that could have triggered or worsened her depression. First, after receiving a full academic scholarship, Liona had switched from attending a public school in her neighborhood to attending an expensive upper-middle-class private school in a distant part of the city in which there were few minority students. The stress associated with the transition to this school was worsened by the fact that Liona's family was very poor and on public assistance. Therefore, Liona had very different social activities and opportunities available to her, compared to her new classmates. Second, Liona's father had recently returned to the United States from Mexico to live with his mother (Liona's paternal grandmother) to receive medical care. Liona's father was very ill, with an extensive history of medical and psychological problems including several heart bypass operations, ulcers, high cholesterol blood levels, lung problems, alcoholism, depression, and Hodgkin's disease. Recently, he had been in and out of the hospital a few times, and Liona was afraid that he might die, even though she was angry at him and spoke very little to him. In fact, Liona's depression was worst shortly before treatment, when her father began calling her house in an effort to participate in child rearing again.

Much of Liona's anger about her father stemmed from the years before her parents' divorce, when she was exposed to many physical fights between her parents. Although her father aimed much of his physical force at her mother, on two occasions he had hit Liona, incidents that had prompted Liona's mother to throw him out of the house for good. Although Liona was mad at her father for his sporadic and unpredictable involvement with and abandonment of the family, she was also angry about the manner in which her mother had interacted with him over the years since the divorce. Specifically, Liona was angry that despite all the hurtful things her father had done to the family, her mother often turned to him when there were problems to be dealt with, and she always accepted him back into the family after he abandoned them without warning or had been physically abusive.

In addition to her father's depression and alcoholism, other members of Liona's family had histories of psychological disorders. Her mother had received outpatient psychotherapy for an episode of depression that occurred shortly after her marital separation. Liona's maternal aunt and paternal grandfather also had had recurring periods of depression. Although Liona's visit to the psychology clinic represented the first time she had received formal treatment for an emotional problem, several years earlier Liona had attended a support group in her old school when she was feeling overwhelmed by her parents' difficulties.

DSM-IV Diagnosis

Based on this information, Liona was assigned the following DSM-IV diagnosis:

Axis I   296.22   Major depressive disorder, single episode,
                       moderate
Axis II   V71.09   No diagnosis on Axis II
Axis III   None
Axis IV   Disruption of family by divorce, health problems in family,
            poverty
Axis V   Global assessment of functioning = 58 (current)

In DSM-IV (American Psychiatric Association, 1994), a major depressive episode is defined by the following features, one or both of which must be present for at least 2 weeks: (a) depressed mood most of the day, nearly every day, as indicated by either the person's report (e.g., feels sad or empty) or observation by others (e.g., appears tearful) and (b) persistent and marked decrease in interest or pleasure in all or almost all activities (e.g., hobbies, social activities, work). As was true with Liona, the depressed mood can also be manifested as irritability in children and adolescents. In addition, a major depressive episode is characterized by at least four of the following symptoms: (a) significant weight loss or weight gain or persistent decrease or increase in appetite, (b) insomnia or sleeping more than usual, (c) agitation or slowing of body movement (e.g., inability to sit still, slowed speech), (d) fatigue or loss of energy, (e) feelings of worthlessness or excessive or inappropriate guilt, (f) lessened ability to think or concentrate or difficulties making decisions, and (g) recurring thoughts of death or suicidal thoughts, plans, or attempts. In addition to causing a significant degree of distress or life-style impairment, in order to meet the DSM-IV definition of major depression, the symptoms cannot be due to biological factors (e.g., the effects of drugs or a general medical condition) and are not better accounted for by bereavement (i.e., grief following the death of a loved one).

In addition to considering the mood disorders involving symptoms of mania (see Case 9), the clinician distinguishes between major depression and dysthymic disorder when establishing a diagnosis. *Dysthymic disorder* is distinguished from major depression by the severity of symptoms and their duration. The essential feature of dysthymic disorder is a chronically depressed mood that occurs for most of the day more days than not for at least 2 years. While most of the symptoms that characterize major depression are also found in dysthymic disorder (e.g., poor appetite or overeating, low energy or fatigue, insomnia or hypersomnia), the symptoms of dysthymic disorder are less severe than those of major depression. In many cases, if the person's symptoms are severe enough to meet criteria for major depression, the diagnosis of dysthymic disorder is not assigned. However, it is appropriate to assign a person both diagnoses, particularly if a major depressive episode follows a long-standing dysthymic disorder, which is often referred to as "double depression." In addition to severity, major depression and dysthymic disorder can often be distinguished by their course: major depressions tends to be more episodic whereas, by definition, dysthymia reflects chronic, less severe depressive symptoms.

As can be seen in Liona's five-axis diagnosis, her major depressive disorder was assigned several specifiers (i.e., "single episode," "moderate"). In addition to specifiers that convey the severity of the disorder (e.g., "mild," "moderate," "severe," "in partial remission," among others), specifiers are used to describe the course of the disorder. These specifiers include whether the person has experienced a "single" episode versus multiple ("recurrent") episodes of depression. For persons who have experienced recurrent depressive episodes, other specifiers may apply, including those that convey more information on the longitudinal course of the illness (i.e., "with/without full interepisode recovery" to indicate whether a full remission of symptoms was attained between the two most recent episodes of depression) and a specifier "with seasonal pattern," which is applied to cases with a regular temporal relationship between the onset and remission of major depressive episodes and a particular time of the year. In most cases that have a seasonal pattern, the depressive episodes begin in the fall or winter and remit in the spring. For both single and recurrent episodes of depression, a specifier termed "with postpartum onset" should be assigned if a woman's depression develops within 4 weeks after delivery of a child.

CASE FORMULATION USING THE INTEGRATIVE MODEL

The integrative theory of the mood disorders (i.e., major depression, dysthymic disorder, bipolar disorder) is based on a diathesis-stress model (Barlow & Durand, 1999). The "diathesis" component of the integrative model refers to the biological vulnerability to develop a mood disorder. Although no specific genetic or biological markers have been confirmed at present as risk factors for major depression, this vulnerability seems to be best described as an overactive neurological response to stressful life events (stressful life events represent the "stress" component of the diathesis-stress model).

Evidence for the biological contribution to major depression can be found in a large number of studies showing that this disorder often runs in families. This was true for Liona whose father, mother, grandfather, and aunt had histories of major depression. This is consistent with research findings showing that the rate of major depression in the families of persons with major depression is considerably higher than the rate of these disorders in families of persons without mood disorders (see Gershon, 1990, for a review). The role of genetics in the origins of major depression has also been supported by findings from twin studies. For example, a study by Bertelsen, Harvald, and Hauge (1977) found that if one twin had major depression, there was a 36% chance that a monozygotic (identical) twin had some form of mood disorder (e.g., major depression, bipolar disorder), which was substantially higher than the rate of mood disorders (17%) in dizygotic (fraternal) twins, if one twin had major depression. Because monozygotic twins have exactly the same genes whereas dizygotic twins share only about 50% of each other's genes (the same number shared among first-order relatives), the higher rate of mood disorders in monozygotic twin pairs suggests that genetic factors contribute to the development of major depression. In this study, severity was also related to the amount of concordance (the degree to which both twin pairs had a mood disorder). If one twin had severe depression (defined as three or more major depressive episodes), then 59% of the identical twins also had a mood disorder, compared with 30% of the fraternal twins (the concordance rates were 33% and 14% for identical and fraternal twins, respectively, for individuals who presented with fewer than three episodes of major depression). These findings suggest that severe mood disorders may have a stronger genetic contribution than less severe disorders, a finding that holds true for most psychological disorders.

Research suggests that the mood and anxiety disorders share a common, genetically determined biological vulnerability. For example, data from family studies indicate that the more signs and symptoms of anxiety and depression in a given patient, the greater the likelihood that anxiety and depression are present in both their first-order relatives and their children (Hammen, Burge, Burney, & Adrian, 1990; Leckman, Weissman, Merikangas, Pauls, & Prusoff, 1983). In two twin studies, Kendler and colleagues found that the same genetic factors contribute to both anxiety and depression (Kendler, Heath, Martin, & Eaves, 1987; Kendler, Neale, Kessler, Heath, & Eaves, 1992). Social and psychological dimensions appeared to account for the factors that differentiate anxiety from depression. These data suggest that the biological vulnerability for mood disorders may not be specific to that disorder but may reflect a more general vulnerability for either anxiety or mood disorders. Whether the person with this general vulnerability develops anxiety or depression would then be influenced later by psychological, social, or other biological factors (Barlow, 1991).

As noted in the beginning of this section, stressful life events appear to play a significant role in the onset of mood disorders. A large body of research indicates that stressful life events (family difficulties, job loss, etc.) are strongly related to the onset of mood disorders, particularly major depression.

How do stressful life events interact with biological factors to produce major depression? The best current thinking on this issue is that stressful life events activate our stress hormones, which, in turn, have wide-ranging effects on our neurotransmitter systems, particularly those involving serotonin and norepinephrine. If these stress hormones remain activated, structural and chemical changes in the brain may occur (e.g., atrophy of neurons in the areas of the brain that contribute to the regulation of emotions and neurotransmitter activity). The extended effects of stress may be associated with disruptions in a person's circadian rhythms, causing them to be susceptible to the recurrent cycling that is a defining feature of major depression (see Case 9).

In addition to this interaction between biological factors and stress, a number of psychological and social dimensions seem to operate as vulnerability and maintaining factors for major depression. Two psychological dimensions that have been linked extensively to depression are *attributional style* and *dysfunctional attitudes*. Attributional style refers to the explanations a person makes for the causes of positive and negative events that occur in his or her life. Originating from animal research on learned helplessness (Seligman, 1975), the basic premise of this theory is that people who make an *attribution* that they have no control over the stress in their lives develop anxiety and depression (Abramson, Seligman, & Teasdale, 1978). Specifically, an attributional style found to be associated with depression has three major characteristics: (a) *internal,* the person attributes the cause of the negative event to their own failings; (b) *stable,* the person attributes the cause of the negative event to be permanent rather than temporary; and (c) *global,* the person attributes the cause of the negative event to factors that extend across a wide range of aspects of their lives or functioning. For example, an attribution that could produce depression is "I'm unintelligent" in explaining why a person did not receive a passing grade on a psychology final, versus explanations that presumably would cause less distress because they are external (e.g., "The exam was unfair"), unstable (e.g., "I didn't have time to study"), or specific (e.g., "I'm good at a lot of things, but not good at psychology"). Although a large number of studies have supported the position that attributions of negative events to internal, stable, and global causes are associated with depression (cf. Sweeney, Anderson, & Bailey, 1986), researchers are still uncertain whether this attributional style is a cause of depression or just a correlated side effect. Findings have been mixed (i.e., some studies have supported the theory, but others have provided evidence against the notion that a pessimistic attributional style is an enduring cause of depression; e.g., Hamilton & Abramson, 1983), and more recently this theory has been revised to deemphasize specific attributions and to highlight the development of a sense of hopelessness as a crucial cause of depression (Abramson, Metalsky, & Alloy, 1989).

Another psychological factor that has received extensive examination and support for its role in depression is dysfunctional thinking (Beck, 1976; Beck, Rush, Shaw, & Emery, 1979). According to Beck, people prone to depression make cognitive errors in which they think negatively about *themselves*, their *immediate world*, and their *future* (these areas are referred to as the *cognitive triad*). Cognitive errors reflect discrete manifestations of deep-seated *negative schemata* that develop in childhood. A *schema* refers to an enduring and stable negative cognitive bias or belief system about some aspect of life. For example, Beck's theory states that depression is often caused by a tendency for a person to distort negative things that have happened in the direction of self-blame, signifying the presence of a self-blame schema in which a person feels responsible for every bad thing that happens (in interpreting why a few guests left the party early, for example, the host concludes, "I'm a failure when it comes to throwing parties" when, in actuality, people had a multitude of reasons for leaving early). Once these schemata and cognitive errors have developed, they are believed to become very automatic; that is, a person who is interpreting events in this fashion may not be consciously aware of their thoughts or of the fact that their interpretations are inaccurate. Thus, the central goals of cognitive therapy for depression are to assist the patient in identifying negative cognitions and evaluating their validity, with the ultimate objective of replacing these thoughts and schemata (underlying assumptions) with more accurate and logical interpretations.

As is the case with attributional style, although a host of studies have documented the connection between negative cognitions and depression, evidence that this thinking style causes and predates depression is less conclusive (cf. Haaga, Dyck, & Ernst, 1991). Although a few studies have found that dysfunctional attitudes may predict the recurrence of depression under some conditions (as opposed to initial onset of depression; e.g., Hammen, Ellicott, Gitlin, & Jamison, 1989), much more research is needed to verify the causal role of negative cognitions in mood disorders.

A variety of social factors may be associated with the origins and maintenance of depression. For example, marital satisfaction and depression are strongly related (e.g., Beach, Sandeen, & O'Leary, 1990), and a marital disruption (e.g., separation, divorce) has often been the stressful life event that acts as the trigger for a depressive episode (e.g., Bruce & Kim, 1992). Similarly, many studies have found that the presence of depression in one spouse may lead to a marked deterioration in the marital relationship (e.g., Beach et al., 1990; Coyne, 1976), which, in turn, may lead to an increase in the spouse's depression. In a broader sense, the extent of a person's *social support* system has also been implicated in depression. In terms of the origins of depression, some studies have found that persons who have experienced a negative life event are less likely to develop depression if they have adequate social support (i.e., access to supportive, caring relationships; e.g., Brown &

Harris, 1978; Monroe, Imhoff, Wise, & Harris, 1983). With regard to the course of depression, studies have found that among people who are experiencing major depression, those who have a supportive spouse and fewer conflicts with friends recover more quickly (McLeod, Kessler, & Landis, 1992). Moreover, living in a family with a lot of nagging, criticism, and emotional outbursts (referred to as "high expressed emotion") has been found to be associated with an increased risk of relapse in persons who have experienced major depression (e.g., Hooley & Teasdale, 1989). Findings such as these have led to a more recently developed psychological treatment for depression, *interpersonal psychotherapy,* which focuses on the role of interpersonal relationships in the maintenance of depression. This treatment is discussed in the remaining sections of this chapter.

Treatment Goals and Planning

Consistent with the findings reviewed in the preceding section, Liona's depression was clearly influenced by social factors, namely, the interpersonal interactions she had with members of her immediate family. Accordingly, Liona's primary treatment was interpersonal psychotherapy (IPT; Klerman, Weissman, Rounsaville, & Chevron, 1984). Although IPT was first developed as a treatment for adults with depression, it has been effectively modified for intervention in adolescent depression (Moreau, Mufson, Weissman, & Klerman, 1991; Mufson, Moreau, Weissman, & Klerman, 1993; Mufson et al., 1994). The underlying principle of IPT is that regardless of the biological, psychological, and environmental (stress) factors that cause the depression, the mood disorder occurs in an interpersonal context that can significantly influence its course. Thus, if problems in the patient's interpersonal relationships can be identified and improved, the depression is lessened. Therefore, the therapy focuses on current interpersonal problems that appear to be associated with the depression. This highly structured, short-term treatment consists of three phases (initial, middle, termination), which are described in the next section.

COURSE OF TREATMENT
AND TREATMENT OUTCOME

Liona received 12 weekly sessions of IPT. Her mother attended two of these sessions, once during the initial phase and once during the termination phase of therapy. The primary goal of the initial phase of treatment was to orient Liona and her mother to the rationale of treatment and to develop a treatment plan. In this phase of treatment, Liona and her mother were educated about the nature of depression; that is, besides learning about the disorder, they were provided information on the causes and factors that maintain a person's depressed mood. In addition to explaining the rationale and goals of treatment, the therapist expressed what she expected of Liona during treatment (e.g., regular session attendance, completion of between-session therapeutic assignments).

A critical component of the initial phase of treatment was reviewing Liona's interpersonal relationships to identify problem areas that would be the focus of intervention during the middle phase of therapy. Based on the rationale of IPT, five different interpersonal problem areas are often associated with the onset or maintenance of depression: grief, interpersonal role disputes, role transitions, interpersonal deficits, and single-parent families. *Grief* is prolonged or abnormal levels of bereavement or sense of abandonment following the loss of a loved one (e.g., death of a parent). *Interpersonal role disputes* are disagreements between the patient and one or more significant others about the expectations about their relationship (e.g., parental expectations that the adolescent should function at a level of maturity higher than she is capable of achieving). *Role transitions* are maladjustments to the changes that occur as the result of progressing from one social role to another (e.g., passage into puberty, separation from parents due to going off to college). *Interpersonal deficits* are lack of the social skills necessary for establishing and maintaining appropriate relationships within and outside of the family (e.g., poor communication skills or inadequate assertiveness to communicate one's needs effectively). *Single-parent families* refer to emotional conflicts between adolescent and parent because of single-parent homes due to divorce, separation, incarceration, death of parent, and other reasons (e.g., distress over feeling pulled in opposite directions by requests for the adolescent's time and attention by parents who are divorced and not communicating with one another).

Liona and her therapist worked together to select one or two of these problem areas to focus on in the next phase of treatment. However, during this time Liona expressed her desire to discontinue treatment. She cited three reasons: (a) she found it uncomfortable to enter a building that said Psychology Clinic on the front of it, (b) a friend had told her that she didn't need treatment, and (c) she felt funny telling her personal business to another person. The therapist explored these concerns with Liona and was able to convince her to try 4 more weeks of treatment, and then the issue of whether to continue therapy would be reevaluated. By the time these 4 weeks had passed, Liona was very engaged in treatment and no longer had any desire to stop.

During this 4-week period, Liona's depression was conceptualized as being related to an interpersonal role dispute with her mother and father. She was often switching back and forth between two roles in her family: (a) the 13-year-old daughter and (b) her mother's companion and protector. Liona was a "parentified" child not only because of the single-parent situation but also because she appeared much older than her 13 years in her dress, her intelligence, and her manner with adults. However, when her father would reenter the picture and try to resume his fatherly role with the children and their mother, Liona would get very angry at having to relinquish her special role as her mother's protector. This anger also stemmed from her feelings of repeated abandonment by and disappointment in her father and her belief that he did not deserve to return to the family, in light of his past behavior. Moreover, Liona worried that she would grow up to be like her father because her mother often compared her to her father in her stubbornness and reluctance to accept help.

Therefore, the primary target of the middle phase of treatment was to help Liona and her mother clarify their expectations for Liona's role in the family in various situations. An additional goal of treatment was to improve Liona and her mother's ability to discuss their feelings with each other. Accordingly, the therapist assisted Liona in learning new communication strategies and skills to improve her relationships with her parents. These issues were addressed through the following methods: (a) using role-playing conversations (e.g., patient-therapist enactments to rehearse how Liona could interact with her parents more effectively; see Case 3 for more details on this technique), (b) encouraging Liona to express her emotions more appropriately (including therapist feedback on what impact Liona's expression of her feelings had on others), (c) exploring and clarifying how Liona felt about various situations or persons, (d) linking the origins of Liona's feelings of anger and depression to events that had occurred in her life, and (e) helping Liona see another person's perspective on a situation so she could learn to negotiate or compromise for a solution.

Indeed, one of the most therapeutic aspects of treatment for Liona was learning about the different roles she had in the family and how they often conflicted. Her high intelligence contributed to her favorable response to the treatment; she could understand abstract concepts and generalize from one situation to another. Thus, once Liona felt comfortable coming to treatment sessions, she devoured the principles of the treatment. Following a session in which her roles in the family were discussed, Liona went home and explained the whole role concept to her mother. She told her mother how sometimes she is the child and sometimes she is more like the adult in the family and that, when her father comes around, she gets confused about who she should be. Her mother listened carefully to Liona and told her that she would help her with the problem, but that most of all, Liona should just be herself. Following this conversation, Liona reported that she felt much closer to and better understood by her mother, and she identified it as a turning point in the treatment. Her mother's support and responsiveness to the treatment principles were also instrumental in Liona's success with therapy.

In addition to the interpersonal issues within her family, Liona's depression appeared to be influenced by her problems in adjusting to her new school. Thus, another topic of treatment was her cultural identity and what it was like for her to be Hispanic in a predominantly white upper-middle-class private school. The therapist and Liona discussed ways in which she could educate her classmates about her culture besides teaching them curse words in Spanish. Also, the therapist encouraged Liona to tell her new friends how she felt to be different culturally and socioeconomically in school and in outside functions. Liona followed through on many of these suggestions and, as a result, began to feel better understood and more accepted by her classmates.

The last few sessions of Liona's treatment were devoted to the termination phase of therapy. During this phase, the therapist reviewed the skills and strategies that Liona learned over the course of treatment. In addition, Liona and her therapist worked to anticipate what situations might be problematic in the future and how Liona's new skills could be applied to these events. The therapist also reminded Liona of what the warning signs and symptoms were for a recurrence of depression and discussed the strategies she could deploy to prevent these early symptoms from culminating into another depressive episode. Finally, the therapist emphasized Liona's wide range of personal assets (e.g., intelligence, sophisticated social skills) to foster Liona's sense that she was highly capable of independently using her new skills of communicating and identifying problematic interpersonal issues.

By the 12th week of treatment, Liona no longer showed any symptoms of depression. She was getting along well with her mother and sisters, and her grades had improved. She still tended to get angry easily, but she now had strategies for handling her anger in a more adaptive and less destructive fashion. For instance, Liona felt as if she had reconciled the situation with her father and was confident that she had learned new methods for handling their difficult situation.

As part of routine procedures of the clinic she attended, Liona underwent another psychological evaluation 1 year after she completed treatment. At this assessment, she continued to report no depressive symptoms. In addition, she reported positive relationships with her mother and sisters, a "tolerable" relationship with her father, good relationships with her peers and many new friends, and excellent school performance.

DISCUSSION

Major depression is very prevalent in the general population. For instance, a community survey of more than 8,000 persons from ages 18 to 54 estimated that 17.1% had experienced a major depressive episode at some time during their lives and that 10.3% had experienced major depression over the prior year (Kessler et al., 1994). The lifetime and 12-month prevalence for dysthymic disorder was found to be much lower (6.4% and 2.5%, respectively). These estimates are higher than the rates of depression observed in earlier large-scale community surveys (e.g., Weissman, Bruce, Leaf, Florio, & Holzer, 1991), for reasons that are not clear. However, consistent with findings of previous community surveys, Kessler et al. (1994) observed that the lifetime prevalence of depression in females (21.3%) was substantially higher than in males (12.7%).

More germane to the present chapter, estimates of the prevalence of depression in children and adolescents have varied widely. The general conclusion is that depressive disorders occur less frequently in children than in adults, but that these numbers rise dramatically in adolescence, when, if anything, depression is more frequent than in adults (Kashani, Hoeper, Beck, & Corcoran, 1987; Lewinsohn, Hops, Roberts, Seeley, & Andrews, 1993). Indeed, in a recent large community survey, the prevalence of emotional disorders was highest in persons ranging from age 15 to 24 (Kessler et al., 1994). There is some evidence that dysthymia is more prevalent than major depression in young children, but that this ratio reverses in adolescence. As with adults, adolescents experience major depression more frequently than dysthymia (Kashani et al., 1987).

Most researchers agree that mood disorders in children and adolescents are fundamentally similar to mood disorders in adults (Lewinsohn et al., 1993). Consistent with Liona's presentation, DSM-IV notes that for children and adolescents, depressed mood may be more apt to take the form of irritable mood or to be accompanied by it (American Psychiatric Association, 1994). Both childhood and adult depression are associated with considerable impairment in psychosocial functioning. For example, in adolescents this impairment includes substance abuse, suicide attempts, school dropout, and antisocial behavior (cf. Fleming & Offord, 1990). Depression and dysthymia often do not occur in isolation with other disorders; anxiety and substance use disorders are quite prevalent in persons with a mood disorder (e.g., Sanderson, Beck, & Beck, 1990). As noted earlier, major depression and dysthymia often occur together, a phenomenon referred to as *double depression*. A large community survey found that 28% of persons with major depression also had dysthymia at some point in their lives. As one might expect, suicide is a prevalent complicating feature of depression. As many as 60% of suicides are associated with an existing mood disorder (Frances, Franklin, & Flavin, 1986), and as many as 75% of adolescent suicides were associated with an existing mood disorder (Brent & Kolko, 1990).

The length of major depressive episodes is variable, with some episodes lasting just 2 weeks, whereas, in more severe cases, an episode may last several years. Studies have indicated that the average duration of major depression is approximately 9 months (e.g., Tollefson, 1993). Even though the vast majority of episodes remit after some period of time, major depression is distinguished by its recurrent nature. Research has found that persons who have episodes that do not remit completely are the most likely to experience full-blown recurrences of depression (hence the utility of the DSM-IV diagnostic specifiers "with/without full interepisode recovery" in conveying the probable course of the disorder). Dysthymia is a much more chronic disorder; a preliminary study has estimated that the median duration of this condition is approximately 5 years (Rounsaville, Sholomskas, & Prusoff, 1988).

A number of treatments, both psychopharmacological (medications) and psychosocial, have been developed for depression. Perhaps the most widely used medications in the treatment of depression are the tricyclic antidepressants (such as imipramine and amitryptyline), which seem to have their most substantial effects on the noradrenergic system, although other neurotransmitter systems are affected as well. A summary analysis of more than 100 studies concluded that tricyclics are effective in roughly 50% of patients, compared to approximately 25% to 30% of patients taking placebo (nonactive) pills (Depression Guideline Panel, 1993). However, because these drugs are associated with a number of side effects (e.g., weight gain, sexual dysfunction, constipation, drowsiness), particularly during the first few weeks after the treatment is started, a considerable proportion of patients (30% to 40%) discontinue their medications prematurely. Although these drugs have been found to be effective in adult and geriatric depression, the available evidence indicates that the tricyclic antidepressants are no more effective than placebos in adolescent patients (e.g., Geller, Cooper, Graham, Marstellar, & Bryant, 1990; Strober, Freeman, & Rigali, 1990).

More recently, another class of medications has been developed called the serotonergic-specific reuptake inhibitors (SSRIs; e.g., fluoxetine [Prozac]), which, as the name implies, operate by inhibiting the reuptake of the neurotransmitter serotonin. Although the existing evidence suggests that the SSRIs are roughly equal in effectiveness to the tricyclic drugs, patients often consider side effects less bothersome (Depression Guideline Panel, 1993). Hence, the SSRIs may be associated with lower treatment dropout rates that are due to patients' inability to tolerate aversive side effects. In addition to medications, the more controversial approach of electroconvulsive therapy (ECT) is an effective biological treatment, particularly for severe depressions that have not responded to medication or psychological treatments (Depression Guideline Panel, 1993).

Two of the leading psychosocial approaches in the treatment of depression are cognitive therapy (Beck et al., 1979) and interpersonal therapy (IPT; Klerman et al., 1984). The nature and goals of IPT have been discussed in detail in the presentation of Liona's treatment. Briefly, the goals of cognitive therapy are to teach patients to carefully examine their thoughts while they are depressed and to recognize "depressive" errors in thinking when these occur. After learning how these thoughts can directly cause their depression, patients learn to correct these cognitive errors and replace them with less depressing and more accurate thoughts and perceptions.

Both cognitive therapy and IPT have been found to be effective, at least in the short term, in the treatment of depressed adults. In the largest study to date (Elkin et al., 1989), cognitive therapy, IPT, and tricyclic antidepressants were compared as treatments of adult major depression in three clinics in North America. When all patients who were treated were considered in the analysis, the results indicated no essential differences in the effectiveness of cognitive therapy, IPT, and tricyclic antidepressants. However, while all three treatments produced considerable improvements in the short term, the long-term results are less encouraging. For instance, Shea et al. (1992) found that among patients who had recovered, only a small percentage (19% to 30%, across treatment conditions) remained well throughout an 18-month follow-up period. Based on this outcome, the investigators concluded that the treatments were not delivered long enough (or well enough) to produce meaningful and durable change. These results also highlight the importance of assessing long-term outcome in the evaluation of treatments for depression. Because major depression is an episodic condition by nature, researchers increasingly concur that the most important indicator of treatment outcome is the extent to which an intervention prevents or delays future depressive episodes (Frank et al., 1990). Encouragingly, recent findings from other studies have indicated that continued use of IPT significantly reduces the recurrences of major depressive episodes in patients who responded to a combination of IPT and tricyclic medication but who, based on their past history, had a substantial risk for relapse (Frank et al., 1990).

Because findings of the effects of a single treatment for depression have often been disappointing, researchers have recently examined whether combining psychosocial and drug treatments produces significantly better therapeutic gains. For example, Hollon et al. (1992) assigned adults with major depression to one of three treatment conditions: cognitive therapy, tricyclic medication, or a combination. Although the differences among treatment conditions were not statistically significant, the combined group had the highest percentage (75%) of patients who were recovered at posttreatment follow-up (compared to 50% and 53% for the cognitive therapy and drug groups, respectively). However, if all patients enrolled in the study were considered (including those who refused or dropped out of treatment), the rates of posttreatment recovery dropped to 52%, 33%, and 32% for the combined groups, cognitive therapy, and drug therapy, respectively.

Thus, these data indicate that much work needs to be done in the development and evaluation of effective treatments for depression. Moreover, work on adapting these treatments for children and adolescents is just beginning, as there are very few controlled outcome studies in the scientific literature ("controlled" refers to comparing a presumably active treatment, such as cognitive therapy, to some form of comparison condition, such as placebos or waiting lists, to determine if the active treatment produces improvement beyond that produced by the comparison condition). Fortunately, as illustrated in the treatment of Liona, important work is underway on the adaptation and extension of interventions such as IPT to depressed children and adolescents (cf. Frank & Spanier, 1995; Moreau et al., 1991; Mufson et al., 1993, 1994).

THINKING CRITICALLY

1. Major depressive disorder (MDD) has been linked to many causes, including biologic and genetic, cognitive, behavioral, and social and interpersonal factors. Which factors do you believe are the most important to the development of MDD? In addition to their roles as causal factors, having MDD can lead to substantial changes in these same domains. How does having MDD affect a person's thoughts, behaviors, and social interactions? What effects can MDD have on how family and friends interact with the depressed person? How can these interpersonal changes result in the maintenance or exacerbation of depression in the afflicted individual?

2. As noted in the case, if all the criteria have been met, a person can be diagnosed as having two depressive disorders at the same time—MDD and dysthymic disorder. What are the differences between MDD and dysthymic disorder? Why might it be clinically important to diagnose both if the features of MDD and dysthymic disorder are present?

3. In addition to the psychosocial intervention described in the treatment of Liona, medications are another widely used method of MDD treatment in children, adolescents, and adults. What do you believe are the major issues and considerations (e.g., ethical, clinical) in using drugs in the treatment of children and adolescents?

4. A recent large community survey found that the prevalence of MDD and other emotional disorders was highest in persons between the ages of 15 and 24. What factors do you believe account for the higher rate of disorders in this age group?

Case

9

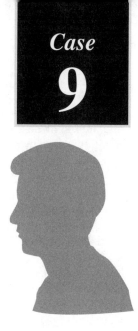

Bipolar Disorder

A t the time of his referral to a psychiatrist working in the outpatient program of a private psychiatric hospital, Buddy King was a 28-year-old married African-American man with two daughters (ages 18 months and 4 years) who worked as a manager in a family food business (he had obtained a degree in business administration at the age of 24). Buddy was referred by his family doctor after his wife had called the doctor to express concern over her observations that her husband was becoming increasingly depressed. Over the prior 2 to 3 months, Buddy's symptoms of depression had indeed escalated. These symptoms included sustained depressed mood and lack of energy, difficulties concentrating, decreased interest and withdrawal from the activities he usually enjoyed, pessimistic views and rumination about the future, and sleep disturbance (i.e., awakening in the morning several hours before he intended). More recently, Buddy had experienced a decrease in his interest in sexual relations with his wife, and occasionally he had thoughts about committing suicide.

Despite these escalations in his symptoms of depression, Buddy was hesitant to see a psychiatrist due to his fear of being revealed as "mentally ill" or "weak." However, these symptoms were beginning to interfere with his work, social life, and marriage. Buddy had previously been very energetic and devoted to his work. He now found it difficult to get up in the morning to go to the office. Furthermore, he had been an avid athlete, but recently he had discontinued nearly all of his athletic activities. Based on these factors, Buddy reluctantly agreed to set up an initial appointment with the psychiatrist.

Clinical History

Buddy's decision to agree to make this appointment was also influenced by his experiences in college. When Buddy was in his senior year at a prestigious university in the midwest, he had also experienced symptoms of depression. During this time, Buddy was under a great deal of stress arising from his family (his parents were upset that he was taking too long in college), and his strong concerns about what he would do for a career after graduation. However, unlike Buddy's more recent experiences (i.e., his symptoms predating his referral to the psychiatrist), these symptoms of depression were followed a few days later by more dramatic symptoms. Specifically, Buddy had experienced a full manic episode, characterized by symptoms of abnormally and persistently elevated mood, grandiose and persecutory delusions, hyperactivity, and a substantially decreased need for sleep (described in more detail later). During this episode, Buddy's school performance diminished greatly, and he often skipped classes altogether. Although he had previously been a sensible drinker (he only drank socially at college parties), Buddy engaged in several alcohol and marijuana binges.

This manic episode was also accompanied by other bizarre and risky activity. During the manic episode, Buddy experienced a marked increase in sexual desire. However, at the time, Buddy was not in a relationship to satisfy his sexual longings. The most significant negative consequence of Buddy's manic episode was his arrest by campus police after he was found naked with a 15-year-old girl in a vacant office building on campus. Although Buddy was arrested and charged with trespassing, these charges were later dropped. The police also threatened to charge him with sexual misconduct with an underage female, but these charges never materialized.

The morning after his arrest, Buddy was taken to a hospital where he was involuntarily hospitalized with the diagnosis of an acute manic episode. This hospitalization lasted 6 weeks. During the first 2 weeks of hospitalization, Buddy was very resistant to treatment and refused most medications. However, he gradually accepted the notion of medications, but refused lithium treatment (lithium carbonate is the most widely used drug for the treatment of mania). He was treated with a combination of Depakote (an antiseizure drug), divalproex (occasionally used in the treatment of mania because it seems to "depress" the central nervous system), and Haldol (haloperidol; an antipsychotic drug used in the treatment of psychotic symptoms such as delusions and hallucinations), which resulted in a gradual reduction in his manic symptoms. At the time of his discharge from the hospital, Buddy insisted on the discontinuation of Haldol, although he reluctantly agreed to continue taking Depakote.

For a time after his discharge, things were rough for Buddy. Although his legal charges were eventually dropped, college authorities refused to allow Buddy to continue in school. Thus, Buddy was forced to transfer and complete his degree at another university. He was somewhat shunned by his friends (who did not understand why Buddy had suddenly acted in a manner so out of character), and his family was very disturbed by the onset of these serious manic symptoms. Although they continually pressured him to comply with his treatment, the family was dismayed that Buddy had become increasingly noncompliant with medical recommendations to continue taking Depakote and submit to regular laboratory tests that were required for his medication regimen (i.e., blood tests that evaluate if the drug is present at a therapeutic level in the person's system and that rule out the presence of negative side effects). This resulted in numerous family conflicts and heated discussions between Buddy and his parents. Buddy rejected his parents' arguments for medication compliance by pointing out that his manic symptoms were no longer present, and so he no longer needed to take the drug.

However, unlike many people who have experienced a manic episode, Buddy, in fact, had had no additional manic episodes since college, despite the fact that he totally stopped taking medications. Buddy completed college at another school and, not having found employment elsewhere, decided to work in the family's food business (where he continued to work at the time of his referral). During the first year after college, Buddy met the woman he eventually married, and he settled into working in the family business. Although Buddy had not experienced any additional manic episodes, he continued to have brief periods of depression from time to time, none of them long or severe enough to cause Buddy to obtain treatment, although his wife had often urged him to do so. Had it not been for his wife's urgings, Buddy may have never agreed to the initial appointment with the psychiatrist.

Buddy was born and raised in a very pressured and high-achieving family. His father was a successful food manufacturer who gradually incorporated all of his children in the family business. Buddy was the youngest of five children; he often struggled with competition with his older brothers. He stated that he often felt that he had to "go the extra mile" in order to measure up to his older brothers in his parents' eyes. Buddy's father was a somewhat harsh, yet supportive man who demanded performance and conscientiousness from all of his children. Differences of opinion were not well-tolerated in the family and each child was pressured to agree with parental views. Although the family was very wealthy, much of the parents' support (both emotional and financial) was tied to such compliant attitudes. For example, those children who rebelled (e.g., had differing views on how aspects of the family business should be run) were often ostracized and would later rejoin after agreeing to give up their "rebellious" attitudes. Buddy described himself as being hyperconscientious and driven during his childhood years, a characteristic that he attributed to his family environment. He also recalled being perfectionistic in high school and college athletics (he played on the basketball team) and to some degree in his school work. Buddy claimed that these family dynamics had resulted in several recent conflicts regarding decisions within the family food business, which he cited as possible contributing factors to his current depression.

Buddy's family had various members with mood disorders. His mother had recurring bouts of depression that had been treated with antidepressant medications. Buddy's maternal grandmother, paternal uncle, and oldest brother had also received outpatient treatment for depression. Buddy's maternal uncle had alcoholism and possible bipolar disorder, although the presence of this latter diagnosis was uncertain because he was estranged from the family and lived in another part of the country.

DSM-IV Diagnosis

Based on the information presented, Buddy was assigned the following DSM-IV diagnosis:

Axis I	296.62	Bipolar I disorder, most recent episode depressed, moderate, with full interepisode recovery
Axis II	V71.09	No diagnosis on Axis II
Axis III	None	
Axis IV	Family conflicts, stressful work environment	
Axis V	Global assessment of functioning = 58 (current)	

Bipolar disorder is the formal diagnostic term that is used in reference to what most people know as "manic depression." Although Buddy did not show any signs of mania at the time of his referral to the psychiatrist, the diagnosis of bipolar disorder is still appropriate because he had a history of a full manic episode. In DSM-IV (American Psychiatric Association, 1994), a *manic episode* is defined as a distinct period of abnormally and persistently elevated, expansive, or irritable mood that lasts at least 1 week (or any duration if hospitalization is necessary, as was the case with Buddy), that is accompanied by at least three of the following symptoms: (a) inflated self-esteem or grandiosity, (b) decreased need for sleep (e.g., feeling rested after only 3 hours of sleep), (c) more talkative than usual or pressure to keep talking, (d) flight of ideas (e.g., jumping from one topic to another in mid-conversation) or subjective experience that thoughts are racing, (e) distractibility (i.e., attention too easily drawn to unimportant or irrelevant external stimuli), (f) increase in goal-directed activity (e.g., writing a torrent of letters to public figures or friends, taking on new business ventures) or psychomotor agitation (e.g., constant pacing, carrying several conversations at the same time), and (g) excessive involvement in pleasurable activities that have a high potential for painful consequences (e.g., buying sprees, foolish business investments, or, as in Buddy's case, sexual indiscretions).

In establishing a diagnosis, the clinician must make the distinction between manic, hypomanic, and mixed episodes. In DSM-IV, both manic and hypomanic episodes have the same characteristic symptoms listed in the preceding paragraph. However, the two types of episodes are distinguished primarily by the extent to which they are accompanied by lifestyle impairment. In contrast to a manic episode, a hypomanic episode is not severe enough to cause marked impairment in social or occupational (or academic) functioning and does not require hospitalization. A mixed episode is characterized by a period of time (lasting at least 1 week) in which the criteria are met for both a full manic episode and a full major depressive episode nearly every day (see Case 8 for the DSM-IV definition of a major depressive episode). Persons meeting the definition of a mixed episode experience rapidly alternating moods (sadness, irritability, euphoria), accompanied by symptoms of manic and major depressive episodes.

If a person presents to a clinic with current or past manic symptoms, a number of potential DSM-IV diagnoses may be applicable. If the person has experienced symptoms that meet criteria for a full manic episode, the diagnosis of *bipolar I disorder* is appropriate (as was the case for Buddy). Although the term *bipolar* may imply otherwise (i.e., two *poles* of mood from extremely high to extremely down), the diagnosis of bipolar I disorder is still appropriate if the person has experienced a manic episode but not a major depressive episode. However, presentations involving full manic episodes only are infrequent, and most patients with bipolar I disorder experience alterations in mood cycling between manic episodes and major depressive episodes (often separated by periods of normal mood).

The diagnosis of *bipolar II disorder* is used in reference to clinical presentations of one or more major depressive episodes and at least one hypomanic episode (and no history of full manic episodes). The defining feature of the diagnosis *cyclothymia* is the chronic (at least 2 years) presence of numerous periods of hypomanic symptoms and numerous periods of depressive symptoms that are not severe enough to meet criteria for major depression. (If the person has at any time met criteria for major depressive, manic, or mixed episodes, the diagnosis of cyclothymia is not assigned.)

As you may have noted from Buddy's five-axis diagnosis, his diagnosis was assigned with several specifiers (i.e., "most recent episode depressed," "moderate," "with full interepisode recovery"). In addition to the use of specifiers to convey the severity of the disorder (e.g., "mild," "moderate," "severe"), specifiers are included with the diagnosis of bipolar disorder to describe the course of the disorder. Specifically, because most persons with this disorder cycle between periods of depression and mania, a specifier is used to indicate the person's current or most recent mood state (e.g., "most recent episode manic," "most recent episode mixed," etc.). Another set of specifiers is used to indicate the longitudinal course of the illness: (a) with or without full interepisode recovery (i.e., whether a full remission of symptoms is attained between the two most recent episodes of mania or depression) and (b) with rapid cycling (used if the person has experienced four or more manic, mixed, depressive, or hypomanic episodes in the past 12 months). (The longitudinal course specifier "with seasonal pattern" is discussed in Case 8.)

CASE FORMULATION USING
THE INTEGRATIVE MODEL

Like each of the anxiety disorders discussed in this book, the integrative theory of mood disorders (bipolar disorder, major depression, dysthymia) is based on a diathesis-stress model (Barlow & Durand, 1999). The "diathesis" component of the integrative model refers to the biological vulnerability to develop a mood disorder. Although no specific genetic or biological markers have been confirmed as risk factors for mood disorders, at present this vulnerability seems to be best described as an overactive neurological response to stressful life events (the "stress" component of the diathesis-stress model). Interestingly, the existing research suggests that the mood and anxiety disorders share a common, genetically determined biological vulnerability (e.g., Kendler, Neale, Kessler, Heath, & Eaves, 1992).

Evidence of the presence of this genetic vulnerability in Buddy was his extensive family history of depression (and possibly bipolar disorder). This is consistent with research findings showing that the rate of mood disorders in the families of persons with bipolar disorder is considerably higher than the rate among others (see Gershon, 1990, for a review). However, one interesting result emerging from these studies is that the most frequent mood disorder in the relatives of persons with bipolar disorder is not bipolar disorder but rather major depression. For persons with major depression, there seems to be a negligible chance that their relatives will have a greater incidence of bipolar disorder than people with no emotional disorder. Thus, among the mood disorders, there may not be a specific or separate genetic contribution to bipolar disorder. Instead, bipolar disorder may represent a more severe manifestation of this underlying genetic vulnerability. This manifestation would be determined by other psychosocial or biological factors that occur in addition to genetic vulnerability. This connection is not yet certain, and researchers continue to disagree as to whether bipolar disorder and major depression are two distinct disorders or one disorder that varies in its severity (Blehar, Weissman, Gershon, & Hirschfeld, 1988).

Findings from twin studies have also supported the role of genetics in the origins of bipolar disorder. For example, in a study by Bertelsen, Harvald, and Hauge (1977), if one twin had bipolar disorder, there was an 80% chance that a monozygotic (identical) twin had some form of mood disorder (e.g., major depression, bipolar disorder). This was substantially higher than the rate of mood disorders (16%) in dizygotic (fraternal) twins, if one twin had bipolar disorder. Because monozygotic twins have exactly the same genes, whereas dizygotic twins share only about 50% of each other's genes (the same amount shared among first-order relatives), the higher rate of mood disorders in monozygotic twin pairs suggests that genetic factors contribute to the development of bipolar disorder. (However, more recent studies have observed somewhat weaker concordance rates in twin pairs compared to those obtained by Bertelsen et al., 1977; e.g., McGuffin & Katz, 1989.)

Numerous studies have attempted to identify neurobiological factors contributing to the development and maintenance of bipolar disorder. Despite this issue's considerable research attention, no neurobiological component has been linked with certainty to this disorder. Researchers generally concur that the balance among a variety of neurotransmitters is more important than the absolute level of any one neurotransmitter in bipolar disorder. For instance, there is increasing interest in the role of dopamine in the context of this balance among neurotransmitters, based on evidence that drugs that increase the activity of dopamine (dopamine "agonists" such as L-dopa) produce mild maniclike states (i.e., "hypomania") in patients with bipolar disorder (Depue & Iacono, 1989; Silverstone, 1985).

Additionally, research has shown that patients with bipolar disorder and their children (who are at greater risk for bipolar disorder) show increased sensitivity to light; that is, when exposed to light at night, they show greater suppression of the hormone melatonin (Nurnberger et al., 1988). Melatonin is a hormone activated by darkness to control the body's biological clock and to induce sleep. There is also evidence that extended bouts of insomnia trigger manic episodes (Wehr, Goodwin, Wirz-Justice, Breitmeier, & Craig, 1982). These findings suggest that mood disorders such as bipolar disorder are related to disruptions in our circadian rhythms (resulting from low levels of the neurotransmitter serotonin; cf. Goodwin & Jamison, 1990).

Other evidence of the role of neurotransmitters in bipolar disorder comes from a host of studies and clinical observations attesting to the effectiveness of the drug lithium in the treatment of this condition. A detailed description of lithium is provided in the next section. The fact that many patients with bipolar disorder respond favorably to lithium has been viewed by some researchers as indicating that the drug is regulating the levels of neurotransmitters contributing to bipolar disorder. However, it is not clear how lithium works. It is possible that lithium reduces the availability of the neurotransmitters dopamine and norepinephrine. Yet, it has also been hypothesized that lithium affects the endocrine system, particularly neurochemicals that affect the production and levels of sodium and potassium, which are electrolytes found in our body fluids (Goodwin & Jamison, 1990). Much more research is needed to identify lithium's mechanisms of action. These findings could potentially lead to more effective drug treatments for bipolar disorder, in addition to a greater understanding of the neurobiological factors contributing to this disturbance.

As noted in the beginning of this section, stressful life events appear to play a significant role in the onset of mood disorders and manic episodes. A large body of research indicates that stressful life events (family difficulties, job loss, etc.) are strongly related to the onset of mood disorders, particularly major depression. A few studies have also produced data that support the connection between stress and the onset of manic episodes (Ellicott, 1988; Goodwin & Jamison, 1990). These findings are consistent with Buddy's experiences, as he connected the emergence of his first manic episode (and subsequent periods of depression) to stress in his life (e.g., senior year of college, familial conflict on how the family business should be run). The limited data that do exist on the role of stress in bipolar disorder suggest that, while stressful life events may trigger initial manic episodes, once the disorder develops, these episodes take a life of their own and occur with no obvious connection to life stress (Post, 1992). According to current diathesis-stress models, stress contributes to the development of bipolar disorder because stressful life events activate our stress hormones, which, in turn, have wide-ranging effects on our neurotransmitter systems (e.g., serotonin, norepinephrine, dopamine). If these stress hormones remain activated, structural and chemical changes in the brain may occur (e.g., atrophy of neurons in the areas of the brain that contribute to the regulation of emotions and neurotransmitter activity). For instance, the extended effects of stress may be associated with disruptions in a person's circadian rhythms, causing them to be susceptible to the recurrent cycling that is a defining feature of many mood disorders. As noted earlier, another psychosocial precipitant of mania appears to be loss of sleep (as might occur in the postpartum period following childbirth), supporting the notion that the emergence of bipolar disorder may be related to a disruption of circadian rhythms (Goodwin & Jamison, 1990).

Many of the psychosocial features that contribute to the onset and maintenance of major depression (e.g., social support, negative perceptions of one's self, world, and future; sense of helplessness or hopelessness) may also play a significant role in bipolar disorder. Because many of these features are discussed in detail in Case 8, the remainder of this section will focus on factors that are more specific to bipolar disorder. One important factor that may contribute to the maintenance of bipolar disorder and predict a poor treatment response is denial or minimization of the problem. Unlike most of the other disorders discussed in this book, the manic or hypomanic aspect of bipolar disorder is often associated with low subjective distress. The patient may find the "high" of a manic episode to be so pleasurable that they consider their symptoms and behavior perfectly reasonable and fail to see the need for treatment. Moreover, this factor is often associated with poor compliance with drug treatment. Specifically, some individuals stop taking their prescribed medications during periods of distress and depression in an attempt to bring on the manic state once again.

This feature was clearly evident in Buddy. During the initial portion of his hospital admission, Buddy did not comply with treatment (he refused all medications). Although he eventually conceded to medications, he quickly stopped taking them following his discharge (against medical advice) because he downplayed the likelihood of his need to continue them to prevent future manic and depressive episodes.

Treatment Goals and Planning

The key intervention that the psychiatrist planned to use in the treatment of Buddy's mood disorder was medication. Because Buddy's principal complaint was depression and because he had experienced only a single manic episode several years ago, the psychiatrist opted to initiate treatment with the tricyclic antidepressants (a group of medications that block the reuptake of neurotransmitters such as serotonin and norepinephrine). Another reason for this strategy was Buddy's refusal to consider taking lithium carbonate, a medication that is commonly used in the treatment of patients with bipolar disorder. Lithium is a common salt that is widely available in the natural environment. For example, it is found in our drinking water in amounts that are too small to have any effect. As noted earlier, in therapeutic doses, lithium is often effective in treating and preventing manic episodes. However, the side effects of therapeutic doses of lithium are potentially more serious than for other antidepressants. The dosage of lithium has to be carefully regulated to prevent toxicity (poisoning) or thyroid problems (lowered thyroid function in particular) that can increase patients' lack of energy associated with their depression. Substantial weight gain is another common side effect of this drug. In addition to the potential for side effects, Buddy's resistance to lithium was based on his difficulty in accepting the diagnosis of bipolar disorder. Although Buddy was resistant to any form of medication treatment, he was especially reluctant to taking lithium because he believed that people who needed lithium must have severe mental illness (based on his limited knowledge from hearing or reading about the uses of lithium on television shows or news articles). This issue is discussed in more detail in the next section.

In addition to pharmacotherapy with antidepressant drugs, Buddy's treatment plan included supportive and cognitive-behavioral therapy. The psychosocial aspect of treatment would address such issues as Buddy's acceptance of the problem and of his need to comply with treatment, his withdrawal from social and occupational activities, identification of sources of family stress, and learning ways to cope effectively with these stressors.

COURSE OF TREATMENT
AND TREATMENT OUTCOME

This section presents a brief summary of Buddy's treatment, which occurred over the span of 8 years. Because of Buddy's refusal to take lithium, the psychiatrist proceeded cautiously with the initiation of tricyclic antidepressant medication. The reason for his caution was that these medications, while potentially effective in reducing Buddy's depression, might possibly induce another manic episode in Buddy if too much of the drug was prescribed. In fact, research has shown that tricyclic antidepressants may induce manic episodes in persons with depression who do not have a preexisting bipolar disorder (Goodwin & Jamison, 1990; Prien et al., 1984). Thus, Buddy had to be closely monitored while he was on the drug, and he had to comply fully with the prescribed medication regimen.

Buddy, in fact, complied very well with the moderate dose of antidepressant medication he was prescribed. Within a few weeks, his symptoms of depression decreased substantially. After his favorable response, he was maintained on a slightly lower dosage of the drug for several months. After 7 months had passed without a recurrence of his depression (and without any signs of mania), Buddy was slowly weaned off the medication. During the first few months, when Buddy was taking a maintenance dosage of antidepressant medication, he also saw the psychiatrist regularly for supportive psychotherapy (the same psychiatrist who monitored Buddy's response to the drug). These sessions occurred with decreasing frequency over the last couple of months that Buddy was taking the medication. After he had fully discontinued the medication without signs of the depression returning, Buddy and his psychiatrist mutually agreed to terminate their sessions of supportive psychotherapy.

Over the next 18 months, Buddy experienced very few symptoms of depression. Although occasional conflicts within the family continued over how certain aspects of the family business should be managed, Buddy found that his sense of devotion and enthusiasm for his work had returned. In fact, he was given a promotion to be the head of a division within the family business. Although Buddy initially was very gratified by his change in job status, he soon experienced a great deal of stress arising from the marked increase in responsibilities that his promotion entailed. In addition, because Buddy was in a position of greater responsibility that required him to make more decisions about the business, he found himself in increasing conflict with one of his older brothers, who often questioned his decisions (partly because his brother had not adjusted well to the fact that Buddy was now at a level of management that was equal to his).

As these stressors continued, Buddy began to notice that he had difficulty falling and staying asleep. Shortly thereafter, he became extremely hyperactive and started having grandiose and suspicious thoughts (grandiose and persecutory delusions), coinciding with changes in his mood that varied between feeling expansive and "on a high" to feeling irritable. He began to work at a feverish pace, often staying at the office 15 to 18 hours a day. He started to develop plans to expand his division of the business to various parts of the country. Increasingly, Buddy was convinced that only he could lead the family business in the direction where it needed to go. Buddy felt that he was "at the top of his game" (grandiose delusions).

However, these plans were considered unrealistic and impractical by his family and co-workers. Buddy became irritated and uncharacteristically enraged with his co-workers and subordinates, who he believed were plotting against him and talking about him behind his back (persecutory delusions). Buddy experienced a gradual increase in the speed of this thoughts. Others noticed that he had become quite distractible and that his speech had become very loud and rapid (pressured speech). Often, in the middle of a conversation about the business, Buddy would utter things that were either nonsensical or totally off the topic (e.g., off-color jokes). When his co-workers tried to give Buddy corrective feedback on his inappropriate behavior, he became very irritated with them and felt that any problem was with them, not him. Consequently, the co-workers began to mistrust Buddy's leadership and approached other members of the family to discuss the importance of controlling some of his actions. Buddy's family, his wife in particular, continually urged Buddy to contact his psychiatrist. Buddy refused and denied the significance of his symptoms. Learning that some of his co-workers had consulted with his family about his conduct in the office had the effect of fanning the flames of his suspicion that people were plotting against him. Buddy's delusions intensified to the point where the family found his behaviors impossible to tolerate. Because Buddy had vehemently refused to seek treatment (even in the face of his wife's threat of marital separation), his wife finally telephoned the psychiatrist behind Buddy's back. The psychiatrist, alarmed at the news that Buddy had been in a full manic episode for nearly 2 weeks, ordered him to be involuntarily admitted to the hospital.

The first few days of Buddy's hospitalization were somewhat reminiscent of his hospital stay during college. However, although Buddy was reluctant to take lithium, he finally accepted this intervention. He quickly responded to the drug and was released from the hospital 8 days later. A central aspect of Buddy's hospital discharge plan was to have him continue on a maintenance dosage of lithium and visit the psychiatrist regularly for individual psychotherapy and drug monitoring. Although Buddy initially complied with this plan, he soon began to attend these sessions quite erratically. The psychiatrist believed that Buddy's resistance to treatment was due in large part to his feeling ashamed, weak, and stigmatized by his bipolar disorder. For the most part, Buddy had accepted his history of depression (because "it is not too unusual for a person to feel down from time to time") but found it very hard to acknowledge his past symptoms of mania, which he regarded as very weird and indicative of significant mental illness. During times when he was not experiencing symptoms of depression or mania, Buddy felt that there was no need to continue using lithium (which served as an unwelcome reminder that he had acted so strangely in the past). The psychiatrist worked hard to assist Buddy to accept his diagnosis (e.g., by challenging his beliefs that the presence of the diagnosis was suggestive of a mental defect, or indicated that he was fundamentally different from everyone else) and to accept the need for continued use of lithium to prevent the occurrence of future manic episodes. Buddy finally voiced his agreement with his psychiatrist's statements, although he did so mainly to placate him. A few months after his hospital discharge, Buddy stopped coming to his outpatient sessions and he stopped taking lithium.

Three months later, Buddy experienced a hypomanic episode. Unlike past incidents when he had experienced manic symptoms, Buddy quickly agreed to his family's pleas to reinitiate treatment. His psychiatrist promptly put him back on lithium, which again produced a rapid therapeutic response. The fact that he had yet another maniclike episode finally convinced Buddy of the need for compliance with treatment. This realization proved to be one of the most important aspects of Buddy's treatment. From then on, Buddy gradually accepted his problem and learned to manage his medications adequately and responsibly. Buddy worked with his therapist to learn to identify the first signs of mood disorder symptoms so that drug and psychosocial interventions could be deployed promptly to prevent an escalation into a full manic or depressive episode. Following several treatment sessions that his wife attended, Buddy enlisted his wife and the rest of his family to help in this endeavor (i.e., monitor early signs of symptom recurrence).

Over the next 4 years, Buddy attended all scheduled follow-up sessions that focused on monitoring and adjusting his dosages of lithium. Once his symptoms and medication were stabilized, these sessions were scheduled less frequently. During this period, Buddy occasionally called his psychiatrist when he was worried about the potential recurrence of symptoms or when he had questions about adjusting his medication to protect against the return of symptoms. Clearly, Buddy's attitude and behavior now differed markedly from his initial presentation, when he resisted treatment, medications, and his diagnosis. This change in attitude was also evident when Buddy developed complications from extended lithium treatment. For example, at one point in treatment, Buddy developed some rashes from the lithium therapy. This side effect was managed through a consultation with a dermatologist. At no time did Buddy use this complication to question the wisdom of continuing on lithium.

Buddy became very self-sufficient in maintaining adequate pharmacological protection against further relapses of manic and depressive symptoms (he learned to adjust his medications accordingly in response to early signs of symptom recurrence). During the last 3 years that the psychiatrist worked with him, Buddy attended sessions on a biyearly basis for medication maintenance checks, renewal of prescriptions, and laboratory blood tests. Although Buddy had initially been very resistant to lithium treatment, the psychiatrist believed that Buddy ultimately exhibited one of the most profound beneficial responses to this medication that he had seen in bipolar disorder (making Buddy a somewhat atypical case of bipolar disorder in terms of his treatment response; see the discussion section). Over the 6 years since Buddy had been stabilized on lithium (the time this chapter was written), he has shown no further signs of manic or depressed symptoms. Buddy went on to form his own food company, which he now directs. He has productively developed new business ventures that continue to prosper. Despite these new occupational responsibilities, Buddy has become more involved in leisure activities. Often, he is able to interrupt his once-driven work habits to spend more time with his wife and children.

DISCUSSION

Bipolar I disorder affects approximately 0.8% of the adult population (estimates from community samples range between 0.4% and 1.6%), and bipolar II disorder affects approximately 0.5% over the course of a lifetime (Weissman, Bruce, Leaf, Florio, & Holzer, 1991). Indeed, the lifetime prevalence of bipolar disorder is much lower than that of the other major mood disorders (i.e., major depression, dysthymia) (Kessler et al., 1994). Unlike major depression, which is much more prevalent in females, bipolar I disorder is about equally common in men and women (e.g., 1.6% versus 1.7% for males and females, respectively; Kessler et al., 1994), although bipolar II disorder appears to be more common in women. There are no known differences among racial groups in the prevalence of either bipolar I or bipolar II disorder.

Similar to Buddy's clinical history, research has found that the average age of onset for bipolar I disorder is about 18 years of age, whereas for bipolar II disorder it is 22 years of age, although cases can begin in childhood (Weissman et al., 1991). In fact, a considerable number of cases of bipolar disorder begin in adolescence (as many as one-third; Taylor & Abrams, 1981). However, there is often a 5- to 10-year interval between the age of onset of symptoms and the age at first treatment or first hospitalization. It is relatively rare for bipolar disorder to begin after a person reaches the age of 40. These ages are somewhat younger than the average age of onset for major depression, and bipolar disorder may begin more abruptly than major depression (Weissman et al., 1991; Winokur, Coryell, Endicott, & Akiskal, 1993). However, the typical pattern of onset in males and females appears to differ. The first episode in males is more likely to be a manic episode, whereas in females the first episode is more likely to be depression. Frequently, a person experiences several episodes of depression before a manic episode occurs (American Psychiatric Association, 1994b).

Once the disorder appears, the course is chronic. Untreated persons with bipolar disorder may have more than 10 total episodes of mania and depression during their lifetime, with the duration of episodes and interepisode symptom-free periods often stabilizing after the fourth or fifth episode (Goodwin & Jamison, 1990). For women with bipolar I disorder, a higher risk for subsequent episodes is present in the immediate postpartum (after childbirth) period. Often 5 or more years may pass between the first and second episode, but the time periods between subsequent episodes usually narrow. However, it should be emphasized that the *variable* and *episodic* nature of bipolar disorder is a hallmark and a unique feature of this condition, as was evident in Buddy, whose initial manic episode emerged abruptly in his senior year of college and was not followed by subsequent episodes until several years later.

Bipolar disorder usually produces substantial disruptions in the afflicted person's life. For instance, marital discord is a common associated feature. Divorce rates are much higher in persons with bipolar disorder, approaching 2 to 3 times the rate of persons without emotional disorders. Compared to persons without emotional disorders, the occupational status of persons with bipolar disorder is twice as likely to deteriorate (Coryell et al., 1993). Persons with bipolar disorder often meet criteria for other disorders; for example, the substance use disorders and the anxiety disorders are quite prevalent in these individuals (Goodwin & Jamison, 1990).

Suicide is an unfortunately common associated feature of bipolar disorder. Among patients with emotional disorders, patients with bipolar disorder have among the highest risks for suicide (Black, Winokur, & Nasrallah, 1987; Fawcett et al., 1987). Estimates of suicide in bipolar disorder range from 9% to as high as 60%, with an average rate of 19% (Goodwin & Jamison, 1990). Suicide occurs more often in males than in females and is most likely to occur during a depressive episode. Persons with bipolar disorder who also have coexisting substance abuse or anxiety disorders are at substantially greater risk of suicide and poor long-term treatment outcome (e.g., Keller, Lavori, Coryell, Endicott, & Mueller, 1993).

Medications, particularly lithium, are currently the treatment of choice for bipolar disorder. Results indicate that 30% to 60% of patients with bipolar disorder respond very well to lithium, 30% to 50% show a partial response, and 10% to 20% have a poor response (Show, 1985; Prien & Potter, 1993). Thus, while lithium is effective, many patients do not show meaningful improvement. However, for the patients who show a favorable acute response, lithium is usually effective in preventing future manic and depressive episodes. For example, a review of 10 well-done treatment outcome studies indicated that patients taking lithium had a significantly lower probability of having future episodes than patients taking a placebo. Overall, 34% of the patients taking lithium had additional manic or depressive episodes during the follow-up period, compared to 81% of the patients taking placebo (Goodwin & Jamison, 1990). Lithium maintenance treatment has also been found to lower the frequency of suicide attempts and completions (Müller-Oerlinghausen, Muser-Causemann, & Volk, 1992). In fact, although untreated bipolar disorder may be associated with a mortality rate that is 2 to 3 times higher than that of the general population, some studies have found that the mortality rate of patients in long-term lithium treatment does not differ from that of persons without emotional disorders (e.g., Coppen et al., 1991).

However, a handful of more recent studies that have examined longer follow-up periods (e.g., 5 or more years) have found less encouraging results of the long-term maintenance effects of lithium (e.g., Gitlin, Swendsen, Heller, & Hammen, 1995; Keller et al., 1993). As noted earlier in this chapter, one problem associated with lithium treatment (or with any drug treatment, for that matter) is noncompliance. Noncompliance with drug treatment is a major cause of relapse in patients with bipolar disorder (Jamison & Akiskal, 1983). Patients with bipolar disorder may be noncompliant with drug therapy for a number of reasons, including denial or failure to believe that they have an emotional disorder (a factor relevant in Buddy's treatment), reluctance to give up the pleasurable experience of mania, and drug side effects. Indeed, as was true for Buddy, up to 75% of patients treated with lithium experience some side effects (Goodwin & Jamison, 1990).

In addition to lithium, several other medications have proven to be of some benefit. For instance, patients who are nonresponsive or intolerant to lithium may benefit from certain antiseizure medications, such as valproates and carbamazepine (Prien & Gelenberg, 1989). Recall that Buddy was initially treated with an antiseizure medication, due in part to his refusal to take lithium. Electroconvulsive therapy (ECT), while typically associated with severe major depression, has also been found to be effective in treating manic episodes (Mukherjee, Sackeim, & Schnuur, 1994). Additionally, many research psychiatrists believe that ECT should be considered as a primary treatment for the depressed phase of bipolar disorder whenever a rapid response is necessary (e.g., due to marked suicidal ideation and intent) or when drug treatments are contraindicated (e.g., in pregnancy, in cases that have not responded to lithium or antiseizure medication) (American Psychiatric Association, 1994b).

Psychosocial treatments for bipolar disorder have not been widely studied. However, the importance of these interventions is increasingly recognized. Specifically, researchers have recognized the potential benefits of these treatments to foster compliance with medications (Cochran, 1984), to address the psychosocial consequences of the disorder (e.g., occupational, marital), and to treat coexisting disorders (e.g., substance use, anxiety disorders) that are associated with an unfavorable long-term course and treatment response. Although lithium was the primary factor in Buddy's favorable treatment response, the psychosocial component of his therapy was very important in addressing acceptance of his problem, dealing with the social (and marital) consequences of his symptoms, and enlisting persons in his social environment (wife, parents, siblings) to assist him in detecting the early signs of possible relapse.

Although a few reports have appeared in the literature on the effects of psychosocial treatments alone in the treatment of bipolar disorder (e.g., Chor, Mercier, & Halpier, 1988), most research has examined the effectiveness of these treatments combined with drug treatment. For example, a pilot study has examined the impact of the addition of family therapy and psychoeducation to standard drug treatment on the long-term outcome of bipolar disorder (Miller, Keitner, Epstein, Bishop, & Ryan, 1991). Compared to patients who received drug treatment alone, patients who received family therapy and psychoeducation plus drugs had lower rates of family separations, greater improvements in the level of family functioning, and lower rates of rehospitalization over the 2 years following treatment. Moreover, the patients receiving psychosocial treatment also had higher rates of full recovery (56%) than patients receiving medications only (20%). These initial findings suggest that the addition of psychosocial elements to the treatment of bipolar disorder holds promise for improving the short- and long-term effectiveness of our current interventions.

THINKING CRITICALLY

1. Noncompliance with the prescribed medication regimen (e.g., lithium) is a frequent complicating factor in the treatment of bipolar disorder. What are the main reasons why patients with this disorder are inclined to avoid their medications, even when they have seen benefits from them?
2. What factors do you think account for the finding that bipolar disorder is associated with one of the highest suicide rates, a rate higher than that found even in major depressive disorder? Why are males more likely to commit a successful suicidal act than females?
3. Although drugs have traditionally been the most common treatment for bipolar disorder, there are possible advantages of using a psychosocial treatment as an additional intervention for this condition. What are these possible advantages? Do you believe that psychosocial treatments could be used effectively as the sole treatment for bipolar disorder? Why or why not?
4. Occasionally, bipolar disorder is misdiagnosed as schizophrenia. What features of bipolar disorder could possibly be mistaken for schizophrenia?

Case

10

Bulimia Nervosa

At the time of her admission as an inpatient to the eating disorders program of a private psychiatric hospital, Jerry Atkins was a 33-year-old single Caucasian woman who had recently graduated from college with a degree in landscaping. With the encouragement of her outpatient therapist, Jerry had decided to admit herself to the hospital for her ongoing, and lately increasing, problems with eating. Specifically, Jerry said that her eating was "out of control." She reported extended periods when she restricted her food intake drastically, fueled by her negative body image (i.e., dissatisfaction with her weight and physical appearance) and her poor self-esteem. Jerry restricted her food intake because she felt that she weighed too much, a conclusion that was very distressing to Jerry, who gauged her value as a person by her perceptions of her physical appearance and weight. Her efforts at reducing the amount of food she ate were often rewarded by marked reductions in weight. In fact, as the result of her most recent period of fasting, Jerry had lost 60 pounds.

However, as had always happened in the past, this period of restriction was followed by a period of binge eating and purging. During a binge, Jerry ate large amounts of food (often sweets, such as cake, cookies, and ice cream,

160

or starches such as mashed potatoes) in a short period of time. She reported that she was totally out of control during these binges and felt as if she could not stop eating or control the amount of food she was ingesting. After the binge, Jerry would experience tremendous distress over the prospect of gaining weight. Consequently, after every binge, Jerry purged the food by sticking her finger down her throat to make herself vomit. Nevertheless, because of her binge eating and changes in her metabolism resulting from her frequent vomiting, Jerry had gained back a lot of weight that she had lost during her period of food restriction. When she admitted herself to the hospital, Jerry weighed 180 pounds (she was 5'6").

At the time of her admission, Jerry was experiencing up to five binge-purge cycles per day. Jerry was purging so frequently that she occasionally vomited a small amount of blood (due to irritation of the esophagus). Her decision to admit herself to the hospital came after her realization that her problem had gotten worse over her last semester of college, despite regular outpatient therapy with a licensed clinical social worker. Jerry was concerned that her eating disorder had become so severe that it would prevent her from obtaining and keeping a steady job in the landscaping business, now that she finally had her college degree. It had taken her 10 years to obtain her degree because her eating disorder (and other emotional problems, discussed later) had interfered with her ability to attend college regularly. When she was not attending classes, Jerry worked odd jobs (e.g., as a cashier at a self-service gas station). However, at the time of her admission to the hospital, Jerry was living on social security disability payments that she received because of her emotional difficulties.

Clinical History

Jerry was adopted by her parents when she was an infant. She grew up as the youngest child in a family of five. Her older brother (by 2 years) and older sister (by 3 years) were the biological children of her parents. Jerry said that she never felt close to her adoptive family. Of her family, she favored her father the most, but noted that throughout her life he had placed a great deal of pressure on her to succeed. Jerry recalled that her focus in her growing years was on excelling in school and in sports and on pleasing her parents. Jerry reported that her relationship with her mother was very poor. She said that her mother was an alcoholic who had been treated on several occasions with little improvement. Jerry felt "unsupported" by her mother and claimed that she never felt that she could confide in her when an issue arose in her life. However, Jerry harbored the most negative feelings for her siblings, especially for her brother. Beginning when she was 10 and continuing through her early 20s, Jerry's brother physically abused her, often beating her up in a violent rage for no apparent reason. Jerry reported that her sister used to beat her as well, although less frequently and much less severely than the beatings that she had suffered at the hands of her brother. From age 13 until she was in her early 20s, Jerry was sexually abused by her brother. In fact, shortly after the sexual abuse began, Jerry began to experience the first signs of her eating disorder. She began dieting due to rising concerns about her physical appearance and body shape. Although 10 years had passed since the sexual abuse had ended, Jerry had never addressed these issues with her brother. Jerry said that her father had become aware of the physical abuse when he discovered a dark bruise on the back of her neck. At this time, when Jerry was 21 years old, Jerry's father forced her brother to leave the household, thus ending her many years of physical and sexual abuse. Her parents were never aware of her sexual abuse until Jerry was 26 years old. At this time, a therapist that Jerry had been consulting for her eating disorder had disclosed the sexual abuse to her parents. Jerry recalled that her parents downplayed the news and said, "Let's never talk about that again."

Jerry said that she grew up wondering what was wrong with her and how she was responsible for being the recipient of such rageful acts by her brother and sister. She reported being an obese child and adolescent who was occasionally teased about her size. Recalling that she felt no control of her environment and of her safety within the home, Jerry hypothesized that one of her methods of coping was to control her weight and shape.

In addition to playing a major role in the development of her eating disorder, Jerry's violent childhood led to other significant psychological difficulties. As is often the case for individuals who have experienced physical or sexual abuse, Jerry suffered from symptoms of posttraumatic stress disorder (PTSD). For example, in her late teens, Jerry began to have a tremendous problem with sleeping because she frequently had distressing nightmares about her physical and sexual abuse. Jerry also reported that for as long as she could remember, she had difficulty trusting other people (especially men) and handling social relationships. She noted that, during the past several years, her eating disorder and her symptoms of PTSD often increased in their severity after she had established a social relationship with a co-worker or classmate. Consequently, Jerry would cut off the friendship in the hopes that her symptoms would decrease. Jerry also reported considerable anxiety and some worsening of her eating disorder symptoms on the infrequent occasions when she developed an interest in sex. At the time of her admission to the hospital, Jerry had never had a steady boyfriend and was living alone in a rented apartment but had maintained friendships with two women she had met at school.

In addition, Jerry had a long history of depression, dating back to her early teens. At age 28, when she was out of school and not working due to her emotional difficulties, Jerry attempted suicide by driving her car off the road into a ravine. Although she totaled the car, Jerry incurred only a few broken ribs and facial cuts. She successfully concealed the fact that she had attempted suicide by claiming that she had veered off the road to avoid hitting a deer. Although

Jerry's depression had waxed and waned through the years, she reported a heightened level of depressed mood over the last several months preceding her admission to the hospital, due to her eating disorder and the resulting sense of hopelessness and impairment.

DSM-IV Diagnosis

Based on this information, Jerry was assigned the following DSM-IV diagnoses at the time she was admitted to the hospital's eating disorders program:

Axis I	307.51	Bulimia nervosa, purging type (principal diagnosis)
	309.81	Posttraumatic stress disorder, chronic
	296.32	Major depressive disorder, recurrent, moderate
Axis II	V71.09	No diagnosis on Axis II
Axis III	None	
Axis IV	Unemployment, discord with family	
Axis V	Global assessment of functioning = 40 (current)	

Jerry's presentation at the time of her admission to the hospital was quite consistent with the DSM-IV definition of bulimia nervosa (American Psychiatric Association, 1994). In DSM-IV, the key features of bulimia nervosa are (a) recurrent episodes of binge eating, characterized by (1) eating in a short period of time (e.g., within 2 hours) an amount of food that is definitely larger than most people eat during a similar period of time and under similar circumstances and (2) a sense of lack of control over eating during the episode; (b) recurrent inappropriate compensatory behavior (purging) in order to prevent weight gain (e.g., self-induced vomiting; misuse of laxatives, diuretics, enemas, or other medications; fasting; excessive exercise); (c) the binge-eating and purging behaviors both occur, on average, at least twice a week for 3 months (or more); and (d) self-evaluation is unduly influenced by body shape and weight. As discussed in the preceding sections, Jerry clearly displayed each of these characteristics. Note that when Jerry's diagnosis was established, it was assigned with the specifier "purging type" because Jerry was regularly engaging in self-induced vomiting (in fact, prior to her admission to the hospital, she purged up to five times per day). The other specifier that the clinician may provide when assigning a DSM-IV diagnosis of bulimia nervosa is "nonpurging type." This specifier is appropriate if the person has inappropriately used fasting or excessive exercise as a means of compensating for binge eating and weight gain prevention but has not regularly engaged in self-induced vomiting or the misuse of laxatives, diuretics, or enemas.

In addition, bulimia nervosa is not assigned as a diagnosis if these symptoms occur exclusively during episodes of anorexia nervosa, the other eating disorder category in DSM-IV, because many persons who meet the criteria for anorexia nervosa also display all of the features of bulimia nervosa. The main difference between these two diagnoses is that patients with anorexia nervosa are substantially underweight, whereas patients with bulimia nervosa are close to or above their normal body weight (in fact, the overwhelming majority of persons with bulimia are within 10% of their normal weight; Hsu, 1990). The key diagnostic features of anorexia nervosa are (a) refusal to maintain a minimally normal body weight (e.g., weight loss leading to the maintenance of body weight less than 85% of that expected), (b) an intense fear of gaining weight or becoming fat, (c) a significant disturbance in the self-perception of the shape or size of the body, and (d) amenorrhea (i.e., absence of at least three consecutive menstrual cycles).

The nature and treatment of bulimia nervosa are discussed more fully in later sections of this chapter. Posttraumatic stress disorder and major depressive disorder are discussed in Cases 4 and 8, respectively.

CASE FORMULATION USING THE INTEGRATIVE MODEL

The integrative model of bulimia nervosa (Barlow & Durand, 1999) highlights a number of factors that may contribute to the development of this eating disorder (as well as other types of eating disorders, such as anorexia nervosa, which is discussed later in this chapter). As with most psychological disorders, eating disorders run in families and seem to have a genetic component. Preliminary studies indicate that the relatives of patients with an eating disorder are 4 to 5 times more likely than the general population to develop an eating disorder themselves (e.g., Hudson, Pope, Jonas, & Yurgelin-Todd, 1983; Strober & Humphrey, 1987). Although a number of twin studies have been conducted to evaluate the extent to which genetics play a factor in the development of eating disorders, the most extensive investigation to date was completed by Kendler and colleagues (1991). In this study, 2,163 female twins were interviewed to determine the prevalence of bulimia nervosa. Twenty-three percent of monozygotic (identical) twins both had bulimia, compared to 9% of dizygotic (fraternal) twins. Because monozygotic twins have exactly the same genes whereas dizygotic twins share only about 50% of each other's genes, the higher rate of bulimia in monozygotic twin pairs supports the notion that genetic factors contribute to the development of bulimia nervosa.

The extent to which biological factors played a role in Jerry's bulimia is not known because she was adopted and had no knowledge of her biological family. Despite some evidence to suggest a genetic contribution to bulimia, it is not known just what is inherited. Research has shown a connection between certain neurobiological functions in the brain and eating disorders (e.g., alterations in levels of neurotransmitters such as norepinephrine, dopamine, and serotonin). However, because these studies have typically been conducted with persons who had already developed an eating disorder (i.e., anorexia nervosa or bulimia nervosa), it has not been determined if these neurobiological abnormalities caused the disorder or if they emerged as a result of semistarvation or multiple binge-purge cycles. Hsu (1990) has suggested that nonspecific personality disorder traits, such as emotional instability and poor impulse control, might be what is inherited. As is considered to be true for the anxiety disorders (see Case 2), one might inherit a tendency to be "emotionally" responsive to stressful life events. In the case of eating disorders, one consequence of this excessive emotionality might be impulsive eating as an attempt to relieve stress and anxiety. Evidence that suggests that eating disorders and anxiety disorders may share some of the same biological vulnerabilities comes from studies showing high rates of anxiety disorders in persons with eating disorders and their families (Pope & Hudson, 1984; Schwalberg, Barlow, Alger, & Howard, 1992). Whereas Jerry may well have possessed a biological or psychological vulnerability of this nature, a reasonable presumption would be that a major source of her emotional overresponsiveness was her long history of physical and sexual abuse.

The integrative model notes that sociocultural factors appear to play the most dramatic and clear-cut role in the development of eating disorders. Eating disorders are most prevalent in Western cultures, where there is tremendous societal pressure for persons, especially females, to be thin. In fact, the increase in the prevalence of the eating disorders, anorexia nervosa and bulimia nervosa, has been attributed to an increase in Western society's emphasis on thinness in women. This phenomenon has been documented in studies examining the characteristics of women found in magazines or other media. For example, Garner, Garfinkel, Schwartz, and Thompson (1980) collected data from *Playboy* magazine centerfolds and Miss America pageants from 1959 to 1978. They found that, over the years, both *Playboy* centerfolds and Miss America contestants had become substantially thinner. A more recent study that covered the years 1979 to 1988 found that Miss America contestants continued to decrease their weight, whereas *Playboy* centerfolds remained at a relatively low level of weight (Wiseman, Gray, Mosimann, & Ahrens, 1992). In fact, 69% of the *Playboy* centerfolds and 60% of Miss America contestants had weights that were 15% or more below their expected weights for their age and height. (As noted earlier in this chapter, being 15% or more underweight is actually one of the DSM-IV diagnostic criteria for anorexia nervosa.)

These studies clearly attest to the fact that Western society's standard of beauty has increasingly emphasized thinness over the last few decades. However, studies have also indicated that, over the same time span, the average American woman between the ages of 17 and 24 has become 5 to 6 pounds heavier (Bureau of the Census, 1983). The result of this collision between Western culture and physiology (Brownell, 1991) has been a marked increase in the number of women with a negative body image (Cash & Pruzinsky, 1990). Consequently, the number of people who diet or exercise to become thinner has increased dramatically, especially in younger females. For example, Hunnicut and Newman (1993) surveyed 3,632 8th- and 10th-grade students and found that 61% of girls and 28% of boys were dieting.

Although most people who diet do not develop eating disorders, dieting has been strongly linked to the onset of eating disorders. For instance, Patton, Johnson-Sabine, Wood, Mann, and Wakeling (1990) found that, in a sample of adolescent girls, those who were dieting were 8 times more likely to develop an eating disorder 1 year later than were those who were not dieting. Similarly, Telch and Agras (1993) have noted a marked increase in the rate of binge eating during or after rigorous dieting in a large sample of obese women. This connection was certainly evident in Jerry, whose eating disorder followed a period of dieting, starting when she was 13 years old. Moreover, Jerry's binge-purge cycles were always preceded by extended periods of food intake restriction. These eating patterns were due, in large part, to Jerry's strong desire to be thinner, because much of her self-esteem was gauged by self-perceptions of her weight and physical appearance. Although growing up in the American culture may have played a key role in the origins of Jerry's desire to be thin, it also seemed that her dysfunctional family life and history of abuse contributed a great deal to the development of her eating disorder (e.g., Jerry's sexual abuse and her history of being teased about her body may have resulted in a disturbance of her body image, placing her at greater risk for developing bulimia).

As discussed in the integrative model, it is not known why a small minority of persons with eating disorders are able to control their food intake successfully, resulting in substantial weight loss (thus, meeting the definition of anorexia nervosa), while the majority, like Jerry, are not successful and compensate by entering a cycle of binging and purging (by self-induced vomiting, use of laxatives, diuretics, or enemas, etc.). However, researchers have explored factors that contribute to binge-purge cycles. For example, Rosen and Leitenberg (1985) have found that persons with bulimia become very anxious before and while they eat, due to their intense fear of weight gain. The act of purging serves to reduce this anxiety (due in part to the person's perception that purging decreases the potential or extent of weight gain). Consequently, this anxiety reduction strongly reinforces the purging (because people tend to repeat behaviors that result in pleasure or relief from emotional distress). This was true for Jerry, who self-induced vomiting to relieve the tremendous distress she experienced after a binge (due to her fear of gaining weight as the result of the binge). This anxiety-reduction perspective of the binge-purge cycle demonstrates another possible connection between the eating disorders and the anxiety disorders. In addition, as discussed in the next section, Rosen and Leitenberg's (1985) findings offer important directions for the treatment of bulimia nervosa.

Treatment Goals and Planning

Jerry's inpatient stay was anticipated to be 1 month. Although Jerry's emotional difficulties were substantial, the hospital staff was optimistic about her prognosis because they regarded her as bright, well-spoken, and very motivated for treatment. During the first few days after Jerry's admission, an extensive treatment plan was generated. In this treatment plan, the following goals were established for her treatment: (a) Jerry will learn how to identify triggers of her binge-purge cycles and will learn methods to divert these cycles, (b) Jerry will discuss her thoughts and feelings about her body and will learn how to identify and challenge negative thoughts about her body image, (c) Jerry will learn more about health and nutrition, (d) Jerry will learn how to identify triggers of her depressed feelings and will learn skills to reduce these feelings, (e) Jerry will discuss her emotions associated with her sexual and physical abuse, and (f) Jerry will develop a plan for continuing her treatment following her discharge from the hospital.

To achieve these goals, Jerry was enrolled in a number of treatment groups that were led by psychologists, psychiatrists, and social workers in the hospital. Each day, Jerry was to attend the following groups: an eating disorders group, a trauma group, and a coping with depression group. In addition, Jerry was scheduled to meet with a psychologist 3 times per week for individual therapy. These sessions were scheduled to address issues relating to bulimia and PTSD symptoms, body image, and discharge planning. Jerry would also have considerable interaction with the nurses working on her floor, who would provide her with valuable information on health and nutrition. The hospital nurses would also contribute to Jerry's treatment in other very important ways. For example, the nurses monitored Jerry's activity on a continual basis; the importance of this function is discussed later.

COURSE OF TREATMENT AND TREATMENT OUTCOME

One of the key techniques used in Jerry's treatment is a strategy referred to as exposure plus response prevention (ERP). Recall that Rosen and Leitenberg's (1985) anxiety model of the binge-purge cycle states that the act of purging is reinforcing to the patient because it relieves them of the anxiety that is triggered by consuming food. This anxiety is due to the patient's intense fear that they will gain weight from what they have eaten. Based on their model, Rosen and Leitenberg (1985) have proposed a treatment strategy to address the binge-purge cycle. The basic notion of ERP is to arrange for the patient, under the supervision of the therapist, to consume a meal (or a food that they often eat during a binge) and then prevent the patient from engaging in their typical response of purging. The rationale for this procedure is that patients who can learn to overcome their anxiety without purging gain control over vomiting (thereby making binge eating less likely). Note that this treatment is very similar to the approach used in the treatment of patients with obsessive-compulsive disorder (OCD). For example, in Case 5, Pat Montgomery was treated with ERP by preventing her from washing after she came in contact with objects that she believed were contaminated with germs.

The structured environment of the hospital provided a good context for the use of ERP in Jerry's treatment. As noted earlier, the hospital nurses provided the important function of monitoring Jerry's actions throughout the day. Most important, the nurses were present at mealtime to ensure that Jerry and the other patients with eating disorders ate their entire meals. In addition, the nurses made sure that the patients remained at the table after the meal was finished. The patients were required to remain at the table until their anxiety and urge to vomit (or, for some patients, urge to use laxatives or diuretics) had dissipated. Therefore, the nurses ensured that the patients did not purge their meals. Sometimes, particularly in the early stages of her hospitalization, Jerry had to sit at the table for nearly an hour after her meal before her anxiety and urge to self-induce vomiting had run their course. During these postmeal periods, the nurses provided reassurance to the patients and reminded them of the value of learning to control their purging behavior. Moreover, the nurses reminded the patients of information that had been presented in their eating disorders group, for example, the ineffectiveness of vomiting or laxative or diuretic use as a means of weight control because these behaviors (a) do not retrieve everything that has been eaten, (b) are habit-forming because they encourage overeating (because patients believe that these behaviors prevent them from absorbing what they've eaten), and (c) can produce many physical complications (e.g., cardiac arrhythmias, kidney damage, seizures, erosion of dental enamel, salivary gland enlargement, electrolyte imbalance). In addition to mealtime monitoring, the nurses carefully watched the patients throughout the day to ensure that they did not engage in other types of purging activities such as excessive exercise. Also, Jerry and the other patients were monitored in the bathroom to make sure that they did not purge on the sly. Early in her stay, Jerry remarked to one of the hospital nurses that she was sure that she needed the structure of the hospital to overcome her eating habits that had become out of control.

The technique of ERP was designed to help patients control their urge to vomit or engage in some other form of purging behavior. Some researchers (e.g., Fairburn, 1985) do not feel it is necessary to focus on purging specifically because this behavior is the direct result of overeating after a period of food intake restriction. Instead, these researchers believe that overeating and restriction should be one of the primary targets in the treatment of bulimia nervosa, because the patient who stops overeating will also cease purging. Therefore, during their hospital stay, Jerry and the other patients were educated on the adverse effects of dieting (e.g., metabolic changes associated with food restriction make the body very resistant to weight loss). Moreover, a plan was developed to assist each patient in restoring a pattern of regular eating behavior. Specifically, the patients were scheduled to eat manageable amounts of food 5 to 6 times per day with no more than a 3-hour interval between planned meals and snacks. This eating pattern was designed to eliminate the patients' abnormal eating pattern, which alternated between dietary restriction and overeating.

In the early stages of Jerry's hospitalization, her meals were planned for her by hospital staff. However, later in her stay, Jerry was requested to plan her own meals with the hopes that she would be able to continue to maintain a normal eating pattern after her discharge. To assist her in planning her own diet, Jerry met with the hospital's nutritionist, who provided her information on the caloric content of foods and the basics for establishing a balanced diet. Because Jerry was now allowed to choose the foods she ate, she was required to keep a food diary so that the hospital staff could monitor her progress in establishing a healthy eating pattern on her own.

At first, Jerry experienced a great deal of difficulty tolerating the responsibility of controlling her own diet. She felt very uncertain about her ability to plan meals successfully and feared that failure would cause her to reinitiate her binge-purge cycles. Through the support and feedback of the hospital staff, she became more confident and adept at planning her meals. However, the staff noticed that Jerry lost 2 pounds over the first week that she was allowed to choose her own meals. Her weight loss was attributed mainly to the fact that Jerry had initiated a sensible exercise program (walking) since her admission to the hospital. Moreover, the staff felt that, if achieved by healthy means, the weight loss was appropriate because Jerry was overweight (180 pounds, 5'6"). Nevertheless, it was also noted that Jerry tended to restrict her food portions when she was uncertain of their caloric content. The staff encouraged Jerry to eat all types of foods, including foods whose caloric content was difficult to determine, given that adherence to a highly selective diet was considered another form of restraint. For these reasons, Jerry was also asked to practice eating in as wide a range of situations as possible. For instance, Jerry was encouraged to eat in restaurants, where she was less likely to be aware of the calories and the ingredients of the food she ordered. Later in her hospital stay, Jerry was granted passes to leave the hospital with a friend to have dinner or attend some type of social function. The frequency and length of these passes increased in the latter part of her stay so that both Jerry and the staff could evaluate her food choices and her ability to retain normal eating behaviors in less structured environments.

Jerry's body-image disturbance was addressed with cognitive restructuring in her eating disorders group and in her individual therapy. Cognitive restructuring involved (a) identification of negative body-image thoughts and the events that triggered the thoughts; (b) illustration of the strong relationship of these thoughts and her emotions, behaviors, and eating disorder symptoms; (c) examination of the origin of the thoughts; (d) exploration of the evidence that supports or refutes the thoughts; and (e) development and rehearsal of more adaptive attitudes about her body shape and physical appearance (Freedman, 1990). Jerry realized that her dysfunctional family life and frequent teasing about being overweight in her childhood contributed strongly to her negative beliefs about her appearance. However, unlike many patients with bulimia nervosa and virtually all patients with anorexia nervosa, Jerry did not have a distorted perception of her current body size. Specifically, many women with eating disorders appear to overestimate the actual size of their bodies (Cash & Brown, 1987). For example, using body-size estimation procedures (such as selecting one's current body shape from a series of body silhouettes ranging from emaciated to very obese), a 75-pound patient with anorexia might judge her body size to be larger than normal. Although Jerry did not perceive her current body size to be larger than she actually was, during treatment she realized that her "target weight" (i.e., the weight she was trying to achieve through food restriction) was unrealistically low. For example, Jerry learned that the weight of women on the hospital floor whom she regarded as having the ideal body size consistently weighed 10 to 15 pounds more than the weight Jerry had been striving for. In addition to modifying her expectations and attitudes about her current and ideal weight and body shape, the body-image therapy helped Jerry question the value and logic of gauging her sense of worth and self-esteem based mainly on her perceptions of her physical appearance.

Given her extensive history of physical and sexual abuse and current symptoms of posttraumatic stress disorder (PTSD), Jerry attended a therapy group for victims of trauma. In addition, many of her individual therapy sessions were spent addressing Jerry's symptoms of PTSD. Because the treatment of PTSD has been discussed extensively in Case 4, this aspect of Jerry's treatment is discussed here briefly. As in the treatment of Cindy Oakley (see Case 4), to help Jerry experience less distress when she encountered recollections or dreams about her traumas, she was asked to write detailed accounts of the most traumatic instances of abuse that she had endured. In her individual sessions, Jerry was asked to read these accounts aloud; following these readings, Jerry and her therapist discussed the thoughts and feelings that Jerry had about her abuse. Shortly after these treatment procedures were initiated, Jerry reported a marked increase in her general anxiety and her nightmares about the abuse; she also noted that her urges to binge and purge had intensified. The hospital staff considered it fortunate that Jerry's trauma issues were being addressed in the structure of a hospital setting; had these issues been addressed after Jerry's discharge, her emotions surrounding the discussion of her trauma history would have placed her at greater risk for a relapse in her bulimia. Throughout the middle 2 weeks of her hospital stay, Jerry was asked to write about and discuss her thoughts, feelings, and recollections of her abuse experiences. Over this time, she reported becoming less upset over thinking about or discussing the abuse.

Early in her admission, the hospital staff observed that Jerry kept herself isolated from other patients. Similarly, they noted that Jerry was very hesitant to communicate her feelings or needs to supportive peers. These features seemed to be related to Jerry's difficulties in trusting or feeling close to others, stemming from her abuse history and her troubled family life. Consequently, Jerry was asked to initiate conversations with her fellow patients and to participate in recreational activities that occurred in the hospital. With the assistance of her therapists, Jerry was asked to identify and contact people who could offer her much-needed social support after her discharge from the hospital. Because Jerry was very much estranged from her family, she identified two of her friends as potential social supports. During her hospital stay, Jerry disclosed to one of these friends her eating disorder and her abuse history. Much to her surprise, this friend was quite supportive and had already guessed that Jerry had problems with binging and purging. Ultimately, this friend visited Jerry at the hospital and accompanied her on her leaves from the hospital to go out to dinner and to attend social functions.

As part of discharge planning, it was decided that Jerry continue her eating disorders treatment with the therapist that she had consulted prior to her hospital admission. To foster the maintenance and increase in the gains that Jerry had achieved while in the hospital, this therapist met with the hospital staff (psychologists and psychiatrists) and Jerry on two occasions before Jerry's discharge to devise a postdischarge treatment plan. In total, Jerry spent 27 days in the hospital. On the day of her discharge, she remarked that this was the first time since the age of 13 that she had not purged in such a length of time. Indeed, the hospital staff felt that Jerry had made considerable strides in her ability to manage her eating disorder symptoms and to recognize the impact that her abuse had on her eating disorder and her level of functioning overall.

DISCUSSION

The overwhelming majority of persons (90% to 95%) with bulimia are women. Estimates of the prevalence of this disorder vary, depending on such factors as the age range or the type of sample that is studied. For example, an investigation of 800 persons in the general population estimated the lifetime prevalence of bulimia among women aged 18 to 44 to be 1.6% (Bushnell, Wells, Hornblow, Oakley-Browne, & Joyce, 1990). However, the prevalence rate was substantially higher in younger women. Although only 0.4% of women aged 45 to 64 years had the disorder, the prevalence of bulimia among women aged 18 to 24 was 4.5%. Somewhat higher prevalence estimates have been obtained in more selective samples. For instance, Schlundt and Johnson (1990) reviewed a large number of studies that examined the prevalence of bulimia. Based on their review, the authors concluded that between 6% and 8% of young women, especially those drawn from college student samples, meet criteria for the disorder.

The age of onset for bulimia nervosa is typically between 16 and 19 (Mitchell & Pyle, 1988). As in the case of Jerry, usually the first signs of the disorder are dietary restriction and body-image dissatisfaction. However, by the time treatment is sought, the overwhelming majority of persons with bulimia nervosa engage regularly in some form of purging behavior. Among the vast majority of patients who do purge, approximately 70% to 90% self-induce vomiting on a regular basis; like Jerry, most of those who vomit do so at least once a day (Mitchell & Pyle, 1988; Pyle, Neuman, Halvorson, & Mitchell, 1991). Roughly 15% of patients abuse laxatives (of this group, 20% use laxatives on a daily basis), 7% use enemas, and approximately 33% use diuretics on occasion. Although this phenomenon has not received much investigation, approximately 65% of patients with bulimia chew and then spit out their food to prevent weight gain.

As with many other types of psychological disorders, bulimia nervosa often does not occur in isolation. This was true for Jerry, who met criteria for major depressive disorder and posttraumatic stress disorder at the time of her admission to the hospital. Research indicates that anywhere from 35% to 78% of patients with bulimia meet criteria for having a mood disorder (major depression or dysthymia) sometime during the course of their eating disorder (for reviews, see Hinz & Williamson, 1987; Striegel-Moore, Silberstein, & Rodin, 1986). Due in part to this high rate of depression and the fact that anti-depressant medication is sometimes effective in the treatment of bulimia (as discussed later), some researchers have argued that bulimia may really be a form of mood disorder, as opposed to a separate diagnostic entity (cf. Hinz & Williamson, 1987). As noted earlier in this chapter, bulimia may share some link with the anxiety disorders, given evidence of high rates of anxiety disorders in persons with bulimia nervosa and their families (Pope & Hudson,

1984; Schwalberg et al., 1992). For example, Schwalberg et al. (1992) found that 80% of patients with bulimia had a history of one or more anxiety disorders, the most frequent diagnoses being generalized anxiety disorder and social phobia. However, the evidence accrued to date on the frequency with which bulimia co-occurs with other disorders is limited by the fact that most studies have been conducted with persons who have sought treatment. Given that persons seeking treatment often have a more severe form of the disorder, it would be important to examine this issue in other populations (e.g., community or college student samples).

The most effective drug treatment for bulimia nervosa appears to be the antidepressant medications. However, the existing evidence suggests that even these types of medications do not produce substantial long-lasting improvements in the symptoms of bulimia. For example, Walsh, Hadigan, Devlin, Gladis, and Roose (1991) found that the average reduction in binge eating and purging was 47% in a group of 80 patients treated with tricyclic antidepressants. However, the remission rate (i.e., number of patients completely free of binging and purging) was only 12%. These investigators also examined the long-term outcome and maintenance of drug treatment. The 29 patients who evidenced at least a 50% reduction in their binge eating by the end of the initial phase of treatment were asked to continue on the medication for a 16-week maintenance period. Of these 29 patients, 8 declined to continue, and another 10 patients dropped out of the study or stopped taking the drug prior to the end of the maintenance period. The primary reason for premature termination was that many patients experienced negative side effects from the drug (e.g., agitation).

More recently, another form of antidepressant medication has been studied as a treatment for bulimia. These drugs, such as fluoxetine (Prozac), inhibit the reuptake of serotonin and therefore belong to a class of drugs called serotonin-specific reuptake inhibitors (SSRIs). Early evidence suggests that the SSRIs may be somewhat more effective than the tricyclic antidepressants in the treatment of bulimia. For example, in a study of 382 patients with bulimia who were treated with Prozac, the average decline in the frequency of binge eating for patients taking a high dosage of the drug was 65%; the rate of patients in remission at the end of treatment was 27% (Walsh, 1991).

The psychosocial treatment that Jerry received at the hospital was modeled after a cognitive-behavioral approach pioneered by Fairburn (1985). The effectiveness of this approach has been examined in several studies. Craighead and Agras (1990) summarized the results of 10 such studies and reported an average reduction in purging of 79%; patients eliminated binging and purging altogether at a rate of 57%. Unlike findings from most of the drug studies conducted to date (e.g., Walsh et al., 1991), cognitive-behavioral treatment appears to produce lasting improvements in bulimic symptomatology. For instance, Fairburn, Jones, Peveler, Hope, and O'Connor (1993) found that, at 1-year follow-up, patients treated with cognitive-behavioral therapy showed more than a 90% reduction in both binge eating and purging. Moreover, 36% of the patients had refrained from binge eating and purging altogether; the remaining patients reported occasional episodes of binging or purging during the 1-year follow-up period. Although such findings suggest that cognitive-behavioral treatments are more effective than drug treatments for bulimia nervosa, this issue awaits future research (i.e., direct comparisons of these two forms of treatment within the same investigation).

THINKING CRITICALLY

1. What do you believe are the main reasons eating disorders are most common in Western cultures and in females? What personality and social characteristics do you think are most relevant to the origin of eating disorders in males?
2. If you were to design a program aimed at the prevention of eating disorders, what components do you believe would be most important to include in this program? In addition to (or in place of) the techniques used in Jerry's treatment, what strategies do you believe would be the most effective for people who have bulimia nervosa or anorexia nervosa?
3. What are the differences between bulimia nervosa and anorexia nervosa, in terms of diagnostic features, causal factors, social and familial variables, and so on? Some researchers believe that bulimia nervosa and anorexia nervosa may not represent distinct syndromes, but differ mainly in the degree of actual weight loss associated with restrictive and purging behaviors. Do you believe this is the case, or do you think that the distinction between bulimia nervosa and anorexia nervosa is valid and important. Why or why not?
4. A negative body image appears to play a key role in the onsets of many cases of eating disorders. Can you think of ways these disorders could develop in the absence of body-image disturbances?

11

Sexual Dysfunction: Male Erectile Disorder

lex Hedges was referred by his urologist to a clinic that specialized in the treatment of sexual dysfunction. At the time of his referral, Alex was a 54-year-old Caucasian man who had worked as a nightclub manager for the past 9 years. He had been married to his wife, Lilly, for 22 years. The couple had no children. Alex was seeking treatment for his 10-year history of difficulties in obtaining erections. Over the past several years, Alex had consulted with many urologists and other physicians about his problem. In each instance, the doctors were unable to identify a medical cause for Alex's erectile difficulties. Nor had any of his prior consultations with these doctors or other health care workers alleviated his problem. Consequently, Alex had essentially given up on trying to remedy the problem until recently, when he learned through magazines and television programs that new treatments had been developed to address problems such as his. Therefore, hoping that new techniques were available that would be effective for his erectile difficulties, Alex contacted his urologist, who arranged for his initial visit to the sexual dysfunction clinic.

At the time of his first visit to the clinic, Alex was having difficulty obtaining an erection every single time he attempted some form of activity (i.e., sexual intercourse, masturbation). During almost every attempt at sexual activity, however, Alex was able to achieve a slight erection; on average, his erections were about 25% to 35% of the tumescence representative of a full erection (*tumescence* refers to erections, or the readiness for sexual activity as indicated by the vascular congestion of the sex organs). Thus, Alex's erections were not sufficient for sexual intercourse with his wife. Nevertheless, the couple usually attempted sexual intercourse at least once per week, despite the fact that Alex's problem had persisted over the years. In these sexual encounters, Alex would achieve a minimal erection based on his excitement and urge to have sex. After his minimal erection was established, Alex would rub his body against his wife's until he ejaculated. Although his erection was always insufficient for intercourse, Alex ejaculated in almost every sexual encounter with his wife. Over the 5 years prior to his initial visit to the clinic, Alex had refrained from attempting to penetrate his wife with his partial erections. During these encounters, Alex's wife did not try to enhance his erections by stimulating his penis manually or orally. Alex stated that he rarely attempted to use sexual fantasies to foster his arousal or erection during sex with his wife. He also reported that he rarely had sexual fantasies at any other time. Nevertheless, Alex claimed that this interest in sex was "moderate" and that his interest or sex drive had not increased or decreased as the result of his erectile problem.

Clinical History

Alex reported that his problem emerged gradually but then became more persistent over the years. He was unable to identify any stressors or factors that contributed to the onset or worsening of his erectile difficulty. Nevertheless, Alex did recall that his employment situation was unstable at the time his problem began. At the time, Alex worked as a welder at a shipyard that was on the verge of shutting down. Eventually, the shipyard closed, leaving Alex unemployed for several months until he secured a new position as a bouncer in a nightclub (the same club where Alex now worked as a manager and part owner). However, Alex did not think that his employment situation was related to the onset of his erectile problems. It was also around this time that the couple, especially Alex's wife, had wished to start a family. Although Alex recalled that he would have liked to have had children, it was at this time that his erectile difficulties had become so persistent and severe that he was unable to have intercourse with his wife. Both Alex and his wife were distressed about this problem, particularly his wife, who was concerned that Alex might no longer be attracted to her or that he really did not want to start a family with her. Alex had reassured his wife that his problem was not due to his feelings toward her or toward having a child.

Shortly after his erectile difficulties began, Alex first saw a urologist (a medical doctor who specializes in the diagnosis and treatment of problems with the urinary or urogenital tract). The urologist conducted a physical examination and ordered a number of tests. The results of the examination indicated that Alex was in good health; the lab tests revealed no abnormalities in Alex's sperm count or hormone levels. Nevertheless, over the ensuing months, the urologist prescribed Alex hormones (testosterone). Later, he prescribed medications to improve Alex's blood circulation. None of these drugs resulted in improvements in Alex's ability to obtain an erection.

Several years later, Alex sought treatment from a clinical psychologist who specialized in hypnotherapy. Alex saw this psychologist for seven sessions of hypnosis. On one occasion during the course of these visits, Alex was able to attain an erection during sex with his wife. However, this gain was temporary, and this was the last time that Alex could recall that he had a full erection.

As more time passed without a remission in his erectile difficulties, Alex became increasingly concerned about his problem. During his sexual interactions with his wife, Alex's worries interfered with his ability to focus on or enjoy sex. At these times, Alex thought about his erectile response and thought to himself that he was definitely not going to be able to achieve an erection that was sufficient for intercourse. He would think to himself that the only way he could sexually satisfy his wife was to have "normal sex." He regarded sexual intercourse as the only form of normal sex. As his problem progressed, Alex felt that he had perhaps become too old or too "deviant" to be able to ever have "normal sex" again.

Alex reported that he masturbated very rarely—approximately once per year. On these occasions, Alex achieved about the same level of erectile response that occurred during sex with his wife. When asked about the low frequency of masturbation, Alex replied that he abstained from this activity due to his religious beliefs. Alex stated that he was raised in a strict Catholic family. Although he recalled a happy childhood and a good family life, he noted that the topic of sex was never discussed in the home. He said that he learned about sex through sexual activity with his wife after they had married.

As part of the initial evaluation at the sexual dysfunction clinic, Alex's wife was asked to come in for an interview to ascertain her perspective on Alex's erectile difficulties and their relationship. Lilly felt that Alex experienced more problems in achieving an erection on the occasions that he attempted vaginal intercourse. Also, she thought that Alex's sexual performance was better when he seemed more relaxed. Although she confirmed Alex's statement that they attempted intercourse roughly once per week, Lilly said that they often had difficulty finding the time for intimate activity. She stated that when they did interact sexually, there was little to no fore-play involved. Lilly said that she had tried to manually stimulate her husband's penis on a few occasions but had ceased doing this because she was not sure if Alex enjoyed this activity. She confessed that their communication about sex and other relationship issues was rather poor. She said that although she felt that Alex was committed to her, she was somewhat dissatisfied with his ability to express his emotions to her; for example, Lilly claimed that Alex rarely told her that he loved her. While acknowledging that Alex's goal of treatment was to regain his ability to achieve erections, she hoped that therapy would result in an improvement in the couple's level of intimacy and communication. Lilly stated that Alex's erectile difficulty had caused the greatest amount of distress during the time when they were attempting to start a family. She recalled that their intent to have a child gradually faded as they became more preoccupied with other aspects of their lives (e.g., careers, friendships). Consequently, she felt that Alex's erectile problem had caused relatively little distress or interference in their lives because they had adapted their sex life around it. Lilly noted that she often experienced an orgasm during these sexual encounters. Finally, she stated that she was very supportive of the prospect of Alex's treatment, and she said that she would be willing to participate in his treatment, if necessary.

To complete his intake evaluation, Alex was given a clinical interview to determine if he was experiencing any other emotional difficulties that contributed to his sexual dysfunction or that were relevant to treatment planning. The results of this interview indicated that Alex had never met criteria for any other form of psychological disorders (including alcohol or drug abuse). During this interview, Alex could not recall a history of psychological disorders in his immediate family (e.g., father, mother, siblings, grandparents).

DSM-IV Diagnosis

On the basis of this information, Alex was assigned the following DSM-IV diagnosis:

Axis I	302.72	Male erectile disorder, acquired type, generalized type, due to psychological factors
Axis II	V71.09	No diagnosis on Axis II
Axis III	None	
Axis IV	None	
Axis V	Global assessment of functioning = 70 (current)	

Alex's presentation before treatment met the DSM-IV definition of male erectile disorder (American Psychiatric Association, 1994). In DSM-IV, the key criteria for this disorder are: (a) persistent or recurrent inability to attain, or to maintain until the completion of sexual activity, an adequate erection and (b) the disturbance causes marked distress or interpersonal difficulty. The diagnosis of male erectile disorder is not made when the person's erectile difficulties are better accounted for by a medical condition or by the effects of alcohol or prescription or illicit drugs. The types of medical problems and drugs that have a negative impact on erectile functioning include cardiovascular disease, use of antihypertensive medication, and persistent abuse of cocaine or alcohol. In addition, this diagnosis is not appropriate if the erectile dysfunction is judged to be due to another psychological disorder. For instance, patients who suffer from a severe major depression may experience erectile problems as a physical manifestation of their disturbance (see Case 8) or as a side effect of their treatment (i.e., use of certain forms of antidepressant medication).

Note that Alex's five-axis DSM-IV diagnosis had three specifiers. These specifiers convey a fuller description of the diagnosis and may imply important information about the anticipated course, treatment, and prognosis of the disorder. In addition to male erectile disorder, the three specifiers are used when the clinician is assigning any type of DSM-IV sexual dysfunction diagnosis (e.g., premature ejaculation, female sexual arousal disorder): (a) nature of onset (i.e., whether the dysfunction has been present since the onset of sexual functioning versus whether it developed after a period of normal functioning), (b) situational context (i.e., whether the dysfunction occurs in a variety of situations versus whether the problem is limited to certain types of stimulation, situations, or partners), and (c) causal factors (i.e., whether psychological factors are judged to fully account for the dysfunction versus whether biological factors such as drugs or medical conditions contribute to the problem to some degree). With regard to the latter specifier, male erectile disorder can be assigned as a DSM-IV diagnosis if biological factors contribute to the disorder, as long as psychological factors contribute strongly to the onset and maintenance of the condition. Accordingly, Alex's diagnosis included the specifier "acquired type" because his erectile difficulties emerged at the age of 44 and were preceded by many years of normal sexual functioning. The specifier "generalized type" was assigned because Alex's erectile problems occurred whenever he attempted to achieve an erection (including masturbation). The specifier "due to psychological factors" was assigned because Alex was not taking any drugs and did not have any medical conditions that could have contributed to the origins or persistence of his erectile difficulties.

More information on the nature of male erectile disorder and its diagnosis and treatment is reviewed in the remaining sections of this chapter.

CASE FORMULATION USING THE INTEGRATIVE MODEL

The integrative model of sexual dysfunction (Barlow & Durand, 1999) highlights a number of factors that are relevant to understanding the causes and planning the treatment of male erectile disorder. Unlike many of the other disorders that are discussed in this casebook, there is no evidence to date suggesting a genetic or familial contribution to this condition (i.e., data showing that this disorder tends to run in families). Nevertheless, a number of biological factors can contribute to the development and maintenance of male erectile disorder. For example, consistent with the impressions of the first urologist that Alex had consulted, who had prescribed hormone therapy, abnormal levels of testosterone can be associated with some sexual dysfunctions. However, researchers have found that it is very rare for hormone levels to contribute substantially to sexual difficulties (cf. Schover & Jensen, 1988). Hormone levels did not seem to play a role in Alex's erectile dysfunction, given that his problem did not respond at all to hormone therapy. Alex's urologist had also prescribed a drug to enhance blood circulation, based on the evidence that vascular disease is responsible for many instances of male erectile disorder (e.g., constricted arteries in the penis). Whereas vascular diseases do account for many cases of erectile dysfunction (cf. Wincze & Carey, 1991), these conditions did not contribute to Alex's problem.

In fact, Alex was in good physical health and did not have a history of any physical condition that could have contributed to his sexual dysfunction. For example, Alex had never experienced physical conditions such as diabetes, kidney disease, or neurological disease, all of which are common causes of sexual dysfunction (Schover & Jensen, 1988). Moreover, Alex did not have a history of alcohol or drug abuse, another factor that has been associated with male erectile disorder (e.g., Cocores, Miller, Pottash, & Gold, 1988; Schiavi, 1990). A number of prescription drugs also have the negative side effect of dampening sexual arousal or desire. These drugs include some forms of antihypertensive medications and the tricyclic and serotonin reuptake inhibitor antidepressants (R. T. Segraves, 1988). However, this could not have contributed to Alex's dysfunction, given that he had never taken any medications other than the drugs prescribed to him by his urologist for his erectile disorder.

Although the integrative model acknowledges many of the biological factors that can contribute to sexual dysfunction, it places greatest emphasis on the psychological features that are associated with the onset and maintenance of these disorders. For example, a number of psychological or social factors can make a person more vulnerable for developing a sexual dysfunction. One such dimension has been termed *erotophobia*, which refers to the tendency for some people to hold negative attitudes about sex (e.g., "sex is dirty"; Byrne & Schulte, 1990). Such beliefs may arise from childhood learning from families or religious figures, or from traumatic experiences such as sexual abuse. Regardless of their source, these attitudes are associated with an increased risk for sexual dysfunction because these beliefs may prevent the person from acquiring adequate knowledge about sex or may make them feel uncomfortable with many aspects of sexual activity (e.g., talking with partner about sexual preferences, engaging in certain forms of sexual behavior such as masturbation or oral sex). The extent of a person's sexual knowledge can play a significant role in their sexual functioning; for instance, many persons with sexual difficulties have never learned enough about sex to afford them the most enjoyment and arousal from sex. This seemed to be the case for Alex, who did not report any form of foreplay during the sexual interactions with his wife; he also did not seem to be aware of the role that tactile stimulation or fantasies could play in enhancing his erections. Although perhaps not having a substantial role in his sexual problem, Alex displayed some erotophobic attitudes. For example, he objected to masturbation, which he attributed to his strict Catholic upbringing.

Social and relationship factors are also highlighted in the integrative model as contributing to some sexual dysfunctions. For example, some instances of sexual dysfunction are preceded by a deterioration of the interpersonal relationship between the sexual partners (e.g., marital discord). In addition, problems in sexual desire or sexual arousal occasionally stem from the person regarding their partner as no longer sexually attractive to them. Although Alex and his wife were generally satisfied and committed to their marriage, aspects of their relationship appeared to contribute to some degree to Alex's erectile difficulties. Specifically, it is possible that Alex would see an improvement in his erectile capacity if he and his wife communicated with each other more effectively and if they increased the level of intimacy in their relationship. The importance of relationship variables is discussed more fully later in this case.

The integrative model provides a detailed account of the types of psychological phenomena that may occur during sexual activity to result in dysfunctional sexual performance (cf. Barlow, 1986). When faced with a sexual situation (e.g., preparing to have sexual intercourse), people may experience anxiety or other negative emotions based on their pessimistic expectancies regarding their ability to perform adequately. During the sexual encounter, these negative thoughts (e.g., "I'm not going to be able to get or maintain my erection") and accompanying negative emotions may keep the person distracted from aspects of the situation that would be arousing to them (i.e., "erotic cues," such as the sensations of being stimulated by one's partner). In other words, because they are so preoccupied with these negative thoughts, the person is not able to focus sufficiently on the erotic cues that would arouse them. Conversely, when the person with normal sexual functioning is sexually aroused, their attention becomes even more strongly focused on the erotic cues in the situation, leading to increases in their level of arousal. As the person with sexual dysfunction continues to experience erectile difficulties, his thoughts, emotions, and expectancies of inadequate performance intensify, resulting in greater erectile dysfunction and often avoidance of sexual situations altogether.

This aspect of the integrative model of sexual dysfunction was quite consistent with Alex's experience. It is possible that his initial erectile problems arose partly from the combination of (a) added pressure to perform sexually to conceive a child and (b) increased likelihood of experiencing occasional problems with achieving or maintaining an erection given his advancing age (Alex was 44 when the first signs of erectile problems occurred) and the fact that the couple never engaged in any form of foreplay prior to intercourse. (As discussed in further detail later in this chapter, older men may require increased physical stimulation to obtain an erection.) Alex's erectile dysfunction intensified and became more persistent as he became more distressed and concerned about the problem. He clearly noted that his worries about obtaining an erection interfered with his ability to focus on or enjoy sex. At these times, Alex thought to himself, "I'll never get an erection," and he considered himself as possibly being "too old" or "too deviant" to be able to ever have "normal sex" again. These negative thoughts and expectancies certainly could have contributed strongly to Alex's inability to become sexually aroused.

Treatment Goals and Planning

Consistent with the information presented in the discussion of the integrative model, Alex's therapist felt that his sexual dysfunction had persisted for the following reasons: (a) inadequate knowledge about sex and limited sexual repertoire (e.g., Alex expected to obtain a full erection in the absence of foreplay or physical stimulation, something that might be particularly difficult to accomplish for a man of his age), (b) a less than ideal level of intimacy and communication in Alex and Lilly's marriage, and (c) negative cognitions and expectancies (e.g., "I'll never get an erection") that were repeatedly reinforced by Alex's unsuccessful attempts at intercourse. Accordingly, the therapist considered these factors as the primary targets of Alex's treatment. Lilly was asked to attend the treatment sessions with Alex. To increase the couple's sexual knowledge, the therapist planned to begin the therapy with a rationale for treatment and general sex education. Secondly, techniques to improve the couple's ability to communicate effectively with one another would be addressed. This aspect of treatment would include techniques to foster their sexual communication and to increase their level of intimacy (e.g., increase the couple's ability to express to one another their preferences for what their sexual activity should involve).

Third, the technique of sensate focus (Masters & Johnson, 1970) would be employed to address Alex's negative emotions and thoughts that arose during sexual activity that prevented him from becoming aroused (this technique would also address improving the couple's level of intimacy). The central goal of this technique is to help the person or couple develop a heightened awareness of, and attentional focus on, the pleasurable sensations of sex, as opposed to focusing on one's level of performance. In so doing, the person experiences less anxiety by striving for something that is immediately obtainable (e.g., emotional comfort and physical pleasure), rather than simply trying to achieve an erection (cf. Carey, Wincze, & Meisler, 1993). In the initial stages of sensate focus, the couple is asked to refrain from attempting sexual intercourse so that they can relearn the basics of being affectionate, receiving pleasure, and so on. In the first phase, called nongenital pleasuring, the couple is asked to explore and enjoy each other's body through touching, kissing, and massaging. After successfully accomplishing this phase, the couple moves to the genital pleasuring phase; however, intercourse and orgasm are still banned, and the male is told that achieving an erection is not the goal of this phase. In the final phase, the couple is asked to gradually reinitiate sexual intercourse, beginning with brief vaginal penetration, then slowly working toward full intercourse.

COURSE OF TREATMENT AND TREATMENT OUTCOME

In the first session, the rationale and goals of treatment were discussed. Alex appeared nervous and uncomfortable throughout the session; he often looked down at the floor and blushed a few times during the discussion of treatment goals and the nature of his erectile difficulties. Once again, it was clear that Alex and Lilly had somewhat differing goals and expectations for treatment. Alex stated that his main goal was to achieve erections that were sufficient for intercourse, at least some of the time. Lilly agreed with this goal, and she also said that she hoped that treatment would lead to improvements in the couple's communication and level of intimacy in the relationship. The therapist replied that treatment would address each of these goals, especially because they were interrelated (e.g., the degree of intimacy in the relationship could have a strong impact on each partner's level of sexual arousal). The therapist asked Alex and Lilly to read the first few chapters of a sex education book to enhance their knowledge about sex. In addition, the first step of sensate focus was initiated: After discussing the rationale of this procedure, the therapist asked the couple to cease their attempts at sexual intercourse for the time being.

In the next session, the couple's communication difficulties were more apparent. For example, both Alex and Lilly had read and enjoyed the chapters of the sex education book that they had been assigned. However, they had not discussed the book with one another. Although Alex had not mentioned this to Lilly, he had become irritated by the fact that she had underlined certain passages of the book, which he thought she had done to point out certain things to him. Lilly was surprised when Alex said this in the session, and she informed both Alex and the therapist that she had underlined these sentences for her own benefit. The couple was also surprised to learn that they had both found a suggestion in the book for enhancing sexual repertoires to be interesting and potentially worth pursuing (i.e., taking showers together). Thus, the therapist spent most of this session addressing communication skills. Lilly noted that the only time that Alex talked to her about their relationship was to say something negative. Alex conceded that his communication with his wife "could be better." To address these issues, the therapist asked the couple to independently complete two tasks before the next session: (a) develop a wish list of things, both sexual and nonsexual, that they would like from each other but have never asked for, and (b) at least once per day, catch your spouse doing something nice and record it on a sheet. The couple was also assigned to read the next few chapters of the sex education book and discuss it with one another. Alex and Lilly reported no difficulty in refraining from their attempts at sexual intercourse. They were asked to continue with this restriction until the procedures of sensate focus had been accomplished.

The therapist began the next session by reviewing the couple's communication homework. Whereas both Alex and Lilly had completed their assignments and discussed the sex education book, Lilly was upset after learning what Alex had recorded on his wish list. Alex's list consisted mostly of things that he wished Lilly would stop doing rather than things that he'd like her to do. Also, he had not recorded many nice things that Lilly had done over the week. One of the things that Alex wished that Lilly would stop doing is speaking on his behalf. The therapist had observed this communication pattern during the therapy sessions. She felt that Alex was not very adept at communicating with his wife or at expressing himself in general. Lilly, by contrast, was quite chatty and did a great deal of the talking in the sessions, sometimes answering questions for her husband. However, Lilly was not very communicative with her husband in some respects as well. For example, if she was dissatisfied with something Alex had done, usually she would not raise the issue for fear that it would upset him. The therapist highlighted these communication problems as examples of "mind reading"—the tendency, based on the belief that they know their partner so well, to guess or assume that one knows what the other is thinking and feeling. For instance, Lilly assumed that Alex preferred that she respond to questions on his behalf.

Another example of mind reading arose in this session during the review of the sex education material that Alex and Lilly had read over the week. The couple realized that their attempts at sexual intercourse rarely, if ever, involved foreplay. When the therapist explored the reasons for this, Lilly stated that shortly after they were first married, she observed that Alex had flinched while she was stimulating his penis manually. Lilly concluded that Alex did not enjoy manual stimulation and thus she never initiated it again. Alex was very surprised at her comments and said that he liked manual stimulation very much, but he had never asked his wife to do this because he was sure that she would not want to. The therapist used this opportunity to emphasize the importance of effective communication as a necessity for both a healthy sexual relationship and a strong marriage. In addition, the therapist pointed out that it might be unreasonable to expect Alex to obtain a full erection with no stimulation whatsoever, given that the need for stimulation to produce erections often increases as a man grows older. The therapist asked them to work on their communication skills and level of intimacy over the next week by (a) spending time discussing an issue in their marriage, while using suggestions that the therapist had offered (e.g., express oneself using the word *I* to foster the ability to communicate thoughts and feelings, asking questions instead of assuming what the other is thinking or feeling), (b) schedule a pleasant activity that they could do together, and (c) review each other's wish list and carry out one of the wishes that the other partner had made. In addition, the nongenital pleasuring component of sensate focus was assigned. The couple was asked to take turns, fully clothed in comfortable dress, giving each other body rubs and focusing on the pleasurable sensations arising from this activity.

The couple returned to the next session having completed all of their homework. The communication homework had gone fairly well, and Lilly was happy to report that Alex had hugged her several times, an item that was on her wish list. Alex and Lilly had completed the body rub homework and said that they had enjoyed it. The couple stated that they felt comfortable moving on to the next step of sensate focus: unclothed massages that involved the entire body with the exception of the genitals and breasts. In addition, Alex was assigned a separate exercise of stimulating his penis to try to become more aware of the sensations of pleasure and arousal (although the therapist emphasized that achieving erections was not a goal of this task). The therapist was hesitant to make this assignment, given Alex's religious and moral convictions about masturbation. However, Alex stated that he had no problem with completing these exercises, if they were important to treatment. The couple was asked to continue practicing the types of communication skills that had been covered thus far.

Although not a goal of the assignment, Alex began the next session by reporting that he had achieved a full erection on two occasions during his self-stimulation exercises. While acknowledging this as a very good sign, the therapist emphasized that the most important thing at the present time was that Alex become more in tune with his sensations, as opposed to getting erections. Nevertheless, because the couple's homework had gone well (including the unclothed body massage), they were asked to proceed to the next stage of sensate focus. Lilly was asked to manually stimulate Alex's penis. To reduce the chances that he would experience performance anxiety, Alex was told not to obtain an erection or reach orgasm.

However, these exercises turned out to be very arousing to Alex because the couple reported at the next session that Alex got an erection on each occasion. When the therapist inquired about this, Alex stated that he found these exercises arousing because Lilly had rarely touched his penis before. Alex, as well as Lilly, began to realize that intercourse was not the only activity that they could engage in to obtain sexual pleasure from one another. The couple expressed interest in expanding their sexual repertoire, perhaps starting with showering together or engaging in more foreplay activities. The therapist agreed that this would be an excellent idea. The couple was asked to continue with the same sensate focus assignment (i.e., manual stimulation without intercourse or orgasm) and to arrange time to discuss with one another how they could enhance the variety of their sexual activity.

Alex continued to achieve erections during the sensate focus exercises. In addition, the couple reported that they had showered together on two occasions between sessions. The therapist responded by saying that it was clear that the couple had improved their ability to communicate about sex and that they were starting to expand their sexual repertoire. The next stage of sensate focus was assigned: Once Lilly had manually stimulated Alex's penis to establish his erection, vaginal penetration would follow, but without movement (thrusting) or orgasm.

Alex and Lilly arrived at the next session and reported that their sensate focus practices had gone very well. Alex stated that, on every occasion, he had felt very aroused and had obtained and maintained his erection. Lilly also reported that she felt that the exercises had gone very well and that she was optimistic and pleased about the progress they had seen. In addition, she felt that the level of intimacy and sense of togetherness had improved considerably since treatment had started. Lilly said that Alex and she had taken a shower together again this week and that they had found it to be very pleasurable. However, the therapist was surprised to hear Alex and Lilly's request that only one more session be scheduled, given that Alex was now getting erections consistently (as well as the fact that regular session attendance was time-consuming and somewhat costly). The therapist suggested that several more sessions be planned because the couple had not yet attempted sexual intercourse and because additional work could be accomplished to produce further improvements in the couple's communication skills. Nevertheless, Alex and Lilly were adamant about scheduling only one more session. Thus, the therapist asked Alex and Lilly to attempt sexual intercourse during the week.

In the final session, Alex and Lilly were pleased to report that they had successfully completed intercourse on the two occasions that they had attempted it. The therapist concluded the therapy by reviewing the techniques of treatment and the gains the couple had made. Alex was now able to obtain erections consistently during self-stimulation and manual stimulation by

Lilly; based on the couple's report in the final session, there was evidence indicating that Alex might now be able to consistently attain erections for sexual intercourse. The couple seemed to feel closer to each other and happier in their relationship. In addition, Alex reported that he was feeling better about himself in general and feeling less like "something was wrong" with him. Despite these considerable gains, the therapist felt that some communication difficulties between Alex and Lilly remained; for example, Alex still seemed somewhat reluctant to express his thoughts and feelings to his wife, and Lilly was still very talkative and continued to speak on Alex's behalf on some occasions. The therapist offered the couple the opportunity for additional sessions to continue to address communication skills or to work on erectile difficulties, if the need arose in the future. Alex and Lilly thanked the therapist for this option but were not heard from again.

DISCUSSION

In addition to the diagnostic guidelines discussed earlier in this chapter, when determining whether to assign male erectile disorder, the clinician must decide if the person's complaint is extensive enough to warrant a full DSM-IV diagnosis. For instance, a DSM-IV diagnosis of male erectile disorder may not be appropriate if the erectile difficulties are due to insufficient sexual stimulation. In fact, it could be argued that Alex's erectile problems did not warrant a full diagnosis because they seemed to be partly accounted for by the fact that he was a 54-year-old man who was attempting to achieve an erection and have intercourse with no physical stimulation whatsoever. (DSM-IV notes that older men may require more stimulation or require more time to achieve an erection.) Nevertheless, Alex was assigned the diagnosis because his problem had become pervasive (lasting 10 years in a variety of contexts) and was associated with considerable distress.

In addition, research indicates that many men have occasional difficulties in obtaining or maintaining an erection at some point. For example, in a survey of 100 well-educated, happily married couples in the community, Frank, Anderson, and Rubenstein (1978) found that 40% of the men reported occasional erectile and ejaculatory problems. Often, these problems are transient and related to situational factors (e.g., fatigue, stress, the effects of alcohol or drugs). Accordingly, the diagnosis of male erectile disorder should be assigned only if the problem is persistent and associated with distress or lifestyle impairment (e.g., interpersonal difficulties).

Nevertheless, the prevalence of erectile dysfunction is startlingly high. Conservative estimates suggest that male erectile disorder may affect between 4% and 9% of the adult male population (Spector & Carey, 1990). However, this figure may underestimate the prevalence in that many men experience erectile difficulties but do not seek treatment (cf. Bancroft, 1989; Bansal, Wincze, Nirenberg, Liepman, & Engle-Friedman, 1990). Yet, in studies conducted on patients seeking treatment for a sexual difficulty, male erectile disorder has been found to be the most common problem for which men seek help, accounting for 50% or more of cases (e.g., Masters & Johnson, 1970; Renshaw, 1988). More recent evidence indicates that the majority of cases of male erectile disorder involve men over the age of 50 (Bancroft, 1989).

The specific types of sexual dysfunction disorders often do not occur in isolation. Frequently, a patient referred to a sexuality clinic complains of a wide assortment of sexual problems, although one problem may be the most prominent or of the most concern to the patient (K. B. Segraves & Segraves, 1991). For instance, DSM-IV notes that male erectile disorders often co-occur with the sexual dysfunctions *hypoactive sexual desire disorder* (characterized by a deficiency or absence of sexual fantasies and desire for sexual activity) and *premature ejaculation* (repeated instances of reaching ejaculation before the person wishes it, with minimal sexual stimulation). Although few studies have examined the temporal sequence of these disorders, presumably the onset of the disorders can occur in any order. For example, as noted in the discussion of the integrative model of male erectile disorder, a deficiency in sexual desire (hypoactive sexual desire disorder) may often predate and contribute to the onset of erectile difficulties. Then again, as was true to some extent for Alex, a decrease in sexual desire is often a consequence of erectile difficulties, associated with a person's avoidance of sexual activity due to repeated failed attempts at sustaining an erection to complete intercourse, masturbation, and so on.

Over the years, a variety of medical and psychosocial treatments have been developed for male erectile disorder. One common medical approach used by urologists is injection of the drug papaverine directly into the penis. Papaverine dilates the blood vessels and allows blood to flow to the penis to quickly produce erections that last from 1 to 4 hours. Some men have benefited from this approach, but a significant drawback of this intervention is that many men refuse or stop using the treatment because it requires that they inject their penis with a hypodermic needle immediately before sexual activity (Gilbert & Gingell, 1991). Moreover, repeated papaverine injections can be associated with major side effects, such as bruising or the development of fibrosis or nodules in the penis (Gregoire, 1992).

An even more drastic procedure involves the surgical insertion of penile implants. The most popular form is an inflatable cylinder. To produce an erection, the man squeezes a small pump that has been surgically implanted into the scrotum to force fluid into the cylinder. Although a number of implant procedures have been developed (including one in which the inflation device is contained in the cylinder itself), these interventions fall short of restoring adequate sexual functioning or satisfaction in most patients (Gregoire, 1992).

In addition, the penile vacuum device has been developed, a procedure that is much less intrusive than surgical implants or injections. The device creates a vacuum in a cylinder placed over the penis, thereby drawing blood to produce an erection. The erection is sustained by temporary placement of a specially designed ring around the base of the penis (to prevent blood from flowing out of the organ). Although awkward to use, many men report satisfaction with this device, particularly those for whom psychosocial treatments were not successful (Witherington, 1988). Medical interventions such as vacuum device therapy are quite appropriate if the erectile dysfunction is due to irreversible organic damage (e.g., vascular disease).

In 1998, the drug sildenafil (Viagra) was approved by the Food and Drug Administration. Based on data from preliminary trials indicating that between 50% and 80% of men benefit from this medication (Goldstein et al., 1998), Viagra has quickly become the medical treatment of choice for erectile dysfunction. Although a widely used intervention for erectile disorder, Viagra is not without its drawbacks. For example, as many as 30% of Viagra users suffer severe headaches as a side effect, particularly in those taking higher dosages. Moreover, it is important to combine Viagra, as well as any other form of medical treatment, with an educational and sex therapy program to ensure maximum benefit (i.e., production of erections through medical means does not address the psychological or interpersonal factors that may have contributed to the sexual dysfunction).

The psychosocial treatment that Alex and Lilly received included components that are frequently used in the treatment of sexual dysfunction (i.e., sex education, communication training, sensate focus). Indeed, most researchers who have examined the effectiveness of psychosocial interventions for sexual dysfunction have studied multicomponent treatments. As noted earlier in this chapter, psychosocial treatments of the nature that Alex and Lilly received emerged from the pioneering work of Masters and Johnson (1970). In their study, Masters and Johnson examined an intensive, multicomponent approach (consisting of sex education, communication training, and sensate focus) that was conducted with daily visits over a 2-week period. A total of 790 patients (both male and female) with a variety of sexual dysfunctions were treated. Masters and Johnson (1970) reported that the majority of these patients recovered from their sexual dysfunction as a result of the intensive program. However, the rates of recovery differed, depending on the type of dysfunction. Yet, it is interesting to note that for patients with a lifelong generalized erectile dysfunction (a condition that could be viewed as very resistant to treatment) a recovery rate of roughly 60% was obtained. Since Masters and Johnson's (1970) work was published, a number of researchers have studied and refined these techniques. More recent results indicate that as many as 70% of patients show a positive treatment outcome from psychosocial treatments for erectile dysfunction (Hawton, Catalan, & Fagg, 1992).

THINKING CRITICALLY

1. Male erectile disorder (MED) has been conceptualized by some researchers to be akin in nature to social phobia. What features that contribute to the development of MED could be seen as similar to those found in social phobia?

2. Although many males in the general population experience occasional erectile failure, most do not subsequently develop MED. What personality, cognitive, behavioral, and social factors do you believe are most important to the development of MED after an occasion of erectile difficulty? How can the reactions of the man's sexual partner contribute to the likelihood that an MED will or will not develop?

3. After the drug Viagra entered the market as a treatment for erectile problems, the incidence of males requesting psychosocial treatment for MED dropped significantly. Do you believe Viagra can be effective as the *sole* treatment of MED? Do you believe psychosocial treatments along the lines of the treatment used for Alex would be important to use in MED, even if Viagra was 100% effective at producing erections? Why or why not?

4. Research has found that the sexual dysfunction premature ejaculation (PE—persistent ejaculation with minimal sexual stimulation before, on, or shortly after penetration and before the person wishes it) often co-occurs with the diagnosis of MED. Why do you think this is the case? Do you think that MED and PE have the same risk (causal) factors or do think that having one of these disorders may lead to having the other? What variables could be viewed as shared causal factors of MED and PE? In persons who have both MED and PE, which disorder do you believe is more likely to arise first, and why?

Case
12

Sexual Disorder
(Paraphilia): Pedophilia

lbert Gatton was referred by a prominent psychiatrist in another
state for assessment and possible treatment of heterosexual
pedophilic behavior. At the time of his presentation, Albert was a
51-year-old married Caucasian minister from the Midwest. He had
three grown children, two girls and a boy, the youngest of whom was a 19-
year-old daughter who was attending college in another state. He was tall and
quite serious and, although he was cooperative, Albert did not volunteer a
great deal of information during the initial interview.

Albert reported that he had been touching and caressing girls between the
ages of 10 and 16 for more than 20 years. He estimated that he had had some
interaction with at least 50 girls. Most typically this interaction was restricted
to hugging or caressing their breasts. On occasion, he would also touch their
genitals. Albert did not expose himself to girls or ask them to touch him in
any way. Generally, he reported achieving a partial erection during these contacts but never ejaculated during any of these encounters. He did not report
this to be primarily an erotic experience but rather continued to suggest that
the emphasis was on an exchange of affection. During the initial interview, in

fact, Albert reported feeling little remorse about his activities for this reason, although he was deeply concerned over the effect on his family and his career from being "found out."

Clinical History

Some 12 years before presenting for treatment, Albert's activities were discovered for the first time, and he was forced to leave his church in another state in the Midwest. The matter was kept relatively quiet, and Albert was able to take up a new position in a different state, a position he retained until just prior to treatment. Although he sought treatment and agreed to refrain from any physical interaction with young girls in his new church, he was soon as sexually active as ever. This behavior continued until several months before he presented for treatment.

According to Albert, in most of the cases the young girls responded positively to his advances and did not seem offended or frightened. In several instances, this activity would continue with the girl for several months, and it was with these girls that genital touching occurred. During these years, although responsible administratively and spiritually for the entire parish, Albert took particular interest in activities involving young adolescent girls such as the local Girl Scout troop. In addition to this activity, Albert, who was particularly attracted to small breasts characteristic of young adolescent girls, would masturbate once or twice a week to pictures of girls with these features that he found in what he referred to as "nudist magazines." In fact, Albert subscribed to a rather extensive series of pedophilic pornographic magazines, which, much to his embarrassment and that of his family, continued to arrive at his old rectory in the Midwest for months, to be received by the new occupants.

Several months before presenting for treatment, Albert was confronted by the parents of an 11-year-old Girl Scout who were hearing "strange stories" about physical touching from their daughter and wanted to discuss them. This behavior was presented by Albert as a misunderstanding, and the incident died down until the parents of another girl who reported similar experiences mentioned them to the parents of the first girl. The story spread and quickly led to outrage, Albert's dismissal from the parish by the bishop, and Albert's suspension as a minister with strong recommendations that he seek treatment.

Albert grew up a rather inhibited teenager with few lasting social contacts with girls. He was married at age 26 and engaged in sexual intercourse for the first time. He had begun dating at approximately age 22, and on only one occasion before marriage had he engaged in even light petting. During high school, most of the fantasies Albert used when masturbating were centered on pubescent girls with developing breasts.

After discovery 12 years ago at his previous parish, Albert had engaged in a number of long-term psychotherapeutic relationships. He reported that none of these treatment programs seemed to have any effect on his sexual arousal patterns. At least one of his previous therapists had taken the approach that there must be something wrong within his marital relationship. In addition to angering Albert, this notion was disconfirmed by his wife who reported a normal and satisfying sexual and marital relationship.

Despite the incident, Albert's relationship with his family remained excellent, and his wife was extremely supportive, determined to stick by him through thick and thin. His children were also quite supportive but seemed to largely dismiss the incidents or deny that they were anything but exaggerations and innuendo. Albert had never approached any of his children sexually.

DSM-IV Diagnosis

On the basis of this information, Albert was assigned the following DSM-IV diagnosis:

Axis I	302.2	Pedophilia, sexually attracted to females, nonexclusive type
Axis II	V71.09	No diagnosis on Axis II
Axis III	None	
Axis IV	Recent job termination	
Axis V	Global assessment of functioning = 60 (current)	

Pedophilia is a form of paraphilia. In DSM-IV, *paraphilias* are defined as "recurrent, intense sexual urges, fantasies, or behaviors that involve unusual objects, activities, or situations that cause clinically significant distress or impairment in social, occupational, or other important areas of functioning." Other types of paraphilias besides pedophilia include *exhibitionism* (recurrent exposure of one's genitals to an unsuspecting stranger), *fetishism* (recurrent and intense sexually arousing fantasies, urges, or behaviors involving the use of nonliving objects such as shoes or undergarments), *frotteurism* (recurrent and intense sexually arousing fantasies, urges, or behaviors involving touching or rubbing against a nonconsenting person), *sexual masochism* (recurrent and intense sexually arousing fantasies, urges, or behaviors involving the act of being humiliated, beaten, bound, or made to suffer), *sexual sadism* (recurrent and intense sexually arousing fantasies, urges, or behaviors involving acts in which the psychological or physical suffering of the victim is sexually exciting to the person), and *voyeurism* (recurrent and intense sexually arousing fantasies, urges, or behaviors involving the observation of an unsuspecting person who is naked, getting undressed, or engaging in sexual activity).

Albert's presentation was quite consistent with the DSM-IV definition of pedophilia (American Psychiatric Association, 1994). In DSM-IV, the key criteria for pedophilia are (a) over a period of at least 6 months, recurrent, intense sexually arousing fantasies, sexual urges, or behaviors involving sexual activity with a prepubescent child or children (generally age 13 years or younger); (b) the fantasies, sexual urges, or behaviors cause clinically significant distress or impairment in social, occupational, or other important areas of functioning; and (c) the person is at least 16 years of age and at least 5 years older than the child or children in Criterion (a). The last criterion was included in DSM-IV in part to prevent the improper diagnosis of pedophilia in adolescent patients. For example, a 16-year-old male would not be diagnosed with pedophilia for having sexual contact with a 12-year-old female. However, for persons who are in late adolescence, DSM-IV does not specify a precise age difference; thus, clinical judgment must be exercised to determine whether a diagnosis of pedophilia is warranted, taking into account both the sexual maturity of the child and the age difference between the child and the patient.

As seen in Albert's five-axis DSM-IV diagnosis, when the diagnosis of pedophilia is assigned, the clinician must indicate the type of pedophilia by three types of specifiers: (a) arousal pattern (sexually attracted to males, sexually attracted to females, sexually attracted to both), (b) whether the pedophilic behavior is limited to incest, and (c) whether the patient is attracted only to children (exclusive versus nonexclusive type). Accordingly, Albert's diagnosis included the specifier "sexually attracted to females" because all his sexual contact involved prepubescent females (no reported history of homosexual fantasies, urges, or behavior). The specifier "nonexclusive type" was assigned because Albert was sexually attracted to both juvenile and adult females (normal sexual relationship with his wife). The specifier "limited to incest" was not assigned because none of Albert's pedophilic behavior occurred with his daughters.

The significance of these specifiers and a fuller discussion of the nature and treatment of pedophilia are provided later in this chapter.

CASE FORMULATION USING THE INTEGRATIVE MODEL

Unlike models of other disorders presented in this book (e.g., panic disorder, major depression), the integrative model of paraphilia has little current scientific support (Barlow & Durand, 1999). For example, the model of paraphilia includes no biological dimensions. However, as is the case with many other psychological disorders, there could be strong biological elements contributing to the development of paraphilias (e.g., excessive sexual arousal). This important question needs future research. Despite its speculative nature, the integrative model of paraphilia can be quite useful in treatment planning. The model asserts the following phenomena, occurring in childhood through late adolescence, as factors that may contribute to the vulnerability for developing a paraphilia: (a) inappropriate sexual associations or experiences, (b) inadequate development of consensual adult arousal patterns, and (c) inadequate development of appropriate social skills. Some evidence in support of the first vulnerability factor comes from findings that individuals with pedophilia very often were victims of childhood sexual abuse themselves (Groth, 1979). With regard to the other two vulnerability factors, inability to develop adequate sexual or social relationships with the appropriate people is associated with the development of inappropriate sexual outlets (Barlow & Wincze, 1980). Certain aspects of Albert's history are consistent with the model. For example, Albert's social development through adolescence was inadequate, as he reported being inhibited and recalled few lasting social contacts with girls. Similarly, Albert was late in his development of appropriate sexual relationships (e.g., he did not begin dating until age 22; heterosexual activity did not occur on a regular basis until he was married at age 26).

These three factors are vulnerability dimensions. As such, they do not ensure the emergence of a paraphilia; many people have early experiences of this nature yet do not develop deviant sexual arousal. Rather, when combined with other factors, these vulnerability dimensions increase the likelihood of a deviant sexual arousal pattern. The most salient of these factors is the recurrent reinforcement of sexual fantasies and behavior through sexual pleasure associated with masturbation. Indeed, almost every current model of sexual disorders underscores deviant masturbatory fantasies as key to the maintenance of the various paraphilias; accordingly, this factor is the primary target of most treatment interventions.

Consider the following as an illustration of the role of masturbatory fantasies in the development of a paraphilia: During masturbation, a person may almost exclusively fantasize about peeping into the bedroom of his neighbor while she is undressing. These fantasies, and later the act of voyeurism itself, are repeatedly reinforced by their pairing with a pleasurable consequence (e.g., orgasm). Accordingly, the deviant arousal pattern is maintained or strengthened by the repeated association of strong sexual arousal with these fantasies, urges, and actions. This dimension of the integrative model was clearly evident in Albert. All of his masturbatory fantasies during high school were centered on girls whose breasts were developing. As an adult, Albert masturbated once or twice a week using pictures in pornographic magazines of adolescent girls with small breasts. By adulthood, Albert's deviant sexual behavior went well beyond masturbating to adolescent fantasies and pictures. Indeed, the actual act of engaging in pedophilic behavior with young girls was quite reinforcing to him (e.g., touching the breasts of young girls always produced at least a partial erection).

After the deviant arousal pattern has developed, paraphilic thoughts, fantasies, and behaviors may increase in their frequency and intensity as the result of a person's repeated attempts to inhibit or suppress them. Like other problems such as the eating disorders, whereby the strong drive to restrict one's food intake may precipitate binge eating, the person with paraphilia who attempts to suppress his deviant fantasies and behaviors may experience a paradoxical increase in them. Albert's attempts to refrain from physical contact with girls after he was first discovered were short-lived. After these brief periods of restraint, Albert was just as active, if not more active, than he had been prior to being forced to leave his church.

In addition to failed attempts at suppression or restraint, Albert displayed a common characteristic of pedophilia: the strong tendency to rationalize one's pedophilic behavior as being acceptable. The primary rationalization found in patients with pedophilia is the notion that they are somehow providing love and affection, or possibly sex education, to children that is beneficial to them and that this affection may be restricted or absent from other sources. One of the most striking aspects of Albert's clinical presentation was his absence of remorse. Albert himself commented on his absence of remorse and seemed puzzled by it because he had at least an intellectual appreciation for the seriousness of his acts. Indeed, the tendency for rationalization was clearly evident in Albert, who considered his behavior to be "affectionate," despite his occasional genital contact with young girls and his masturbatory activity to "nudist magazines."

Treatment Goals and Planning

Before attempting formal intervention to directly target his deviant sexual arousal patterns, the therapist would have to address Albert's motivation for change, which would most likely affect his compliance with other treatment procedures. Thus, the initial treatment goal was to strip away some of Albert's rationalizations.

The primary component of Albert's treatment would be *covert sensitization* (Cautela, 1967; Cautela & Kearney, 1993). It would target Albert's pattern of deviant sexual arousal, which is considered in the integrative model to be the most important factor in the maintenance of paraphilia. The goal of this procedure is to change the associations and context of deviant arousal patterns from arousing and pleasurable to neutral or aversive. It is accomplished through repeated pairing, in the patient's imagination, of the pleasurable but undesirable scene of paraphilic behavior with an aversive or noxious consequence. If performed systematically, this procedure reconditions the patient's deviant thoughts, fantasies, and behaviors. Through covert sensitization, material that was once linked to pleasurable consequences becomes associated with aversive consequences, thereby breaking down a key factor contributing to the maintenance of the paraphilia.

Another treatment technique for altering deviant sexual arousal patterns is masturbatory extinction (sometimes referred to as masturbatory satiation or orgasmic reconditioning; Alford, Morin, Atkins, & Schoen, 1987; Marshall,

1979). Although there are variants of this technique (e.g., Davison, 1968), this procedure usually entails having the patient masturbate to orgasm in the presence of appropriate sexual stimuli (e.g., videos of heterosexual intercourse). Following orgasm, the patient is instructed to masturbate for protracted periods of time (often 1 hour or more) in the presence of stimuli depicting his deviant sexual behavior (e.g., for Albert, pictures of unclothed, prepubescent females). That the patient has just reached orgasm prevents him from becoming sexually aroused to the deviant stimuli. As per principles of learning (classical or operant conditioning), the repeated pairing of the patient's typical deviant stimuli in the absence of sexual arousal breaks the association between the paraphilic material and arousal (a process referred to as extinction). In addition to extinguishing arousal responses to deviant stimuli, these procedures may help establish appropriate sexual arousal patterns because they involve the repeated pairing of sexual arousal and orgasm to material depicting normal sexual behavior.

COURSE OF TREATMENT
AND TREATMENT OUTCOME

Beginning in the first session and continuing throughout treatment, Albert was provided self-monitoring forms to record the frequency and intensity of normal and pedophilic sexual thoughts, fantasies, and behaviors. Prior to the first treatment session, a physiological assessment of sexual arousal patterns was conducted with penile strain gauge measures (Abel, Blanchard, Barlow, & Mavissakalian, 1975; Barlow, Becker, Leitenberg, & Agras, 1970). This assessment involved the presentation of videotapes depicting adult heterosexual activity and pictures of unclothed school-age girls. While Albert viewed these materials, his sexual response was recorded with a gauge designed to measure the circumference of his penis (i.e., his erectile response). The results of this assessment revealed a high level of responsiveness to pedophilic stimuli.

As noted previously, it was important first to address Albert's motivation for treatment because he displayed a strong tendency to rationalize his pedophilic activities. Albert was instructed to make a list of various specific rationalizations. He began working on these rationalizations at home. He was also asked to contemplate how his contacts were received by the girls and whether he was oblivious to any negative cues. It became apparent that he had established a strong boundary between "proper and improper" pedophilic behavior. For example, intercourse with a child or sexual coercion of a child was just as repugnant to him as it would be to most people. But Albert considered fondling breasts and genitals to be affectionate. Evidence for this rationalization was present in the following: (a) Albert reported that most children were very responsive to his advances; (b) his description of many of his episodes was objectified by his use of third-person speech; (c) he was very indignant over the angry manner with which most of his congregation responded to him after his discovery, thinking they were somehow ungrateful for all of his years of service to the parish (including his bishop, whom he accused of not providing appropriate support); and (d) he established boundaries between "good and bad" pedophilic behavior.

To break down some of these barriers, Albert was requested to consider two scenarios. First, Albert was asked how he would react if he had discovered that one of his daughters had been fondled or molested by a strange adult male. Initially, Albert digressed into problems of hypothetical questions but then replied that he had never considered that possibility and had probably blocked it out. In fact, in the remainder of the session he refused to consider the topic despite the therapist's subsequent attempts to introduce it. Second, in regard to the reaction of his parishioners, Albert was asked what his response would be if his bishop were discovered to have been raping women in the back alleys of the city for several years on Saturday nights. He was able to admit that his behavior was at least as repugnant as the hypothetical behavior of his bishop and that it would seem quite shocking indeed.

Thinking about these issues during and between the first several sessions sensitized Albert to several facets of his problem. Consequently, he was able to recognize, at least at a rational level, the horror that his behavior evoked in others and, by inference, the repugnant nature of the behavior itself. Nevertheless, he was now requested within sessions to imagine that his daughter was being molested and to picture it as vividly as possible. He was instructed to "feel it emotionally" and then report his reactions. Second, he was asked to imagine a similar situation in which he was engaging in genital contact with his most recent victim with all of the parishioners watching.

During this time, Albert was also given materials to read on the consequences of sexual abuse of children. In fact, he reported that he had been familiar with some of these materials before but had read them in a more abstract, intellectual manner. During the next several weeks, Albert reported that his masturbatory fantasies began to incorporate images of nameless, faceless people watching him and that his fantasies became fuzzy, much like static on a television set.

By the fourth session, Albert clearly began to experience some of the horror and aversiveness of his behavior and actually demonstrated some negative affect and a few tears. This was a marked change from previous sessions in which Albert displayed little or no emotion while discussing his behavior. Albert's self-monitoring records indicated that masturbation of any kind had stopped. At this point, steps preliminary to implementing covert sensitization were begun.

Detailed descriptions of Albert's behavior were obtained during the early sessions. Self-monitoring revealed infrequent pedophilic fantasies at this time. Most likely, the decrease in the frequency of his fantasies was related to the punishing effect of his recent discovery of the aversiveness of his pedophilic activities. Nevertheless, Albert's pattern of pedophilic behavior was fairly consistent. Typically, he would playfully approach a young girl who happened to be alone in a room at the church recreation center or perhaps in his car if he were driving her somewhere. Albert would then put his arms on her or around her and gradually move his hands to the breast area or, on occasion, the genital area. He would be very careful to ascertain if the girl was likely to be responsive beforehand and if she remained responsive during the encounter. If there was any sign of resistance or lack of responsiveness, Albert would quickly desist or revert to a wrestling or playing type of activity that did not involve breast or genital contact. On rare occasions, the same behavior might occur during the summer while he was swimming in a nearby lake.

In addition to these rather restricted behavioral patterns, Albert experienced urges upon seeing young girls in various locations. These urges ranged from a full-blown sexual thought sequence while watching a young girl to what he called a "glimpse," during which Albert was not aware of any frank sexual thoughts but would notice himself glancing at a young girl who was not directly in his line of sight and, therefore, represented someone who probably would not attract his attention if she were not the appropriate age and sex.

Because no deviant behavior was occurring at this time and because fantasies (sexual thoughts in the absence of young girls) were also absent, self-monitoring was restricted to "urges," defined as sexual thoughts, images, or impulses upon seeing a young adolescent girl. Albert recorded all sexual urges on a self-monitoring record that he was instructed to continue to carry with him at all times. The record was divided into daily segments in which he could total the number of full-blown urges and "glimpses" each day. Albert was instructed to record these urges and glimpses as soon as possible.

One further assessment procedure that precedes covert sensitization is the determination of the worst possible consequences of the behavior in the patient's own mind. Consistent with his reaction during the first several sessions of treatment, Albert reported that being observed while engaging in this behavior provoked a particularly strong negative emotional reaction in him. He also displayed some sensitivity to images of nausea and vomiting, which comprise a common set of aversive scenes in covert sensitization. If nausea and vomiting are not particularly aversive, scenes of blood and injury or of snakes or spiders crawling on one's skin can be very effective. With this information, Albert was ready to begin covert sensitization trials.

Prior to initiating covert sensitization, Albert was presented with a therapeutic rationale. After determining that Albert understood the rationale, the covert sensitization sessions were begun. Because Albert had identified being "caught in the act" or being observed by his family and close friends as perhaps the most aversive naturally occurring event he could think of and because he showed some sensitivity to nausea and vomiting, two aversive scenes were utilized throughout covert sensitization trials. The first scene entailed the following:

> Sit back in the chair and get as relaxed as possible. Close your eyes and concentrate on what I'm saying. Imagine yourself in the recreation room of the church. Notice the furniture . . . the walls . . . and the feelings of being in the room. Standing to one side is Joan (a 13-year-old girl). As she comes toward you, you notice the color of her hair . . . the clothes she is wearing . . . and the way she is walking. She comes over and sits by you. She is being flirtatious and very cute. You touch her playfully and begin to get aroused. She is asking you questions about sex education and you begin to touch her. You can feel your hands on her smooth skin . . . on her dress . . . and on her breasts under her shirt.
>
> As you become more and more aroused, you begin taking off her clothes. You can feel your fingers on her dress as you slip it off. You begin touching her arms . . . her back and her breasts. . . . Now your hands are on her thighs and her buttocks. As you get more excited, you put your hands between her legs. She begins rubbing your penis. You're noticing how good it feels. You are stroking her thighs and genitals and getting very aroused.
>
> You hear a scream! As you turn around you see your two daughters and your wife. They see you there—naked and molesting that little girl. They begin to cry. They are sobbing hysterically. Your wife falls to her knees and holds her head in her hands. She is saying "I hate you, I hate you!" You start to go over to hold her but she is afraid of you and runs away. You start to panic and lose control. You want to kill yourself and end it all. You can see what you have done to yourself.

The aversive scenes were presented in great detail in order to elicit arousal and to facilitate the imagery process. Initially, they were presented late in the chain of behavior (e.g., after Albert had begun to fondle the girl). As treatment progressed, the aversive scenes were introduced earlier into the arousing sequence (e.g., after Albert experienced the urge to touch the girl).

In addition to these scenes where Albert was caught by his family, other images involving nausea and vomiting were utilized. In these images, as Albert would begin genital contact with young girls, he was guided in imagery to feel himself becoming more and more nauseous: "Feel the nausea working its way up into your throat and as you begin to swallow hard to attempt to keep it down. You begin to gag uncontrollably until the nausea and mucus begins to spill out of your mouth and nose all over your clothes and the clothes of the young girl." In later sessions, this scene was embellished by having Albert imagine that he was continuing to vomit all over the lap of the young girl until the girl's flesh would actually begin to rot before his eyes and worms and maggots would begin crawling around in it. Although these embellishments are not effective with everyone, they were very effective with Albert. During these scenes, Albert would become visibly tense, rise in his chair, and be quite drained by the end of the session. In later sessions, Albert occasionally brought a fresh shirt for fear that he might actually vomit during the covert sensitization trial.

The initial trials allowed Albert to progress rather far into the chain of sexual behaviors before the aversive scene was introduced. However, in later sessions, the aversive scenes were introduced earlier in the arousing sequence. In this fashion, aversive scenes were paired with the very early parts of the chain, often the first glimpse, by the end of treatment. These scenes were presented to Albert in two different formats. In the first format, referred to as "punishment," the sexually arousing scene was presented and resulted in aversive outcomes. In the second format, described as "escape," Albert was instructed, in imagination, to begin the sexually arousing scene, briefly contemplate the aversive consequences, and then turn and flee the situation as quickly as possible, feeling greatly relieved and relaxed as he got farther away from the situation.

During this phase of treatment, a typical session usually involved presenting five of the scenes, either three punishment and two escape, or vice versa. The location of the scenes conformed to the typical locations that were relevant to Albert. The two aversive scenes would also be alternated in a random fashion or sometimes integrated or combined.

When Albert could imagine these images vividly and was fully processing the information, he was asked to go through the trial himself in the presence of his therapist. Methods for overcoming difficulties in achieving clear images were discussed and practiced. The self-administered practices within sessions were interspersed with therapist-conducted trials. After several sessions, when it was clear that Albert could self-administer the procedure as effectively as his therapist, homework was assigned. Albert monitored the intensity of his self-administered sessions on a scale of 0 to 100, where 0 equaled no intensity whatsoever and 100 represented an intensity as vivid as real life. Albert rated his initial practice sessions in the 10% to 50% range. As time went on, Albert more consistently rated the practice sessions in the 50% to 70% range. Albert's therapist judged this range to be sufficiently intense to produce the desired effects. Initially, sessions were prescribed once a day in which he would be asked to imagine three scenes. After several weeks, this schedule was cut back to two practices a week in order to maximize the intensity.

During this time, self-monitoring revealed occasional urges and glimpses but still no fantasies or masturbatory activity. In fact, Albert had cut back on masturbatory activity shortly after his apprehension and ceased altogether just before treatment began. Nevertheless, occasional interviews with his wife, who remained extremely supportive, revealed some increase in sexual relationships, averaging two to three times per week. Both described these relationships as improved and entirely satisfactory.

At this time the final phase of covert sensitization was introduced. In this phase, Albert used the aversive images in real-life situations whenever an urge or even a glimpse occurred. Accordingly, Albert was instructed that any urge or glimpse should be immediately followed by an aversive image. Albert reported initial difficulties and then increasing facility in carrying out his part of the treatment, and he noted a gradual decrease in the number of urges and glimpses.

Rather early in the course of treatment, a community reaction to Albert's behavior threatened to disrupt progress. Although Albert had moved out of the rectory and away from the church, some of his family remained in his hometown. On occasion, Albert would return to town from his temporary residence to assist with some practical matters concerning an upcoming move that he and his wife were planning. He would also see a few old friends. During this period, a very ugly reaction to his earlier apprehension occurred in the community. Rumors circulated with very exaggerated accounts of his behavior and claims that he was living in another state simply to wait out the statute of limitations and avoid criminal charges. It was also rumored that he had stopped seeking treatment and had a cavalier attitude toward his problem. This community reaction, which also affected his family, had a serious impact on therapy. Brief but deep depression retarded his progress and forced the covert sensitization sessions to stop temporarily while the implications of the community reaction were discussed. In fact, Albert was deeply distressed by the incident, not only because of the vicious allegations but also because of the illusions he still harbored that the community, which had showed deep support and respect for him during his years of service, would somehow welcome him back with open arms once his treatment was completed. Only when Albert fully appreciated that this was not going to happen and began to make realistic plans about permanently relocating was he able to continue on with therapy.

Four months after treatment, his pedophilic urges had dropped to zero and remained there. At this time, Albert and his wife permanently relocated to another state, where he obtained work in a local hardware store. He would continue to commute approximately 5 hours each way for the remaining treatment sessions to attend one long session every 2 weeks. A full assessment was completed 6 months after treatment began. The results of this evaluation indicated an excellent treatment response. Treatment was terminated, with plans for the first follow-up session to occur 1 month later and then at decreasing intervals as indicated.

Periodic follow-ups were conducted during the ensuing 18 months. A full evaluation at that time, which included a physiological assessment with the penile strain gauge, revealed no return of pedophilic arousal patterns. This pattern of results was supported by lengthy interviews with Albert, as well as separate interviews with his wife. Both Albert and his wife reported a satisfactory adaptation to their new location, where Albert had worked steadily and productively for the same employer and had been asked to take on supervisory responsibilities. The marital relationship, if anything, had continued to improve during the past year. Albert had begun to engage in extensive volunteer activity in his community.

More than 2 years after this contact and nearly 4 years after treatment began, another follow-up visit confirmed that no pedophilic arousal patterns had returned. Albert continued to do extremely well in his new job and was now second in command of a small chain of hardware stores. He continued to be active in the community. The church continued to ignore his occasional letters asking for clarification of his status, and he had given up all hope of any return to even part-time duties. Nevertheless, Albert still hoped against hope that some day the church that he had served so long might at least lift the suspension and allow him to occasionally conduct religious services for his immediate family. Beyond that, Albert's thoughts centered on his day-to-day life in his new community and a distant plan of retirement with his wife somewhere in the South in another 10 or 15 years.

DISCUSSION

Although estimates of the prevalence of pedophilia are not available, surveys have indicated that 10% to 20% of people have been victims of sexual molestation as children or adolescents (Finkelhor, 1979; Lanyon, 1986; Mrazek, 1984). These studies indicate that girls are approximately twice as likely to be victimized as boys. Indeed, available data suggest that close to three-quarters of male abusers choose female victims exclusively, about one-quarter choose male victims, and a small minority abuse both sexes (Lanyon, 1986). The offender is usually a friend or relative of the victim. Usually, the molestation does not include physical violence; instead, the perpetrator often uses his authority as an adult to persuade the child to acquiesce to his sexual advances (Finkelhor, 1979). As is the case with the other paraphilias, pedophilia is diagnosed almost exclusively in males. Left untreated or if treated with nonspecialized interventions, the disorder runs a chronic course (Hanson, Steffy, & Gauthier, 1993); some evidence suggests that the average child molester has abused 73 victims (McCall, 1984). Whereas a person with paraphilia was previously thought to usually participate in one type of deviant sexual behavior, more recent evidence indicates otherwise. For example, in a large study of 561 nonincarcerated men with paraphilia, 89.6% had engaged in more than one type of paraphilic behavior (Abel, Becker, Cunningham-Rathner, Mittelman, & Rouleau, 1988); in fact, 37.6% of the sample had committed 5 to 10 different types of deviant sexual activities. Although Albert had an extensive abuse history (he had fondled at least 50 girls), fortunately he had participated in only one type of paraphilia (heterosexual pedophilia)—fortunate in light of recent evidence that multiple paraphilias are associated with poorer treatment outcomes (Maletzky, 1991).

Recall that Albert's diagnosis of pedophilia was assigned with the specifiers "sexually attracted to females" and "nonexclusive type" (versus "sexually attracted to males/both sexes" and "exclusive type," respectively). In addition to conveying a fuller diagnostic picture, this information has relevance for the course, treatment, and prognosis of the disorder. For example, although the scientific literature is not extensive on the long-term effectiveness of treatments for sex offenders (cf. Furby, Weinrott, & Blackshaw, 1989), the recidivism rate (frequency of committing more sexual offenses following treatment or criminal action) for persons with pedophilia involving a preference for males is roughly twice that for those who prefer females (American Psychiatric Association, 1994; although some studies have not observed differences in the recidivism rate between heterosexual and homosexual pedophiles, cf. Maletzky, 1991; Marshall & Barbaree, 1988). One study has indicated that, on the basis of penile strain gauge responses, males with a history of incest are, in general, more aroused to adult females than are males with pedophilia without a history of incest (Marshall, Barbaree, & Christophe, 1986). Although this was not the case with Albert, this study suggested that men with pedophilia and without a history of incest may be more likely to display a sexual arousal pattern that is exclusively focused on children. This information would be quite important in treatment planning because, in addition to decreasing arousal over children, therapy should focus on developing an arousal pattern for adults.

Though effective treatments such as the one described in this chapter are available for paraphilias, they are usually available only in specialized clinics. In addition to the techniques described earlier (e.g., restructuring rationalizations of deviant sexual behaviors, covert sensitization, masturbatory extinction), these treatment programs typically address interpersonal and familial aspects of the problem (Lanyon, 1986; Marshall, Eccles, & Barbaree, 1991). For example, social skills training is frequently used to treat sex offenders, given the high prevalence of social skills deficiencies in these patients, a characteristic that is, in the integrative model, a vulnerability factor for the development of paraphilias. This chapter focused on the application of covert sensitization in Albert's treatment, but effective treatments for paraphilias consist of several components, including cognitive, behavioral, and interpersonal and familial elements. In addition, these programs usually contain procedures aimed at relapse prevention (Laws, 1989; Marshall, Hudson, & Ward, 1992). Relapse prevention procedures are designed to assist the patient in (a) recognizing the early signs of urges to engage in deviant sexual behavior and (b) deploying a variety of self-control procedures (e.g., covert sensitization) before their arousal or urges intensify. Certain drugs (e.g., medroxyprogesterone, an anti-androgen drug [Depo-Provera]) are also available for the treatment of paraphilias. These medications produce drastic reductions in testosterone levels, thereby decreasing sexual desire and fantasy. Recent evidence indicates that these medications are used infrequently because most paraphilias are responsive to psychosocial interventions (Maletzky, 1991).

Whereas early studies examining the effectiveness of psychosocial treatments of paraphilia involved single-case experiments or very few patients, large sample outcome studies are beginning to appear in the literature. For example, Maletzky (1991) reported on the long-term outcome (patients were followed for as long as 17 years) of 5,000 sex offenders treated at the University of Oregon Medical School. In order to be deemed a "treatment success," the patient was required to meet the following criteria: (a) complete all treatment sessions, (b) evidence no deviant sexual arousal on any follow-up penile strain gauge evaluation, (c) report no deviant arousal or behavior at any time since the conclusion of treatment, and (d) have no legal record of deviant sexual activity, even if the activity was not ultimately substantiated. The percentage of offenders classified as treatment successes ranged from 71.7% to 100%. Treatment success rates of at least 90% were found for the following categories: zoophilia (sex with animals), obscene telephone calls, heterosexual pedophilia, exhibitionism, and public masturbation. Persons with multiple paraphilias (including men who had both heterosexual and homosexual pedophilia) or a history of rape had the poorest outcome. Similar outcomes have recently been obtained in large samples of adult (Pithers & Cumming, 1989) and adolescent sex offenders (Becker, 1990). Other factors Maletzky (1991) found to be associated with treatment failure included a history of unstable social relationships, an unstable employment history, and a strong denial that the problem exists. This last factor emphasizes why it was so important to address Albert's cognitive rationalizations prior to beginning covert sensitization. Had these issues not been addressed, then there would have been a strong chance that Albert would not have been compliant with other treatment initiatives, thereby severely jeopardizing the possibility of a favorable treatment outcome. In addition, Albert received deep and sustaining support from his family, not only during the initial crisis of being discovered but also throughout treatment. This support extended to at least some of his old friends in his community who were aware of his problem and, increasingly, friends that he met in his new community who, of course, were not aware of his problem. This support was very valuable to Albert and undoubtedly contributed to his positive and durable treatment response.

THINKING CRITICALLY

1. Although persons who have committed pedophilic acts are handled by the criminal justice system, pedophilia is nonetheless considered to be a form of mental disorder characterized by intense, uncontrollable urges to have sexual contact with children. Should the status of pedophilia as a mental disorder have any bearing on how persons with this condition are managed by the legal system? Why or why not? Do you agree that pedophilia is a mental disorder or do you believe it should just be regarded as a criminal act?

2. What factors do you believe are most important in the development of pedophilia and other types of paraphilias?

3. What do you believe accounts for the fact that persons with pedophilia often evidence a strong tendency to rationalize their behavior as being acceptable, sometimes showing no signs of remorse (as in the case of Albert)?

4. As in the case of Albert, psychophysiological assessment (penile strain gauge) is frequently used to monitor whether treatment has had an impact on the patient's deviant sexual arousal patterns. Do you believe that such assessments accurately characterize these patients' arousal patterns or do you think it is possible for patients to "fake good" on these evaluations (i.e., manipulate their erectile responses to indicate no arousal to pedophilic stimuli and sufficient arousal to appropriate cues)? Provide justification for your answer.

Alcohol Dependence

A t the time of his referral to the Psychology Service of the Veterans Administration Medical Center (VAMC), Steve Johnson was a 45-year-old divorced African-American man. Steve presented with an extensive history of prior treatments for alcohol abuse and dependence, all of which had been unsuccessful. Indeed, Steve's referral to the VAMC was mandated by the courts after a hearing on his recent charge of driving while intoxicated.

Steve presented to his first meeting with the psychologist at the VAMC as attractive, well-groomed, and highly intelligent. During this session, Steve appeared depressed, anxious, and somewhat irritable. Though he was restless and fidgeted frequently during the meeting, Steve was very quiet and spoke only in response to the psychologist's questions. Steve gazed fixedly at the psychologist throughout the session. Although his fixed gaze appeared hostile, Steve usually responded in an overly polite manner to the inquiries of the psychologist. While acknowledging that his motivation for treatment was largely related to his fear that he would not be permitted to drive again if his drinking did not change, Steve did cite some other reasons for initiating his contact with the VAMC. One reason related to the physical effects of his drinking. In addition to noting increasing difficulties with his memory, Steve reported a poor result from a recent physical exam indicating elevated liver function. Second, Steve stated that, under the influence of alcohol, he often became verbally abusive and occasionally physically abusive to his "wife," who had recently given Steve the ultimatum of "clean up or get out by the end of the month." Steve's "wife" was actually his ex-wife from his second marriage. Although Steve had received a divorce from her when he was 42, he had reconciled and resumed living with her and their child (age 12) a year after the divorce. Though they had not remarried, the couple had a second child (age 1½) since their reconciliation. Thus, Steve cited the problems that drinking had caused his wife as another important factor in his decision to seek treatment. Noting his unsuccessful prior attempts at curtailing his drinking, Steve told the psychologist, "I'm a failure, and my family doesn't care about me anymore." Indeed, much of Steve's negative affect in this session seemed to be related to the social effects of his drinking.

When asked about his current drinking patterns and associated symptoms, Steve reported that he drank 1 pint of vodka per day. Beginning in the mid to late morning, he kept the bottle of vodka by his side throughout the day, until he finished it off by early evening. Almost every night, Steve drank a six-pack of beer "so that I can sleep." In addition to this excessive intake of alcohol, Steve clearly showed signs of two other hallmark features of alcohol dependence: (a) tolerance (markedly diminished effect of alcohol [e.g., feeling "high"] with continued use of the same amount) and (b) withdrawal (unpleasant behavioral and physical effects from stopping or reducing the amount of alcohol that is ingested). In previous attempts to stop or cut back his drinking, Steve reported experiencing sweating, trembling, insomnia, anxiety, nausea, and restlessness. In some past instances, Steve had resumed his drinking to eliminate these unpleasant withdrawal symptoms.

Clinical History

Steve reported that he began drinking when he was 18 years old when he started his career in the military. For 17 years (between the ages of 18 and 35), Steve served as a chief steward on a ship in the U.S. Navy. To begin his military training in California, Steve was separated from his high school sweetheart whom he was dating at the time and married 5 years later (and divorced at age 26). Steve stated that his drinking was due mainly to feeling alone and homesick during this year on the West Coast. However, Steve recalled that his drinking was not abusive during this time: he drank primarily on weekends and during rest and recreation with his buddies.

However, Steve's drinking increased substantially at the age of 19 after the mysterious death of his mother. Steve reported that his father had an extensive history of being physically abusive to him and his mother. This abuse had been so brutal on some occasions that Steve continued to suffer the psychological effects of it (discussed later). Despite pleading repeatedly with his mother (with whom Steve had a strong and loving bond) to leave the household, she had remained with Steve's father and had continued to be a victim of occasional physical abuse. While Steve was completing a tour of duty on a ship in the middle of the Pacific Ocean, he learned from his father of his mother's death. Steve's father told him that she had died after "falling down the stairs." During this conversation, Steve discovered that his mother's death had occurred 3 months earlier. When asked why he had not been informed of his mother's death sooner, Steve's father replied that he had held off because he was concerned about upsetting Steve. Though Steve regarded the circumstances surrounding his mother's death as suspicious, police ruled the death accidental, and his father was never questioned about having a role in this incident.

After Steve learned of his mother's death, he began to drink more heavily and more frequently. He recalled that, during this time, he found alcohol to be "consoling" and useful in controlling his feelings of rage and sadness. In addition, Steve reported that he discovered that alcohol reduced the frequency of his nightmares and thus made him sleep better. When asked about these experiences, Steve related that the nightmares involved recollections of episodes of brutal physical abuse that were committed by his father, uncle, and paternal grandfather when Steve was between the ages of 6 and 16. Later, during the course of his treatment, Steve revealed that he had also been a victim of recurrent sexual abuse, perpetrated by his uncle (his father's brother). In addition to the recurrent nightmares, these experiences had led Steve to experience considerable generalized anxiety, social withdrawal, distrust of others, and avoidance of his family of origin. Even at the time of his first visit to the Psychology Service at the VAMC, Steve reported that much of his drinking was motivated by the reduction of the nightmares and associated symptoms (e.g., persistent anxiety) stemming from the memories of these experiences.

From the age of 19 on, Steve's drinking was problematic. His drinking typically worsened when at home on leave from the ship. While he was on duty, Steve began drinking after finishing his job responsibilities for the day. Steve also recalled that the frequency and amount of his drinking increased on the anniversaries of his mother's death and during the Christmas holidays. His alcohol use was a key factor in ending his first marriage. Steve's first wife was very concerned about how much he drank when he was home on leave. She had repeatedly threatened to leave him if he did not stop drinking. During one drinking episode, Steve responded to these threats by severely beating his wife. The following day she left him, taking with her their two daughters (who were aged 22 and 20 at the time of

Steve's first visit to the VAMC). At that time, as well as following his second divorce, Steve's drinking became heavier due to boredom and distress over living alone.

Steve's drinking also had serious negative effects on his military career. On five different occasions (at ages 24, 27, 34, and twice at the age of 35), Steve was ordered by the Navy to undergo detoxification and alcohol rehabilitation. Because none of these treatments resulted in lasting improvement, Steve was discharged from the military at age 35 because of his alcohol dependence. After his discharge, Steve made several attempts at outpatient treatment that resulted in periods of abstinence (the longest period was 14 months) and then resumption of heavy drinking, despite his continued belief that he could control his drinking and "be like everyone else—just have one or two drinks and stop."

Steve had not been steadily employed since his discharge. At the time of his first visit to the VAMC, Steve was unemployed but, given his strong interest and talent in painting, was taking classes part-time to earn a Master of Fine Arts degree. Soon after his discharge from the military, Steve had earned a B.A. degree in Culinary Arts and Science. However, his frequent absenteeism due to drinking prevented him from holding down a series of chef positions he had obtained after getting his degree. His unsteady employment created financial problems because the household of four (Steve, his ex-wife, and their two children) was living off his ex-wife's income (she was a legal secretary for a major law firm).

In addition to physical abuse and occasional sexual abuse, Steve grew up in a family characterized by extensive alcohol abuse and dependence. Steve's father, paternal grandfather, paternal uncle (the same uncle who sexually abused him), and three older brothers either abused alcohol or were alcohol dependent (one of Steve's brothers was killed in the Vietnam War). In fact, Steve recalled that he did not drink when he lived with his family because he "didn't ever want to be a drunk like they were." Based on Steve's description, his father displayed symptoms of antisocial personality disorder in addition to alcoholism. Steve's father was an accomplished jazz musician who traveled extensively and was therefore not home for more than a week per month. When his father was at home, however, Steve characterized him as a "strict disciplinarian" and "inaccessible." Besides battering Steve and his mother, his father had numerous extramarital affairs throughout Steve's childhood.

Despite these problems in the family, Steve excelled in school. Although he did have a few friends, Steve was somewhat of a loner who enjoyed solitary activities such as reading, painting, drawing, and gourmet cooking. During adulthood, Steve's social withdrawal increased as a function of his adjustment difficulties stemming from past physical and sexual abuse and the effects of his persistent and excessive drinking.

DSM-IV Diagnosis

On the basis of this information, Steve was assigned the following DSM-IV diagnosis:

Axis I	303.90	Alcohol dependence, with physiological dependence (principal diagnosis)
	309.81	Posttraumatic stress disorder, chronic
Axis II	V71.09	No diagnosis on Axis II
Axis III		Elevated liver function
Axis IV		Unemployment, inadequate finances, discord with significant other
Axis V		Global assessment of functioning = 48 (current)

Steve's history and presentation to the VAMC were consistent with the DSM-IV definition of alcohol dependence (American Psychiatric Association, 1994). The DSM-IV makes a distinction between *alcohol dependence* and *alcohol abuse* (i.e., they are separate diagnoses in DSM-IV). The diagnosis of alcohol abuse may be appropriate if any of the following are evident as a function of recurrent alcohol use: (a) failure to fulfill major obligations at work, school, or home (e.g., frequent absences or poor performance at work); (b) use in physically hazardous situations (e.g., drinking and driving); (3) legal problems (e.g., arrests for alcohol-related disorderly conduct); and (4) continued use despite its causing or increasing social or interpersonal problems (e.g., arguments with spouse about consequences of intoxication). Because Steve showed each of these features when he first arrived at the VAMC, you might wonder why he did not receive a diagnosis of alcohol abuse. However, the DSM-IV specifies that alcohol abuse is not assigned as a diagnosis when the person meets the criteria for alcohol dependence. The reason is that individuals who meet criteria for alcohol dependence, while displaying most if not all of the features of alcohol abuse, present with other important symptoms: (a) *tolerance,* a need for markedly increased amounts of alcohol to achieve intoxication or the desired effect, or a markedly diminished effect with continued use of the same amount of alcohol, and (b) *withdrawal,* the characteristic syndrome resulting from cessation of alcohol use that had been heavy and prolonged (including symptoms of accelerated heart rate, sweating, hand tremor, nausea, agitation, anxiety, and sometimes hallucinations and seizures) or the recurrent ingestion of alcohol to relieve or avoid symptoms of withdrawal.

Although tolerance and withdrawal are considered to be the defining features of alcohol dependence that are useful in differentiating the disorder from alcohol abuse, DSM-IV specifies that these features do not have to be present in order to assign the diagnosis of alcohol dependence. Instead, this diagnosis can be assigned if three or more of the following features are present: (a) alcohol is often taken in larger amounts or over a longer time period than was intended; (b) persistent desire or unsuccessful efforts to cut down or control use of alcohol; (c) a great deal of time is spent in activities necessary to obtain or use alcohol or to recover from its effects; (d) important social, occupational, or recreational activities are given up or reduced because of use of alcohol (e.g., Steve was unemployed and was taking only one college course due to his drinking); and (e) alcohol use is continued despite knowledge of physical or psychological problems that are caused or increased by its use (e.g., continued drinking despite medical evidence of ulcer or, in Steve's case, elevated liver function). The case description presented earlier in this chapter showed that Steve possessed each of these features at the time of his first visit to the VAMC. You may also note that when Steve was assigned the diagnosis of alcohol dependence, it was given with the specifier "with physiological dependence." Under DSM-IV, this specifier is included in the diagnosis if symptoms of tolerance or withdrawal are present. If the criteria for alcohol dependence are met in the absence of symptoms of tolerance or withdrawal, the specifier "without physiological dependence" is appropriate.

The nature and treatment of alcohol dependence are presented in more detail in the remainder of this chapter. Steve's additional diagnosis of post-traumatic stress disorder is discussed in Case 4.

CASE FORMULATION USING
THE INTEGRATIVE MODEL

As with the other disorders discussed in this book, the integrative model of alcohol dependence is a diathesis-stress model emphasizing both biological and psychological factors (Barlow & Durand, 1999). Part of the diathesis component of this model is biological vulnerability. Indeed, both twin and adoption studies have indicated that genetic factors play a role in alcoholism (e.g., Cloninger, Bohman, & Sigvardsson, 1981; Goodwin, 1979; Kendler, Heath, Neale, Kessler, & Eaves, 1992). This was clearly evident in Steve, who had an extensive history of alcoholism in his family.

Exactly how these genetic influences contribute to the development of alcoholism are multifold. For instance, some persons may inherit a greater sensitivity to the effects of alcohol. Some evidence indicates that those at risk for developing alcoholism (e.g., offspring of people with alcohol dependence) are more sensitive to the initial euphoric effects of drinking and less sensitive to the depressant effects that occur for several hours after this initial and transient "high" (Newlin & Thomson, 1990; Schuckit, 1994). Because they experience these highs more extensively and because they escape the lows, these individuals may be more susceptible to continued drinking. In addition, genetic factors may be manifested in a person's ability to metabolize alcohol more quickly, thereby tolerating higher and more dangerous amounts of the drug. Remember, however, that these are theories of "vulnerability" in that these factors make one more likely to develop alcoholism but not guarantee it.

Besides these neurobiological factors, the integrative model of alcoholism specifies other forms of vulnerability. This vulnerability concerns the presence of preexisting emotional disorders. For example, persons with antisocial personality disorder (such as Steve's father, perhaps), a disorder characterized by the frequent violation of social norms, are thought to have lower levels of arousal than others, helping to explain why these individuals report minimal anxiety when confronting threatening situations (e.g., driving at high speeds) or when committing unlawful acts (Lykken, 1957). This factor may account for the increased prevalence of substance abuse in these individuals; in the absence of anxiety, a person may be more likely to engage in risky behaviors such as taking illicit drugs or drinking and driving. Moreover, as was discussed in Case 2, there is a high rate of co-occurrence (comorbidity) between the anxiety disorders and the alcohol use disorders (see Kushner, Sher, & Beitman, 1990, for a review). The association between these two types of disorders may be related to the use of alcohol to relieve anxiety. Recall in Case 2 that John Donahue developed problems with alcohol after he began using it to try to reduce the frequency of his panic attacks and associated symptoms (e.g., generalized anxiety). Similarly, Steve's alcohol use increased dramatically after hearing the news of his mother's death. Moreover, Steve stated that much of his ongoing alcohol use was to remedy his sleeping problems. However, the source of his sleep difficulties seemed to be his symptoms of posttraumatic stress disorder (i.e., nightmares of prior experiences of physical and sexual abuse). Thus, in the cases of both Steve and John, these preexisting anxiety disorders (posttraumatic stress disorder, panic disorder) appeared to contribute to the development and maintenance of alcoholism. But, again, we consider anxiety disorders only to be a vulnerability to developing alcohol abuse because they make abuse more likely. Many people with anxiety disorders do not develop alcohol abuse or alcohol dependence. Nevertheless, the role of anxiety and negative affect as triggers for increased drinking was further evident in Steve, who noted that he drank more after his marital separations and on the anniversary of his mother's death.

The integrative model states that factors other than these vulnerability dimensions must be present for alcohol abuse or dependence to develop. One of these factors is the extent of exposure to alcohol. The legal status of alcohol consumption helps to explain why the prevalence of alcohol use disorders is much higher than that of other substance use disorders (e.g., cocaine, heroin, hallucinogens). The extent to which a child or adolescent is exposed to the use of alcohol in the home may also contribute to their later use of the substance. Although Steve vowed he would never drink because he did not want to end up like the "drunks" in his family, his extensive exposure to drinking while growing up may have influenced his later use of alcohol. Similarly, one's peers can contribute to the onset of excessive drinking. As Steve recalled, he really began drinking with his Navy buddies.

Once a person uses alcohol repeatedly, reactions in the brain contribute to the development of alcohol dependence. Continued use of alcohol causes *tolerance,* which means that the person must ingest greater and greater amounts of the drug to experience the same effect. In addition, symptoms of *withdrawal* appear after continued use, which means that a person experiences negative physical responses when the substance is no longer taken. Steve recalled sweating, trembling, insomnia, anxiety, nausea, and restlessness during his previous attempts to stop or cut back his drinking. However, the withdrawal effects of long-term heavy drinking can be even more severe than Steve had experienced. At its most extreme, withdrawal can lead to alcohol *withdrawal delirium* (or delirium tremens or DTs), a condition that can produce frightening hallucinations and body tremors. The experience of withdrawal symptoms represents another potential maintaining factor of alcohol dependence. Specifically, consistent with Steve's history, many drinkers are motivated to continue drinking to reduce the intensity of the increasingly unpleasant negative feelings and symptoms that follow the use of alcohol.

In addition, cognitive factors often contribute to the maintenance of excessive alcohol use over time. Such factors include "alcohol myopia" (the inability to evaluate accurately the risks involved in continued drinking) and cognitive distortions pertaining to the positive effects of the drug or the presence of a drinking problem. For example, despite his ongoing alcohol dependence, Steve had always maintained the belief that he could control his drinking and "be like everyone else—just have one or two drinks and stop." Similarly, during the course of therapy (discussed later in this chapter), Steve was somewhat resistant to maintaining his abstinence because he believed that he was a better painter when he was under the influence of alcohol.

Treatment Goals and Planning

Because Steve was still using alcohol at the time of his first consultation to the VAMC (a pint of vodka and a six-pack of beer per day), the first treatment initiative was to discontinue his alcohol use. Given that Steve had a longstanding alcohol dependence, it was imperative that he be admitted to the VA hospital for detoxification to monitor and treat the very unpleasant and potentially dangerous symptoms of alcohol withdrawal that would inevitably arise upon his cessation of alcohol use. Knowing exactly what was to come from his five previous attempts to discontinue his alcohol intake after periods of prolonged and excessive use, Steve agreed to be admitted to the hospital for detoxification. After completing detoxification, the plan was to have Steve attend a relapse prevention group on a weekly basis. In addition, he would meet weekly with a psychologist at the VA for individual outpatient therapy.

The group that Steve was to attend targeted factors that are believed to be associated with triggering a "relapse" (the reinitiation of problem drinking). Based on the model of relapse prevention (Marlatt & Gordon, 1985), relapse is viewed as a failure of a person's cognitive and behavioral coping skills. This treatment involves identifying and challenging the patient's faulty beliefs concerning the use of alcohol (e.g., "I perform much better after I drink") as well as helping the patient confront the negative consequences of drinking (e.g., Steve's tendency to become violent when he was under the influence of alcohol). Situations in which the person is at greater risk for drinking are identified (e.g., in Steve's case, these situations might include times of boredom or getting together with his Navy buddies) so that these scenarios can be addressed (e.g., by staying clear of these situations or, if the situation must be confronted, preparing ahead of time by developing coping strategies to deal with urges or demands by others to drink). When incidences of relapse actually occur, the relapse prevention treatment is designed to help the patient view this occurrence as something from which they can recover, as opposed to viewing the episode as catastrophic and inevitably leading to more alcohol use.

While participating in the relapse prevention group, Steve would attend weekly one-on-one sessions with a VA psychologist. Given Steve's particular problems, these individual sessions would address such issues as stabilization of his mood (increasing positive affect while targeting areas contributing to his anxiety and dysphoria), skills to assist Steve in effectively managing his anger, and enhancement of Steve's repertoire of social skills while decreasing his tendency for social withdrawal. Because Steve's posttraumatic stress disorder (PTSD) also seemed to contribute to his motivation to drink (i.e., he would drink in attempt to reduce the symptoms of this disorder such as nightmares and sleep difficulties), Steve would be referred to a VA PTSD group upon completion of his individual treatment at the VA for alcohol dependence.

COURSE OF TREATMENT
AND TREATMENT OUTCOME

After completing a 3-week period of detoxification at the VAMC, Steve began attending individual treatment sessions with a VA psychologist. As noted earlier, Steve also attended a relapse prevention group during this time. At his first session of individual therapy, Steve's psychologist provided an overview and the ground rules of treatment. In addition to the typical ground rules (e.g., importance of attending sessions regularly and completing between-sessions homework assignments), Steve was informed that he would be asked to complete a Breathalyzer test at the beginning of each session to ensure that he was maintaining sobriety and to enhance his motivation to remain sober. Steve was upset to hear that he would be asked to submit to Breathalyzer tests; he saw the use of this procedure as a sign that the therapist did not trust him. The therapist reassured him that this procedure was routine and often a strong motivator for maintaining abstinence. During this session, Steve was given self-monitoring forms to record his mood daily (levels of anxiety, depression, and pleasantness) and the frequency and extent of his drinking and urges to drink.

In the first few sessions, Steve and his therapist completed a functional analysis of Steve's drinking patterns to identify the following aspects: (a) situations or emotions that trigger drinking episodes, (b) the patient's thoughts about drinking or about situations that lead to urges to drink, and (c) both the positive and negative consequences of drinking. The functional analyses made Steve aware that his urges to drink were often prompted by specific emotional states. In addition to anxiety related to memories of prior physical and sexual abuse (which would be addressed in a separate referral to a therapist with extensive experience in the treatment of PTSD), many of Steve's urges to drink were triggered by feelings of boredom or anger. The procedure also highlighted certain thoughts that Steve had about alcohol that contributed to his urges to drink. For example, Steve equated drinking with "having a good time," and he "deserved" to have a good time if he was bored or had been working hard all day. Moreover, Steve held the belief that drinking got his creative juices flowing, that he was a better painter when he was under the influence of alcohol. Thus, the functional analysis identified important targets for treatment.

This information was helpful in the sessions when Steve was taught coping skills to resist his urges to drink or avoid situations associated with a higher risk of drinking (e.g., when bored or when around others who were drinking). These urge-specific coping skills have five components. The first is self-statements to cope with the urge itself. For example, when Steve experienced an urge to drink, he was taught to remind himself, "My urge can't last forever," "I'm stronger than this urge," and "Just because I have an urge doesn't mean I'll drink." The second component outlined the negative consequences that drinking had caused in the past. For this part of urge coping, Steve reminded himself that drinking had resulted in such things as loss of jobs, discharge from the military, marital and family problems, memory and potential liver problems, DWI charges and fines, low self-esteem, financial trouble, and often feeling sick and hungover. Conversely, the third component specified the positive consequences of sobriety, which for Steve were better physical and emotional health, "wife and children enjoy being with me," saving money, thinking more clearly, doing better at school, getting more things accomplished, and no fights with family. The fourth component required

Steve to list alternative activities that would either distract him from an urge to drink or reduce the emotions that prompted the urge. Here, Steve listed the following: listen to jazz, paint, cook, do homework assignments, go out to dinner or see a movie with my wife, play with children, or exercise. The final component involved listing other food or drinks that Steve could consume to reduce his urge to drink alcohol. Steve suggested drinking tonic water, soda, or lemonade, or eating pizza, ice cream, or a piece of fruit. Steve was instructed to write down these five components on a "toolbox," which was actually a sheet of paper that he kept with him so that he would have ready access to it in the event of an urge to drink.

Also, because Steve's urges to drink were often triggered by feelings of boredom, the techniques of time management were discussed and used, particularly in the first several weeks after Steve's detoxification. Specifically, Steve was encouraged to plan each hour of the day in advance so that he kept busy and had no down time for feelings of boredom to develop. Time management also helped make Steve's mood more positive because it assisted him in getting more accomplished during the day (e.g., class assignments, cooking, activities with family, work around the house).

Next, Steve and his therapist addressed Steve's beliefs about alcohol that had contributed to his continued problems with drinking. From the functional analysis described earlier, it appeared that much of Steve's drinking was triggered by feeling bored and regarding alcohol as a relief from boredom and having a good time. The therapist assisted Steve in challenging his belief that drinking alcohol would provide him with a good time. Using the information that Steve had already generated for his toolbox to cope with urges to drink, the therapist challenged this belief by noting that the initial pleasant effects of alcohol (e.g., feelings of relaxation and mellowness) were short-lived and followed by a wide assortment of negative consequences (e.g., hangover, family conflict, loss of jobs). This thought was also challenged by helping Steve learn that he could experience a good time (a *better* time, at that) in many alternative activities such as painting, cooking, or going out for the evening with his wife. In fact, one helpful component of Steve's treatment was arranging for him to increase the number of pleasant activities he participated in. This strategy helped Steve reduce the negative emotions that had often led to urges to drink in the past and also emphasized to him the good time he could have in ways other than drinking (or as he later stated, "Good things and good times aren't going to come from a bottle of vodka").

Another example of the type of thoughts that Steve and his therapist addressed was Steve's belief that he was a better artist when he drank. This belief stemmed in part from a critical comment that Steve's art professor had made about one of his paintings. Through their discussion during the session, the therapist helped Steve realize that, of the 30 evaluations that his professor had made of his paintings, this comment was the only negative evaluation.

Thus, Steve was focusing on the 1 negative comment and dismissing all 29 of his professor's positive comments, as well as his classmates' positive reactions. Nevertheless, Steve was still concerned that his paintings were less natural, less daring, and more effortful since he became sober. Through some additional discussion with his therapist, Steve began to consider the possibility that in the past, when he was painting under the influence of alcohol, he was not concerned at all about artistic technique. His paintings therefore had lately been less "natural" and had taken more effort because he was trying to catch up on learning painting techniques he had disregarded in the past. However, a stronger challenge of Steve's belief that he was a better painter when he drank came from having several people (classmates and friends) evaluate a set of his completed paintings—half of which were painted when he had been drinking, the other half, when he was sober. To Steve's amazement, these people generally preferred the paintings that Steve had completed after his most recent detoxification (although Steve had not told them which paintings were done when). Based on this experience, Steve began to believe that the paintings he had completed when he was drinking were "gloomy" and had no depth or perspective. The belief that his paintings had improved since he became sober was supported later when Steve managed to sell a few of his works at a local art gallery.

Because anger had frequently precipitated Steve's drinking, the therapist addressed the techniques of anger control. Steve was told, as the first step in controlling anger, to learn to be aware of angry feelings as soon as they arise, before they grow and get out of hand. Hence, the therapist helped Steve become aware of the types of things that made him angry and the types of thoughts that Steve had in connection with these situations that led to anger. Steve was taught to use calming self-statements (e.g., "take a deep breath," "count to 10") and to identify and challenge thoughts that caused him to feel angry. For example, one day during the course of his treatment, Steve had a flat tire while driving and wound up spending a hundred dollars on a new tire and the cost of having the car towed. Initially, this situation provoked anger. Steve thought, "My wife was supposed to get the car serviced last Tuesday— she's so irresponsible." However, using the techniques of anger control, Steve first used calming self-statements. Once he began to simmer down, Steve challenged his initial thoughts by telling himself, "My wife has been busy— maybe she forgot to bring the car in" and "Even if the car had been serviced, I could have had a flat tire—maybe I ran over a nail or something." Because this situation had provoked an urge to drink, Steve had used his "toolbox" to cope with this urge, particularly emphasizing to himself the negative consequences that would result from having a drink.

As noted earlier, Steve exhibited a strong tendency to be socially withdrawn. This characteristic seemed partly attributable to the effects of chronic alcohol dependence and partly reflective of PTSD. Nevertheless, social skills training was addressed both in Steve's groups and in his individual therapy. This treatment component contained modules to address giving and receiving criticism, listening and conversation skills, providing positive feedback and compliments, conflict resolution skills, and assertiveness training. A detailed discussion of many of these aspects of social skills training is presented in Case 3, Adolescent Social Phobia. However, one facet that was specific to problems with alcohol was learning techniques for refusing offers to drink and resisting pressure to drink. Steve was told that usually these offers can be handled with a simple "No, thank you," but occasionally more direct, assertive behavior is necessary. In addition to refusing the offer of a drink, these techniques include (a) suggesting an alternative activity or beverage ("Let's go to a movie instead of a bar" and "No, thanks, but I will have a ginger ale"); (b) changing the subject to avoid getting into a discussion about drinking; (c) avoiding excuses ("I can't drink because I'm taking medication right now") or vague answers ("Maybe later"); and (d) in response to persons who repeatedly pressure one to drink, directly request that they not offer drinks in the future (e.g., if the person says, "Oh, come on, just have one drink for friendship," respond by saying "If you want to be my friend, then don't offer me a drink"). As with other aspects of social skills training, these behaviors were shaped in the therapy session through role playing so that Steve could practice and get feedback on his ability to respond to this situation effectively. (For a more detailed discussion of role playing, see Case 3.)

Although Steve continued to attend group meetings at the VAMC (as well as Alcoholics Anonymous meetings, which he began attending at the VAMC 8 weeks after he completed detoxification), Steve and his therapist agreed to terminate his individual therapy after the 22nd session. At this time, Steve had maintained his abstinence. In fact, in his last individual therapy session Steve confessed that the routine Breathalyzer tests he had resisted at first were a big motivation for him to remain sober during the first few months after his detoxification. Although he still had mild memory problems, Steve was heartened to learn that his recent liver tests were within normal limits. Steve reported that his problems with sleeping had improved over the course of treatment; however, he still experienced nightmares on occasion, as well as other PTSD symptoms (e.g., distress over seeing scenes of violence on television). Therefore, the original plan for a referral for PTSD treatment was carried out. Steve also stated that treatment—and his continuing sobriety—had resulted in a "much improved" family life: He was spending much more time with his children and wife and he no longer exhibited tendencies toward domestic violence. However, at the end of his individual treatment sessions, Steve could still be best described as a "loner" who had made few friends outside a few contacts he had established with fellow patients attending the relapse prevention group. Nevertheless, around this time Steve was finishing his Master of Fine Arts degree and beginning to search for jobs as an instructor of art.

Psychologists at the VAMC continued to monitor Steve's progress over the next 2 years. Over this time, Steve reported one drinking episode: He drank four vodka and tonics at his daughter's wedding. Steve responded to this slip by contacting the psychologist he had seen for individual treatment. Three "booster" sessions were scheduled to address this slip and to review certain aspects of treatment (e.g., urge coping skills). Steve otherwise maintained his abstinence despite several other urges to drink that were usually triggered by a flare-up in his PTSD symptoms, particularly at the beginning of his PTSD treatment sessions when he was required to confront the most distressing memories of his past physical and sexual abuse (a treatment technique referred to as imaginal exposure; see Case 4 for a discussion). Shortly after receiving his M.F.A., Steve found a position as an art instructor at a local community college. Consequently, he noted that his family's finances had been much improved.

DISCUSSION

Recent estimates indicate that about 10% of people in the United States experience some problems with drinking alcohol. About 10.5 million adults are considered to meet criteria for alcohol dependence (McCreery & Walker, 1993). Other estimates indicate that about 8% of the adult population in the United States have had alcohol dependence in their lives and about 5% have had alcohol abuse (American Psychiatric Association, 1994). Studies indicate that men are more likely than women to drink alcohol and to drink heavily (U.S. Department of Health and Human Services, 1990). Men seem most vulnerable to drinking problems when they are between the ages of 18 and 29. Approximately 14% of males in this age group report symptoms of alcohol dependence, and 20% report some negative drinking-related consequences (U.S. Department of Health and Human Services, 1990). Steve's racial group (African-American) has been found in studies (e.g., U.S. Department of Health and Human Services, 1990) to be associated with the highest rates of abstinence within the U.S. population (along with Hispanics and Asian-Americans) and the lowest rates of heavy drinking (along with Asian-Americans); however, in the DSM-IV, it is asserted that whites and African-Americans have nearly identical prevalence rates of alcohol dependence and alcohol abuse.

The negative effects of chronic alcohol use are numerous. In addition to the heightened comorbidity rate with other emotional problems such as the anxiety disorders, discussed earlier in this chapter, the alcohol-related disorders are associated with increased risk for accidents, violence, and suicide. Half of all highway fatalities involve either a driver or a pedestrian who has been drinking. Numerous studies have found that people who commit violent acts such as murder, rape, and assault are often intoxicated at the time of the crime (U.S. Department of Health and Human Services, 1990). These statistics should not be interpreted as indicating that alcohol *causes* violent behavior, but alcohol may contribute to aggression by reducing fear of punishment or impairing a person's ability to think through the consequences of acting impulsively. This seemed to be the case for Steve, whose aggressive acts toward his wives were confined to instances when he was under the influence of alcohol. Consistent with recent research evidence (O'Farrell & Murphy, 1995), Steve no longer displayed tendencies toward family violence after his successful treatment for alcohol dependence.

Moreover, long-term heavy alcohol use has been linked to many medical complications, particularly those involving the gastrointestinal tract, cardiovascular system, and central and peripheral nervous systems. Gastrointestinal effects include gastritis, ulcers, and, in about 15% of heavy alcohol users, liver cirrhosis and pancreatitis. Steve was developing elevated liver function at the time of his first visit to the VAMC. Cardiovascular effects include low-grade hypertension and elevated risk of heart disease. Nervous system effects include severe memory impairment (which Steve had begun to show signs of), dementia, and Wernicke's disease (manifested by confusion, loss of muscle coordination, and unintelligible speech). Pregnant women who abuse alcohol are at risk for delivering babies with fetal alcohol syndrome, a condition in which the baby has cognitive deficits, behavior problems, learning difficulties, and, in many cases, alterations in facial appearance (Phelps & Grabowski, 1992).

Unlike many of the disorders covered in this book, the long-term success of treatments, both psychosocial and biological (drugs), is quite limited. Indeed, studies indicate that only 20% to 30% of patients are able to maintain abstinence or nonproblematic levels of drinking over the long term. The most popular biological treatment for alcohol dependence is the drug disulfiram (Antabuse). A person who has been taking this drug experiences the effects of alcohol as very unpleasant, leading to feelings of nausea. The rationale for Antabuse is that by associating alcohol with the feelings of illness produced by the physical interaction of Antabuse and alcohol, the patient will subsequently avoid using alcohol. However, noncompliance is a significant limitation to the usefulness of this intervention because avoiding Antabuse for a few days is sufficient for a person to begin drinking again (Nathan, 1993).

The most popular psychosocial treatment for alcoholism is Alcoholics Anonymous (AA). The AA program, delivered in a group format, is based on the assumption that alcoholism is a disease and that persons with alcoholism must acknowledge their addiction and the fact that their addiction is more powerful than they are. Moreover, AA possesses a strong religious component: Persons attending AA meetings are encouraged to look to God to pray in order to have their "shortcomings" removed. Despite the enormous popularity of AA as a treatment for alcohol dependence over the past 60 years (Nathan, 1993), very few scientific studies have evaluated its effectiveness. What data do exist indicate that, although AA can be an effective treatment for some people with alcoholism, a very large number of people who contact AA for their drinking problems ultimately drop out of the program (50% after 4 months, 75% after 12 months; Alcoholics Anonymous, 1990).

In addition to the strategies described in Steve's treatment (Monti, Abrams, Kadden, & Cooney, 1989), another cognitive-behavioral treatment of alcohol dependence is controlled drinking (Sobell & Sobell, 1978), which has been very controversial because its philosophy is counter to other established treatments such as AA that champion complete abstinence. The notion behind this treatment approach is that at least some persons with alcoholism may be capable of becoming "social users" who do not relapse. Despite the controversy and the opposition to its use, research has indicated that controlled drinking is at least as effective as abstinence approaches (e.g., Marlatt, Larimer, Baer, & Quigley, 1993). However, this statement should be tempered by again noting that the long-term outcomes of alcoholism treatments of any form are modest at best.

Finally, researchers have disagreed about the best setting for the treatment of alcohol dependence. Indeed, the relative effectiveness of inpatient versus outpatient rehabilitation is one of the more actively debated issues in alcoholism treatment (Institute of Medicine, 1989). However, recent evidence indicates that day hospitals and other forms of outpatient treatment are as effective as inpatient treatment for most persons with alcohol dependence (McKay, Alterman, McLellan, Snider, & O'Brien, 1995; Miller & Hester, 1986). This finding is quite important given that outpatient treatment can cost 90% less than inpatient treatment, which often exceeds fifteen thousand dollars (cf. Miller & Hester, 1986).

THINKING CRITICALLY

1. Often, the DSM-IV diagnosis of alcohol abuse is not straightforward in college students, given the prevalence and social acceptance of binge drinking in this group (e.g., frequent fraternity or tailgate parties). Based on the DSM-IV definitions provided in this case, how would you differentiate such drinking patterns from alcohol abuse? At what level does such drinking cross over to the DSM-IV diagnosis of alcohol abuse?

2. How important do you believe a person's familial and social environment is to the long-term success in overcoming alcohol dependence? Why? What factors do you think could contribute most to a relapse of problem drinking? Do you think that a person who has been treated for alcohol dependence should ever consider having an occasional drink? Why or why not?

3. What do you think accounts for the strong racial and ethnic differences in the prevalence of abstinence and heavy drinking? What factors do you believe underlie the finding that while alcohol use is quite prevalent in some cultures (e.g., certain countries in Europe), alcohol dependence is rare?

4. Anxiety and mood disorders often co-occur with alcohol abuse and dependence. Why do you think this is the case? Do you think anxiety and mood disorders are more likely to occur before or after the onset of alcohol abuse or dependence? Why?

Borderline Personality Disorder

obin Henderson was a 30-year-old married Caucasian woman with no children who lived in a middle-class urban area with her husband. Robin was referred to a clinical psychologist by her psychiatrist. The psychiatrist had been treating Robin with pharmacotherapy (primarily antidepressant medication) for more than 18 months. During this time, Robin had been hospitalized at least 10 times (one hospitalization had lasted 6 months) for treatment of suicidal ideation (and one near-lethal suicide attempt) and numerous instances of suicidal gestures, including at least 10 instances of drinking Clorox bleach and self-inflicting multiple cuts and burns.

Robin was accompanied by her husband to the first meeting with the clinical psychologist. Her husband stated that both he and the patient's family considered Robin too lethal to be outside a hospital setting. Consequently, he and her family were seriously contemplating the viability of securing long-term inpatient care. However, Robin expressed a strong preference for outpatient treatment, although no therapist had yet appeared to be willing to take her as an outpatient case. The clinical psychologist agreed to accept Robin into therapy, so long as Robin committed to work toward behavioral change and stay in treatment for at least 1 year; the therapist later pointed out repeatedly that this also meant that Robin agreed not to attempt suicide.

Clinical History

Robin was raised as an only child. Both her father (who worked as a salesman) and her mother had histories of depression and alcohol abuse. Although the therapist did not learn of this until well into therapy, Robin had suffered severe physical abuse by her mother throughout childhood. When Robin was 5, her father began sexually abusing her. Although the sexual abuse had been nonviolent for the first several years, her father's sexual advances became physically abusive when Robin was about 12 years old. These abuses continued through Robin's first years of high school.

Beginning about age 14, Robin had difficulties with alcohol abuse and bulimia nervosa (see Cases 13 and 10, respectively). In fact, Robin met her husband at an Alcoholics Anonymous meeting while she was attending college. Robin continued to show symptoms of these two disorders (intermittent alcohol binges, restriction of food intake followed by eating binges), as well as the symptoms of major depressive disorder, at the time of her first visit with the clinical psychologist. Despite these difficulties, until she was age 27, Robin had been able to function well in work and school settings. She had earned her college degree and completed 2 years of medical school. However, during her second year of medical school, a classmate that Robin knew only slightly committed suicide. Robin reported that when she heard about the suicide, she immediately decided to kill herself as well. Yet, Robin had very little insight as to why the situation had provoked her inclination to kill herself. Within weeks, Robin dropped out of medical school and became severely depressed and actively suicidal.

A certain chain of events often seemed to precede Robin's suicidal behavior. This chain began with an interpersonal encounter, usually with her husband, which culminated in Robin feeling threatened, criticized, or unloved (usually with no clear or objective basis for this perception). These feelings were frequently followed by urges to either self-mutilate or kill herself, depending to some degree on how hopeless or angry Robin felt. Robin's decision to self-mutilate or attempt suicide was often accompanied by her thought, "I'll show you" ("you" being the person she believed was slighting her or abandoning her). At other times, these behaviors seemed related to Robin's sense of hopelessness or her desire to permanently end her emotional pain and persistent feeling of emptiness.

Similar to the experiences of Wendy Howe, who suffered from dissociative identity disorder (formerly called "multiple personality disorder"; see Case 7), these stressful interpersonal encounters occasionally led Robin to experience symptoms of dissociation (recall that, in DSM-IV, *dissociation* refers to disruption in a person's consciousness, memory, identity, or perception of the environment). Following her conscious decision to self-mutilate or commit a suicidal act, Robin would immediately dissociate and, at some later point, cut or burn herself while in a state of "automatic pilot." Consequently, Robin often had difficulty remembering the specifics of the actual act. At one point, Robin burned her leg so badly (and injected it with dirt to convince the doctor that he should give her more attention) that reconstructive surgery was required.

Although she had been able to function competently in school and at work, Robin's interpersonal behavior was erratic and unstable; she would quickly—and without apparent reason—fluctuate from one extreme to the other. She was an enigma to her few friends and family members. At times, Robin was personable and reasonable and behaved appropriately; at other times, she seemed irrational and enraged. After verbally berating her friends for no valid reason, Robin would become frightened and worried that she had alienated them permanently, which created a situation that Robin feared the most—feeling alone. Consequently, Robin would frantically do something kind for her friends to attempt to bring them emotionally closer to her.

As might be expected from her behavior, Robin had alienated many people. When friends or family members tried to distance themselves from her, Robin would either threaten to commit suicide to keep them from leaving her (thereby holding them hostage, in a sense) or beat them to the punch by ending the relationship abruptly.

Robin expected to have all of her needs met, yet she was unable to verbalize what those needs were. As mentioned earlier, when a friend disappointed her (e.g., canceled lunch plans), Robin would take this as a personal affront, feel unaccepted and unloved, and want to prove how much she needed them. She viewed people (including herself) as all good or all bad rather than seeing people as possessing a mixture of good and bad qualities. This polarity (sometimes referred to as *splitting*) was also evident when others commented on her competency (e.g., compliment her on her school performance). Because she would interpret such remarks as a sign that others viewed her as self-sufficient and gifted, Robin would react by showing them how incompetent she was (e.g., seek more reassurance for the quality of her work, demand extra study sessions) to prove to them that she needed their help and attention.

DSM-IV Diagnosis

On the basis of this information, Robin was assigned the following DSM-IV diagnosis:

Axis I	296.32	Major depressive disorder, recurrent, moderate
	305.00	Alcohol abuse
	307.51	Bulimia nervosa (in partial remission)
Axis II	301.83	Borderline personality disorder (principal diagnosis)

Axis III   None
Axis IV   None
Axis V   Global assessment of functioning = 28 (current)

Robin's presentation was consistent with the DSM-IV definition of borderline personality disorder (BPD; American Psychiatric Association, 1994). In DSM-IV, BPD is defined as a pervasive pattern of instability of interpersonal relationships, self-image, and emotions, as well as marked impulsivity, as indicated by five (or more) of the following features: (a) frantic efforts to avoid real or imagined abandonment; (b) a pattern of unstable and intense interpersonal relationships characterized by alternating between extremes of idealization and devaluation; (c) identity disturbance (i.e., markedly and persistently unstable self-image or sense of self); (d) impulsivity in at least two areas that are potentially self-damaging (e.g., spending, sex, substance abuse, reckless driving, binge eating); (e) recurrent suicidal behavior, gestures, or threats, or self-mutilating behavior; (f) emotional instability due to a marked reactivity of mood (e.g., intense episodic dysphoria, irritability, or anxiety lasting a few hours); (g) chronic feelings of emptiness; (h) inappropriate, intense anger or difficulty controlling anger; and (i) transient, stress-related paranoid thinking or severe dissociative symptoms. As stated in the criteria for all of the DSM-IV personality disorders, the features comprising BPD must be evident by early adulthood and present in a variety of contexts (e.g., not specific to certain situations) to be counted toward the diagnosis.

The nature and treatment of borderline personality disorder are discussed in more detail throughout the remainder of this chapter.

CASE FORMULATION USING THE INTEGRATIVE MODEL

As with many other types of personality disorders, the causes of borderline personality disorder (BPD) are not well understood (cf. Barlow & Durand, 1999). Existing data suggest that both biological and psychological factors play significant roles in the origins of this condition. With regard to biological factors, the results of almost 20 family studies indicate that BPD is more prevalent in families of persons with the disorder (e.g., Baron, Gruen, Asnis, & Lord, 1985; Links, Steiner, & Huxley, 1988; Zanarini, Gunderson, Marino, Schwartz, & Frankenburg, 1988). These studies have also discovered a high rate of mood disorders (e.g., major depression) in the families of persons with BPD, thereby suggesting that BPD is somehow linked or related to the mood disorders. In addition, the possible connection of BPD to the mood disorders is reflected by the fact that these conditions have overlapping symptoms (e.g., suicidal tendencies, feelings of emptiness). At any rate, although these family studies indicate that BPD may involve some traits that are inherited (e.g., impulsivity, intense emotional reactivity), there appears to be a great deal of room for the role of environmental influences in the development of this disorder.

One such environmental factor that has received considerable attention is the possible contribution of early trauma, especially sexual and physical abuse. Consistent with Robin's presentation, researchers have found that among women with a history of both BPD and parasuicidal behavior (which includes both suicide attempts and self-mutilative behavior), 76% report some type of childhood sexual abuse (Wagner & Linehan, 1994). Moreover, those women with a history of early sexual abuse were found to have engaged in more serious attempts to commit suicide. In addition to this study, several other studies have found that people with BPD are more likely to report abuse than are individuals with other psychological disorders (e.g., Goldman, D'Angelo, DeMaso, & Mezzacappa, 1992; Ogata et al., 1990). Given these findings, investigators have argued that BPD is similar to posttraumatic stress disorder (PTSD; Gunderson & Sabo, 1993; Herman, Perry, & van der Kolk, 1989). For example, you might recall from Case 4 that PTSD is often characterized by difficulties in the regulation of mood, impulse control, and interpersonal relationships, key characteristics of BPD. In both BPD and PTSD (as well as in dissociative identity disorder), the symptoms of dissociation are sometimes present (e.g., amnesia; a sense of numbing, detachment, or absence of emotional responsiveness). These observations seem to support the hypothesis that BPD may be caused by early trauma.

However, as you may have noticed from reading other chapters, a history of sexual or physical abuse is prevalent in, and has been implicated as a risk factor for, many disorders (e.g., posttraumatic stress disorder, dissociative identity disorder, bulimia nervosa). Thus, it is unclear why or if sexual or physical abuse is directly linked to the development of BPD. In addition, roughly 20% to 40% of persons with BPD have no apparent history of such abuse (Gunderson & Sabo, 1993), thereby highlighting the fact that a history of sexual or physical abuse is not necessary to produce BPD.

Linehan (1993) has emphasized a particular environment that is necessary for the development of BPD. In her model, the crucial developmental circumstance is the "invalidating environment," which is defined by the parents' tendency to negate or respond erratically and inappropriately to the child's emotions or private experiences. According to this model, patients with BPD had childhoods in which their emotional responses or interpretations of events are often reacted to by family members as invalid responses to events; are punished, trivialized, dismissed, or disregarded; or are attributed to socially unacceptable characteristics such as overreactivity, inability to see things realistically, or lack of motivation or discipline. For example, in response to a child crying out of distress and frustration from trying to complete a difficult homework assignment, the parent says, "Stop acting like a baby—just sit down and finish your work." This trivializes and fails to acknowledge the basis for the child's distress and implies that the child is not disciplined. As a function of such a childhood environment, the person never learns how to label and regulate emotional arousal, how to tolerate emotional distress, or when to trust his or her emotional responses as reflections of valid interpretations of events. Thus, the person learns to mistrust internal states and instead scans the environment for cues about how to act, think, or feel. This general reliance on others results in a person's failure to develop a coherent sense of self. Impairments in the person's ability to develop and maintain interpersonal relationships are due to the fact that these goals depend on both a stable sense of self and a capacity to self-regulate emotions. Finally, the model views the invalidating family's tendency to trivialize or ignore negative emotion to be linked to an expressive style seen in patients with BPD, a style that vacillates between inhibition or suppression of emotions and extreme emotional and behavioral displays (e.g., the person who was shaped by the childhood environment to suppress emotions also learned that excessive emotions or behaviors, such as temper tantrums or impulsive acts, are the only way to solicit attention or help from significant others).

Treatment Goals and Planning

Robin was to be treated with a psychosocial treatment approach referred to as *dialectical behavior therapy* (Linehan, 1993; Linehan & Kehrer, 1993). In this treatment, the following symptoms and goals are targeted: (a) life-threatening and suicidal behaviors, including parasuicidal episodes (*parasuicidal acts* refer to any intentional self-injurious behavior with or without suicidal intent, including both suicide attempts and self-mutilative behaviors); (b) behaviors that interfere with treatment (e.g., noncompliance or premature dropout); (c) behavioral patterns that have a severe effect on quality of life, including those that necessitate inpatient psychiatric care (e.g., substance abuse, binge eating or food intake restriction); and (d) increasing general coping and social skills. To address these issues, dialectical behavior therapy combines weekly individual therapy sessions with psychoeducational skills training groups. In individual therapy, motivational issues are given the primary focus, including the patient's motivation to stay alive. Much of the individual sessions are spent with crisis intervention and management, and the specific session agenda is dictated by the patient's behavior (or crises) since the previous session. Thus, in these weekly sessions patients are provided with support and are taught how to identify and regulate their emotions. When appropriate, patients receive a treatment similar to that used for people with posttraumatic stress disorder; prior traumatic events are reexperienced to help reduce the fear associated with them (see Case 4).

In dialectical behavior therapy, group therapy sessions are held weekly with each lasting 2 to 2½ hours. In contrast to individual therapy, in which the session agenda is determined primarily by the problem (or crisis) at hand to be solved, group therapy follows a predetermined schedule of skills to be taught. Thus, group skills training is more highly structured than individual therapy. Half of the session is devoted to review of homework practice of skills being taught, and the other half is devoted to presenting new skills. Areas addressed in group treatment include those to improve social skills and methods of identifying and regulating emotional reactions.

COURSE OF TREATMENT
AND TREATMENT OUTCOME

Shortly into treatment, Robin reported that she felt that she could no longer keep herself alive. When reminded of her previous commitment to stay alive for 1 year of therapy, Robin replied that things had changed and she could not help herself. From this session forward, almost every therapy session for the next 6 months revolved around the topic of whether (and how) to stay alive versus committing suicide. Robin began to come to sessions wearing mirrored sunglasses and would slump in her chair or ask to sit on the floor. Questions from the therapist were often met with minimal comment or long silences. In response to the therapist's attempts to discuss prior suicidal behavior, Robin would become very angry and withdraw. Occasionally, Robin would display marked dissociative reactions during the therapy session. During these reactions, Robin appeared unable to concentrate on or hear much of what was being said. She described these experiences as feeling "spacy" and distant. Robin stated that she felt that she could no longer engage in many activities, such as driving, working, or attending school. Overall, she viewed herself as incompetent in all areas.

Through the use of self-monitoring (Robin's daily recordings of her symptoms), the therapist carefully monitored Robin's suicidal ideation, misery, and urges to self-harm as well as actual parasuicidal acts. An important focus of therapy was to identify the sequence of events that led up to and followed Robin's suicidal behavior. As noted earlier in this chapter, Robin's suicidal acts were often triggered by her feelings of being criticized, unloved, or abandoned following a negative interpersonal encounter (often with her husband). At every point, the therapist told Robin that, given its strength, her parasuicidal behavior was to be expected but was ultimately beatable. The therapist also pointed out that if Robin succeeded at suicide, therapy would be over, so they had better work really hard now, while she was alive.

Several months into therapy, a long-standing pattern of suicidal behavior leading to inpatient hospitalization was apparent. Robin would report intense suicidal ideation, express doubts that she could resist the urge to kill herself, and request admission to her preferred hospital. Or without warning she would cut or burn herself severely and require hospitalization for medical treatment. Any attempts to persuade Robin to stay out of the hospital or to leave before she felt she was ready typically resulted in an escalation of suicidal thinking. At this point, her psychiatrist would insist on her admission, or the hospital would agree to extend her stay. This pattern led the therapist to hypothesize that the hospitalization itself was reinforcing suicidal behavior. The therapist tried to help Robin understand how hospitalization might be strengthening the very behavior they were working to eliminate.

This issue became an intense point of disagreement in therapy. Robin viewed her therapist's position as unsympathetic and lacking in understanding. In her opinion, the intensity of her emotional pain made the probability of suicide so high that hospitalization was necessary in order to guarantee her safety. Robin supported her position by pointing out her dissociative reactions, which she reported as extremely aversive and apt to make her feel unable to function much of the time. From the therapist's perspective, the long-term risk of suicide created by repeated hospitalization in response to suicidal behavior was higher than the short-term risk of suicide if hospitalization stays were reduced. Nevertheless, Robin viewed these explanations as the therapist's direct attack on her. Although the therapist stood her ground on this matter (i.e., maintained her assertion that repeated hospitalization influenced Robin's chronic suicidal thinking), she compensated by doing three things: First, the therapist repeatedly validated Robin's experience of almost unbearable pain. Second, she repeatedly addressed Robin's dissociative symptoms by explaining them to be an automatic reaction to intensely painful affect. Third, the therapist frequently addressed the quality of the therapeutic relationship between her and Robin in order to strengthen the relationship and keep Robin in therapy, even though it was a source of even more emotional pain.

By the fifth month of therapy, the therapist began to worry that the current approach to treatment was going to have the unintended effect of killing Robin (via suicide). Thus, the therapist decided to arrange a consultation meeting in which Robin and all of her treatment providers (e.g., her current therapist, psychiatrist, staff from her preferred hospital, health insurance monitor) addressed Robin's hospitalizations. At the case conference, the therapist presented her hypothesis that hospitalization was reinforcing Robin's suicidal behavior. Also, she assisted Robin in making her case that the therapist was wrong. The therapist requested that a new system be agreed on to disrupt the relationship between Robin's suicidal behavior and hospitalization. A plan was therefore developed whereby Robin was not required to be suicidal in order to gain admission to the hospital. Under this new system, Robin could elect at will to enter the hospital for a stay of up to 3 days, at the end of which she would always be discharged. If she convinced people that she was too suicidal for discharge, Robin would be transferred to her least preferred hospital for safety.

Parasuicidal behavior would no longer be grounds for admission except to a medical unit when required. Although there was some disagreement as to whether hospitalization was reinforcing Robin's suicidal behavior, this system was agreed to by Robin and the consulting team.

After this consultation meeting, Robin's husband announced that he was no longer able to live with or tolerate his wife's suicidal behavior and that the constant threat of finding her dead had led to his decision to file for divorce. The focus of therapy then shifted to helping Robin grieve this event and find a suitable living arrangement. Robin alternated between fury that her husband would desert her in her hour of need (or illness as she put it) and despair that she could never cope alone. She decided that "getting her feelings out" was the only useful therapy. This led to many tearful sessions, with the therapist simultaneously validating the pain and cheerleading Robin's ability to manage without going back into the hospital. However, during this time Robin engaged in several alcohol binges, and she began to restrict her food intake severely. The reemerging symptoms of Robin's alcohol abuse and eating disorder became the immediate targets of therapy. In addition to trying to eliminate these symptoms, the therapist's strong attention to these behaviors communicated to Robin that that the therapist would take her problems seriously even if she was not suicidal. Nevertheless, due to these symptoms and Robin's high level of distress and suicidal risk, both she and her therapist decided that she would enter a residential treatment facility for a 3-month period. At the end of this period, the arrangement was for Robin to return to her home with a roommate.

Individual therapy sessions with the clinical psychologist continued during Robin's stay at the residential treatment facility. Following Robin's release from the facility, she resumed attending the weekly skills training group. Although Robin initially committed to attending the group for the first year of therapy, her attendance was quite erratic. She often missed entire sessions, or she left during the break. Robin usually responded to therapists' attempts to address this issue by stating that she could not drive at night due to night blindness. Although this behavior was considered to interfere with treatment and was addressed frequently over the course of therapy, this issue was not made out to be a major focus of treatment due to the continuing presence of higher priority suicidal behavior. In addition, the therapist's attempts to engage Robin in skills acquisition during individual therapy sessions were somewhat limited. Instead, these sessions often focused on attempts to strengthen the therapeutic relationship and to ensure that the relationship was not reinforcing Robin's suicidal or dissociative behaviors. Strategies to foster the therapeutic alliance included between-sessions therapist-initiated telephone calls to see how Robin was doing, routinely giving out telephone numbers when the therapist was traveling, and sending Robin postcards when the therapist was out of town.

During the 8th through 14th months of her therapy, considerable progress was observed in Robin. A few months after returning home from the residential treatment facility, Robin returned to school. Therapy focused on maintaining Robin in school and expanding her social network. In addition, therapy continued to focus on changing the factors that increased the risk of Robin's suicidal behavior, reducing emotional pain, and becoming more tolerant of distress. During this time, Robin's hospital stays were greatly reduced, as was the frequency of her parasuicidal behavior.

However, this period of improvement ended abruptly in the 14th month of Robin's treatment when she committed suicide by consuming an overdose of a prescription drug and alcohol. The primary trigger for this was Robin's telephone call to her estranged husband. During this call, Robin discovered that her husband was living with another woman. As she told her therapist during a phone call the next morning, Robin's unverbalized hope that they might someday get back together, or at least be close friends, had been shattered. Robin telephoned the therapist again that evening, in tears, stating that she just drank half a fifth of liquor. Such drinking incidents had occurred several times before, and thus the phone call was spent offering Robin hope, assisting her to see how she could indeed live without her husband, and contracting with her to agree to get through that evening to attend her therapy appointment the next day. Robin's roommate was home, and she agreed to talk with her, watch a TV movie together, and go to bed (plans she did follow through on). Robin stated that although she felt suicidal, she would stop drinking and would not do anything self-destructive until her therapy appointment. She was instructed to call the therapist back later that evening if she wanted to talk again. The next day, when Robin was not at her appointment, the therapist called her home just as her roommate discovered her dead, still in bed from the night before.

DISCUSSION

Borderline personality disorder (BPD) is one of the more common personality disorders. In DSM-IV, the prevalence of this disorder in the general population is estimated at about 2% (American Psychiatric Association, 1994); about 70% to 77% of persons with BPD are women (Widiger & Frances, 1989). However, because BPD is one of the most debilitating personality disorders, it is quite prevalent in psychiatric settings. In psychiatric settings, persons with BPD make up approximately 15% of the patient population, and about 50% of the people in these settings who have personality disorders have BPD (Widiger & Weissman, 1991).

Persons with BPD are likely to have additional emotional disorders. The mood disorders are quite common in patients with BPD; studies indicate that

24% to 74% of patients with BPD also have major depression, and 4% to 20% have a coexisting bipolar disorder (Widiger & Rogers, 1989). The eating disorders (bulimia nervosa, in particular) and BPD have also been found to frequently co-occur. For example, one study found that almost 25% of persons with bulimia nervosa also had BPD (Levin & Hyler, 1986). Substance abuse is also quite common in patients with BPD—up to 67% of these patients also receive a diagnosis of at least one substance abuse disorder (Dulit, Marin, & Frances, 1993).

As is illustrated in Robin's case, suicidal inclinations are a prevalent feature of BPD. From 70% to 75% of patients with BPD have a history of at least one parasuicidal act (Clarkin, Widiger, Frances, Hurt, & Gilmore, 1983; Cowdry, Pickar, & Davies, 1985). Recall that a *parasuicidal act* is defined as any intentional, acute, self-injurious behavior (with or without suicidal intent) and therefore includes both suicide attempts and self-mutilative behaviors. Suicidal threats and crises are frequent even among those patients who never engage in any parasuicidal behaviors. Although many patients who evidence parasuicidal behavior never kill themselves, roughly 5% to 10% of persons with BPD eventually commit suicide (Frances, Fyer, & Clarkin, 1986; Paris, Brown, & Nowlis, 1987; Stone, 1989).

The long-term course of BPD is variable. As is the case for some personality disorders (e.g., antisocial personality disorder), many people with BPD seem to improve when they reach their 30s or 40s (Stone, Stone, & Hurt, 1987). However, many persons continue to have difficulties into old age (Rosowsky & Gurian, 1992).

Very little research has been conducted on the development and evaluation of treatments for BPD. Many people with BPD may respond favorably to a variety of medications, including tricyclic antidepressants (Soloff et al., 1989; Stone, 1986), tranquilizers (Cowdry & Gardner, 1988), and lithium (Links, Steiner, Boiago, & Irwin, 1990). However, persons with BPD often have problems with drug abuse, compliance with treatment, and suicide attempts, and these features complicate efforts to provide safe and successful drug treatments.

Most studies of the effectiveness of psychosocial treatments of BPD have been descriptive in nature (e.g., Stevenson & Meares, 1992; Tucker, Bauer, Wagner, Harlam, & Sher, 1987); that is, these studies have described the outcome of a treatment for BPD without determining whether the treatment is more effective than alternative treatments or no treatment at all. One of the most extensive studies to evaluate a psychosocial treatment for BPD was conducted by Linehan and her colleagues. In this study, dialectical behavior therapy (the approach used in the treatment of Robin) was compared to "treatment as usual," which referred to general therapeutic support from any type of treatment that was available in the community. Forty-four female patients with BPD who displayed marked parasuicidal behavior were randomly assigned to either dialectical behavior therapy or community treatment. The treatment lasted 1 year with assessments every 4 months. During and at the end of this 1-year period, dialectical behavior therapy was more effective than community treatment as indicated by less frequent and less severe suicidal behavior, fewer treatment dropouts (only 16.7% in dialectical behavior therapy), and fewer days of inpatient psychiatric hospitalization (Linehan, Armstrong, Suarez, Allmon, & Heard, 1991). Compared to patients assigned to the community treatment condition, patients treated with dialectical behavior therapy showed significantly greater improvement on measures of anger and social adjustment (Linehan, Tutek, Heard, & Armstrong, 1994). These treatment gains were generally maintained during the 1-year follow-up period (Linehan, Heard, & Armstrong, 1993).

Although these findings need to be replicated and extended in future studies, the treatment developed by Linehan and her colleagues may help in easing the suffering of patients with BPD and the enormous burden that these persons place on their families and the health care system. Moreover, as was dramatically illustrated in Robin's case, some patients do not benefit at all from our existing treatments for BPD, and thus considerable work needs to be done to make these interventions more effective.

THINKING CRITICALLY

1. What factors do you think contribute to the finding that borderline personality disorder (BPD) is much more common in women than in men?
2. BPD is associated with an elevated suicide rate. What reasons do you believe account for the surprisingly high incidence of parasuicidal behaviors in these persons? What do you think are the best ways to respond to a person who displays suicidal gestures?
3. What similarities do you see in the features and risk factors of BPD and in the features and risk factors of dissociative identity disorder? Do you believe the similarities of these disorders are more prominent than their differences? Why or why not?
4. Do you think Robin's suicide could have been prevented? If so, how?

Case

15

Schizophrenia

A t the time of his admission to a private psychiatric hospital, Sonny
Ford was a 21-year-old single Caucasian man who lived with his
adoptive parents. Sonny had been referred for hospital admission
by his outpatient psychotherapist. Over the past 2 years, Sonny had
struggled with symptoms such as concentration difficulties, anxiety, and
obsessional thinking. More significantly, within the year prior to his admission, Sonny began to experience paranoid and delusional thoughts that had
become quite persistent. These difficulties started after Sonny smoked marijuana. While experiencing the effects of the marijuana, Sonny believed that
his mind had gone "numb." From that time on, Sonny believed that the marijuana had permanently "warped" his mind. Moreover, he had experienced
considerable distress and frustration over his inability to get others to agree
that the marijuana had this effect on him. More recently, Sonny had developed
paranoid concerns that the police and FBI were out to get him (persecutory
delusions). In addition, he had begun to feel that certain television shows had
special importance to him, in that information embedded in these programs
was directed especially to Sonny to remind him that he was at risk for some
sort of persecution by the authorities (delusions of reference; i.e., all events

that occurred somehow "referred" to Sonny). On a few occasions, Sonny also heard voices in his head (auditory hallucinations). Although he could not make out what they were saying, Sonny perceived the voices as angry and critical.

Over the past several months, Sonny's symptoms had worsened to the point that they were interfering substantially with his attendance at work as a state office janitor. Because of these factors, and because Sonny had not responded to outpatient treatment thus far, his outpatient therapist made the referral for hospital admission.

At the intake evaluation for his inpatient admission, Sonny's emotions were quite restricted. Although appearing very tense and anxious, Sonny's face was, for the most part, immobile throughout the intake. He engaged in very little eye contact with his doctors, and his body movements were quite constricted, with the exception of restless movements in his legs and the occasional rocking back and forth of his body as he sat in his chair. His speech was very hesitant and deliberate, and he often responded to the interviewer's questions with terse and empty replies. For instance, when the interviewer asked, "What difficulties are you having that you would like help for?" Sonny replied, "I think it was the marijuana."

Clinical History

Sonny was adopted at birth, and no records were available about the medical and psychiatric history of his family of origin. Sonny was raised in a household of four: In addition to his parents, he had a sister 4 years older who had also been adopted. He could recall very few memories from his early childhood. However, Sonny said that throughout his life he had always been a loner who, to this day, never had any friends. Sonny's parents, who were present at the time of his admission to the hospital, confirmed that Sonny had always been very frustrated by social interactions and added that their son had always been hypersensitive to real or perceived criticism during his school years. They also noted that Sonny had great difficulty at college in classes that required some form of oral presentation or class participation. Sonny was very attached to his father and, for many years, experienced considerable distress and loneliness when he was separated from the family's home or his father for extended periods. Whereas Sonny regarded his father to be very understanding and accepting, he later described his mother as "not accepting of me as a person." Sonny claimed that his mother, with her excessively critical demeanor, had significantly affected his self-esteem in a negative way. Sonny also claimed that his mother was an alcoholic, a statement that was not upheld by either of his parents.

When Sonny was approximately 16, he began to realize that he had a homosexual preference. Although his father had been accepting,

Sonny reported that his mother had been very unaccepting of his homosexuality and had often referred to him with pejorative labels such as "fag." While Sonny had accepted his sexual orientation, he said that being gay had caused him many troubles in that the lifestyle was a difficult one that could often be lonely. Many of Sonny's current obsessive thoughts pertained to persistent thoughts about the possibility of having contracted the HIV virus from having unprotected sex on one occasion. Sonny's fears of having HIV had not been allayed by the fact that the person with whom he had sex did not have HIV or by the fact that all of his recent HIV testing was negative.

Despite his lifelong difficulties with social adjustment, Sonny had been able to meet most of the demands and responsibilities of adolescence. Following his graduation from high school (with a C+ grade average), Sonny decided to attend a local college to take introductory courses. This decision was strongly influenced by his apprehension of moving out of his parents' house to attend a school away from his immediate community. However, it was during his freshman year of college that Sonny had smoked the marijuana that he believed had permanently damaged his brain. Following this incident, Sonny's functioning worsened steadily. He dropped out of college but later enrolled in a different local college. Sonny took classes at the second school for only one semester before dropping out once again, because of his inability to cope with sitting in crowded classrooms and completing required assignments and tests. Over the 2 years preceding his referral to the psychiatric hospital, Sonny had experienced considerable difficulties in maintaining part-time employment in a handful of jobs (e.g., fast-food restaurant busboy, printer's apprentice). Yet, Sonny had held his current position as a janitor in a state office for 7 months, in part because this position allowed him to work alone for the most part and did not require extensive social interaction (although Sonny's symptoms had progressed to the point that his attendance in this job had become sporadic).

DSM-IV Diagnosis

Based on this information, Sonny was assigned the following DSM-IV diagnosis at the time of his admission to the psychiatric hospital:

Axis I	295.30	Schizophrenia, paranoid type, continuous
Axis II	799.9	Diagnosis deferred on Axis II
Axis III	None	
Axis IV	Academic and work problems, conflict with mother	
Axis V	Global assessment of functioning = 40 (current)	

Schizophrenia is a syndrome composed of positive and negative symptoms. Positive symptoms reflect an excess or distortion of normal functions (e.g., hallucinations, delusions, disorganized speech and behavior). Negative symptoms reflect a paucity or absence of normal functions (e.g., restriction in the range of emotional expression or speech). In DSM-IV (American Psychiatric Association, 1994), schizophrenia is defined by two (or more) of the following symptoms, which must be present for a significant portion of time during at least a 1-month period (or less, if the symptoms were successfully treated): (a) delusions (i.e., false beliefs based on incorrect inferences about external reality that the person firmly and persistently sustains despite the fact that almost everyone else believes otherwise and despite the presence of obvious proof or evidence to the contrary; e.g., Sonny's belief that the police and FBI were out to get him); (b) hallucinations (perceptual disturbances in which things are seen or heard or otherwise sensed, although they are not real and not actually present; e.g., Sonny's auditory hallucinations of hearing voices in his head); (c) disorganized speech (e.g., *derailment,* verbally slipping off track from one topic to another; *tangentiality,* answering questions with weakly or totally unrelated responses); (d) grossly disorganized or catatonic behavior (e.g., *disorganized behavior,* childlike activity, unpredictable agitation, dressing in an unusual or disheveled manner; *catatonic behavior,* unresponsitivity to the environment, maintaining a rigid posture and resisting efforts to be moved); and (e) negative symptoms (e.g., flattened affect; *alogia,* deficiency in the amount or content of speech; *avolition,* inability to initiate or persist in important activities, such as work).

In addition to the presence of at least two of these five symptoms, the criteria for schizophrenia require that marked social or occupational dysfunction be present for a significant portion of time since the onset of the disturbance. Also, DSM-IV requires that continuous signs of the disturbance must have persisted for at least 6 months. In many cases of schizophrenia, the continuous features of the disorder are negative symptoms (e.g., flat affect) or one or more of the five characteristic symptoms in a less severe form (e.g., odd beliefs instead of full-blown delusions). In assigning the diagnosis of schizophrenia, the clinician must rule out the possibility that the symptoms are better accounted for by a mood disorder (e.g., as was illustrated in Case 9, psychotic symptoms such as hallucinations and delusions may also occur during manic episodes or severe depressive episodes), by the effects of a substance (e.g., hallucinogenic drugs such as LSD), or by a general medical condition.

Sonny's diagnosis of schizophrenia, was assigned as "paranoid type." In DSM-IV, there are five major types of schizophrenia: (a) *paranoid type,* with a preoccupation with one or more delusions (usually persecutory or grandiose) or frequent auditory hallucinations; (b) *disorganized type,* with disorganized speech and behavior, as well as flat or inappropriate affect; (c) *catatonic type,* with motoric immobility, excessive and purposeless motor activity, or bizarre posturing; (d) *undifferentiated type,* in which the diagnostic criteria for schizophrenia are met, but the patient does not fully meet the criteria for any of the three preceding specific types; and (e) *residual type,* in which the patient has met criteria for schizophrenia in the past, but currently only milder symptoms are present (e.g., negative symptoms) and prominent positive psychotic symptoms (e.g., delusions, hallucinations) are absent.

CASE FORMULATION USING THE INTEGRATIVE MODEL

As highlighted in the integrative model of schizophrenia (Barlow & Durand, 1999), the evidence strongly points to a significant genetic contribution to the development of schizophrenia. For example, Gottesman (1991), in a review of about 40 family and twin studies of schizophrenia, concluded that if an identical (monozygotic) twin had schizophrenia, there was roughly a 48% chance that the other twin would develop the disorder as well; however, the rate of schizophrenia in both twins was significantly lower (17%) for fraternal (dizygotic) twins. Because monozygotic twins have exactly the same genes whereas dizygotic twins share only about 50% of each other's genes (the same amount shared by first-order relatives), the higher rate of schizophrenia in monozygotic twin pairs suggests that genetic factors contribute to the development of this disorder. While twin and other studies (e.g., adoption research) have strongly documented the role of genetics in schizophrenia, the specific gene or genes that make one vulnerable to develop the disorder have yet to be identified. Moreover, because identical twins can be discordant for schizophrenia (i.e., only one of the twins may ever develop the disorder) despite having exactly the same genetic material, other factors (e.g., environmental variables) must contribute to the origins of the disorder.

Considerable research has been conducted to examine neurobiological factors that may be involved in schizophrenia. One of the most enduring theories of the cause of schizophrenia posits that schizophrenia is related to an excess of the neurotransmitter dopamine (Davis, Kahn, Ko, & Davidson, 1991). Evidence in its favor is (a) that antipsychotic drugs (neuroleptics), which are often effective in the treatment of schizophrenia, interfere with the release of dopamine (are dopamine antagonists) and partially block the brain's use of it (e.g., Creese, Burt, & Snyder, 1976) and (b) that drugs that increase or foster dopamine transmission (e.g., dopamine agonists such as L-dopa) may produce schizophrenia symptoms in some people (Davidson et al., 1987). Despite these and other observations, more recent evidence has countered the relationship of schizophrenia to excess dopamine (e.g., Carson & Sanislow, 1993; Davis et al., 1991). For instance, research has shown that a significant number of people with schizophrenia do not improve with drugs that hamper the activity and levels of dopamine. In addition, a relatively new medication, clozapine, is effective in treating some patients with schizophrenia; however, this drug has very weak effects on the dopamine system (Kane, Honigfeld, Singer, & Meltzer, 1988). Accordingly, most researchers have revised their conceptualization of the role of dopamine in schizophrenia and are increasingly considering the possibility that the balance and interaction of this neurotransmitter with other neurotransmitters (such as serotonin) may better account for many of the symptoms of the disorder.

Studies have also indicated that schizophrenia is associated with alterations in brain structure. For instance, many studies have found that persons with schizophrenia often have abnormally large lateral ventricles (Pahl, Swayze, & Andreasen, 1990). The size of the ventricles alone may not be a problem, but the dilation or enlargement of the ventricles may indicate that parts of the brain adjacent to the ventricles have atrophied or have not developed fully. Nevertheless, enlarged ventricles are not found in all persons with schizophrenia, and the reasons for this abnormality are unclear. Another structural problem that has been linked to schizophrenia involves the frontal lobes of the brain. Specifically, this area of the brain may be less active in people with schizophrenia than in those without the disorder (Gur & Pearlson, 1993). This phenomenon may account for many of the negative symptoms of schizophrenia (Andreasen et al., 1992), and may produce effects in other areas of the brain that are responsible for positive symptoms (Davis et al., 1991).

As noted earlier, the fact that identical twins can be discordant for schizophrenia suggests that environmental, psychological, and social factors may play important roles in the origins and course of schizophrenia. Within this domain, many researchers have examined the effects of life stressors on schizophrenia. For instance, Dohrenwend and Egri (1981) observed that otherwise healthy people who engage in wartime combat often display temporary symptoms that resemble those of schizophrenia. Investigators who have looked back on the histories of persons with schizophrenia have often found that stressful life events precede the emergence of the initial signs of the disorder (e.g., Day et al., 1987). Similarly, relapses of schizophrenia symptoms are often linked to stressful life events, although a considerable proportion of relapses occur in the absence of life stress (e.g., Ventura, Nuechterlein, Lukoff, & Hardesty, 1989). Nonetheless, such findings have led researchers to propose diathesis-stress models of schizophrenia in which the presence of environmental stress is highlighted as necessary in the activation of an underlying genetic or biological diathesis (vulnerability) to develop schizophrenia (e.g., Zubin & Spring, 1977).

A great deal of research has examined whether aspects of the person's social or family environment are related to the emergence or course of the symptoms of schizophrenia. The most extensively researched phenomenon in this area has been on an emotional communication style referred to as *expressed emotion*. Early research indicated that, among patients who were discharged from a hospital after an episode of schizophrenia, those most likely to relapse were patients whose families expressed high levels of criticism, hostility, and emotional overinvolvement (Brown, Monck, Carstairs, & Wing, 1962). More recent research has also verified the notion that residing in a family with high expressed emotion is associated with a significantly greater likelihood of relapse of persons who have experienced a schizophrenic episode (Hooley, 1985). Whereas high expressed emotion may be an important factor contributing to the *course* of schizophrenia once it develops (i.e., risk for relapse), most researchers do not believe that this communication style is instrumental in the *causes* of the disorder.

Treatment Goals and Planning

During Sonny's hospitalization, the treatment attempted to (a) reduce Sonny's psychotic symptoms (i.e., hallucinations, paranoid delusions) via medications, (b) ensure that Sonny used his antipsychotic (neuroleptic) medications consistently, (c) teach Sonny skills to structure his time better and to allow him to gradually resume social and occupational functioning, (d) teach Sonny methods to reduce his tendencies toward self-criticism and social withdrawal, and (e) offer family therapy to educate Sonny's parents about his disorder and teach them new ways to communicate that may increase their son's chances of a better long-term outcome of his illness.

A primary intervention in Sonny's hospital stay was identifying the type and proper dosage of a neuroleptic medication that would have the most therapeutic effect on his psychotic symptomatology. Discovered in the 1950s, neuroleptic medications provided a significant advance in the treatment for persons suffering from schizophrenia (Potkin, Albers, & Richmond, 1993). When effective, these drugs help people think more clearly and reduce or eliminate hallucinations and delusions. Accordingly, neuroleptic medications work by affecting positive symptoms, presumably through their effects on neurotransmitter systems such as those involving dopamine and serotonin. These drugs do not have any appreciable effects on the negative symptoms of schizophrenia (e.g., social skills deficits) and thus psychosocial interventions (e.g., social skills training) are always involved. Most researchers agree that medication should never be the sole treatment for schizophrenia.

In addition to addressing the negative symptoms of schizophrenia, psychosocial interventions increase the chances that patients comply with their medication regimen. Neuroleptic medications work only if they are taken properly, and many people with schizophrenia do not regularly or routinely take their medication. In fact, research on the prevalence of noncompliance indicates that the majority of people with schizophrenia stop taking their medication from time to time. For example, a recent study found that 75% of patients refused to take their neuroleptic medication for at least 1 week over a 2-year period (Weiden et al., 1991).

A major reason for medication noncompliance with neuroleptic drugs is negative side effects. For instance, these drugs can produce a number of unwanted physical symptoms such as grogginess, blurred vision, and dry mouth. Because neuroleptic drugs affect neurotransmitter systems, more serious side effects, called extrapyramidal symptoms, can occur, including tardive dyskinesia, which involves involuntary movements of the tongue, face, mouth, or jaw and can include protrusions of the tongue, puffing of the cheeks, puckering of the mouth, and chewing movements. Tardive dyskinesia results from long-term use of high doses of neuroleptic medications and may occur in as many as 20% of people who remain on these drugs over long periods of time (Morgenstern & Glazer, 1993). Once they emerge, the symptoms are chronic and must be controlled with additional medication.

COURSE OF TREATMENT
AND TREATMENT OUTCOME

At the time of his admission, the estimated length of Sonny's hospital stay was 6 weeks. Sonny was tearful on the first day, and he reported feeling hopeless about the future. It took very little to move him to tears. Because he claimed that he was feeling very confused in his new surroundings, the staff encouraged him to remove himself from the hospital milieu when he was feeling overstimulated. It was clear that Sonny was struggling both physically and mentally on his medication regimen at the time of admission. Prior to his hospitalization, Sonny had been prescribed clonazepam (Klonopin, an antianxiety medication) and loxapine (Loxitane, a neuroleptic medication). Hospital doctors confirmed Sonny's complaints that the neuroleptic drug was producing unwanted side effects of restlessness and, more significantly, some pronounced tongue movement. Therefore, Sonny was taken off the Loxitane and a trial of perphenazine (Trilafon, another form of neuroleptic medication) was started at an initial dose of 24 milligrams per day. Beginning the second day of his admission, Sonny attended individual and group therapy sessions to work on the issues discussed earlier (e.g., medication compliance, social skills training).

Within a week of hospitalization, Sonny was clear about the fact that his problems were not just related to his use of marijuana. He was able to acknowledge long-standing problems interacting with people as well as a very dependent attachment to his father. Sonny was also able to discuss his unfounded belief that his mother was an alcoholic and that her behavior toward him had affected his self-esteem in a negative way. Moreover, in therapy, Sonny talked about how his mother had not accepted his sexual preference.

Quite soon after his medication change, Sonny appeared more physically comfortable, less restless, and more animated. He reported feeling more hopeful and having more emotions accessible to him. Because of his quick, favorable response to the Trilafon, Sonny began to become somewhat focused on the possibility of an earlier hospital discharge date. However, he was able to respond to feedback from the staff that he should remain hospitalized long enough to ensure that his medication was appropriate for him. Nevertheless, Sonny conveyed how difficult he found being away from home for the first time.

Throughout his hospital stay, Sonny made excellent attempts to socialize on the unit, and he reported comfortable interactions with a few of his fellow patients. Although Sonny attended all of his group therapy sessions, his participation was usually limited. He reported discomfort in groups, and he was observed to be better at relating to others on a one-to-one basis. Yet, Sonny was very verbal in family therapy sessions, during which he expressed his concerns about his mother's drinking. In these sessions, Sonny's mother clearly did not consider drinking to be a problem for her, a point that was reinforced by Sonny's father. Accordingly, Sonny was encouraged not to focus on his parents' issues but instead to deal with his own struggles separate from them. This suggestion was particularly difficult for both Sonny and his father because his father had grown accustomed to stepping in to take over his son's responsibilities. Nonetheless, Sonny did report feeling very good about the fact that he had been able to "survive" in the hospital without his parents for a reasonable period of time.

In family therapy, Sonny's father questioned his son's diagnosis, and he appeared quite upset about the prospect that Sonny had schizophrenia. In addition to being supportive and providing information about the disorder and its treatment, the therapists told Sonny's parents that often making a diagnosis is an ongoing process and that the diagnosis could change, depending on Sonny's pattern of later symptoms.

After 4 weeks of hospitalization, Sonny was discharged (2 weeks earlier than anticipated at admission). At the time of his discharge, Sonny was offered the option of attending the hospital's day treatment program, an offer that Sonny and his parents accepted. In the day treatment program, Sonny would come to the hospital for 8 hours, 5 days a week for further treatment and monitoring of his medications. Now that he was residing with his parents once again, the day treatment program therapists would continue to work with Sonny on handling family issues and begin work on assisting Sonny in his reentry to social and work environments.

During the time Sonny attended the hospital's day treatment program, he began to fail to take his medications as prescribed because his extrapyramidal symptoms (tongue movements, monotonous speech) began to emerge from the Trilafon. After attempts at adjusting his dosage to a lower level were unsuccessful and produced a temporary recurrence of mild delusional thoughts (e.g., the police were out to get him), Sonny's doctors decided to take him off the Trilafon and begin him on a newly developed neuroleptic medication, clozapine (Clozaril). The switch to Clozaril turned out to be important for Sonny's treatment because, in addition to working as well as the Trilafon in managing the positive symptoms of his condition, it ultimately produced a markedly reduced level of extrapyramidal symptoms. Therefore, Sonny stayed compliant with his prescribed regimen of Clozaril.

Over the next several months, Sonny had occasional relapses of transient delusions (particularly about the permanent effects of marijuana) and agitation. However, these symptom recurrences did not approach the severity of his initial presentation to the hospital and were easily managed on an outpatient basis (i.e., medication dose adjustment). Sonny's supportive family (particularly his father) and structured environment (e.g., residing in his parents' home) continued to be very significant in allowing him to maintain consistency, structure, and self-esteem in his daily life. The transient relapses he experienced were usually related to various environmental stressors that tended to continue to overwhelm him. One such stressor was Sonny's reentry into the work environment part-time. With the aid of the hospital's employee assistance program, Sonny was able to resume his prior position as a janitor, initially on a part-time basis. With the assistance and support of his therapists, Sonny was able to adjust to the responsibilities of working again.

At the time this chapter was written, Sonny's adjustment had progressed to the point where he had returned to full-time employment and was responsibly taking care of his finances. His delusions and hallucinations have decreased to near absence with the continued use of Clozaril, although Sonny's belief that his use of marijuana produced permanent brain damage and is responsible for all his symptoms continues to surface from time to time and must be dealt with continually in therapy. Currently, Sonny is able to socialize more readily, although he continues to live at his parents' house and has a relatively circumscribed social life. In addition to regular visits with his psychiatrist for monitoring and adjustment of his medications, Sonny and his parents continue weekly visits with an outpatient psychotherapist (the same one who referred him for hospitalization) for family therapy and other issues (e.g., learning to detect early signs of relapse, social skills training).

DISCUSSION

The prevalence of schizophrenia in the general population has been estimated at 0.2% to 2% (American Psychiatric Association, 1994). In the United States alone, approximately 4.5 million people are believed to have active symptoms of schizophrenia at any given time (Carson & Sanislow, 1993). Although schizophrenia has usually been thought to affect an equivalent number of women and men over the course of a lifetime, more recent evidence suggests that schizophrenia is more prevalent in men (Iacono & Beiser, 1992). The onset of schizophrenia typically occurs between the late teens and the mid-30s, with onsets prior to adolescence rare. Women are more likely to have a later onset than men. In addition, schizophrenia in women has more prominent mood symptoms (e.g., depression, flat affect). Although the onset of the disorder may be abrupt, the majority of persons who develop schizophrenia display some type of *prodromal* phase that is manifested by the slow and gradual development of a variety of signs and symptoms such as social withdrawal, deterioration in hygiene and grooming, unusual behavior, or outbursts of anger. Eventually, symptoms of an *active* phase (e.g., delusions, hallucinations) emerge. In addition to the sex differences, the age of onset of schizophrenia has been found to be associated with other important factors. For instance, persons with an early age of onset are more apt to have had poorer premorbid adjustment, lower educational achievement, more evidence of structural brain abnormalities, and more prominent negative symptoms, and they are more likely to have a poorer long-term outcome. Conversely, research has shown that persons with a later age of onset are less likely to show structural brain abnormalities and are more likely to display a better long-term outcome.

As illustrated in Sonny's case, schizophrenia is a debilitating disorder that is usually associated with marked impairment in most areas of life functioning. In addition, the life expectancy of a person with schizophrenia is slightly less than average, partly due to the higher rate of suicide among people with this disorder (Potkin et al., 1993). When researchers have considered schizophrenia across the life span, most have presumed that the natural course of the disorder is associated with progressive deterioration through late adulthood. However, some evidence suggests that this is not necessarily the case. For example, studies that have followed patients with schizophrenia into late life (e.g., Winokur, Pfohl, & Tsuang, 1987) have generally found that older adults tended to display fewer positive symptoms (e.g., delusions, hallucinations) and perhaps more negative symptoms (e.g., speech difficulties). In fact, one study that followed 118 patients who had been treated in Vermont State Hospital for schizophrenia in the 1950s found that one-half to two-thirds had achieved considerable improvement or recovered, as indicated by assessments conducted in the 1980s (Harding, Brooks, Ashikaga, Strauss, & Breier, 1987). Thus, persons with schizophrenia do not appear to continue to deteriorate over time but in some ways may show improvement as they enter later adulthood.

Nevertheless, most studies of the course and outcome of schizophrenia suggest that the course is variable, with some persons displaying exacerbations and remissions and others remaining chronically ill. Roughly 20% may display a single episode of schizophrenia and then improve and show no lasting impairment. However, most people experience several episodes of schizophrenia (i.e., symptoms of the active phase such as hallucinations and delusions), with differing degrees of impairment between these episodes (Zubin, Steinhauer, & Condray, 1992).

As noted earlier in this chapter, neuroleptic medications, such as those prescribed to Sonny (e.g., Clozaril, Trilafon), represent the primary treatment of schizophrenia. Some of the limitations of neuroleptic treatments were noted previously, including high rates of patient noncompliance, the potential for serious side effects (e.g., extrapyramidal symptoms such as tardive dyskinesia), and the fact that these drugs typically do not have an appreciable therapeutic impact on the negative symptoms of schizophrenia (e.g., social withdrawal). Researchers had hoped that Clozaril, introduced in 1990, would reconcile some of the problems associated with other neuroleptic drugs. While Clozaril has been used effectively with some patients who were unresponsive to other medications and is associated with fewer side effects, it does produce some undesirable effects, and its use must be monitored closely to avoid rare but potentially life-threatening physical effects of the drug (Kane & Marder, 1993).

Although most researchers agree that schizophrenia cannot be treated effectively with psychosocial treatments alone, these interventions are nonetheless an important aspect of the management of this disorder (Bellack & Mueser, 1993). For instance, as was true in Sonny's treatment, psychosocial treatments are often used to increase compliance with drug interventions by helping patients communicate better with their doctors about their concerns about side effects. In addition, because social withdrawal and social skills deficits are common negative symptoms of schizophrenia, social skills training is very frequently included in treatment. With these treatments, therapists break down social skills (e.g., being assertive) into their component parts, then model the behaviors, and then have patients role play their parts and ultimately practice their new skills in the real world, while receiving therapist feedback and encouragement. There is some disagreement about how effective social skills training is in the treatment of schizophrenia (cf. Bellack & Mueser, 1992); one problem is that patients often do not retain their newly learned skills after treatment has ended.

As shown in Sonny's case, family therapy is another common psychosocial approach included in the treatment of schizophrenia. The need for this form of treatment was highlighted in part from the evidence discussed earlier that patients who resided with families with high expressed emotion were at greater risk for relapse or poor long-term outcome (Hooley, 1985). In family therapy for schizophrenia, family members are typically provided with information about the disorder and its treatment and are taught skills to be more supportive of the patient (Mueser, Liberman, & Glynn, 1990). For instance, family members are taught to be more empathetic listeners, learn more constructive ways of expressing negative feelings, and learn problem-solving skills to help resolve problems or conflicts when they arise. Collectively, the research on social skills training and family therapy has indicated that these interventions are effective in avoiding or delaying recurrences of schizophrenic episodes, particularly if these interventions are delivered on an ongoing basis (Falloon, Brooker, & Graham-Hole, 1992).

THINKING CRITICALLY

1. How important do you believe familial and social factors are in the development and maintenance of schizophrenia? Do you believe that schizophrenia is mainly a biological disorder, such that these psychosocial variables have little influence on onset and course? Why or why not?
2. Consider the studies discussed in this case that found that the long-term course of schizophrenia is often associated with a surprisingly favorable outcome. What factors do you believe account for the fact that older persons may show almost full recovery from the schizophrenia for which they had been hospitalized as young adults?
3. Based on the information presented in this case, do you think it is possible for some persons to abruptly experience an active psychotic phase with little or no warning, or do you think that these symptoms are virtually always preceded by longstanding warning signs? Why? If you think psychotic symptoms can emerge abruptly, under what conditions are they likely to do so?
4. John Hinckley, who was confirmed as having schizophrenia, successfully used the insanity plea in his trial for his assassination attempt on Ronald Reagan. Do you believe such a plea is justified, or do think persons with schizophrenia should be held fully accountable for their criminal acts? Why?

Autistic Disorder

A t the time of his initial consult at a university-based clinic, Ritchie Firkins was a 5-year-old Caucasian boy who had for 2 months been attending kindergarten, where he was in a special education class with children who had developmental delays (e.g., delays in intellectual, social, or verbal development) or emotional problems. Ritchie had been diagnosed with autistic disorder at the age of 2½. From the age of 2 years on, Ritchie had engaged in frequent temper tantrums, during which he screamed, banged his head, and hit others. When Ritchie started attending kindergarten, however, the frequency and severity of his tantrums increased markedly, both at school and at home. Every day, Ritchie typically had five tantrums at home and six tantrums at school. In addition, Ritchie refused to sit at his desk at school for more than a few minutes. He often ran around the classroom, and he rarely paid attention to the teacher.

During a school meeting, Ritchie's teacher and parents agreed that they were all having a great deal of difficulty managing Ritchie's behavior problems and that these problems were getting worse. Ritchie's parents believed that the increased structure and the higher expectations for good behavior in a kindergarten classroom were the likely reasons for their son's increased tantrum problems. Ritchie's tantrums produced considerable disruption at home. For instance, because of the tantrums, the family had canceled a vacation and had gone on fewer local outings to such places as zoos and museums. When Ritchie's parents went on outings, such as dining out, attending a movie, or shopping, they frequently left Ritchie at home with a babysitter (to ensure that others were not exposed to their son's behavior). At the end of the school meeting, Ritchie's mother agreed to call the local university in order to reach someone who could assist both her and Ritchie's teacher in managing his behavior problems.

Clinical History

The first signs of Ritchie's autistic disorder appeared when he was 2 years old. At that time, Ritchie's parents noticed that he was quite withdrawn and that he did not demonstrate an interest in or preference for being with his parents or his older brother (who was 4 years older than Ritchie). For example, Ritchie's parents observed that, unlike their older son, Ritchie did not appear to enjoy being held. He often pulled away when they tried to hug him, and he rarely sought them out when he was distressed.

From that time forward, Ritchie's parents noted that their son did not appear interested in other children, including his older brother. Over his entire 5 years of life, Ritchie never had any friends. In addition to his lack of interest in others, his peers did not seem to enjoy being around Ritchie. Several of his kindergarten classmates had demonstrated jealousy toward Ritchie because he was the only child in the class who could easily get away with not sitting still and not paying attention to the teacher. Also, some children feared Ritchie because of his frequent tantrums. In addition to his lack of interest in others, Ritchie had never developed an interest in doing things independently, such as dressing or cleaning himself. If his parents insisted that he do something (such as brush his hair), Ritchie usually responded by having a tantrum.

Ritchie had also demonstrated a severe language delay; in fact, he had not developed any speech whatsoever. Occasionally, Ritchie had been able to communicate with his parents by taking one of their hands and placing it on an object that he wanted. For example, if Ritchie wanted to watch television, he would take his father's hand and guide it to the TV remote control. Most often, however, Ritchie communicated by crying and by temper tantrums. If Ritchie wanted something, such as milk that was out of his reach, he would often scream or bang his head against something. His parents typically responded by looking around to find what Ritchie wanted so that they could give it to him and he would stop his tantrum.

In addition, Ritchie had engaged in repetitive and ritualistic behaviors. From an early age, he had spent much time rocking back and forth and flapping his hands. Also, he frequently spun objects, such as toy cars, pens, and pencils. Ritchie's parents reported that they had never seen him play with toys appropriately.

Particularly problematic were Ritchie's ritualistic behavior and intense desire for things to stay unchanged. Ritchie often became very upset when things were not exactly the way he wanted them to be. For instance, Ritchie would frequently have a severe tantrum if his mother opened the living room blinds. Ritchie insisted that they remain down at all times. Moreover, Ritchie would get upset if the dinner table was not set in a very particular manner. He also did not allow anyone to rearrange objects in his bedroom.

In addition to autistic disorder, Ritchie had previously been diagnosed by the school psychologist as having attention deficit hyperactivity disorder (ADHD), a disorder characterized by a persistent pattern of inattention, hyperactivity-impulsivity, or both, that is clearly more frequent and severe than would be expected for the person's age. As is often the case, Ritchie was not diagnosed with ADHD until he began kindergarten. There were few demands for Ritchie to sit still and pay attention at home and at preschool. In kindergarten, however, Ritchie was expected to sit for long periods several times a day. For instance, Ritchie was expected to sit still for a morning circle and he was expected to pay attention while his teacher read the class a story each afternoon. As noted earlier, Ritchie did not meet these expectations. He typically ran around the room while the other children paid attention to the teacher. Prior to Ritchie's first visit to the university clinic, the family doctor had prescribed methylphenidate (Ritalin) as a treatment for Ritchie's ADHD symptoms. The Ritalin had seemed to have some benefit because the teacher believed that Ritchie's inattention and hyperactivity had decreased since he began taking the medication.

Ritchie came from an affluent family. His father was a biochemist and his mother was an accountant who owned and ran a successful accounting firm. As is virtually always the case with autistic disorder, no significant stressors or other environmental factors were evident that could be linked to the origins of Ritchie's problem. Throughout his entire life, Ritchie had been in excellent physical health and had never had any known medical problems. He had been raised in a very supportive and loving family. He attended an excellent school that had many resources. Ritchie's family did not have a history of developmental disabilities or emotional disorders. Ritchie's older brother was quite well adjusted and doing very well in school.

DSM-IV Diagnosis

Based on this information, Ritchie was assigned the following DSM-IV diagnosis:

Axis I	299.00	Autistic disorder (principal diagnosis)
Axis II	318.0	Moderate mental retardation
Axis III	None	
Axis IV	None	
Axis V	Global assessment of functioning = 25 (current)	

In DSM-IV (American Psychiatric Association, 1994), autistic disorder resides in a section entitled "pervasive developmental disorders." Pervasive developmental disorders are characterized by severe and wide-ranging impairment in several areas of development, including social interaction and communication skills, and the presence of stereotyped behavior, interests, and activities. Although children vary in their rate of development, the impairments that define the pervasive developmental disorders are clearly deviant relative to the afflicted child's developmental level or mental age. All pervasive developmental disorders are usually evident in the first 5 years of life, and each is often associated with some degree of mental retardation. In addition to autistic disorder, other types of DSM-IV pervasive developmental disorders include Rett's disorder, childhood disintegrative disorder, and Asperger's disorder (described and differentiated later).

As is the case with the other pervasive developmental disorders, autistic disorder is defined by the presence of markedly abnormal or impaired development in social interaction and communication and a markedly restricted repertoire of activity and interests. Accordingly, the key DSM-IV criteria for autistic disorder are organized into these three symptom areas: (a) impairment in social interaction; (b) impairment in communication; and (c) restricted, repetitive, and stereotyped patterns of behavior, interests, and activities. Each of these three key features is broken down into four specific symptoms. The symptoms of impairment in social interaction are (a) marked impairment in the use of multiple nonverbal behaviors (e.g., eye contact, facial expression); (b) failure to develop peer relationships appropriate to the child's developmental level; (c) a lack of spontaneous seeking to share enjoyment, interests, and achievement with other people; and (d) a lack of social or emotional reciprocity (e.g., not actively participating in simple social play or games). The symptoms of impairment in communication are (a) delay in, or total lack of, the development of spoken language; (b) in children with speech, marked impairment in the ability to initiate or maintain a conversation with others; (c) stereotyped and repetitive use of language or idiosyncratic language (e.g., repeating jingles or commercials); and (d) lack of varied, spontaneous make-believe play or lack of social imitative play appropriate to developmental level (e.g., absence of playing games such as "Cowboys and Indians" or pretending to be a superhero). The symptoms of restricted, repetitive, and stereotyped patterns of behavior, interests, and activities are (a) encompassing preoccupation with one or more stereotyped and restricted patterns of interest that is abnormal either in intensity or focus (e.g., persistently amassing baseball statistics at the expense of being involved in anything else); (b) inflexible adherence to specific, nonfunctional routines or rituals (e.g., insistence on walking the exact same route to school each day with acute distress or temper tantrum if this routine is disrupted, limiting one's diet to a few foods); (c) stereotyped and repetitive motor mannerisms (e.g., hand or finger flapping or twisting, body rocking); and (d) persistent preoccupation with parts of objects (e.g., emotional attachment to a piece of string, fascination with the movement of an electric fan or the spinning wheel of a toy). The DSM-IV diagnosis of autistic disorder requires the presence of at least 6 of the aforementioned 12 symptoms, with clear evidence of at least 2 symptoms of social impairment, 1 symptom of communication impairment, and 1 symptom of restricted repertoire of activity and interests. Moreover, to meet the definition of autistic disorder, delays or abnormal functioning should be evident in at least one of these three main symptom areas prior to the child's third birthday.

Asperger's disorder, childhood disintegrative disorder, and Rett's disorder are comprised of symptoms that are quite similar and often identical to the symptoms of autistic disorder. For instance, like autistic disorder, Asperger's disorder is also characterized by impairments in social relationships and restricted or unusual behaviors. However, delays in language skills are not present in Asperger's disorder, leading some researchers to conclude that this condition is simply a milder form of autistic disorder. Childhood disintegrative disorder consists of the same symptoms as those found in autistic disorder but is differentiated by a severe developmental regression (in language, adapative behavior, and motor skills) after a period of normal development over the first 2 to 4 years of the child's life. Like childhood disintegrative disorder patients, children who develop Rett's disorder also show normal development in the first several months of life. However, beginning some point after the fifth month of life, evidence of a progressive neurological disorder emerges, characterized by constant handwringing, mental retardation, and impaired motor skills. Curiously, unlike the other pervasive developmental disorders, Rett's disorder occurs almost exclusively in females.

Autistic disorder is discussed in more detail throughout the remainder of this chapter. You will note that, although Ritchie had been diagnosed by the school psychologist as having attention deficit hyperactivity disorder (ADHD), this diagnosis was not assigned by psychologists at the university-based clinic. Despite Ritchie's ADHD symptoms, the DSM-IV criteria for ADHD specify that this diagnosis should not be given if the symptoms occur exclusively during the course of a pervasive developmental disorder such as autistic disorder (based on the notion that symptoms of inattention and hyper-activity are better construed as associated features of the pervasive develop-mental disorder rather than signs of a separate condition). This was true for Ritchie, and hence he was not diagnosed with ADHD.

CASE FORMULATION USING
THE INTEGRATIVE MODEL

Like all of the other disorders discussed in this book, the working model of autistic disorder concludes that this problem cannot be attributed to a single cause. However, as noted by Barlow and Durand (1999), research on autistic disorder is in its infancy, and this area still awaits an integrative theory. Currently, very few researchers believe that psychological or social influences play a major role in the *origins* of autistic disorder (although, as discussed later, psychological and social factors may contribute strongly to associated features and the course of the disorder). The conclusion that social factors do not cause autistic disorder comes as a great relief to many parents of children with this condition. Early prominent theories (e.g., Bettelheim, 1967; Ferster, 1961; Tinbergen & Tinbergen, 1972) asserted that autistic disorder arises from poor parenting, but subsequent research has strongly contradicted these assertions. Parents of children with autistic disorder do not differ from other parents on various measures of personality and adjustment (Koegel, Schriebman, O'Neill, & Burke, 1983; McAdoo & DeMyer, 1978). In Ritchie's case, there was clearly no evidence that parenting or other social factors contributed to the onset of his disorder.

The available evidence suggests that biological factors are associated with autistic disorder. Autism has a clear genetic component (Smalley, 1991). Although the sample sizes have been quite small (due largely to the rarity of autistic disorder), twin studies have routinely found higher rates of concor-dance for autistic disorder in monozygotic twins than in dizygotic twins (e.g., Folstein & Rutter, 1977; Steffenburg et al., 1989). For instance, a study of 21 twin pairs by Steffenburg et al. (1989) found that if one twin had an autistic disorder, there was a 91% chance that a monozygotic (identical) twin had autism as well, which is substantially higher than the rate of autistic disorder in dizygotic (fraternal) twins; in fact, the concordance rate for autism in dizy-gotic twins was 0 (i.e., in all of the dizygotic twin pairs, only one twin had autistic disorder). Because monozygotic twins have exactly the same genes whereas dizygotic twins share only about 50% of each other's genes (the same percentage shared among first-order relatives), the markedly higher rate of autistic disorder in monozygotic twin pairs suggests that genetic factors have a strong contribution to the development of autism. However, researchers have not identified a gene or genes responsible for this condition.

Investigators do concur that the genetics of autism are not straightforward and that several genes are likely to contribute to the disorder.

Neurological factors have been linked rather strongly to autistic disorder. Indirect evidence of a neurological component comes from the clinical observation that roughly 75% of persons with autism have some degree of mental retardation. Moreover, an appreciable proportion of individuals with autistic disorder show some other form of neurological abnormality, such as clumsiness or abnormal posture or gait (Tsai & Ghaziuddin, 1992). Further evidence of neurological dysfunction comes from studies involving the use of computerized axial tomography (CAT) and magnetic resonance imaging (MRI), procedures used to generate pictures of a living person's brain. Investigators using these imaging procedures have observed abnormalities in the brains of persons with autistic disorder, namely, that some people with autism have abnormally small cerebellums (the cerebellum is located in the hindbrain, the lowest portion of the brain stem, and is known to be involved in the control of motor coordination). Although this abnormality has not been observed in every person who has the disorder, it does appear to be one of the more consistent findings in autism research thus far (cf. Courchesne, 1991). The fact that all persons with autism do not have reduced cerebellar size reinforces the idea that autistic disorder has multiple causes (in fact, recent preliminary studies using MRI techniques have found that many persons with autism evidence *larger* overall brain volume than those without the condition; e.g., Piven et al., 1995).

Even though genetic and neurological factors appear to play prominent roles in the origins of autistic disorder, psychological and social factors nevertheless may have important contributions to the course and complications of the condition. One such factor is social reinforcement, a principle emanating from learning theory (Skinner, 1971). Reinforcement is discussed in detail in the next section in the context of Ritchie's treatment planning.

Treatment Goals and Planning

Although Ritchie displayed problems in many areas, his parents and teachers had the most difficulty coping with his behavior problems. Of greatest concern was the fact that Ritchie often banged his head on the floor during these tantrums. On several occasions, this behavior had resulted in large bumps on his head. In some tantrums, Ritchie screamed loudly or hit others. Therefore, his parents requested assistance in reducing Ritchie's tantrums. Interestingly, despite Ritchie's diagnosis of autistic disorder nearly 3 years before, he had not received any professional interventions prior to his visit to the university-based treatment clinic (although Ritchie's mother had been very active in learning about autism, having attended many workshops and read several books on the topic).

Ritchie's therapists believed that, although his autistic disorder was likely due to a neurological abnormality, his behavior problems were being maintained by *reinforcement.* Reinforcement refers to environmental consequences for behavior that strengthen it or increase its frequency. Children with autistic disorder appear to be at great risk for developing behavior problems (such as tantrums) because they are unable to communicate by speaking. These children often learn to receive things by engaging in their problem behaviors. As discussed earlier, Ritchie seemed to have learned to communicate by throwing tantrums. If he wanted milk that was out of reach, he would scream and bang his head. Like most parents, Ritchie's parents would become distressed at the sight of their son crying or hurting himself. Thus, they responded by quickly giving Ritchie the milk (or whatever else he wanted) to stop his tantrum. However, while offering the milk was successful in ending the tantrum, Ritchie's parents were reinforcing their son's behavior problems and were making these behaviors more likely to recur. In essence, Ritchie learned that he could promptly receive what he wanted by throwing a tantrum (i.e., the positive consequence of getting milk reinforced the behavior of having a tantrum). In addition, children with autistic disorder often learn to avoid things by engaging in problem behaviors. For instance, Ritchie could get out of doing work by throwing a tantrum. Ritchie often cried when his father asked him to brush his hair or learn some other grooming skill. Typically, his father responded to the tantrum by telling Ritchie that it was all right and that they could work on it later.

In addition to his parents, Ritchie's teachers also seemed to be reinforcing some of his problem behaviors. For instance, the teachers allowed Ritchie to get out of doing work (like sitting still during the reading hour) or gave him what he wanted whenever Ritchie threw a tantrum. Hence, the goals of treatment were (a) to teach Ritchie how to communicate in more adaptive ways so that he did not throw tantrums to communicate his needs and (b) to teach Ritchie's parents and teachers how to respond to Ritchie's problem behaviors in a fashion that would not reinforce them. To achieve these goals, Ritchie's therapists intervened with functional communication training (Durand, 1990), a treatment that is discussed in some detail in the next section.

COURSE OF TREATMENT
AND TREATMENT OUTCOME

In total, 15 treatment sessions were held over a 6-month period. Nine of these sessions were held at Ritchie's school, and six sessions took place in Ritchie's home. The first objective of treatment was to identify the things that were maintaining or reinforcing Ritchie's tantrums. Ritchie's therapists obtained this information by interviewing his parents and teachers and by observing

Ritchie at home and at school. Consistent with the therapists' impressions from the initial meeting, it became obvious that Ritchie displayed behavior problems in order to get what he wanted and to avoid work. More specifically, Ritchie threw a tantrum when he wanted food, when he wanted someone to restore his environment in a particular manner (e.g., lower the blinds in the living room), and when someone asked him to do a chore (such as grooming). Having identified the manners in which Ritchie was being reinforced for having tantrums, the next goal of functional communication training was to teach him new, more adaptive ways to gain access to these reinforcers (in Ritchie's case, food, assistance in arranging his environment, and escape from work).

The next step of treatment was to teach Ritchie to request the reinforcers that were maintaining his behavior problems. The therapists had to decide on the best form of communication for Ritchie. Because Ritchie had never developed any speech, the therapists decided not to try to teach Ritchie to communicate vocally. Instead, they decided to teach Ritchie to point to pictures of the things he wanted. Accordingly, a "communication book" was assembled that contained pictures of various types of food. Ritchie was prompted to touch the picture of the food. After he touched the picture, he quickly received something to eat. Over time, the therapists (as well as the parents and teachers) gradually reduced their prompts for Ritchie to touch pictures until he learned to independently touch the picture of food in order to receive something to eat.

After Ritchie learned to touch pictures to communicate his desire for food, the therapists added new pictures to the communication book. One of these pictures said, "Fix it, please." This aspect of treatment began by raising the blinds in Ritchie's living room and prompting Ritchie to touch the new picture. After Ritchie touched the picture, the blinds were quickly lowered. Using such strategies, Ritchie learned to independently request to have his environment rearranged by touching the appropriate picture. Later, another picture was added to the book that said, "Break, please." The therapists used this picture to teach Ritchie that he could receive a break from work by touching this picture. The instructions that the therapists provided to Ritchie's parents and teachers for this aspect of treatment are presented in Table 16.1.

One of the most significant points of Ritchie's treatment was the first time that he independently requested food with his communication book. Ritchie had never communicated in such a manner before and was, for the first time, able to request what he wanted without engaging in problem behaviors. Conceptually, the reason for this positive outcome is a learning theory principle referred to as *functional equivalence.* That is, both Ritchie's tantrums and his new communicative activities served the same function for him—obtaining food. With two functionally equivalent methods of acquiring food—throwing tantrums or pointing to pictures—Ritchie most frequently chose the response that presumably was easier for him: pointing to pictures.

It took Ritchie roughly 2 weeks of daily training (carried out by his parents and teachers after the therapists introduced the technique) to learn to use his communication book to request food. However, once Ritchie learned the benefits of using the book, he seemed more motivated to learn new responses. For instance, Ritchie learned to use his second and third phrases ("Fix it, please," and "Break, please") in about 1 week.

Nevertheless, Ritchie's treatment did not proceed without complications. One came up shortly after Ritchie began to communicate with his picture book. Once Ritchie began to request food independently, at school he started asking for it at a very high rate (approximately every 30 minutes). The teacher felt that it would be very difficult for her to offer Ritchie food this often. In response to this concern, the therapists decided to teach Ritchie to tolerate a delay in reinforcement. Initially, the teacher was instructed to provide Ritchie a snack immediately after he requested food. After 2 weeks had passed, the teacher was told to respond to Ritchie's requests by saying, "Yes, you can have something to eat, but please wait 2 minutes." After 2 minutes had elapsed, the teacher gave Ritchie a snack. Three days later, the teacher added another 2 minutes to the length of time that Ritchie had to wait before he received food. Over the next several weeks, the delay for reinforcement was increased further (on average, she added 2 minutes every 3 days).

Some of Ritchie's tantrums reappeared during the first week of delay of reinforcement. The teacher was advised to be sure not to add more time to the delay than Ritchie could tolerate. Although the teacher proceeded slowly, Ritchie's tantrums indicated that the rate of increase in the delay was too great for him to handle. Thus, the teacher had to occasionally remain at a specific time delay for up to 1 week. On two occasions, she had to decrease the length of the delay. However, after 3 months had gone by, Ritchie was handling a delay of 30 minutes by displaying very infrequent tantrums. Once Ritchie could tolerate waiting 30 extra minutes to receive food (which translated into his receiving a small snack roughly once per hour), no more time was added to the delay. The teacher felt that offering Ritchie food at this rate was not disruptive to the class.

Another complication in Ritchie's treatment was that the frequency of tantrums remained essentially unchanged in his music and gym classes. In other words, the use of the intervention had not generalized to other settings. In addition, Ritchie did not use his book with new teachers. Following these observations, all of Ritchie's specialty teachers (i.e., music, gym, library, and art) were asked to attend a brief workshop to learn about functional communication training. These teachers also received hands-on training on how to prompt Ritchie to communicate with his picture book and how to fade these prompts. Following this training, the frequency of Ritchie's tantrums remained low in all classrooms and with all teachers. In fact, Ritchie's main teacher reported that, on a day when there was a substitute teacher in art

Table 16.1 Example of Instructions for Functional Communication
Training Provided to Ritchie's Parents and Teacher

The goal is to teach Ritchie to request a break from work by using the communication book. This will be done by beginning with full physical prompts and then fading the prompts as quickly as possible until Ritchie responds independently. Initially, training will require 1:1 training, and it is important that sessions are run daily and consistently.

INITIAL TRAINING—PHASE I

All sessions should be done while Ritchie is asked to work. First, full physical prompts should be used to assist Ritchie in using the communication book to request a break.

1. Have Ritchie briefly attempt the task.

The duration of time that Ritchie should be required to work before prompting begins should be less than the amount of time that he can typically tolerate before becoming upset. For example, if Ritchie typically tolerates working for 2 minutes, the prompts should begin after 1 minute. If Ritchie begins to tantrum during the 1 minute, it is important to work through the problem behavior and still wait a full minute before prompting him to request a break.

2. After the specified amount of time, say to Ritchie, "Ask for a break."
3. Guide Ritchie's hand to the communication book and help him to point to the picture representing a request for a break.
4. After he points, pull his materials away and allow Ritchie to take a break for about 1 minute.
5. Once again, briefly present work materials to Ritchie and then repeat from step 1.

Once Ritchie successfully points to the picture 3 to 5 times in a row using the above steps, the full physical prompts can begin to be faded. This will be done by following the steps described in Phase II.

PHASE II

1. Have Ritchie briefly attempt the task.
2. After the specified amount of time, say to Ritchie, "Ask for a break."
3. Guide Ritchie's hand to the communication book and wait about 5 seconds to see if he will point to the picture independently. If he does not, physically prompt him to do so.
4. When Ritchie points to the picture, pull his materials away and allow Ritchie to take a break for about 1 minute.
5. Once again, briefly present work materials to Ritchie and then repeat from step 1.

Once Ritchie successfully points to the picture 3 to 5 times in a row, once his hand has been guided to it, the physical prompts can be faded further. This will be done by following the steps described in Phase III.

Table 16.1 *(Continued)*

PHASE III

1. Have Ritchie briefly attempt the task.
2. After the specified amount of time, say to Ritchie, "Ask for a break."
3. Guide Ritchie's hand only part way to the communication book and wait about 5 seconds to see if he will continue to bring his hand to the communication book himself and point to the picture. If he does not, physically prompt him to do so.
4. When Ritchie points to the picture, pull his materials away and allow Ritchie to take a break for about 1 minute.
5. Once again, briefly present work materials to Ritchie, and then repeat from step 1.

Once Ritchie successfully points to the picture 3 to 5 times in a row using the above steps, the prompts should be faded further. This will be done by following the steps described in Phase IV.

PHASE IV

1. Have Ritchie briefly attempt the task.
2. After the specified amount of time, say to Ritchie, "Ask for a break."
3. Now, only touch Ritchie's elbow and wait about 5 seconds to see if he will bring his hand to the communication book himself and point to it. If he does not, physically prompt him to do so.
4. Following the message, pull his materials away and allow Ritchie to take a break for about 1 minute.
5. Once again, briefly present work materials to Ritchie and then repeat from step 1.

Once Ritchie successfully points to the picture 3 to 5 times in a row using the above steps, the physical prompts should be completely faded. This will be done by following the steps described in Phase V.

PHASE V

1. Have Ritchie briefly attempt the task.
2. After the specified amount of time, say to Ritchie, "Ask for a break."
3. Wait about 5 seconds to see if he will bring his hand to the communication book and point to it independently. If he does not, gently touch his arm.
4. After Ritchie points to the picture, pull his work materials away and allow Ritchie to take a break for about 1 minute.
5. Once again, briefly present work materials to Ritchie and then repeat from step 1.

Once Ritchie begins to request a break without any physical prompts, the verbal prompt can be faded by following the steps in Phase VI.

Table 16.1 *(Continued)*

PHASE VI
1. Have Ritchie briefly attempt the task.
2. Gradually increase the amount of time before you say to Ritchie, "Ask for a break."

This should be done until Ritchie requests a break without any prompts.

class, Ritchie had indeed requested a break from work by using his communication book. Thus, these generalization training procedures were very important in Ritchie's treatment because they helped him learn that he could use his book with a variety of people and in a variety of places.

After Ritchie's behavior problems had been reduced to a level that his parents and teachers could tolerate, and after he was reliably using all three communication pictures in various situations, the formal treatment sessions were discontinued. Nonetheless, Ritchie's parents and teachers were encouraged to contact the therapists if any further problems arose. By the end of treatment, Ritchie's tantrums were infrequent. Most important, Ritchie no longer banged and injured his head, and his parents felt quite confident that his self-injurious behaviors were not likely to recur. Because Ritchie was no longer having a high rate of tantrums, he was able to participate in many activities that he had not experienced in several months. For instance, his parents began taking him out to dinner and bringing him on shopping trips. In addition, Ritchie enjoyed again going on trips and vacations with his parents and older brother. At school, Ritchie's classmates no longer seemed to fear him. Moreover, a major goal of Ritchie's teacher was to place each of her students into an integrated class for the first grade. At first, she was quite convinced that Ritchie would not be a candidate for integration. However, midway through the school year she seriously entertained this possibility, and she had Ritchie visit several integrated first-grade classes for the following year. Around this time, the teacher slowly began to add pictures to Ritchie's communication book to increase his vocabulary. She successfully added "Bathroom," "Drink, please," "Music, please," and "May I play with the computer?" Ritchie demonstrated proficiency in using each of these additions, and at the time this chapter was written, his teacher was continuing to add new pictures in the hopes that Ritchie will develop a larger vocabulary.

Despite these encouraging outcomes, Ritchie continues to display significant symptoms and deficits. Though the frequency of his tantrums has decreased substantially as the result of treatment, he continues to have many symptoms of autistic disorder (and associated symptoms of ADHD). Ritchie continues to be somewhat withdrawn, and he still engages in stereotyped and ritualistic behaviors (e.g., body rocking). Despite the fact that the Ritalin appeared to significantly decrease his hyperactivity and increase his attention span, Ritchie continues to have some difficulty remaining in his seat and attending to his teachers for long periods of time. Although Ritchie may eventually attend integrated classes, he will likely always require a special education teacher to ensure that he is provided with the intense level of teaching that children with autistic disorder typically require to learn new things. In addition, making friends will probably always be difficult for Ritchie.

DISCUSSION

Autistic disorder is relatively rare in comparison to most, if not all, of the other disorders covered in this book. Although prevalence estimates have varied to some degree from study to study (cf. Gillberg, 1984), most researchers agree that autistic disorder occurs at a rate of approximately 2 to 5 per 10,000 people (American Psychiatric Association, 1994). Rates of autistic disorder are roughly 4 to 5 times higher in males than in females, although its prevalence between the sexes appears to vary, depending on the IQ of the child. As noted earlier, approximately 75% of all persons with autistic disorder have at least a mild level of mental retardation (Waterhouse, Wing, & Fein, 1989). However, autistic disorder is more prevalent in females with IQs under 35, whereas autistic disorder is more prevalent in males with higher IQ ranges. Thus, females who develop autistic disorder are more likely to exhibit more severe mental retardation. The reasons for this sex difference are not known (Volkmar, Szatmari, & Sparrow, 1993). No other demographic differences in the prevalence or nature of autistic disorder (e.g., racial, cultural) have been firmly established.

In addition to the features that make up the formal DSM-IV definition of autistic disorder, the disturbance is frequently associated with other problematic symptoms. For instance, persons with autistic disorder may have a range of behavioral problems including hyperactivity (as was true for Ritchie); short attention span; poor impulse control; aggressive, self-injurious behaviors (e.g., head banging); and temper tantrums. Children with autism may display peculiar or unusual reactions to various forms of environmental stimulation (e.g., high pain threshold, extreme aversion to being touched). Disturbances in mood or the expression of emotions are common associated features of autistic disorder (e.g., laughing or crying for no apparent reason). Moreover, persons with autistic disorder may show no emotional reaction to situations or objects that most individuals would react to (e.g., display no fear to a large, aggressive dog), yet respond with excessive emotionality to harmless or trivial objects or situations (e.g., extreme distress upon discovering that a piece of furniture has been moved). In adolescence or early adulthood, persons with autistic disorder who have the intellectual capacity for insight have been observed to develop depression in response to the realization of their serious impairment.

By definition, the onset of autistic disorder is prior to age 3. Once it emerges, autistic disorder follows a continuous course (i.e., unlike some disorders, it is not generally characterized by alternating periods of improvement and recurrence). Nevertheless, the long-term course of autistic disorder is variable across individuals. Some children with autism deteriorate behaviorally when they reach adolescence, whereas other children show improvement. Research has indicated that the presence of language skills (i.e., ability for communicative speech) and higher overall intelligence may strongly predict a more positive long-term prognosis. Nevertheless, the little research that does exist on the long-term course of autistic disorder shows that only a small proportion of these children enter adulthood with the capability of living and working independently. Those who do achieve some degree of independence nonetheless continue to display problems with social interaction and communication, along with constricted interests and activities (American Psychiatric Association, 1994).

Thus far, there are no powerful treatments for autistic disorder. Most of the treatments developed to date have focused on problematic associated features of the disorder, such as disruptive or self-injurious behaviors. Biological treatments such as psychoactive drugs (e.g., Ritalin, frequently used in the treatment of ADHD; fenfluramine, an appetite suppressant) and vitamin therapy (e.g., vitamin B_6) have not produced significant or lasting improvements in intellectual level, sociability, or hyperactivity (for a review, see Holm & Varley, 1989). Many of the psychosocial interventions for autism have relied heavily on the learning theory principles of reinforcement and punishment to improve patients' skills of living and to curtail behavior problems. As was illustrated in Ritchie's case, these treatments have been used in the effort to improve the communication skills of children with autism (Durand, 1990; Lovaas, 1977). In addition, such treatments have been employed to improve socialization skills (i.e., increase the interest and frequency of social interaction with other people). Whereas behavior therapy has increased the frequency of social behaviors, such as playing with toys or other children, these treatments have not shown considerable positive effects in changing the quality of these interactions (e.g., the ability to initiate and maintain friendships with other children; Durand & Carr, 1988). However, an investigation that included an extremely time-intensive behavioral treatment (more than 40 hours per week for more than 2 years) found the psychosocial interventions could produce meaningful and lasting improvements in the intellectual and social abilities of children with autistic disorder (Lovaas, 1987). For instance, Lovaas (1987) reported that 47% of children with autism who were treated with the intensive program had achieved normal intellectual and educational functioning by the first grade (compared to none of a group of children with autism who received a less intensive treatment). Despite these promising results, some researchers have noted that these treatments may be seriously limited by their poor practicality (i.e., very expensive and time-intensive); others have argued that, given the potential for substantial benefits (i.e., intellectual functioning within the normal range), the "ends" provide resounding support for the intensive "means." Nevertheless, considerable work must be done in the future to develop more effective and practical treatments for autistic disorder.

THINKING CRITICALLY

1. Often, it is difficult to diagnostically distinguish autistic disorder from Asperger's disorder, childhood disintegrative disorder, or Rett's disorder. What features distinguish each of these conditions?
2. Given the clear evidence for the strong role of genetic, neurological, and biological factors in autism, what justifies the use of behavioral treatments for this disorder?
3. What do you believe is the best approach to educating children with developmental disorders within the public educational system? What do you believe are the advantages and disadvantages of special education programs versus programs aiming to integrate these students into normal classes?
4. What factors do you believe account for the higher rates of autism in boys than in girls?

Trichotillomania

A fter seeing a segment on a television network news program, Stevie Betts arranged an initial visit with a local clinical psychologist in private practice. At the time, Stevie was a 30-year-old single Caucasian woman who worked as a police officer. She contacted the psychologist because of a recent worsening of her long-standing habit of pulling out the hairs on her head and body. Although she had received treatment on two occasions in the past for her negative habit (described later), Stevie's problem had not fully responded to these interventions. However, the television show had described treatments that were different from the types that Stevie had received. Thus, the show prompted her hope that other treatment approaches would be helpful to her.

Clinical History

During her first visit with the psychologist, Stevie reported that, using either hand or tweezers, she pulled out hairs from most areas of her body—her head, arms, pubic area, stomach, and legs. She reported that her hair pulling was so frequent and had persisted for so long that she was totally bald except for a fringe of hair around the back of her head. She also noted that very few hairs remained in her pubic area. Being very ashamed and embarrassed about her hair loss, Stevie wore a wig at all times. In fact, Stevie's boyfriend, who had lived with her for 3 years, had never seen Stevie without the wig. Stevie had led her boyfriend to believe that her hair loss was due to a chemical imbalance. Believing that the therapist might ask her to show the extent of her hair loss, Stevie stated that she would never remove the wig, even in therapy. Although her hair loss was extensive, Stevie said that she had not noticed any scarring or physical damage to her head or other body areas resulting from the hair pulling.

The therapist asked Stevie for more specific information about her problem. Stevie said that, at the present time, she engaged in episodes of hair pulling that lasted approximately 10 to 15 minutes; these episodes occurred anywhere from 2 to 5 times per day. Stevie reported that the number of hairs that she pulled out varied from episode to episode, ranging from 10 to 50 hairs. Stevie said that she usually pulled out hairs that were short, thick, and coarse. With considerable embarrassment, Stevie reluctantly told the therapist that after she pulled out the hair, she would usually bite off the top of the hair (the follicle) before discarding it.

Stevie reported that her episodes of hair pulling always occurred at home, usually in the afternoon or evening. She said that she never had urges to pull hairs when she was in public. These episodes were often preceded by worrisome or depressive thoughts (discussed later). Stevie felt that the hair pulling distracted her from these negative thoughts. Nevertheless, she noted that this distraction was temporary because she would then feel depressed and frustrated about her inability to keep herself from pulling out her hair. When the therapist asked Stevie for more details about what occurred during her episodes of hair pulling, Stevie replied that a worrisome or depressive thought would lead to an urge to pull hair. When the urge occurred, Stevie would try to resist it at first, but she would then experience more discomfort because the urge intensified. Finally, she would give in to the urge and start to pull out her hair. The urge did not subside right after she began to pull out hair. During a hair-pulling episode, Stevie experienced an intensifying sense of frustration and guilt over her lack of control of the habit. In fact, Stevie said that most of her hair-pulling episodes would stop after her feelings of frustration and guilt overrode her urges to pull more hair.

Stevie recalled that her habit began when she was a senior in high school, shortly after a crisis in her family. Stevie's mother asked her father to leave the household upon learning that he had been having an affair with his secretary. Stevie's mother also learned that he had been squandering the family's savings through gambling and buying lavish gifts for his secretary. Her father had initially left the household without much ado and moved in with his secretary. After this relationship ended 3 months later, however, Stevie's father tried to move back into the household. When Stevie's mother refused, he became violent, smashed objects around the house, and threatened to beat up or kill her mother. Stevie and her little sister witnessed such incidents on several occasions. In fact, Stevie's mother was forced to get a restraining order from the courts to keep her father away from the family. Her father complied with the restraining order but blamed Stevie for what had happened to the family and accused her of not sticking up for him by not persuading her mother to allow him back into the household. Even at the time of her initial visit with the psychologist, Stevie was much estranged from her father and would often refer to him as her ex-father. Although she associated these incidents with the onset of her problem, Stevie did not understand why the stress in her family caused her to develop the habit of pulling out hair.

Stevie reported that she had undergone treatment on two occasions for her hair pulling. Four years prior to her initial visit with the psychologist, Stevie had consulted with a psychiatrist who treated her problem with clomipramine (Anafranil), a tricyclic antidepressant medication that has been frequently used in the treatment of obsessive-compulsive disorder (OCD). Patients with OCD often have nonsensical urges that produce discomfort and behavioral actions to reduce the urges and their associated distress; for example, they may report discomfort in attempting to resist the nonsensical urge to count objects in their environment, and they are able to reduce this discomfort only by giving into the urge to count (see Case 5). The psychiatrist prescribed Stevie a drug that is commonly used in the treatment of OCD because some researchers believe that the problem of persistent hair pulling is related to OCD. The potential link between hair pulling and OCD is discussed later in this chapter.

Stevie took clomipramine for 1 year. Stevie recalled that her problem responded quite well to the drug during the first 8 months she took it. During this time, she stated that she was "98% better" and would pull out only a few hairs on rare occasions. However, she said that she experienced a number of negative side effects from clomipramine, including decreased sex drive, constipation, persistent dry mouth, a tendency to stutter, and eye twitching. Because of these side effects and the fact that she was beginning to resume her habit of hair pulling despite her initial favorable response to the drug, Stevie's psychiatrist tapered her off the medication. Over the next several months, the psychiatrist then prescribed other antidepressant medications, none of which had any effect on Stevie's problem. Later, Stevie consulted another psychiatrist who treated her problem with psychodynamic psychotherapy. After 3 months, she stopped seeing this psychiatrist because she felt that therapy was not helping her.

As part of the intake evaluation, the psychologist administered a clinical interview to determine if Stevie had any other psychological disorders that contributed to her current difficulties. Stating that she felt sad and had low self-esteem for as long as she can remember, Stevie reported ongoing problems with depression. She said that for most of her adulthood, including the present, she felt depressed. At the time of her evaluation, Stevie's depressed mood was accompanied by the symptoms of loss of interest and pleasure in her usual activities and hobbies, fatigue, excess sleepiness (frequent naps, sleeping more than 8 hours per night), increased appetite, feelings of guilt, slowed body movement, and difficulty concentrating and making decisions. Stevie said that her depression was also associated with her tendency to worry excessively. She claimed that, on average, she worried 75% of the day about matters such as finances, her job performance, personal relationships, and the health of her mother (whose mammogram indicated possible precancerous tissue). She said much of her current depression and worry related to her relationship with her current boyfriend; Stevie felt that the relationship was going nowhere, and she worried that he was going to break up with her and move out. In addition, Stevie stated that her inability to gain control of her bad habit of hair pulling contributed to her depression a great deal. As noted earlier, Stevie reported that her urges to pull hair usually were prompted by depressive or worrisome thoughts and that she felt that she engaged in hair pulling to distract herself from these thoughts.

Stevie recalled that her problems with depression began several years before she started pulling her hair. When she was 22, Stevie's depression had become so bad that she attempted suicide by taking an overdose of allergy medication. Stevie told her mother about the overdose immediately after taking the pills. Her mother took Stevie to the hospital, where she had her stomach pumped. Stevie reported that depression seemed to run in her mother's side of the family in that her mother and both of her maternal grandparents had a history of this problem. She recalled that her depression was another reason why her first psychiatrist had prescribed an antidepressant medication for her hair pulling.

During the clinical interview, Stevie also reported anxiety in social situations where she might be negatively evaluated by others and thus be embarrassed or humiliated. She stated that she was apprehensive of and often avoided social situations such as parties, attending or participating in meetings, eating in public, being assertive, and initiating or maintaining conversations with people she did not know well. Although she recalled that she had been shy and somewhat anxious in social situations since she was a child, Stevie reported that her social anxiety and avoidance had increased after she developed the habit of pulling out her hair. Indeed, some of her apprehension of entering social situations related to Stevie's concern that others would ask about her wig or discover that she had no hair on her head. Stevie also reported being very tense on the job as a police officer about the concern that her wig might get knocked off in a scuffle. Stevie stated that many of her fellow officers knew about her lack of hair, but as with her boyfriend, she had led them to believe that her hair loss was caused by a chemical imbalance.

DSM-IV Diagnosis

Based on this information, Stevie's psychologist assigned the following DSM-IV diagnosis:

Axis I	312.30	Trichotillomania (principal diagnosis)
	296.33	Major depressive disorder, recurrent, severe without psychotic features, chronic
	300.23	Social phobia
Axis II	V71.09	No diagnosis on Axis II
Axis III	None	
Axis IV	Familial discord, conflict with boyfriend	
Axis V	Global assessment of functioning = 50 (current)	

Prior to beginning treatment, Stevie clearly evidenced all of the symptoms of the DSM-IV impulse control disorder trichotillomania (American Psychiatric Association, 1994), which is defined by the following features: (a) recurrent pulling out of one's hair, resulting in noticeable hair loss; (b) an increasing sense of tension immediately before pulling out the hair or when attempting to resist the behavior; (c) pleasure, gratification, or relief while pulling out the hair; and (d) the disturbance causes clinically significant distress or impairment in social, occupational, or other important areas of functioning. In DSM-IV, it is also specified that trichotillomania should not be diagnosed if the symptoms are better accounted for by another emotional disorder or a general medical condition (e.g., a dermatological condition). Social phobia and major depression are discussed in Cases 3 and 8, respectively.

CASE FORMULATION USING THE INTEGRATIVE MODEL

To date, research conducted on the nature and treatment of trichotillomania is sparse. Accordingly, very little is known about the factors that are responsible for the causes and maintenance of this problem. In fact, trichotillomania was not included as a disorder in the DSM classification system until 1987 (American Psychiatric Association, 1987). Researchers have disagreed on the possible causes of trichotillomania. Consistent with the way in which the problem is currently classified in DSM-IV (American Psychiatric Association, 1994), many investigators believe that trichotillomania is a form of impulse control disorder. The essential feature of impulse control disorders is the failure to resist an impulse, drive, or temptation to perform an act that the person knows is harmful to self or others. Other impulse control disorders listed in DSM-IV include kleptomania (stealing objects that are not needed for personal use or monetary value), pyromania (setting fires), and pathological gambling (persistent and maladaptive gambling). As was true for Stevie, a person with an impulse control disorder may experience an increasing sense of tension or arousal before committing the act (e.g., hair pulling, stealing) and then experience a sense of relief (or gratification or pleasure) while engaging in the behavior. Like Stevie's experience, this sense of relief is often followed by a feeling of regret or guilt for having given in to the impulse.

As noted earlier, some researchers (e.g., Jenike, 1989) have conceptualized trichotillomania as a form of OCD. To support this conceptualization, these investigators point out that OCD and trichotillomania share many clinical features. For example, both sets of patients recognize that their compulsive behaviors (i.e., hair pulling in trichotillomania; washing, checking, counting, etc., in OCD) are senseless, yet feel driven to complete the behavior despite knowledge that doing so creates significant distress and interference in their lives. Moreover, there is evidence, albeit quite preliminary and in need of replication, that patients with trichotillomania may have a higher incidence of OCD in their immediate families than other persons (e.g., Lenane et al., 1992), which would suggest that trichotillomania and OCD may share biological or genetic factors that contribute to the development of these conditions. This familial pattern was not observed in Stevie, who reported only a history of depression in her mother's side of the family. Nevertheless, Stevie's father may have had another form of impulse control disorder, pathological gambling, given that his gambling was one of the reasons why Stevie's mother demanded that he leave the household when Stevie was 17. You may recall that Stevie's first treatment for her trichotillomania was the drug clomipramine (Anafranil), an antidepressant medication that has been frequently used in the treatment of OCD. As was initially the case for Stevie, some patients with trichotillomania show a favorable response to clomipramine. These studies are reviewed in the discussion section of this chapter. Because both OCD and trichotillomania may respond to the same drug treatment, some researchers feel that this is evidence for a relationship between these two disorders.

Because little research has been done on trichotillomania, these conceptualizations of this disorder are quite tentative. For example, other investigators have disputed the idea that trichotillomania and OCD are related conditions by noting important differences between these two disorders, one of which is that most patients with OCD engage in their compulsive behavior to reduce anxiety associated with their belief that if they do not complete this act, a negative or harmful consequence will occur. Recall that in Case 5 Pat Montgomery spent at least 4 hours per day washing herself and objects in her home because she feared that if she did not complete these actions, she would become contaminated with germs that would cause her to contract a deadly disease. Although trichotillomania is similar to OCD with regard to the presence of repetitive behavior (e.g., hair pulling versus excessive washing), unlike OCD the compulsive act of hair pulling is not performed to reduce anxiety or to decrease the perceived likelihood of an aversive or harmful event (cf. Stanley, Borden, Mouton, & Breckenridge, 1995). In fact, over time the act of hair pulling can become so habitual that a person often may not even be aware of doing it.

Treatment Goals and Planning

Despite limited evidence on the nature of trichotillomania, Stevie's therapist used an OCD-like model in conceptualizing her problem and planning her treatment. Consistent with Stevie's report during the intake evaluation, the therapist felt that Stevie's urges to pull out her hair were more likely to occur in the afternoon or evening when she was home by herself and when she focused on depressing or worrisome thoughts. If Stevie attempted to resist the urge to pull, she would experience an increase in discomfort and an intensification of her urge. The only way that Stevie could reduce the urge and discomfort was to give in to the urge by pulling out her hair. In addition to reducing the urge and its associated discomfort, hair pulling was somewhat rewarding to Stevie because it distracted her from her worries or depressing thoughts. However, this relief was temporary because Stevie would feel very guilty and ashamed after a hair-pulling episode over the fact that she had not been able to resist the urge. The therapist realized that this formulation did not account for all of Stevie's symptoms. For example, it did not address why Stevie developed the problem to begin with or why Stevie usually bit the top off each hair that she pulled. (Stevie could not offer any insight into this either and noted that biting the hairs did not seem to affect how quickly her urge to pull more hair was reduced.)

Although Stevie had considerable difficulties with depression, Stevie and her therapist agreed to focus the treatment on her trichotillomania. This decision was based on the fact that Stevie considered trichotillomania to be her biggest problem and because the therapist was planning to take an extended vacation 3 months from the date that Stevie's treatment would begin (potentially not affording sufficient time to address both trichotillomania and depression thoroughly). Thus, the therapeutic plan was to treat Stevie's trichotillomania, then provide her with a referral to another clinical psychologist in private practice who specialized in the cognitive-behavioral treatment of depression. The primary treatment technique that the therapist planned to employ was gradual exposure to situations that triggered Stevie's hair-pulling urges while, at the same time, guiding her to deploy behaviors that would compete or interfere with her habitual tendency to pull out hair. This technique is referred to as habit reversal (Azrin & Nunn, 1973).

COURSE OF TREATMENT
AND TREATMENT OUTCOME

In the first treatment session, Stevie was asked to begin daily self-monitoring of her hair pulling. On forms provided to her by the therapist, Stevie was instructed to record the following information each time she pulled out hair: the date and time of day, the situation she was in (e.g., watching TV alone), the manner in which the hair was pulled (e.g., tweezers, right or left hand), the number of hairs pulled, the body site from which hair was pulled, emotions or thoughts preceding the hair pulling, and emotions or thoughts after the episode. In addition to providing an index of Stevie's progress throughout treatment, the self-monitoring had a number of other useful purposes. For example, the act of self-monitoring would assist Stevie to become more aware of the instances when she was pulling out hair. As noted earlier, hair pulling can become so habitual that people may often not realize when they are engaging in this act. In addition, self-monitoring would assist Stevie and her therapist in learning more about the circumstances that Stevie's urges to pull hair were most likely to occur—information that would be very important for designing strategies to break or reverse Stevie's habit.

In the second session, Stevie noted the value of self-monitoring because it had made her aware of the fact that she often pulled out hair when she did not realize that she was doing so. Her monitoring records were consistent with her report that she had "unconsciously" pulled out hairs on several occasions. However, Stevie said that she had found it easy to stop pulling hair when she had become conscious that she had unknowingly started the action. Nevertheless, she reported considerable difficulty resisting the urges to pull hair deliberately; she had engaged in two episodes of deliberate hair pulling between the first and second sessions. As the initial step of habit reversal, the remainder of this session was spent discussing further the contexts in which Stevie was most likely to pull hair (i.e., awareness training). Because of the approaching Christmas holidays, the third session was scheduled for 2 weeks later.

Stevie came to the third meeting with a startling revelation. Two days after the second session, Stevie and several of her fellow police officers were assigned to patrol and act as crowd control at a rock concert. A "mini-riot" had erupted outside the theater after several people were not allowed into the sold-out concert, even though they had tickets (in error, more tickets had been printed and sold than the number of seats actually available). During the altercation, Stevie had been bitten on the arm by a rioting concert-goer she was helping to restrain. She later learned that this person, who was placed under arrest, had AIDS. Because the bite had broken her skin, there was now concern that Stevie had been exposed to the HIV virus. As would be expected, Stevie was very upset about what had occurred and the fact that she would not know for several months whether the virus had been passed on to her (because evidence of the HIV does not show up on medical tests until many months after exposure). Nevertheless, Stevie seemed to be dealing with the incident appropriately. She also noted that her colleagues and supervisors at work had been very supportive.

Remarkably, this incident had a very strong and unexpected effect on her symptoms of trichotillomania. Stevie reported that her emotions and thoughts surrounding her possible exposure to HIV had "overshadowed" her urges to pull hair. In fact, Stevie stated that she had not pulled out a single hair since the mishap had occurred, nearly 2 weeks ago. When the therapist learned of this, she thought to herself that the remission of Stevie's trichotil-lomania might be temporary, given that the symptoms had abated for only a brief time and could possibly recur after the "shock" of the distressing event began to wane. However, the therapist quite appropriately used most of this session to help Stevie sort out her emotions surrounding the event, instead of focusing solely on trichotillomania.

Over the next 7 weeks, Stevie did not pull any hair, although she did experience some urges to pull hair on occasion. Despite the fact that Stevie's trichotillomania had remitted to a considerable degree, she and her therapist continued with the treatment. Stevie had agreed with her therapist's sugges-tion that it would be a good idea for her to learn techniques to treat tri-chotillomania to reduce the remaining urges and to increase the likelihood that her symptoms did not resurface in the future. Based on Stevie's self-monitoring, a list was constructed of situations that had prompted episodes or strong urges for hair pulling. This list included such situations as looking in the mirror after a shower, leaving her head bare (no wig) at home, sitting in front of the TV worrying about work or relationships, and sitting on the bed with tweezers and a mirror. After this list was constructed, the therapist introduced the technique of graduated exposure plus habit reversal. Starting with the situations that had prompted mild urges to pull hair (and gradually working up the list to situations that produced strong urges), the therapist asked Stevie to repeatedly confront these situations on a daily basis. If Stevie experienced an urge to pull hair while she was in the situation, she was instructed to engage in a behavior that would be incompatible with the actions required to pull out hair. For example, if she experienced an urge to pull hair while she was looking at herself in the mirror after a shower, Stevie squeezed her hands into fists until the urge subsided. Stevie was also instructed to squeeze her hands into fists when the urges to pull hair occurred naturally during the day. Based on the guidelines of habit reversal (Azrin & Nunn, 1973), "making fists" was considered to be an appropriate competing response to hair pulling because (a) it was the opposite of movements needed to pull hair, (b) it could be maintained for several minutes until the urge passed, and (c) it was socially inconspicuous and readily deployable during the course of normal activity.

Despite the fact that Stevie's symptoms of trichotillomania had subsided, her depression had gotten increasingly worse since she was bitten by the person with AIDS. Interestingly, Stevie's depression did not seem to be related to her thoughts and feelings about possible HIV exposure. Indeed, she had been coping with these issues very well. Rather, Stevie's depression was largely attributable to her uncertainty about her relationship with her boyfriend. Two weeks after she was bitten, her boyfriend had left their home on short notice to visit friends in a town 150 miles away. Because several weeks had gone by and Stevie had not heard from him, she assumed that this was his way of breaking up with her. However, Stevie had made no effort to reach him, and she expressed humiliation at the thought of contacting him and being rejected. Stevie's depression had gotten so bad that she had discontinued all her usual activities other than going to work.

Stevie's mood also had a negative impact on her compliance with treatment. As her depression increased, Stevie completed less and less of her self-monitoring and homework assignments (e.g., exposure plus habit reversal exercises). Also, she usually did not complete tasks that the therapist had assigned to address her depression (e.g., to schedule and participate in pleasant activities to enhance her positive affect and to counteract her tendency to withdraw from usual activities; see Case 8). Part of Stevie's noncompliance with self-monitoring was due to her belief that the act of monitoring increased her feelings of guilt by emphasizing her perceived lack of control over pulling. The therapist pointed out that Stevie could use the self-monitoring to increase her sense of control by showing that the urges to pull and episodes of actual hair pulling had decreased. The therapist also observed that Stevie exhibited an all-or-nothing thinking pattern that contributed to her noncompliance with homework. Specifically, if Stevie failed to complete a task early in the week, she would not complete any other assignments for the remainder of the week based on the belief that it was of no use because she had "screwed up" from the start. Stevie also felt that she was not capable of completing everything that she was being assigned (i.e., self-monitoring, exposure plus habit reversal, pleasant events scheduling), although she had handled a similar workload prior to the worsening of her depression. The therapist responded by (a) temporally reducing the amount of homework Stevie was assigned and gradually working up to the level that she had completed before the depression had worsened and (b) contacting Stevie by phone during the week to ensure that she was completing her assignments and to offer her advice and support in completing tasks over the rest of the week. Overall, these maneuvers were successful in restoring Stevie's compliance and in fostering her expectations that she could complete therapeutic tasks well.

Although Stevie had refrained from hair pulling for the 7 weeks after she'd been bitten by a person with AIDS, these symptoms resurfaced following Stevie's final break-up with her boyfriend, when she was bedridden for 4 days with the flu. Stevie reported that, on a few occasions while she was bedridden, she had pulled many hairs from her pubic area. She also stated that she had pulled hairs from her head but had been successful at stopping after pulling out only a couple of hairs. Stevie was very distressed over this turn of events. Only with considerable difficulty did the therapist assist Stevie in entertaining the notion that this minor recurrence of hair pulling did not signify that Stevie had altogether failed to respond to treatment or that she had regressed back to where she was prior to treatment.

Over the next several weeks, Stevie routinely pulled 5 to 10 hairs from her head daily, usually in the evening while she was watching TV. During this time, Stevie usually was unaware that she was pulling and was able to stop upon realizing what she was doing. In addition to repeatedly noting that the frequency of pulling had decreased markedly since the onset of treatment (a point that Stevie usually minimized or downplayed), the therapist had Stevie focus most of her exposure plus habit reversal practices around watching TV.

One reason why Stevie's urges to pull hair had increased was that her hair had started to grow back. For example, the hair on her head was now 1 inch long. (Despite this sign of considerable progress, Stevie felt that her hair was still too short to dispose of the wig.) In addition to now having more hair to pull, Stevie's short hair was very itchy under the wig. Because Stevie had to scratch her itchy scalp often, her hands were in contact with her hair several times per day. Stevie was asked to practice habit reversal after she touched the short hairs on her head. In addition, Stevie maintained some strong beliefs that contributed to her urge to pull hair, especially from her arms. For example, Stevie believed that the hair on her arms was usually too thick and too long and that others would notice it and be disgusted. The therapist attempted to use cognitive restructuring to assist Stevie in changing these beliefs. As noted in several other cases, cognitive restructuring involves a set of procedures to identify faulty thoughts or erroneous assumptions, followed by a thorough evaluation of the validity of these thoughts and assumptions by examining the factual evidence to support or refute these beliefs. The successful end result is to assist the person in replacing a faulty belief with an accurate perception.

The therapist only had limited success with cognitive restructuring in changing Stevie's negative beliefs about her hair. Stevie's depression was a key factor for this technique's lack of success. For instance, with the assistance of her therapist, Stevie often began to challenge her negative beliefs appropriately. For example, she would challenge the prediction that "people would be grossed out by the hair on my arms" by saying, "Why would anyone stare at my arms anyhow? Most people do not pay attention to other people's arms." However, these statements would usually be followed by depressive self-statements such as "Nobody wants to look at me anyway."

Moreover, Stevie's specific beliefs about the appearance of hair were quite rigid and firmly ingrained in her. The therapist considered these beliefs to be more discrete manifestations of Stevie's overarching view that she was an unattractive person with no positive qualities.

Despite the limited value of cognitive restructuring in changing her beliefs about her appearance, Stevie's trichotillomania did go into another remission over the next several weeks. During this time, Stevie's compliance with homework was exemplary. Her urges to pull continued, but episodes of actual hair pulling were infrequent and usually stopped after one hair. However, Stevie did not express much satisfaction over the positive change in her symptoms or her increased homework compliance; instead, she expressed frustration and self-denigration over the fact that some symptoms of trichotillomania remained. Nevertheless, Stevie's depression lifted to some degree during this period. She started to view the break-up with her boyfriend as having the potential of providing new opportunities. Accordingly, Stevie began to resume her usual activities and hobbies and reinitiated contact with several friends. With the encouragement of her therapist, Stevie bought new clothes for herself and joined a fitness club.

Because it was nearing the time when the therapist was leaving the area for an extended vacation, the focus of Stevie's treatment increasingly was on relapse prevention and fostering her transition to the new therapist. As is discussed in greater detail in Case 13, relapse prevention involves techniques to reduce the likelihood of the recurrence of symptoms, as well as strategies to assist the person in holding a realistic perspective on the long-term course of symptoms and how to respond to instances of the reemergence of symptoms (cf. Marlatt & Gordon, 1985). This latter component was very important in Stevie's case, given that she regarded the considerable progress that she had made as trivial and because she still expressed guilt and dejection over the fact that some symptoms remained.

Although Stevie was fully aware of the fact that her treatment with her current therapist would last 3 months and had agreed to this arrangement at the start of therapy, she did not handle the transition to a new therapist well. Although the hair on her head was now 2 inches long, Stevie continued to berate her progress and expressed considerable pessimism over the prospect of holding or furthering her gains with a new therapist. The therapist attempted to allay these issues by emphasizing the objective aspects of Stevie's favorable response to treatment (e.g., her extensive hair growth). In addition, the therapist pointed out that the original plan had been to have Stevie continue on with this particular therapist, given his considerable training and experience in the cognitive-behavioral treatment of depression. These efforts were not successful in assisting Stevie to handle the transition better. In fact, treatment ended after Stevie canceled a therapy session and did not reschedule. She did not respond to phone messages or to letters from the therapist. Prior to leaving the area, the therapist called the psychologist to whom Stevie had been referred. He stated that Stevie had completed an initial assessment session and promised to call him to arrange for the first treatment session. However, she had not contacted him, and his efforts to reach her by phone and by mail had been unsuccessful.

DISCUSSION

Research on the nature and treatment of trichotillomania is sparse. Perhaps the most extensive study of this disorder was by Christenson, Mackenzie, and Mitchell (1991), who evaluated 60 patients (56 females, 4 males) with trichotillomania by using a semistructured clinical interview. In this study, the majority of patients reported that the onset of their disorder occurred before the age of 16; very few patients reported an age of onset in their 20s or later. All patients reported that their condition had a chronic course; the mean duration of hair pulling in this sample was 21 years. Sites of hair pulling included every region of the body in which hair may grow, although the most common sites were the scalp (75% of patients), eyelashes (53%), eyebrows (42%), and pubic area (17%). The majority of patients (62%) pulled hair from two or more sites of the body. Consistent with Stevie's presentation, more than half (57%) of the patients reported that hairs perceived as coarse or thick were the most likely targets of pulling. Also consistent with Stevie's clinical history was the observation that nearly half (48%) of patients reported engaging in some form of oral behavior associated with hair pulling. A third of the sample (33%) chewed or bit off the ends of hair, 25% rubbed hair around their mouths after pulling it out, and 10% ate their hair. Like Stevie, most patients (95%) reported that their hair pulling was worse in the evening and while they were engaged in sedentary activities such as watching television or reading.

As noted in the first paragraph of this section, in order to satisfy the definition of trichotillomania, DSM-IV requires that the person must evidence an increasing sense of tension immediately before pulling out the hair (or when attempting to resist pulling) and pleasure, gratification, or relief when pulling out the hair. Whereas most of the chronic hair pullers studied by Christenson, Mackenzie, and Mitchell (1991) reported these characteristics, a significant minority (17%) did not evidence both of these features (i.e., tension, followed by tension reduction or gratification when the hair is pulled). Indeed, some patients reported that their hair pulling *always* occurred without their full awareness (which occasionally happened to Stevie when she was watching TV). Thus, these authors raised the argument that the DSM-IV criteria for trichotillomania may be too restrictive because the criteria do not provide diagnostic coverage for persons who persistently pull hair but who do not report a tension-reduction cycle.

Although trichotillomania was previously thought to be an uncommon condition, it is now believed to occur more frequently. Most of the studies that have examined the prevalence of trichotillomania have used college student samples. In one of the first and largest studies of this nature, Christenson, Pyle, and Mitchell (1991) found that less than 1% (0.6%) of a sample of 2,534 college freshmen had experienced the full diagnostic syndrome of trichotillomania at some point during their lives. However, hair pulling that resulted in visible hair loss but did not meet the full diagnostic criteria for trichotillomania was identified in 1.5% of males and 3.4% of females. Subsequent studies have obtained even higher rates of nonclinical hair pulling in college student samples (i.e., regular hair pulling that is not associated with all of the features necessary to meet DSM-IV criteria for trichotillomania). For instance, two studies have found that 10% to 15% of college students report repetitive hair pulling that does not lead to significant hair loss (Rothbaum, Shaw, Morris, & Ninan, 1993; Stanley, Borden, Bell, & Wagner, 1994). In all these studies, persons who reported a current or past history of hair pulling or trichotillomania were more likely to be female.

Initial evidence suggests that trichotillomania does not often occur in the absence of other emotional disorders. In the Christenson, Mackenzie, and Mitchell (1991) study, only 11 (18%) of the 60 patients did not have a history of current or past emotional disorders other than trichotillomania. Consistent with Stevie's presentation, mood disorders were the most common additional diagnosis in this sample. Indeed, 65% of the patients had experienced a mood disorder at some point during their lives; the most common mood disorder diagnosis was major depression (55% of the sample had major depression at some point in their lives; 23% had major depression at the time of their evaluation). Anxiety disorders were also quite prevalent; the lifetime prevalence of these disorders was 57%, with the most common diagnoses being specific phobia (32%), generalized anxiety disorder (27%), and panic disorder with or without agoraphobia (18%). The lifetime prevalence of eating disorders (e.g., bulimia) and substance use disorders (e.g., alcoholism) was also quite high (20% and 22%, respectively). Interestingly, and perhaps counter to the argument for the similarities between these two conditions, obsessive-compulsive disorder (OCD) occurred less frequently in this sample (15%) than a number of other disorders.

Despite the low rate of co-occurrence between trichotillomania and OCD in the Christenson, Mackenzie, and Mitchell (1991) study, a great deal of the research that has been conducted on chronic hair pulling has been done in reference to their potential similarities and overlap. Much of this research was discussed in the case formulation section of this chapter (e.g., similarity of clinical features, rates of OCD in the immediate families of persons with trichotillomania). In support of the position that trichotillomania may be a variant of OCD, researchers often point to the evidence indicating that both disorders respond to the same medication. As detailed in Case 5, the tricyclic antidepressant clomipramine (Anafranil) is frequently used in the OCD treatment. Initial evidence suggests that clomipramine can be effective in the treatment of trichotillomania as well (Swedo et al., 1989). In the Swedo et al. (1989) study, 13 women with trichotillomania were treated with clomipramine and another form of tricyclic antidepressant drug, desipramine, in a cross-over design (patients are given both treatments at separate times, and their clinical response to each treatment is evaluated). On nearly all measures of treatment outcome, clomipramine resulted in greater improvement than did desipramine. Immediately following the 5-week treatment, 12 of 13 patients showed significant improvement while they were taking clomipramine; 3 patients had a total remission. Although the authors concluded that clomipramine appears to be an effective treatment for trichotillomania, these findings should be tempered by (a) the small number of patients studied and (b) the lack of long-term results (i.e., what is the success rate of clomipramine several months after the treatment has been initiated?).

In addition to these caveats, considering trichotillomania and OCD to be related conditions because of their similar treatment response to clomipramine is problematic for another reason. Specifically, many different types of emotional disorders have been found to respond to antidepressant medications. For instance, if you read through the cases on panic disorder, OCD, major depression, and bulimia nervosa, you will see that antidepressant drugs have been used in the treatment of each of these conditions. Thus, the fact that both OCD and trichotillomania may respond to the same antidepressant drug is not unique, given the common finding that several disorders may respond to a similar treatment (cf. Hudson & Pope, 1990; Tyrer, 1989).

Cognitive-behavioral treatments, such as the habit reversal approach used with Stevie, represent the most common psychosocial interventions for trichotillomania (Friman, Finney, & Christophersen, 1984). However, most evidence in support of these procedures has come from single-case studies. To date, one of the most extensive psychosocial treatment studies to be completed was by Azrin, Nunn, and Frantz (1980). In this study, 34 hair-pullers were assigned to either habit reversal treatment or negative practice training (requiring the person to rapidly perform the habitual behavior at predetermined times to eliminate the rewarding properties of the habit). Habit reversal was more effective, reducing hair pulling by more than 90%, whereas negative practice reduced it by only 50%. Although the results were promising, they are limited by the fact that outcome was gauged by subject self-report only (i.e., subjects' report that they were pulling less hair was not verified by objective means such as extent of hair growth). In addition, this study was conducted before trichotillomania was listed in the DSM system and thus it is reasonable to presume that many of the participants engaged in subclinical levels of hair pulling (and less severe symptoms may be more responsive to treatment). The study also did not contain any form of control group (e.g., waiting list condition) and did not examine the long-term effects of treatment. Therefore, consistent with a theme touched on throughout this case, much more research is needed on the development and evaluation of effective treatments, both psychosocial and drug, for trichotillomania.

THINKING CRITICALLY

1. Some researchers have pursued the possible link between trichotillomania and obsessive-compulsive disorder. In what ways are these disorders similar? Do you think that trichotillomania is best classified as an impulse-control disorder, as it is currently categorized in DSM-IV?

2. What do you believe are the most common and most likely pathways to developing trichotillomania? Do you think that excessive hair-pulling may reflect an overlearned habit that occurs outside the person's awareness, or instead emanates from one or more psychological factors, such as a response to an uncontrollable impulse, a body-image disturbance (e.g., self-perceptions of excessive body hair), or a form of self-mutilation as is found in depressive disorders or borderline personality disorder? Provide justification for your answer. Do you believe trichotillomania simply reflects a "bad habit" in some cases, or is it always a sign of a deeper psychological disturbance?

3. What do you believe would be the most successful strategies for treating excessive hair-pulling? Critics of the techniques used in Stevie's treatment (e.g., habit reversal) might say that these interventions are too narrowly focused because they only deal with hair-pulling urges and do not address the factors that lead to such urges. Would you agree or disagree with this appraisal? Why? Do you think that trichotillomania is sufficiently heterogeneous that different types of treatments must be tailored for each individual in order to successfully intervene in that person's disorder?

4. What factors do you believe account for the finding that some persons with trichotillomania perform some type of ritual after the hair has been pulled (e.g., biting off the follicle before discarding the hair or storing the pulled hair in small piles around the house)?

Case

18

Diagnosis Not Provided: Case #1

At the time of his admission to the psychiatric hospital, Carl Landau was a 19-year-old single Caucasian man. Carl was a college freshman majoring in philosophy who had withdrawn from school because of his incapacitating symptoms and behaviors. He had an 8-year history of behavioral and emotional problems that had become increasingly severe, including excessive washing and showering; ceremonial rituals for dressing and studying; compulsive placement of any objects he handled; grotesque hissing, coughing, and head tossing while eating; and shuffling and wiping his feet while walking.

These behaviors interfered with every aspect of his daily functioning. Carl had steadily deteriorated over the past 2 years. He had isolated himself from family and friends, refused meals, and neglected his personal appearance. His hair was very long, as he had not allowed it to be cut in 5 years. He had never shaved or trimmed his beard. When Carl walked, he shuffled and took small steps on his toes while continually looking back, checking, and rechecking. On occasion, he would run in place. Carl had withdrawn his left arm completely from his shirt sleeve, as if it were injured and his shirt were a sling.

Seven weeks prior to his admission to the hospital, Carl's behaviors had become so time-consuming and debilitating that he refused to engage in any personal hygiene for fear that grooming and cleaning would interfere with the time needed to study. Although Carl had previously showered almost continuously, at this time he did not shower at all. He stopped washing his hair, brushing his teeth, and changing his clothes. He left his bedroom infrequently, and he had begun defecating on paper towels, urinating in paper cups while in his bedroom, and storing the waste in a corner of the closet in his room. His eating habits had degenerated from eating with the family, to eating in an adjoining room, to eating in his own room. In the 2 months prior to his admission, Carl had lost 20 pounds and would eat only late at night, when others were asleep. He felt that eating was "barbaric"; this described well his grotesque eating rituals, which consisted of hissing noises, coughs and hacks, and severe head tossing. His food intake had been narrowed to ice cream or a mixture of peanut butter, sugar, cocoa, milk, and mayonnaise. Carl did not eat several foods (e.g., cola, beef, and butter) because he felt that these foods contained germs and diseases and were poisonous. In addition, he was preoccupied with the placement of objects. Excessive time was spent ensuring that wastebaskets and curtains were in the proper places. These preoccupations had progressed to tilting of wastebaskets and twisting of curtains, which Carl periodically checked throughout the day.

Most of Carl's problem behaviors were associated with distressing thoughts that he could dismiss or get out of his mind only by engaging in these actions. As noted before, many of his bizarre eating behaviors and narrow diet related to his extreme fear that he would be poisoned. In fact, Carl reported that some of his rituals while eating were attempts to reduce the probability of being contaminated or poisoned. For example, the loud hissing sounds and coughing before he put food in his mouth were part of his attempt to exhale all air from his system, thereby allowing any food that he did swallow to enter an air-free and somewhat sterile environment (his stomach). Carl realized that this was not rational but was strongly driven by the idea of reducing any chance of contamination.

In addition, his cessation of washing or going to the bathroom to eliminate waste was also related to his failure to cut his hair or shave. Carl's thoughts centered around the possibility that nicking himself while shaving would allow contaminants that might kill him to enter his body. Therefore, when shaving, even with an electric razor, he had to be excruciatingly careful, and this process would often take hours. Similarly, if he did not wash according to some preconceived stereotypical patterns, he would feel that he had not removed all of the contaminants and therefore would have to start all over again. These behaviors had progressed from taking several hours to taking all day; thus, the only possibility open to Carl was to cease doing them altogether in order to have some time to devote to other activities.

Finally, Carl's placement of objects in a certain way, including waste-baskets and curtains, and withdrawing his arm from his shirt sleeve and carrying it inside his shirt as if he were wearing a sling were also methods, in Carl's mind, to protect him and his family from some future catastrophe such as contracting AIDS. Once again, Carl realized that there was no rational connection between these stereotypical behaviors and contracting AIDS or dying from some other means, but he would be haunted by thoughts of disasters and catastrophes befalling him and his family if he did not engage in these behaviors. Indeed, although early in the course of his disorder Carl had regarded the thoughts he was having as senseless, over time these ideas had become intense and distressing to him. The more Carl tried to dismiss these thoughts or resist engaging in a problem behavior such as shuffling his feet, the more intense and distressing his thoughts became.

Clinical History

Carl was raised in a very caring family consisting of himself, a younger brother, his mother, and his father, who was minister of a local Protestant church. Carl was quiet and withdrawn and had only a few friends. Nevertheless, he did very well in school and was functioning reasonably well until approximately the seventh grade, when he became the object of jokes, ridicule, and scorn by a group of students in his class. Under their constant harassment, Carl began experiencing severe emotional distress, and many of his problem behaviors began to emerge. Although he performed very well academically throughout junior high school and into high school, Carl's behavioral problems deteriorated to the point where he began missing school and went from having a few friends to having no friends. Increasingly, Carl started withdrawing to his bedroom to engage in the problem behaviors described previously. This marked deterioration in Carl's behavior prompted his parents to bring him in to treatment.

DSM-IV Diagnosis

Based on this information, what five-axis diagnosis do you think best applies to Carl?

Axis I

Axis II

Axis III

Axis IV

Axis V   Global assessment of functioning =   (current)

Diagnosis Not Provided: Case #2

At the time of his presentation to the outpatient clinic of a psychiatric hospital, Eric Beck was a 32-year-old single Caucasian man who lived with his parents. Although he had worked as a stockbroker after college and had also been trained as a paralegal, Eric had been underemployed over the preceding several years. Currently, Eric was working part-time as a night watchman for a large professional building in the city. Although he had a few close heterosexual relationships during college, Eric had not been in a steady relationship for more than 8 years.

Eric had a long history of emotional difficulties dating back to his high school years. He had been hospitalized on three occasions when his symptoms had become severe. The most recent of these hospitalizations, occurring a year before his initial visit to the outpatient clinic, had lasted 2 months. Over the past 13 years, Eric had continually taken some form of medication for his symptoms.

During his initial visit to the clinic, Eric stated that the primary reason for seeking treatment was for help with his persistent symptoms of concentration difficulties and chronic worry and anxiety. Eric reported that he worried about everything, including his inability to hold a job to be self-supporting, losing support from his family or being too much of a burden on them, the possibility of his car breaking down, accidentally insulting people, and his lack of a girlfriend. He claimed that he was having considerable difficulty controlling these worries to put them out of his mind and concentrate on something else. Because his worries hindered his ability to concentrate, Eric routinely repeated information in his head in an attempt not to forget things that he felt might be important later (e.g., the name of a company to which he might apply for a job at some point in the future).

Eric's inability to sustain a career and his self-perception that he may perhaps always be a "failure" were key areas of concern to him. Behaviors associated with these worries included difficulty throwing away newspapers (due to his concern that he might discard suitable job announcements from the classified ads), excessive overpreparation for job interviews, excessive rewriting of cover letters for job applications, and frequent revisions to his job resume. Moreover, all of Eric's worries were accompanied by other symptoms such as irritability, feelings of shakiness, muscle tension, rapid heart rate, and extreme restlessness. Eric's restlessness was so severe that he often paced back and forth in his bedroom when he was feeling keyed up and worried about some matter. In fact, Eric's pacing had been so extensive and persistent that he had actually worn holes in the carpet of his bedroom.

However, while Eric reported that his primary reason for seeking treatment at the present time was for his generalized anxiety and worry, the psychologist who conducted his intake evaluation soon realized that, as had always been true over the past 15 years, these difficulties were occurring in the context of other prominent symptoms. Specifically, Eric had an extensive history of depression dating back to his high school years. Over the years, these periods of depression were characterized by depressed mood, a loss of interest in pleasurable activities (at the intake evaluation, Eric stated, "I suffer even when doing things I should enjoy"), concentration difficulties and problems making decisions, and feelings of guilt and worthlessness (e.g., feeling that he was not a contributing member of his family or society, with little expectation of becoming one). In addition, Eric experienced recurrent thoughts of suicide and had a history of four suicide attempts. Eric's first suicide attempt occurred during high school when he "crashed the family car on purpose because I wanted to die." Each of his other suicide attempts had occurred over the past 3 years; on all three occasions, Eric had tried to hang himself.

During his freshman year of college, Eric experienced a 2-week period when his mood was both excessively elevated and excessively agitated. In addition to feeling like he was on a high and very energetic, Eric became quite talkative and spoke very loudly and very quickly. He became even more distractible and was often late or missed classes and appointments because he would be engrossed in some trivial task (such as rearranging the furniture in his room). In addition, during this time Eric engaged in a number of reckless behaviors, one of the most noteworthy being, over this 2-week period, experimentation with almost every recreational drug available around campus, except heroin. Due to the combination of the effects of the drugs he had taken and his agitated mood, Eric had also gotten in several fistfights during this time. This episode ended when Eric crashed his parents' car (by accident, not as a suicide attempt) at 3:00 in the morning when he lost control of the vehicle doing 95 miles per hour on the highway. He was hospitalized for 4 days because of his injuries from the accident, and at this time the hospital physicians recognized Eric's emotional disorder and placed him on medications for the first time.

Over the ensuing years, Eric continued to experience bouts of depression as well as periods when his mood was elevated, agitated, or expansive. In fact, during subsequent "high" periods, Eric wrecked a car by driving at dangerous speeds on two other occasions. At one point, he had his driver's license revoked for 1 year. In another instance involving the family car, Eric burned up the car's engine because he had turned on the ignition, got distracted by something, walked away from the car, and left it running for hours. In other episodes, Eric had gone on buying sprees, spending thousands of dollars (primarily his parents' money because Eric had not held down a steady job since his position as a stockbroker) on vitamins, gifts for his family, and books. Although Eric paced a lot when he was worried about something, most of his pacing had occurred during periods when he felt excessively energetic or agitated. In later years when he was unemployed or working part-time, Eric would channel this energy into such activities as writing and then rewriting his job resume, or going through the yellow pages of the phone book to try to arrange an interview at every company or office that he felt had the potential for hiring him.

Six months after he had landed a job as a stockbroker (a position he obtained 1 year after college graduation), Eric quit because he felt that he could not handle the stress of this career. After his resignation, Eric experienced an extended period of severe depression related to his self-perception of being a failure. However, unlike other times when his mood was down, this episode of depression eventually was associated with other problematic symptoms. Specifically, Eric concluded that because both his father and his brother had once been employed in high-security jobs with the federal government, the CIA was monitoring his actions continuously. Eric began to believe firmly and persistently that he was being set up to fail, career-wise and relationship-wise, by the CIA. Upon learning about these beliefs, Eric's doctors, who had been treating him with medications designed to regulate mood, decided that Eric should be taking drugs to manage psychotic symptoms. Consequently, Eric was put on antipsychotic drugs. As is often the case with these types of medication, Eric experienced a number of aversive side effects and often would not comply with his prescription regimen. As a result, Eric often had a recurrence of his symptoms (either a period of feeling very down or very high), and his unusual beliefs would return. In later episodes, Eric began to hear voices, which he said were the CIA telling him to keep taking his medications. This would lead Eric to be even less compliant with his drug regimen because he believed that the CIA wanted him to be on drugs because the drugs were designed to keep him down and make him fail. Eric's suicide attempts usually occurred when he was very despondent and hopeless about his prospects of being a "useful citizen" if the government was against him.

However, when Eric was not feeling very down or very high, he experienced few symptoms. For instance, during these between-episode periods, Eric did not entertain any thoughts or hear any voices involving the CIA or federal government. At these times, Eric's excessive worries would also diminish, and he recalled that his only worries would be (a) his fear that another episode would might soon occur and (b) his concern about the potential for negative and permanent effects from taking medications continuously.

Clinical History

There appeared to be no history of psychological disorders in Eric's first-order relatives (i.e., parents, grandparents, siblings). Eric was raised in a close-knit and religious middle-class family. His older brother and two younger sisters were quite well adjusted, and each had graduated from college and had sustained productive careers (a fact that added to Eric's perception of being a failure). As noted earlier, the first evidence of Eric's emotional difficulties arose during his high school years, when Eric struggled with some of his classwork. His grades fluctuated between A's and C's, and for some courses Eric had considerable difficulty in keeping up with assigned readings and in taking exams (due to high test anxiety). Consequently, Eric became very stressed out over whether he would gain admission to college. These issues were compounded by Eric's feeling that he was constantly being compared, by his parents and teachers, to his older brother, who was in his junior year of college on a full scholarship studying to be an electrical engineer. Eric's symptoms quickly progressed into the more debilitating symptoms that were discussed at the beginning of this chapter.

In general, Eric's family was quite supportive of him. In addition to allowing him to move back into their home after he quit his job as a stockbroker, Eric's parents were quite involved in his treatment and care over the years. They had done everything possible to keep Eric at home and to prevent him from being hospitalized, partly because the most recent of Eric's three hospitalizations had used up all of their insurance money for hospital coverage. However, his parents also felt that Eric's condition had deteriorated further as the result of prolonged hospitalization. Eric's father charted his son's symptoms and medication use daily in order to try to predict when Eric was at risk for an escalation of symptoms. Moreover, in an effort to avoid some of the serious complications of Eric's condition, his father had routinely engaged in some preventative actions. For example, he had taken away Eric's credit card permanently and had put him on an allowance to try to prevent Eric's tendency for overspending when he was on a high. Because Eric had either wrecked or damaged the car on several occasions, his father prevented the car from starting (by secretly disengaging the wire to the car's ignition when he was not using the car) to keep his son from driving at all times. While these maneuvers were done in an attempt to keep Eric from further harm, they resulted in substantial discord within the family because Eric felt like he was being treated like a child, even though he was in his early 30s. Occasionally, there was also some conflict between Eric's parents because his mother felt that his father was sometimes overinvolved in Eric's affairs (e.g., charting Eric's symptoms and medication use). For example, Eric's father often did not drive his son to therapy appointments at times when Eric was very symptomatic, in order to keep him "safe" at home. Eric's mother disagreed with this decision strongly because she felt that it was especially during times of increased symptoms that Eric needed to be going for treatment. However, Eric and his father usually won this argument—an unfortunate victory because it appeared to be a factor in why Eric had not responded well to treatment over the years (i.e., irregular attendance of treatment sessions).

Indeed, while the numerous drugs Eric had been prescribed over the years had controlled his initial tendencies for aggressive behavior (e.g., getting into fistfights), they had been ineffective in altering Eric's cycles of depression and overagitation-elation. Eric regarded the "cure" to be as bad as his problems because the drugs made him feel "fuzzy" and interfered with his memory and ability to concentrate, including staying focused on basic things such as on reading a newspaper or book or watching a television program. As noted earlier, besides these side effects, Eric's compliance with drug treatment was often severely compromised by his belief that the CIA wanted him on drugs, a thought he routinely had during extreme depression or extreme agitation and elation (but not at other times).

DSM-IV Diagnosis

Based on this information, what five-axis diagnosis (or diagnoses) do you think best applies to Eric?

    Axis I

    Axis II

    Axis III

    Axis IV

    Axis V   Global assessment of functioning =   (current)

References

Abel, G. G., Becker, J. V., Cunningham-Rathner, J., Mittelman, M., & Rouleau, J. L. (1988). Multiple paraphilic diagnoses among sex offenders. Bulletin of the American Academy of Psychiatry and Law, 16, 153–168.

Abel, G. G., Blanchard, E. B., Barlow, D. H., & Mavissakalian, M. (1975). Identifying specific erotic cues in sexual deviations by audiotaped descriptions. Journal of Applied Behavior Analysis, 8, 247–260.

Abramson, L. Y., Metalsky, G. I., & Alloy, L. B. (1989). Hopelessness depression: A theory-based subtype of depression. Psychological Review, 96, 358–372.

Abramson, L. Y., Seligman, M. E. P., & Teasdale, J. D. (1978). Learned helplessness in humans: Critique and reformulation. Journal of Abnormal Psychology, 87, 49–74.

Alcoholics Anonymous (1990). Comments on A.A.'s triennial surveys. New York: Alcoholics Anonymous World Services.

Alford, G. S., Morin, C., Atkins, M., & Schoen, L. (1987). Masturbatory extinction of deviant sexual arousal: A case report. Behavior Therapy, 18, 265–271.

American Psychiatric Association (1980). Diagnostic and statistical manual of mental disorders (3rd ed.). Washington, DC: Author.

American Psychiatric Association (1987). Diagnostic and statistical manual of mental disorders (3rd ed., rev.). Washington, DC: Author.

American Psychiatric Association (1994a). Diagnostic and statistical manual of mental disorders (4th ed.). Washington, DC: Author.

American Psychiatric Association (1994b). Practice guideline for the treatment of patients with bipolar disorder. American Journal of Psychiatry (Suppl.), 151, 1–36.

Andreasen, N. C., Rezai, K., Alliger, R., Swayze, V. M., Flaum, M., Kirchner, P., Cohen, G., & O'Leary, D. S. (1992). Hypofrontality in neuroleptic-naive patients and in patients with chronic schizophrenia: Assessment with xenon 133 single-photon emission computed tomography with the Tower of London. Archives of General Psychiatry, 49, 943–958.

Andrews, G., Stewart, G., Allen, R., & Henderson, A. S. (1990). The genetics of six neurotic disorders: A twin study. Journal of Affective Disorders, 19, 23–29.

Arias, I., Samios, M., & O'Leary, K. D. (1987). Prevalence and correlates of physical aggression during courtship. Journal of Interpersonal Violence, 2, 82–90.

Arkowitz, H. (1977). The measurement and modification of minimal dating behavior. In M. Hersen, R. M. Eisler, & P. M. Miller (Eds.), Progress in behavior modification (Vol. 5). New York: Academic Press.

Azrin, N. H., & Nunn, R. G. (1973). Habit-reversal: A method of eliminating nervous habits and tics. Behaviour Research and Therapy, 11, 619–628.

Azrin, N. H., Nunn, R. G., & Frantz, S. E. (1980). Treatment of hairpulling: A comparative study of habit reversal and negative practice training. Journal of Behavior Therapy and Experimental Psychiatry, 11, 13–20.

Bancroft, J. (1989). Human sexuality and its problems (2nd ed.). Edinburgh: Churchill Livingstone.

Bansal, S., Wincze, J. P., Nirenberg, T., Liepman, M. J., & Engle-Friedman, M. (1990). Sex-steroid levels in chronic alcoholic males: Relationship to age and liver functions. Unpublished manuscript, Brown University.

Barlow, D. H. (1986). Causes of sexual dysfunction: The role of anxiety and cognitive interference. Journal of Consulting and Clinical Psychology, 54, 140–148.

Barlow, D. H. (1988). Anxiety and its disorders: The nature and treatment of anxiety and panic. New York: Guilford Press.

Barlow, D. H. (1991). Disorders of emotion. Psychological Inquiry, 1, 58–71.

Barlow, D. H. (1994). Psychological interventions in the era of managed competition. Clinical Psychology: Science and Practice, 1, 109–122.

Barlow, D. H., & Craske, M. G. (1994). Mastery of your anxiety and panic (MAP II). Albany, NY: Graywind Publications.

Barlow, D. H., & Durand, V. M. (1999). Abnormal psychology: An integrative approach. Belmont, CA: Wadsworth Publishing Company.

Barlow, D. H., & Wincze, J. P. (1980). Treatment of sexual deviations. In S. R. Leiblum & L. A. Pervin (Eds.), Principles and practice of sex therapy (pp. 347–375). New York: Guilford Press.

Barlow, D. H., Becker, H., Leitenberg, H., & Agras, W. S. (1970). A mechanical strain gauge for recording penile circumference change. Journal of Applied Behavior Analysis, 3, 73–76.

Barlow, D. H., O'Brien, G. T., & Last, C. G. (1984). Couples treatment of agoraphobia. Behavior Therapy, 15, 41–58.

Baron, M., Gruen, R., Asnis, L., & Lord, S. (1985). Familial transmission of schizotypal and borderline personality disorders. American Journal of Psychiatry, 142, 927–934.

Basoglu, M., Lax, T., Kasvikis, Y., & Marks, I. M. (1988). Predictors of improvement in obsessive-compulsive disorder. Journal of Anxiety Disorders, 2, 299–317.

Beach, S. R. H., Sandeen, E. E., & O'Leary, K. D. (1990). Depression in marriage: A model for etiology and treatment. In D. H. Barlow (Ed.), Treatment manuals for practitioners. New York: Guilford Press.

Beasley, R., & Stoltenberg, C. D. (1992). Personality characteristics of male spouse abusers. Professional Psychology, 23, 310–317.

Beck, A. T. (1976). Cognitive therapy and the emotional disorders. New York: Harper & Row.

Beck, A. T., & Emery, G. (1985). Anxiety disorders and phobias: A cognitive perspective. New York: Basic Books.

Beck, A. T., Rush, A. J., Shaw, B. F., & Emery, G. E. (1979). Cognitive therapy of depression. New York: Guilford Press.

Becker, J. V. (1990). Treating adolescent sexual offenders. Professional Psychology: Research and Practice, 21, 362–365.

Becker, J. V., Skinner, L. J., Abel, G. G., & Cichon, J. (1986). Level of post-assault sexual functioning in rape and incest victims. Archives of Sexual Behavior, 15, 37–49.

Bellack, A. S., & Mueser, K. T. (1992). Social skills training for schizophrenia? Archives of General Psychiatry, 49, 76.

Bellack, A. S., & Mueser, K. T. (1993). Psychosocial treatment for schizophrenia. Schizophrenia Bulletin, 19, 317–336.

Berk, R. A., Berk, S. F., Loseke, D. R., & Rauma, D. (1983). Mutual combat and other family violence myths. In D. Finkelhor, R. J. Gelles, G. T. Hotaling, & M. A. Straus (Eds.), The dark side of families: Current family violence research (pp. 197–212). Beverly Hills, CA: Sage.

Bertelsen, B., Harvald, B., & Hauge, M. (1977). A Danish twin study of manic-depressive disorders. British Journal of Psychiatry, 130, 330–351.

Bettelheim, B. (1967). The empty fortress. New York: Free Press.

Black, D. W., Noyes, R., Goldstein, R. B., & Blum, N. (1992). A family study of obsessive-compulsive disorder. Archives of General Psychiatry, 49, 362–368.

Black, D. W., Winokur, G., & Nasrallah, A. (1987). The treatment of depression: Electroconvulsive therapy vs. antidepressants: A naturalistic evaluation of 1,495 patients. Comprehensive Psychiatry, 28, 169–182.

Blazer, D. G., George, L., & Hughes, D. (1991). The epidemiology of anxiety disorders: An age comparison. In C. Salzman & B. D. Lebowitz (Eds.), Anxiety disorders in the elderly (pp. 180–203). New York: Free Press.

Blehar, M. C., Weissman, M. M., Gershon, E. S., & Hirschfeld, R. M. A. (1988). Family and genetic studies of affective disorders. Archives of General Psychiatry, 45, 289–292.

Borkovec, T. D. (1994). The nature, functions, and origins of worry. In G. Davey & F. Tallis (Eds.), Worrying: Perspectives on theory, assessment, and treatment (pp. 5–33). New York: Wiley & Sons.

Borkovec, T. D., & Costello, E. (1993). Efficacy of applied relaxation and cognitive behavioral therapy in the treatment of generalized anxiety disorder. Journal of Consulting and Clinical Psychology, 61, 611–619.

Boudewyns, P. A., & Hyer, L. (1990). Physiological response to combat memories and preliminary treatment outcome in Vietnam veteran PTSD patients treated with direct therapeutic exposure. Behavior Therapy, 21, 63–87.

Brent, D. A., & Kolko, D. J. (1990). The assessment and treatment of children and adolescents at risk for suicide. In S. J. Blumenthal & D. J. Kupfer (Eds.), Suicide over the life cycle: Risk factors, assessment, and treatment of suicidal patients. Washington, DC: American Psychiatric Press.

Brown, G. W., & Harris, T. O. (1978). Social origins of depression: A study of psychiatric disorder in women. London: Tavistock.

Brown, G. W., Monck, E. M., Carstairs, G. M., & Wing, J. K. (1962). Influence of family life on the course of schizophrenic illness. British Journal of Preventive and Social Medicine, 16, 55–68.

Brown, T. A., & Barlow, D. H. (1992a). Comorbidity among anxiety disorders: Implications for treatment and DSM-IV. Journal of Consulting and Clinical Psychology, 60, 835–844.

Brown, T. A., & Barlow, D. H. (1992b). Long-term clinical outcome following cognitive-behavioral treatment of panic disorder and panic disorder with agoraphobia. In P. H. Wilson (Ed.), Principles and practice of relapse prevention (pp. 191–212). New York: Guilford Press.

Brown, T. A., Abueg, F. R., & Fairbank, J. A. (1992). Patterns of adjustment following exposure to extreme events: Psychological aftermath of combat and sexual assault. In M. S. Gibbs, J. R. Lachenmeyer, & J. Sigal (Eds.), Community psychology and mental health (2nd ed., pp. 259–276). New York: Gardner Press.

Brown, T. A., Antony, M. M., & Barlow, D. H. (1992). Psychometric properties of the Penn State Worry Questionnaire in a clinical anxiety disorders sample. Behaviour Research and Therapy, 30, 33–37.

Brown, T. A., Barlow, D. H., & Liebowitz, M. R. (1994). The empirical basis of generalized anxiety disorder. American Journal of Psychiatry, 151, 1272–1280.

Brown, T. A., Marten, P. A., & Barlow, D. H. (1995). Discriminant validity of the symptoms constituting the DSM-III-R and DSM-IV associated symptom criterion of generalized anxiety disorder. Journal of Anxiety Disorders, 9, 317–328.

Brown, T. A., Moras, K., Zinbarg, R. E., & Barlow, D. H. (1993). Diagnostic and symptom distinguishability of generalized anxiety disorder and obsessive-compulsive disorder. Behavior Therapy, 24, 227–240.

Brown, T. A., O'Leary, T. A., & Barlow, D. H. (1993). Cognitive-behavioral treatment of generalized anxiety disorder. In D. H. Barlow (Ed.), Clinical handbook of psychological disorders: A step-by-step treatment manual (2nd ed., pp. 137–188). New York: Guilford Press.

Browne, A. (1987). When battered women kill. New York: Free Press.

Browne, A. (1993). Violence against women by male partners: Prevalence, outcomes, and policy implications. American Psychologist, 48, 1077–1087.

Browne, A., & Williams, K. R. (1989). Exploring the effect of resource availability and the likelihood of female-perpetrated homicides. Law and Society Review, 23, 75–94.

Brownell, K. D. (1991). Dieting and the search for the perfect body: Where physiology and culture collide. Behavior Therapy, 22, 1–12.

Bruce, M. L., & Kim, K. M. (1992). Differences in the effects of divorce on major depression in men and women. American Journal of Psychiatry, 149, 914–917.

Bruch, M., Heimberg, R. G., Berger, P., & Collins, T. M. (1989). Social phobia and perceptions of early parental and personal characteristics. Anxiety Research, 2, 57–63.

Bureau of the Census (1983). Statistical abstract of the United States. Washington, DC: U.S. Government Printing Office.

Burnam, M. A., Stein, J. A., Golding, J. M., Siegel, J. M., Sorenson, S. B., Forsythe, A. B., & Telles, C. A. (1988). Sexual assault and mental disorders in a community population. Journal of Consulting and Clinical Psychology, 56, 843–850.

Bushnell, J. A., Wells, J. E., Hornblow, A. R., Oakley-Browne, M. A., & Joyce, P. (1990). Prevalence of three bulimia syndromes in the general population. Psychological Medicine, 20, 671–680.

Byrne, D., & Schulte, L. (1990). Personality dispositions as mediators of sexual responses. Annual Review of Sex Research, 1, 93–117.

Caeser, P. L., & Hamberger, K. (1989). Treating men who batter: Theory, practice, and programs. New York: Springer.

Calhoun, K. S., & Resick, P. A. (1993). Post-traumatic stress disorder. In D. H. Barlow (Ed.), Clinical handbook of psychological disorders: A step-by-step treatment manual (2nd. ed., pp. 48–98). New York: Guilford Press.

Carden, A. D. (1994). Wife abuse and the wife abuser: Review and recommendations. The Counseling Psychologist, 22, 539–582.

Cardena, D., Lewis-Fernandez, R., Bear, D., Pakianathan, I., & Spiegel, D. (in press). DSM-IV sourcebook for dissociative disorders. In T. A. Widiger, A. J. Frances, H. A. Pincus, M. J. First, R. Ross, & W. Davis (Eds.), DSM-IV sourcebook (Vol. 4). Washington, DC: American Psychiatric Press.

Carey, M. P., Wincze, J. P., & Meisler, A. W. (1993). Sexual dysfunction: Male erectile disorder. In D. H. Barlow (Ed.), Clinical handbook of psychological disorders: A step-by-step treatment manual (2nd ed., pp. 442–480). New York: Guilford Press.

Carlson, E. B., & Putnam, F. W. (1989). Integrating research on dissociation and hypnotizability: Are there two pathways to hypnotizability? Dissociation, 2, 32–38.

Carroll, E. M., Rueger, D. B., Foy, D. W., & Donahoe, C. P. (1985). Vietnam combat veterans with posttraumatic stress disorder: Analysis of marital and cohabitating adjustment. Journal of Abnormal Psychology, 95, 329–337.

Carson, R. C., & Sanislow, C. A. (1993). The schizophrenias. In P. B. Sutker & H. E. Adams (Eds.), Comprehensive handbook of psychopathology (pp. 295–333). New York: Plenum Press.

Carter, W. R., Johnson, M. C., & Borkovec, T. D. (1986). Worry: An electrocortical analysis. Advances in Behaviour Research and Therapy, 8, 193–204.

Cascardi, M., O'Leary, K. D., Lawrence, E. E., & Schlee, K. A. (1995). Characteristics of women physically abused by their spouses and who seek treatment regarding marital conflict. Journal of Consulting and Clinical Psychology, 63, 616–623.

Cash, T. F., & Brown, T. A. (1987). Body image in anorexia nervosa and bulimia nervosa: A review of the literature. Behavior Modification, 11, 487–521.

Cash, T. F., & Pruzinsky, T. (Eds.) (1990). Body images: Development, deviance, and change. New York: Guilford Press.

Cautela, J. R. (1967). Covert sensitization. Psychological Reports, 20, 459–468.

Cautela, J. R., & Kearney, A. J. (1993). The covert sensitization casebook. Pacific Grove, CA: Brooks/Cole Publishing Co.

Chambless, D. L., Cherney, J., Caputo, G. C., & Rheinstein, B. J. G. (1987). Anxiety disorders and alcoholism: A study with inpatient alcoholics. Journal of Anxiety Disorders, 1, 29–40.

Chemtob, C., Roitblat, H., Hamada, R., Carlson, J., & Twentyman, C. (1988). A cognitive action theory of posttraumatic stress disorder. Journal of Anxiety Disorders, 2, 253–275.

Chor, P. N., Mercier, M. A., & Halpier, I. S. (1988). Use of cognitive therapy for treatment of a patient suffering from a bipolar affective disorder. Journal of Cognitive Psychotherapy, 2, 51–58.

Christensen, H., Hadzi-Pavlovic, D., Andrews, G., & Mattick, R. (1987). Behavior therapy and tricyclic medication in the treatment of obsessive-compulsive disorder: A quantitative review. Journal of Consulting and Clinical Psychology, 55, 701–711.

Christenson, G. A., Mackenzie, T. B., & Mitchell, J. E. (1991). Characteristics of 60 adult chronic hair pullers. American Journal of Psychiatry, 148, 365–370.

Christenson, G. A., Pyle, R. L., & Mitchell, J. E. (1991). Estimated lifetime prevalence of trichotillomania in college students. Journal of Clinical Psychiatry, 52, 415–417.

Clark, D. M. (1986). A cognitive approach to panic. Behaviour Research and Therapy, 24, 461–470.

Clark, D. M. (1988). A cognitive model of panic attacks. In S. Rachman & J. D. Maser (Eds.), Panic: Psychological perspectives (pp. 71–89). Hillsdale, NJ: Lawrence Erlbaum.

Clark, D. M., Salkovskis, P. M., Hackmann, A., Middleton, H., Anastasiades, P., & Gelder, M. (1994). A comparison of cognitive therapy, applied relaxation, and imipramine in the treatment of panic disorder. British Journal of Psychiatry, 164, 759–769.

Clarkin, J. F., Widiger, T. A., Frances, A. J., Hurt, S. W., & Gilmore, M. (1983). Prototypic typology and the borderline personality disorder. Journal of Abnormal Psychology, 92, 263–275.

Cloninger, C. R., Bohman, M., & Sigvardsson, S. (1981). Inheritance of alcohol abuse. Archives of General Psychiatry, 38, 861–868.

Cochran, S. D. (1984). Preventing medical noncompliance in the outpatient treatment of bipolar affective disorders. Journal of Consulting and Clinical Psychology, 52, 873–878.

Cocores, J. A., Miller, N. S., Pottash, A. C., & Gold, M. S. (1988). Sexual dysfunction in abusers of cocaine and alcohol. American Journal of Drug and Alcohol Abuse, 14, 169–173.

Conner, K. R., & Ackerley, G. D. (1994). Alcohol-related battering: Developing treatment strategies. Journal of Family Violence, 9, 143–155.

Coon, P. M. (1986). Treatment progress in 20 patients with multiple personality disorder. Journal of Nervous and Mental Disease, 174, 715–721.

Cooper, N. A., & Clum, G. A. (1989). Imaginal flooding as a supplementary treatment for PTSD in combat veterans: A controlled study. Behavior Therapy, 20, 381–391.

Coppen, A., Standish-Barry, H., Bailey, J., Houston, G., Silcocks, P., & Hermon, C. (1991). Does lithium reduce the mortality of recurrent mood disorders? Journal of Affective Disorders, 23, 1–7.

Coryell, W., Scheftner, W., Keller, M., Endicott, J., Maser, J., & Klerman, G. L. (1993). The enduring psychosocial consequences of mania and depression. American Journal of Psychiatry, 150, 720–727.

Courchesne, E. (1991). Neuroanatomic imaging in autism. Pediatrics, 87, 781–790.

Cowdry, R. W., & Gardner, D. L. (1988). Pharmacotherapy of borderline personality disorder: Alprazolam, carbamazepine, trifluoperazine, and tranylcypromine. Archives of General Psychiatry, 45, 111–119.

Cowdry, R. W., Pickar, D., & Davies, R. (1985). Symptoms and EEG findings in the borderline syndrome. International Journal of Psychiatric and Medicine, 15, 202–211.

Coyne, J. C. (1976). Toward an interactional description of depression. Psychiatry, 39, 28–40.

Craighead, L. W., & Agras, W. S. (1990). Mechanisms of action in cognitive-behavioral and pharmacological interventions for obesity and bulimia nervosa. Journal of Consulting and Clinical Psychology, 59, 115–125.

Craske, M. G., & Barlow, D. H. (1993). Panic disorder and agoraphobia. In D. H. Barlow (Ed.), Clinical handbook of psychological disorders: A step-by-step treatment manual (2nd ed., pp. 1–47). New York: Guilford Press.

Craske, M. G., Barlow, D. H., & O'Leary, T. A. (1992). Mastery of your anxiety and worry. Albany, NY: Graywind.

Craske, M. G., Brown, T. A., & Barlow, D. H. (1991). Behavioral treatment of panic disorder: A two-year follow-up. Behavior Therapy, 22, 289–304.

Creese, I., Burt, D. R., & Snyder, S. H. (1976). Dopamine receptor binding predicts clinical and pharmacological potencies of anti-schizophrenic drugs. Science, 192, 481–483.

Davidson, J., Swartz, M., Storck, M., Krishnan, R. R., & Hammett, E. (1985). A diagnostic and family study of posttraumatic stress disorder. American Journal of Psychiatry, 142, 90–93.

Davidson, M., Keefe, R. S. E., Mohs, R. C., Siever, L. J., Losonczy, M. F., Horvath, T. B., & Davis, K. L. (1987). L-Dopa challenge and relapse in schizophrenia. American Journal of Psychiatry, 144, 934–938.

Davis, K. L., Kahn, R. S., Ko, G., & Davidson, M. (1991). Dopamine in schizophrenia: A review and reconceptualization. American Journal of Psychiatry, 148, 1474–1486.

Davison, G. C. (1968). Elimination of a sadistic fantasy by a client-controlled counter-conditioning technique: A case study. Journal of Abnormal Psychology, 73, 91–99.

Day, R., Nielsen, J. A., Korten, A., Ernberg, G., Dube, K. C., Gebhart, J., Jablensky, A., Leon, C., Marsella, A., Olatawura, M., Sartorius, N., Stromgren, E., Takahashi, R., Wig, N., & Wynne, L. C. (1987). Stressful life events preceding the acute onset of schizophrenia: A cross-national study from the World Health Organization. Cultural Medicine and Psychiatry, 11, 123–205.

Depression Guideline Panel (1993, April). Depression in primary care: Vol. 1 Detection and diagnosis (AHCPR publication no. 93-0550). Clinical practice guideline, No. 5. Rockville, MD: U.S. Department of Health and Human Services, Public Health Service, Agency for Health Care Policy and Research.

Depue, R. A., & Iacono, W. G. (1989). Neurobehavioral aspects of affective disorders. Annual Review of Psychology, 40, 457–492.

Devinsky, O., Feldman, E., Burrowes, K., & Bromfield, E. (1989). Autoscopic phenomena with seizures. Archives of Neurology, 46, 1080–1088.

Dohrenwend, B. P., & Egri, G. (1981). Recent stressful life events and episodes of schizophrenia. Schizophrenia Bulletin, 7, 12–23.

Dulit, R. A., Marin, D. B., & Frances, A. J. (1993). Cluster B personality disorders. In D. L. Dunner (Ed.), Current psychiatric therapy (pp. 405–411). Philadelphia: W. B. Saunders.

Durand, V. M. (1990). Severe behavior problems: A functional communication training approach. New York: Guilford Press.

Durand, V. M., & Carr, E. G. (1988). Autism. In V. B. Van Hasselt, P. S. Strain, & M. Hersen (Eds.), Handbook of developmental and physical disabilities (pp. 195–214). Elmsford, NY: Pergamon Press.

Dutton, D., & Strachan, C. E. (1987). Motivational needs for power and spouse-specific assertiveness in assaultive and non-assaultive men. Violence and Victims, 2, 145–156.

Dutton, D. G. (1995). Male abusiveness in intimate relationships. Clinical Psychology Review, 15, 567–581.

Elkin, I., Shea, M. T., Watkins, J. T., Imber, S. D., Sotsky, S. M., Collins, J. F., Glass, D. R., Pilkonis, P. A., Leber, W. R., Docherty, J. P., Fiester, S. J., & Parloff, M. B. (1989). National Institute of Mental Health Treatment of Depression Collaborative Research Program: General effectiveness of treatments. Archives of General Psychiatry, 46, 971–982.

Ellicott, A. G. (1988). A prospective study of stressful life events and bipolar illness. Unpublished doctoral dissertation, University of California, Los Angeles.

Ellis, E. M., Atkeson, B. M., & Calhoun, K. S. (1981). An assessment of long-term reaction to rape. Journal of Abnormal Psychology, 90, 263–266.

Eysenck, H. J. (1967). The biological basis of personality. Springfield, IL: Charles C. Thomas.

Fairbank, J. A., & Brown, T. A. (1987). Current behavioral approaches to the treatment of posttraumatic stress disorder. The Behavior Therapist, 10, 57–64.

Fairbank, J. A., Hansen, D. J., & Fitterling, J. M. (1991). Patterns of appraisal and coping across different stressor conditions among former prisoners of war with and without posttraumatic stress disorder. Journal of Consulting and Clinical Psychology, 59, 274–281.

Fairburn, C. G. (1985). Cognitive-behavioral treatment for bulimia. In D. M. Garner & P. E. Garfinkel (Eds.), Handbook of psychotherapy for anorexia nervosa and bulimia (pp. 160–192). New York: Guilford Press.

Fairburn, C. G., Jones, R., Peveler, R. C., Hope, R. A., & O'Connor, M. (1993). Psychotherapy and bulimia nervosa: The longer-term effects of interpersonal psychotherapy and cognitive behaviour therapy. Archives of General Psychiatry, 50, 419–428.

Falloon, I. R. H., Brooker, C., & Graham-Hole, V. (1992). Psychosocial interventions for schizophrenia. Behaviour Change, 9, 238–245.

Faulkner, K., Stoltenberg, C. D., Cogen, R., Nolder, M., & Shooter, E. (1992). Cognitive-behavioral group treatment for male spouse abusers. Journal of Family Violence, 7, 37–55.

Fawcett, J., Scheftner, W., Clark, D., Hedeker, D., Gibbons, R., & Coryell, W. (1987).

Clinical predictors of suicide in patients with major affective disorders: A controlled prospective study. American Journal of Psychiatry, 144, 35–40.

Feldman, C. M. (1997). Childhood precursors to adult interpartner violence. Clinical Psychology: Science and Practice, 4, 307–333.

Ferster, C. B. (1961). Positive reinforcement and behavioral deficits of autistic children. Child Development, 32, 437–456.

Finkelhor, D. (1979). Sexually victimized children. New York: Free Press.

Fleming, J. E., & Offord, D. R. (1990). Epidemiology of childhood depressive disorders: A review. Journal of the American Academy of Child and Adolescent Psychiatry, 29, 571–580.

Flournoy, P. S., & Wilson, G. L. (1991). Assessment of MMPI profiles of male batterers. Violence and Victims, 6, 81–95.

Foa, E. B., & Kozak, M. J. (1989). Obsessions, overvalued ideas, and delusions in obsessive-compulsive disorder (Report to the DSM-IV Anxiety Disorders Workgroup). Philadelphia, PA: Eastern Pennsylvania Psychiatric Institute, Medical College of Pennsylvania.

Foa, E. B., & Kozak, M. J. (1995). DSM-IV field trial: Obsessive-compulsive disorder. American Journal of Psychiatry, 152, 90–96.

Foa, E. B., Kozak, M. J., Goodman, W. K., Hollander, E., Jenike, M. A., & Rasmussen, S. A. (1998). DSM-IV field trial: Obsessive-compulsive disorder. In T. A. Widiger, A. J. Frances, H. A. Pincus, R. Ross, M. B. First, W. Davis, & M. Kline (Eds.), DSM-IV sourcebook (Vol. 4; pp. 761-776). Washington, DC: American Psychiatric Press.

Foa, E. B., Grayson, J. B., & Steketee, G. (1982). Depression, habituation, and treatment outcome in obsessive-compulsives. In J. C. Boulougouris (Ed.), Practical applications of learning theories in psychiatry (pp. 129–142). New York: John Wiley & Sons.

Foa, E. B., Rothbaum, B. O., Riggs, D. S., & Murdock, T. B. (1991). Treatment of posttraumatic stress disorder in rape victims: A comparison between cognitive-behavioral procedures and counseling. Journal of Consulting and Clinical Psychology, 59, 715–723.

Foa, E. B., Steketee, G., & Rothbaum, B. O. (1989). Behavioral/cognitive conceptualizations of post-traumatic stress disorder (PTSD). Behavior Therapy, 20, 155–176.

Foa, E. B., Steketee, G. S., Kozak, M. J., & McCarthy, P. R. (1990). Treatment of depressive and obsessive-compulsive symptoms in OCD by imipramine and behavior therapy. Manuscript submitted for publication.

Folstein, S., & Rutter, M. (1977). Genetic influences and infantile autism. Nature, 265, 726–728.

Foy, D. W., Carroll, E. M., & Donahoe, C. P. (1987). Etiological factors in the development of PTSD in clinical samples of Vietnam combat veterans. Journal of Clinical Psychology, 43, 17–27.

Foy, D. W., Sipprelle, R. C., Rueger, D. B., & Carroll, E. M. (1984). Etiology of posttraumatic stress disorder in Vietnam veterans: Analysis of premilitary, military, and combat exposure influences. Journal of Consulting and Clinical Psychology, 52, 79–87.

Frances, A. J., Franklin, J., & Flavin, D. (1986). Suicide and alcoholism. Annals of the New York Academy of Science, 287, 316–326.

Frances, A. J., Fyer, M., & Clarkin, J. F. (1986). Personality and suicide. Annals of the New York Academy of Sciences, 487, 281–293.

Frank, E., & Spanier, C. (1995). Interpersonal therapy for depression: Overview, clinical efficacy, and future directions. Clinical Psychology: Science and Practice, 2, 349–369.

Frank, E., Anderson, C., & Rubenstein, D. (1978). Frequency of sexual dysfunction in "normal" couples. New England Journal of Medicine, 299, 111–115.

Frank, E., Kupfer, D. J., Perel, J. M., Cornes, C., Jarrett, D. B., Mallinger, A. G., Thase, M. E., McEachran, A. B., & Grochocinski, V. J. (1990). Three year outcomes for maintenance therapies in recurrent depression. Archives of General Psychiatry, 47, 1093–1099.

Freedman, R. (1990). Cognitive-behavioral perspectives on body-image change. In T. F. Cash & T. Pruzinsky (Eds.), Body images: Development, deviance, and change (pp. 272–295). New York: Guilford Press.

Friman, P. C., Finney, J. W., & Christophersen, E. R. (1984). Behavioral treatment of trichotillomania: An evaluative review. Behavior Therapy, 15, 249–265.

Frost, R. O., Sher, K. J., & Geen, T. (1986). Psychological and personality characteristics of nonclinical compulsive checkers. Behaviour Research and Therapy, 24, 133–143.

Frye, S., & Stockton, R. (1982). Discriminant analysis of post-traumatic stress disorder among a group of Vietnam veterans. American Journal of Psychiatry, 139, 52–56.

Furby, L., Weinrott, M. R., & Blackshaw, L. (1989). Sex offender recidivism: A review. Psychological Bulletin, 105, 3–30.

Fyer, A. J., Mannuzza, S., Chapman, T. F., Liebowitz, M. R., & Klein, D. F. (1993). A direct interview family study of social phobia. Archives of General Psychiatry, 50, 286–293.

Garner, D. M., Garfinkel, P. E., Schwartz, D., & Thompson, M. (1980). Cultural expectation of thinness in women. Psychological Reports, 47, 483–491.

Geller, B., Cooper, T. B., Graham, G. L., Marstellar, F. A., & Bryant, D. M. (1990). Double-blind placebo-controlled study of nortriptyline in depressed adolescents using a "fixed plasma level" design. Psychopharmacological Bulletin, 26, 85–91.

Gershon, E. S. (1990). Genetics. In F. K. Goodwin & K. R. Jamison (Eds.), Manic-depressive illness (pp. 373–401). New York: Oxford University Press.

Gilbert, H. W., & Gingell, J. C. (1991). The results of an intracorporeal papaverine clinic. Sexual and Marital Therapy, 6, 49–56.

Gillberg, C. (1984). Infantile autism and other childhood psychoses in a Swedish urban region: Epidemiological aspects. Journal of Child Psychology and Psychiatry, 25, 35–43.

Gitlin, M. J., Swendsen, J., Heller, T. L., & Hammen, C. (1995). Relapse and impairment in bipolar disorder. American Journal of Psychiatry, 152, 1635–1640.

Goldfried, M. R., & Davison, G. C. (1994). Clinical behavior therapy. New York: John Wiley & Sons.

Goldman, M. S., D'Angelo, E. J., DeMaso, D. R., & Mezzacappa, E. (1992). Physical and sexual abuse histories among children with borderline personality disorder. American Journal of Psychiatry, 149, 1723–1726.

Goldstein, I., Lue T. F., Padama-Nathan, H., Rosen, R. C., Steers, W. D., & Wicker, P. A., for the Sildenafil Study Group (1998). Oral sildenafil in the treatment of erectile dysfunction. New England Journal of Medicine, 338, 1397–1404.

Goodwin, D. S. (1979). Alcoholism and heredity. Archives of General Psychiatry, 36, 57–61.

Goodwin, F. K., & Jamison, K. R. (1990). Manic-depressive illness (pp. 373–401). New York: Oxford University Press.

Gottesman, I. I. (1991). Schizophrenia genesis: The origins of madness. New York: W.H. Freeman.

Gregoire, A. (1992). New treatments for erectile impotence. British Journal of Psychiatry, 160, 315–326.

Greist, J. H. (1990). Treatment of obsessive-compulsive disorder: Psychotherapies, drugs, and other somatic treatments. Journal of Clinical Psychiatry, 51, 44–50.

Groth, N. A. (1979). Sexual trauma in the life histories of rapists and child molesters. Victimology, 4, 10–16.

Gunderson, J. G., & Sabo, A. N. (1993). The phenomenological and conceptual interface between borderline personality disorder and PTSD. American Journal of Psychiatry, 150, 19–27.

Gur, R. E., & Pearlson, G. D. (1993). Neuroimaging in schizophrenia research. Schizophrenia Bulletin, 19, 337–353.

Haaga, D. A. F., Dyck, M. J., & Ernst, D. (1991). Empirical status of cognitive theory of depression. Psychological Bulletin, 110, 215–236.

Halford, W. K., & Markman, H. J. (1997). Clinical handbook of marriage and couples interventions. New York: John Wiley & Sons.

Hamilton, E. W., & Abramson, L. Y. (1983). Cognitive patterns and major depressive disorders: A longitudinal study in a hospital setting. Journal of Abnormal Psychology, 92, 173–184.

Hammen, C., Burge, D., Burney, E., & Adrian, C. (1990). Longitudinal study of diagnoses in children of women with unipolar and bipolar affective disorder. Archives of General Psychiatry, 47, 1112–1117.

Hammen, C., Ellicott, A., Gitlin, M., & Jamison, K. R. (1989). Sociotropy/autonomy and vulnerability to specific life events in patients with unipolar depression and bipolar disorders. Journal of Abnormal Psychology, 98, 154–160.

Hanson, R. K., Steffy, R. A., & Gauthier, R. (1993). Long-term recidivism of child molesters. Journal of Consulting and Clinical Psychology, 61, 646–652.

Harding, C. M., Brooks, G. W., Ashikaga, T., Strauss, J. S., & Breier, A. (1987). The Vermont longitudinal study of persons with severe mental illness, II: Long-term outcome of subjects who retrospectively met DSM-III criteria for schizophrenia. American Journal of Psychiatry, 144, 727–735.

Hastings, J., & Hamberger, K. (1988). Personality correlates of spouse abusers: A cross-validation study. Violence and Victims, 3, 31–48.

Hawton, K., Catalan, J., & Fagg, J. (1992). Sex therapy for erectile dysfunction: Characteristics of couples, treatment outcome, and prognostic factors. Archives of Sexual Behavior, 21, 161–175.

Heimberg, R. G., & Barlow, D. H. (1988). Psychosocial treatments for social phobia. Psychosomatics, 29, 27–37.

Heimberg, R. G., Dodge, C. S., & Becker, R. E. (1987). Social phobia. In L. Michelson & M. L. Ascher (Eds.), Anxiety and stress disorders: Cognitive-behavioral assessment and treatment (pp. 280–309). New York: Guilford Press.

Heimberg, R. G., Dodge, C. S., Hope, D. A., Kennedy, C. R., Zollo, L. J., & Becker, R. E. (1990). Cognitive-behavioral group treatment for social phobia: Comparison with a credible placebo control. Cognitive Therapy and Research, 14, 1–23.

Heimberg, R. G., Liebowitz, M. R., Hope, D. A., & Schneier, F. R. (Eds.) (1995). Social phobia: Diagnosis, assessment, and treatment. New York: Guilford Press.

Heimberg, R. G., Salzman, D. G., Holt, C. S., & Blendell, K. A. (1995). Cognitive-behavioral group treatment for social phobia: Effectiveness at five-year follow-up. Cognitive Therapy and Research, 17, 325–339.

Helzer, J. E., Robins, L. N., & McEvoy, M. A. (1987). Post-traumatic stress disorder in the general population: Findings from the Epidemiologic Catchment Area survey. New England Journal of Medicine, 317, 1630–1634.

Herman, J. L., Perry, J. C., & van der Kolk, B. A. (1989). Childhood trauma in borderline personality disorder, American Journal of Psychiatry, 146, 490–495.

Himmelfarb, S., & Murrell, S. A. (1984). The prevalence and correlation of anxiety symptoms in older adults. Journal of Psychiatry, 116, 159–167.

Hinz, L. D., & Williamson, D. A. (1987). Bulimia and depression: A review of the affective variant hypothesis. Psychological Bulletin, 102, 150–158.

Hoehn-Saric, R., Hazlett, R. L., & McLeod, D. R. (1993). Generalized anxiety disorder with early and late onset of anxiety symptoms. Comprehensive Psychiatry, 34, 291–298.

Hoehn-Saric, R., McLeod, D. R., & Zimmerli, W. D. (1989). Somatic manifestations in women with generalized anxiety disorder. Archives of General Psychiatry, 46, 1113–1119.

Hollon, S. D., DeRubeis, R. J., Evans, M. D., Weiner, M. J., Garvey, M. J., Grose, W. M., & Tuason, V. B. (1992). Cognitive therapy and pharmacotherapy for depression: Singly and in combination. Archives of General Psychiatry, 49, 772–781.

Holm, V. A., & Varley, C. K. (1989). Pharmacological treatment of autistic children. In G. Dawson (Ed.), Autism: Nature, diagnosis, and treatment (pp. 386–404). New York: Guilford Press.

Holtzworth-Munroe, A., & Anglin, K. (1991). The competency of responses given by maritally violent versus nonviolent men to problematic marital situations. Violence and Victims, 6, 257–269.

Holtzworth-Munroe, A., & Hutchinson, G. (1993). Attributing negative intent to wife behavior: The attributions of maritally violent versus nonviolent men. Journal of Abnormal Psychology, 102, 206–211.

Holtzworth-Munroe, A., & Stuart, G. L. (1994). Typologies of male batterers: Three subtypes and differences among them. Psychological Bulletin, 116, 476–497.

Hooley, J. M. (1985). Expressed emotion: A review of the critical literature. Clinical Psychology Review, 5, 119–139.

Hooley, J. M., & Teasdale, J. D. (1989). Predictors of relapse in unipolar depressives: Expressed emotion, marital distress, and perceived criticism. Journal of Abnormal Psychology, 98, 229–235.

Hornung, C. A., McCullough, B. C., & Sugimoto, T. (1981). Status relationships in marriage: Risk factors in spouse abuse. Journal of Marriage and the Family, 43, 675–692.

Hsu, L. K. G. (1990). Eating disorders. New York: Guilford Press.

Hudson, J., Pope, H., Jonas, J. M., & Yurgelin-Todd, D. (1983). Family history study of anorexia nervosa and bulimia. British Journal of Psychiatry, 142, 133–138.

Hudson, J. L., & Pope, H. G. (1990). Affective spectrum disorder: Does antidepressant response identify a family of disorders with a common pathophysiology? American Journal of Psychiatry, 147, 552–564.

Hunnicut, C. P., & Newman, I. A. (1993). Adolescent dieting practices and nutrition knowledge. Health Values, 17, 35–40.

Iacono, W. G., & Beiser, M. (1992). Are males more likely than females to develop schizophrenia? American Journal of Psychiatry, 149, 1070–1074.

Insel, T. R., Zahn, T., & Murphy, D. L. (1985). Obsessive-compulsive disorder: An anxiety disorder? In A. H. Tuma & J. D. Maser (Eds.), Anxiety and the anxiety disorders (pp. 577–589). Hillsdale, NJ: Erlbaum.

Institute of Medicine (1989). Prevention and treatment of alcohol problems: Research opportunities. Washington, DC: National Academy Press.

Jamison, K. R., & Akiskal, H. S. (1983). Medication compliance in patients with bipolar disorder. Psychiatric Clinics of North America, 6, 175–192.

Jasinski, J. L., Asdigian, N. L., & Kantor, G. K. (1997). Ethnic adaptations to occupational strain: Work-related stress, drinking, and wife assault among Anglo and Hispanic husbands. Journal of Interpersonal Violence, 12, 814–831.

Jenike, M. (1989). Obsessive-compulsive and related disorders. New England Journal of Medicine, 321, 539–541.

Jenike, M. A., Baer, L., Ballantine, H. T., Martuza, R. L., Tynes, S., Giriunas, I., Buttolph, M. L., & Cassem, N. H. (1991). Cingulotomy for refractory obsessive-compulsive disorder: A long-term follow-up of 33 patients. Archives of General Psychiatry, 48, 548–555.

Jones, J. C., & Barlow, D. H. (1990). The etiology of posttraumatic stress disorder. Clinical Psychology Review, 10, 299–328.

Kagan, J., & Snidman, N. (1991). Infant predictors of inhibited and uninhibited profiles. Psychological Science, 2, 40–44.

Kagan, J., Reznick, J. S., & Snidman, N. (1988). Biological bases of childhood shyness. Science, 240, 167–171.

Kane, J., Honigfeld, G., Singer, J., & Meltzer, H. Y. (1988). Clozapine for the treatment resistant schizophrenic. Archives of General Psychiatry, 45, 789–796.

Kane, J. M., & Marder, S. R. (1993). Psychopharmacologic treatment of schizophrenia. Schizophrenia Bulletin, 19, 287–302.

Kantor, G. K., Jasinski, J. L., & Aldarondo, E. (1994). Sociocultural status and incidence of marital violence in Hispanic families. Violence and Victims, 9, 207–222.

Karno, M., & Golding, J. M. (1991). Obsessive-compulsive disorder. In L. N. Robins & D. A. Regier (Eds.), Psychiatric disorders in America: The Epidemiologic Catchment Area study (pp. 204–219). New York: Free Press.

Kashani, J. H., Hoeper, E. W., Beck, N. C., & Corcoran, C. M. (1987). Personality, psychiatric disorders, and parental attitude among a community sample of adolescents. Journal of the American Academy of Child and Adolescent Psychiatry, 26, 879–885.

Keane, T. M., Fairbank, J. A., Caddell, J. M., & Zimering, R. T. (1989). Implosive (flooding) therapy reduces symptoms of PTSD in Vietnam combat veterans. Behavior Therapy, 20, 245–260.

Keane, T. M., Fairbank, J. A., Caddell, J. M., Zimering, R. T., & Bender, M. E. (1985). A behavioral approach to assessing and treating posttraumatic stress disorders in Vietnam veterans. In C. R. Figley (Ed.), Trauma and its wake: The assessment and treatment of posttraumatic stress disorders (pp. 257–294). New York: Brunner/Mazel.

Keller, M. B., Lavori, P. W., Coryell, W., Endicott, J., & Mueller, T. I. (1993). Bipolar I: A five-year prospective follow-up. Journal of Nervous and Mental Disease, 181, 238–245.

Kendler, K. S., Heath, A. C., Martin, N. G., & Eaves, L. J. (1987). Symptoms of anxiety and symptoms of depression: Same genes, different environments? Archives of General Psychiatry, 44, 451–457.

Kendler, K. S., Heath, A. C., Neale, M. C., Kessler, R. C., & Eaves, L. J. (1992). A population-based twin study of alcoholism in women. Journal of the American Medical Association, 268, 1877–1882.

Kendler, K. S., Maclean, C., Neale, M., Kessler, R., Heath, A., & Eaves, L. (1991). The genetic epidemiology of bulimia nervosa. American Journal of Psychiatry, 148, 1627–1637.

Kendler, K. S., Neale, M. C., Kessler, R. C., Heath, A. C., & Eaves, L. J. (1992). Major depression and generalized anxiety disorder: Same genes, (partly) different environments? Archives of General Psychiatry, 49, 716–722.

Kendler, K. S., Neale, M. C., Kessler, R. C., Heath, A. C., & Eaves, L. J. (1992). Generalized anxiety disorder in women: A population-based twin study. Archives of General Psychiatry, 49, 267–272.

Kessler, R. C., McGonagle, K. A., Zhao, S., Nelson, C. B., Hughes, M., Eshleman, S., Wittchen, H. U., & Kendler, K. S. (1994). Lifetime and 12-month prevalence of DSM-III-R psychiatric disorders in the United States. Archives of General Psychiatry, 51, 8–19.

Kilpatrick, D. G., Best, C. L., Veronen, L. J., Amick, A. E., Villeponteaux, L. A., & Ruff, G. A. (1985). Mental health correlates of criminal victimization: A random community survey. Journal of Consulting and Clinical Psychology, 53, 866–873.

Kilpatrick, D. G., Edmunds, C. N., & Seymour, A. K. (1992). Rape in America: A report to the nation. Arlington, VA: National Victim Center.

Klerman, G. L., Weissman, M. M., & Rounsaville, B. J., & Chevron, E. S. (1984). Interpersonal psychotherapy for depression. New York: Basic Books.

Kluft, R. P. (1991). Multiple personality disorder. In A. Tasman & W. Goldinger (Eds.), Review of psychiatry (Vol. 10). Washington, DC: American Psychiatric Press.

Koegel, R. L., Schriebman, L., O'Neill, R. E., & Burke, J. C. (1983). The personality and family interaction characteristics of parents of autistic children. Journal of Consulting and Clinical Psychology, 51, 683–692.

Koss, M. P. (1983). The scope of rape: Implications for the clinical treatment of victims. The Clinical Psychologist, 36, 88–91.

Koss, M. P., Gidycz, C. A., & Wisniewski, N. (1987). The scope of rape: Incidence and prevalence of sexual aggression and victimization in a national sample of higher education students. Journal of Consulting and Clinical Psychology, 55, 162–170.

Kulka, R. A., Schlenger, W. E., Fairbank, J. A., Hough, R. L., Jordan, B. K., Marmar, C. R., & Weiss, D. S. (1990). Trauma and the Vietnam War generation. New York: Brunner/Mazel.

Kushner, M. G., Sher, K. J., & Beitman, B. D. (1990). The relation between alcohol problems and the anxiety disorders. American Journal of Psychiatry, 147, 685–695.

Lanyon, R. I. (1986). Theory and treatment in child molestation. Journal of Consulting and Clinical Psychology, 54, 176–182.

Laws, D. R. (Ed.) (1989). Relapse prevention with sex offenders. New York: Guilford Press.

Leckman, J. F., & Chittenden, E. H. (1990). Gilles de la Tourette's syndrome and some forms of obsessive-compulsive disorder may share a common genetic diathesis. L'Encephale, 16, 321–323.

Leckman, J. F., Weissman, M. M., Merikangas, K. R., Pauls, D. L., & Prusoff, B. A. (1983). Panic disorder and major depression. Archives of General Psychiatry, 40, 1055–1060.

Lenane, M. C., Swedo, S. E., Rapoport, J. L., Leonard, H., Sceery, W., & Guroff, J. J. (1992). Rates of obsessive-compulsive disorder in first degree relatives of patients with trichotillomania: A research note. Journal of Child Psychology and Psychiatry, 33, 925–933.

Levin, A., & Hyler, S. (1986). DSM-III personality diagnosis in bulimia. Comprehensive Psychiatry, 27, 47.

Lewinsohn, P. M., Hops, H., Roberts, R. E., Seeley, J. R., & Andrews, J. A. (1993). Adolescent psychopathology: I. Prevalence and incidence of depression and other DSM-III-R disorders in high school students. Journal of Abnormal Psychology, 102, 133–144.

Liebowitz, M. R., Schneier, F., Campeas, R., Hollander, E., Hatterer, J., Fyer, A., Gorman, J., Papp, L., Davies, S., Gully, R., & Klein, D. F. (1992). Phenelzine vs. atenolol in social phobia: A placebo controlled comparison. Archives of General Psychiatry, 49, 290–300.

Linehan, M. M. (1993). Cognitive-behavioral treatment of borderline personality disorder. New York: Guilford Press.

Linehan, M. M., Armstrong, H. E., Suarez, A., Allmon, D., & Heard, H. L. (1991). Cognitive-behavioral treatment of chronically parasuicidal borderline patients. Archives of General Psychiatry, 48, 1060–1064.

Linehan, M. M., Heard, H. L., & Armstrong, H. E. (1993). Naturalistic follow-up of a behavioral treatment for chronically parasuicidal borderline patients. Archives of General Psychiatry, 50, 971–974.

Linehan, M. M., & Kehrer, C. A. (1993). Borderline personality disorder. In D. H. Barlow (Ed.), Clinical handbook of psychological disorders: A step-by-step treatment manual (2nd ed., pp. 396–441). New York: Guilford Press.

Linehan, M. M., Tutek, D. A., Heard, H. L., & Armstrong, H. E. (1994). Interpersonal outcome of cognitive behavioral treatment for chronically suicidal borderline patients. American Journal of Psychiatry, 151, 1771–1776.

Links, P. S., Steiner, M., Boiago, I., & Irwin, D. (1990). Lithium therapy for borderline patients: Preliminary findings. Journal of Personality Disorders, 4, 173–181.

304 • *References*

Links, P. S., Steiner, M., & Huxley, G. (1988). The occurrence of borderline personality disorder in families of borderline patients. Journal of Personality Disorders, 2, 14–20.

Lovaas, O. I. (1977). The autistic child: Language development through behavior modification. New York: Irvington.

Lovaas, O. I. (1987). Behavioral treatment and normal educational and intellectual functioning in young autistic children. Journal of Consulting and Clinical Psychology, 55, 3–9.

Lykken, D. T. (1957). A study of anxiety in the sociopathic personality. Journal of Abnormal and Social Psychology, 55, 6–10.

Magdol, L., Moffitt, T. E., Caspi, A., Newman, D. L., Fagan, J., & Silva, P. A. (1997). Gender differences in partner violence in a birth cohort of 21-year-olds: Bridging the gap between clinical and epidemiological approaches. Journal of Consulting and Clinical Psychology, 65, 68–78.

Maiuro, R. D., Cahn, T. S., Vitaliano, P. P., Wagner, B. C., & Zegree, J. B. (1988). Anger, hostility, and depression in domestically violent versus generally assaultive men and nonviolent control subjects. Journal of Consulting and Clinical Psychology, 56, 17–23.

Maletzky, B. M. (1991). Treating the sexual offender. Newbury Park, CA: Sage.

Margolin, G., & Burman, B. (1993). Wife abuse versus marital violence: Different terminologies, explanations, and solutions. Clinical Psychology Review, 13, 59–73.

Margolin, G., John, R. S., & Gleberman, L. (1988). Affective responses to conflictual discussions in violent and nonviolent couples. Journal of Consulting and Clinical Psychology, 56, 24–33.

Marks, I. M., Lelliott, P., Basoglu, M., Noshirvani, H., Monteiro, W., Cohen, D., & Kasvikis, Y. (1988). Clomipramine, self-exposure, and therapist-aided exposure for obsessive-compulsive rituals. British Journal of Psychiatry, 152, 522–534.

Marlatt, G. A., & Gordon, J. R. (Eds.) (1985). Relapse prevention: Maintenance strategies in the treatment of addictive behaviors. New York: Guilford Press.

Marlatt, G. A., Larimer, M. E., Baer, J. S., & Quigley, L. A. (1993). Harm reduction for alcohol problems: Moving beyond the controlled drinking controversy. Behavior Therapy, 24, 461–504.

Marshall, W. L. (1979). Satiation therapy: A procedure for reducing deviant sexual arousal. Journal of Applied Behavior Analysis, 12, 377–389.

Marshall, W. L., & Barbaree, H. E. (1988). The long-term evaluation of a behavioral treatment program for child molesters. Behaviour Research and Therapy, 26, 499–511.

Marshall, W. L., Barbaree, H. E., & Christophe, D. (1986). Sexual offenders against female children: Sexual preferences for age of victims and type of behaviour. Canadian Journal of Behavioural Science, 18, 424–439.

Marshall, W. L., Eccles, A., & Barbaree, H. E. (1991). The treatment of exhibitionists: A focus on sexual deviance versus cognitive and relationship features. Behaviour Research and Therapy, 29, 129–135.

Marshall, W. L., Hudson, S. M., & Ward, T. (1992). Sexual deviance. In P. H. Wilson (Ed.), Principles and practice of relapse prevention (pp. 235–254). New York: Guilford Press.

Masters, W. H., & Johnson, V. E. (1970). Human sexual inadequacy. Boston: Little, Brown.

Mattick, R. P., & Peters, L. (1988). Treatment of severe social phobia: Effects of guided exposure with and without cognitive restructuring. Journal of Consulting and Clinical Psychology, 56, 251–260.

Mattick, R. P., Peters, L., & Clarke, J. C. (1989). Exposure and cognitive restructuring for social phobia: A controlled study. Behavior Therapy, 20, 3–23.

Mavissakalian, M., Turner, S. M., & Michelson, L. (1985). Future directions in the assessment and treatment of obsessive-compulsive disorder. In M. Mavissakalian, S. M.Turner, & L. Michelson (Eds.), Psychological and pharmacological aspects of obsessive-compulsive disorder. New York: Plenum Press.

McAdoo, W. G., & DeMyer, M. K. (1978). Research related to family factors in autism. Journal of Pediatric Psychology, 2, 162–166.

McCahill, T. W., Meyer, L. C., & Fischman, A. W. (1979). The aftermath of rape. Lexington, MA: D.C. Heath.

McCall, C. (1984, December). The cruelest crime. Life, 35–52.

McCreery, J. M., & Walker, R. D. (1993). Alcohol problems. In D. L. Dunner (Ed.), Current psychiatric therapy (pp. 92–98). Philadelphia: W. B. Saunders.

McGuffin, P., & Katz, R. (1989). The genetics of depression and manic-depressive disorder. British Journal of Psychiatry, 155, 294–304.

McKay, J. R., Alterman, A. I., McLellan, T., Snider, E. C., & O'Brien, C. P. (1995). Effect of random versus nonrandom assignment in a comparison of inpatient and day hospital rehabilitation for male alcoholics. Journal of Consulting and Clinical Psychology, 63, 70–78.

McLeod, J. D., Kessler, R. C., & Landis, K. R. (1992). Speed of recovery from major depressive episodes in a community sample of married men and women. Journal of Abnormal Psychology, 101, 277–286.

Mellman, T. A., & Davis, G. C (1985). Combat-related flashbacks in posttraumatic stress disorder: Phenomenology and similarity to panic attacks. Journal of Clinical Psychiatry, 46, 379–382.

Miller, I. W., Keitner, G. I., Epstein, N. B., Bishop, D. S., & Ryan, C. E. (1991). Families of bipolar patients: Dysfunction, course of illness, and pilot treatment study. In Proceedings of the 22nd meeting of the Society for Psychotherapy Research, Pittsburgh, PA.

Miller, W. R., & Hester, R. K. (1986). Inpatient alcoholism treatment: Who benefits? American Psychologist, 41, 794–805.

Mitchell, J. E., & Pyle, R. L. (1988). The diagnosis and clinical characteristics of bulimia. In B. J. Blinder, B. F., Chaitin, & R. S. Goldstein (Eds.), The eating disorders: Medical and psychological bases of diagnosis and treatment (pp. 267–273). New York: PMA.

Monroe, S. M., Imhoff, D. F., Wise, B. D., & Harris, J. E. (1983). Prediction of psychological symptoms under high-risk psychosocial circumstances: Life events, social support, and symptom specificity. Journal of Abnormal Psychology, 92, 338–350.

Monti, P. M., Abrams, D. B., Kadden, R. M., & Cooney, N. L. (1989). Treating alcohol dependence: A coping skills training guide. New York: Guilford Press.

Moras, K., Di Nardo, P. A., Brown, T. A., & Barlow, D. H. (1995). Comorbidity, functional impairment, and depression among the DSM-III-R anxiety disorders. Unpublished manuscript.

Moreau, D., Mufson, L., Weissman, M. M., & Klerman, G. L. (1991). Interpersonal psychotherapy for adolescent depression: Description of modification and preliminary application. Journal of the American Academy of Child and Adolescent Psychiatry, 30, 642–651.

Morgenstern, H., & Glazer, W. M. (1993). Identifying risk factors for tardive dyskinesia among long-term outpatients maintained with neuroleptic medications: Results of the Yale tardive dyskinesia study. Archives of General Psychiatry, 50, 723–733.

Mrazek, F. J. (1984). Sexual abuse of children. In B. Lahey & A. E. Kazdin (Eds.), Advances in child clinical psychology (Vol. 6, pp. 199–215). New York: Plenum Press.

Muehlenhard, C. A., & Linton, M. A. (1987). Date rape and sexual aggression in dating situations: Incidence and risk factors. Journal of Counseling Psychology, 34, 186–196.

Mueser, K. T., Liberman, R. P., & Glynn, S. M. (1990). Psychosocial interventions in schizophrenia. In A. Kales, C. N. Stefanis, & J. A. Talbott (Eds.), Recent advances in schizophrenia (pp. 213–235). New York: Springer-Verlag.

Mufson, L., Moreau, D., Weissman, M. M., & Klerman, G. L. (1993). Interpersonal psychotherapy for depressed adolescents. New York: Guilford Press.

Mufson, L., Moreau, D., Weissman, M. M., Wickramaratne, P., Martin, J., & Samoilov, A. (1994). The modification of interpersonal psychotherapy with depressed adolescents (IPT-A): Phase I and II studies. Journal of the American Academy of Child and Adolescent Psychiatry, 33, 695–705.

Mukherjee, S., Sackeim, H. A., & Schnuur, D. B. (1994). Electroconvulsive therapy of acute manic episodes: A review. American Journal of Psychiatry, 151, 169–176.

Müller-Oerlinghausen, B., Muser-Causemann, B., & Volk, J. (1992). Suicides and parasuicides in a high risk patient group on and off lithium long-term medication. Journal or Affective Disorders, 25, 261–269.

Murphy, C. M., & O'Leary, K. D. (1989). Psychological aggression predicts physical aggression in early marriage. Journal of Consulting and Clinical Psychology, 57, 579–582.

Nathan, P. E. (1993). Alcoholism: Psychopathology, etiology, and treatment. In P. B. Sutker & H. E. Adams (Eds.), Comprehensive handbook of psychopathology (pp. 451–476). New York: Plenum Press.

Neidig, P. H., & Friedman, D. H. (1984). Spouse abuse: A treatment program for couples. Champaign, IL: Research Press.

Newlin, D. B., & Thomson, J. B. (1990). Alcohol challenge with sons of alcoholics: A critical review and analysis. Psychological Bulletin, 108, 383–402.

Noyes, R., & Kletti, R. (1977). Depersonalization in response to life-threatening danger. Comprehensive Psychiatry, 18, 375–384.

Noyes, R., Clarkson, C., Crowe, R. R., Yates, W. R., & McChesney, C. M. (1987). A family study of generalized anxiety disorder. American Journal of Psychiatry, 144, 1019–1024.

Noyes, R., Garvey, M. J., Cook, B., & Suelzer, M. (1991). Controlled discontinuation of benzodiazepine treatment for patients with panic disorder. American Journal of Psychiatry, 148, 517–523.

Noyes, R., Woodman, C., Garvey, M. J., Cook, B. L., Suelzer, M., Clancy, J., &

Anderson, D. J. (1992). Generalized anxiety disorder vs. panic disorder: Distinguishing characteristics and patterns of comorbidity. Journal of Nervous and Mental Disease, 180, 369–379.

Nurnberger, J. I., Berrettini, W., Tamarkin, L., Hamovit, J., Norton, J., & Gershon, E. S. (1988). Supersensitivity to melatonin suppression by light in young people at risk for affective disorder: A preliminary report. Neuropsychopharmacology, 1, 217–223.

O'Farrell, T. J., & Murphy, C. M. (1995). Marital violence before and after alcoholism treatment. Journal of Consulting and Clinical Psychology, 63, 256–262.

O'Hanlon, J. F., Haak, J. W., Blaauw, G. J., & Riemersma, J. B. J. (1982). Diazepam impairs lateral position control in highway driving. Science, 27, 79–81.

O'Leary, K. D. (1988). Physical aggression between spouses: A social learning theory perspective. In V. B. Van Hasselt, R. L. Morrison, A. S. Bellack, & M. Hersen (Eds.), Handbook of family violence (pp. 31–55). New York: Plenum Press.

O'Leary, K. D., Barling, J., Arias, I., Rosenbaum, A., Malone, J., & Tyree, A. (1989). Prevalence and stability of physical aggression between spouses: A longitudinal analysis. Journal of Consulting and Clinical Psychology, 57, 263–268.

O'Leary, K. D., Malone, J., & Tyree, A. (1994). Physical aggression in early marriage: Prerelationship and relationship effects. Journal of Consulting and Clinical Psychology, 62, 594–602.

O'Leary, K. D., Heyman, R. E., & Jongsma, A. E. (1998). The couples psychotherapy treatment planner. New York: John Wiley & Sons.

Ogata, S. N., Silk, K. R., Goodrich, S., Lohr, N. E., Westen, D., & Hill, E. M. (1990). Childhood sexual and physical abuse in adult patients with borderline personality disorder. American Journal of Psychiatry, 147, 1008–1013.

Öst, L. G. (1987). Age of onset in different phobias. Journal of Abnormal Psychology, 96, 223–229.

Pahl, J. J., Swayze, V. M., & Andreasen, N. C. (1990). Diagnostic advances in anatomical and functional brain imaging in schizophrenia. In A. Kales, C. N. Stefanis, & J. A. Talbott (Eds.), Recent advances in schizophrenia (pp. 163–189). New York: Springer-Verlag

Paris, J., Brown, R., & Nowlis, D. (1987). Long term follow-up of borderline patients in a general hospital. Comprehensive Psychiatry, 28, 530–535.

Parkinson, L., & Rachman, S. (1981a). The nature of intrusive thoughts. Advances in Behaviour Research and Therapy, 3, 101–110.

Parkinson, L., & Rachman, S. (1981b). Intrusive thoughts: The effects of an uncontrived stress. Advances in Behaviour Research and Therapy, 3, 111–118.

Pato, M. T., Zohar-Kadouch, R., Zohar, J., & Murphy, D. L. (1988). Return of symptoms after discontinuation of clomipramine in patients with obsessive-compulsive disorder. American Journal of Psychiatry, 145, 1521–1525.

Patton, G. C., Johnson-Sabine, E., Wood, K., Mann, A. H., & Wakeling, A. (1990). Abnormal eating attitudes in London school girls—a prospective epidemiological study: Outcome at twelve month follow-up. Psychological Medicine, 20, 383–394.

Pauls, D. L. (1989). The inheritance and expression of obsessive-compulsive behaviors. Proceedings of the American Psychiatric Association, San Francisco, CA.

Pauls, D. L., Towbin, K. E., Leckman, J. F., Zahner, G. E., & Cohen, D. J. (1986).

Gilles de la Tourette's syndrome and obsessive-compulsive disorder. Archives of General Psychiatry, 43, 1180–1182.

Phelps, L., & Grabowski, J. (1992). Fetal alcohol syndrome: Diagnostic features and psychoeducational risk factors. School Psychology Quarterly, 7, 112–128.

Pithers, W. D., & Cumming, G. F. (1989). Can relapse be prevented?: Initial outcome data from the Vermont Program for sexual aggressors. In D. R. Laws (Ed.), Relapse prevention with sex offenders (pp. 313–325). New York: Guilford Press.

Piven, J., Arndt, S., Bailey, J., Havercamp, S., Andreasen, N. C., & Palmer, P. (1995). An MRI study of brain size in autism. American Journal of Psychiatry, 152, 1145–1149.

Pope, H. G., & Hudson, J. I. (1984). New hope for binge-eaters: Advances in the understanding and treatment of bulimia. New York: Harper & Row.

Post, R. M. (1992). Transduction of psychosocial stress into the neurobiology of recurrent affective disorder. American Journal of Psychiatry, 149, 999–1010.

Potkin, S. G., Albers, L. J., & Richmond, G. (1993). Schizophrenia: An overview of pharmacological treatment. In D. L. Dunner (Ed.), Current psychiatric therapy (pp. 142–154). Philadelphia: W. B. Saunders.

Prien, R. F., & Gelenberg, A. J. (1989). Alternatives to lithium for preventive treatment of bipolar disorder. American Journal of Psychiatry, 146, 840–848.

Prien, R. F., Kupfer, D. J., Mansky, P. A., Small, J. G., Tuason, V. B., Voss, C. B., & Johnson, W. E. (1984). Drug therapy in the prevention of recurrences in unipolar and bipolar affective disorders: Report of the NIMH collaborative study group comparing lithium carbonate, imipramine, and a lithium carbonate-imipramine combination. Archives of General Psychiatry, 41, 1096–1104.

Prien, R. F., & Potter, W. Z. (1993). Maintenance treatment for mood disorders. In D. L. Dunner (Ed.), Current psychiatric therapy. Philadelphia: W. B. Saunders.

Putnam, F. W. (1989). Diagnosis and treatment of multiple personality disorder. New York: Guilford Press.

Putnam, F. W. (1991). Dissociative phenomena. In A. Tasman & W. Goldinger (Eds.), Review of psychiatry (Vol. 10). Washington, DC: American Psychiatric Press.

Putnam, F. W., Guroff, J. J., Silberman, E. K., Barban, L., & Post, R. M. (1986). The clinical phenomenology of multiple personality disorder: Review of 100 recent cases. Journal of Clinical Psychiatry, 47, 285–293.

Pyle, R. L., Neuman, P. A., Halvorson, P. A., & Mitchell, J. E. (1991). An ongoing cross-sectional study of the prevalence of eating disorders in freshman college students. International Journal of Eating Disorders, 10, 667–677.

Rainey, J. M., Manov, G., Aleem, A., & Toth, A. (1990). Relationships between post-traumatic stress disorder and panic disorder: Concurrent psychiatric illness, effects of lactate infusions, and erythrocyte lactate production. In J. C. Ballenger (Ed.), Clinical aspects of panic disorder (pp. 47–54). New York: John Wiley & Sons.

Rasmussen, S. A., & Eisen, J. L. (1989). Clinical features and phenomenology of obsessive-compulsive disorder. Psychiatric Annals, 19, 67–73.

Rasmussen, S. A., & Eisen, J. L. (1990). Epidemiology of obsessive-compulsive disorder. Journal of Clinical Psychiatry, 51, 10–14.

Rasmussen, S. A., & Tsuang, M. T. (1986). Clinical characteristics and family history in DSM-III obsessive-compulsive disorder. American Journal of Psychiatry, 143, 317–382.

Ray, W. A., Gurwitz, J., Decker, M. D., & Kennedy, D. L. (1992). Medications and the safety of the older driver: Is there a basis for concern? Human Factors, 34, 33–47.

Renshaw, D. C. (1988). Profile of 2,376 patients treated at Loyola Sex Clinic between 1972 and 1987. Sexual and Marital Therapy, 3, 111–117.

Resick, P. A. (1983). The rape reaction: Research findings and implications for intervention. The Behavior Therapist, 6, 129–132.

Resick, P. A., & Schnicke, M. K. (1993). Cognitive processing therapy for rape victims. Thousand Oaks, CA: Sage Publications.

Rickels, K., Schweizer, E., Case, W. G., & Greenblatt, D. J. (1990). Long-term therapeutic use of benzodiazepines: I. Effects of abrupt discontinuation. Archives of General Psychiatry, 47, 899–907.

Riggs, D. S., & Foa, E. B. (1993). Obsessive-compulsive disorder. In D. H. Barlow (Ed.), Clinical handbook of psychological disorders: A step-by-step treatment manual (2nd ed., pp. 189–239). New York: Guilford Press.

Rosen, J. C., & Leitenberg, H. (1985). Exposure plus response prevention treatment of bulimia. In D. M. Garner & P. E. Garfinkel (Eds.), Handbook of psychotherapy for anorexia nervosa and bulimia (pp. 193–209). New York: Guilford Press.

Rosenbaum, A., & O'Leary, K. D. (1981). Marital violence: Characteristics of abusive couples. Journal of Consulting and Clinical Psychology, 49, 63–71.

Rosowsky, E., & Gurian, B. (1992). Impact of borderline personality disorder in late life on systems of care. Hospital and Community Psychiatry, 43, 386–389.

Ross, C. A. (1989). Multiple personality disorder: Diagnosis, clinical features, and treatment. New York: John Wiley & Sons.

Ross, C. A., Miller, S. D., Reagor, P., Bjornson, L., Fraser, G. A., & Anderson, G. (1990). Structured interview data on 102 cases of multiple personality disorder from four centers. American Journal of Psychiatry, 147, 596–601.

Ross, S. M. (1996). Risk of physical abuse to children of spouse-abusing parents. Child Abuse and Neglect, 20, 589–598.

Rothbaum, B. O., Shaw, L., Morris, R., & Ninan, P. T. (1993). Prevalence of trichotillomania in a college freshman population. Journal of Clinical Psychiatry, 54, 72.

Rounsaville, B. J., Sholomskas, D., & Prusoff, B. A. (1988). Chronic mood disorders in depressed outpatients: Diagnosis and response to pharmacotherapy. Journal of Affective Disorders, 2, 72–88.

Russell, D. E. H. (1984). Sexual exploitation: Rape, child sexual abuse, and workplace harassment. Beverly Hills, CA: Sage Publications.

Sakheim, D. K., & Devine, S. E. (Eds.) (1992). Out of darkness: Exploring Satanism and ritual abuse. New York: Lexington Books.

Salkovskis, P. M. (1985). Obsessional-compulsive problems: A cognitive-behavioral analysis. Behaviour Research and Therapy, 23, 571–583.

Salkovskis, P. M. (1989). Cognitive-behavioral factors and the persistence of intrusive thoughts in obsessional problems. Behaviour Research and Therapy, 27, 677–682.

Salkovskis, P. M., & Campbell, P. (1994). Thought suppression induces intrusion in naturally occurring negative intrusive thoughts. Behaviour Research and Therapy, 32, 1–8.

Salkovskis, P. M., & Westbrook, D. (1989). Behaviour therapy and obsessional ruminations: Can failure be turned into success? Behaviour Research and Therapy, 27, 149–160.

Salzman, C. (1991). Pharmacologic treatment of the anxious elderly patient. In C. Salzman & B. D. Lebowitz (Eds.), Anxiety disorders in the elderly (pp. 149–173). New York: Free Press.

Sanderson, W. C., & Barlow, D. H. (1990). A description of patients diagnosed with DSM-III-R generalized anxiety disorder. Journal of Nervous and Mental Disease, 178, 588–591.

Sanderson, W. C., Beck, A. T., & Beck, J. (1990). Syndrome comorbidity in patients with major depression or dysthymia: Prevalence and temporal relationships. American Journal of Psychiatry, 147, 1025–1028.

Schenk, L., & Bear, D. (1981). Multiple personality and related dissociative phenomena in patients with temporal lobe epilepsy. American Journal of Psychiatry, 138, 1311–1316.

Schiavi, R. C. (1990). Chronic alcoholism and male sexual dysfunction. Journal of Sex and Marital Therapy, 16, 23–33.

Schlundt, D. G., & Johnson, W. G. (1990). Eating disorders: Assessment and treatment. Boston: Allyn & Bacon.

Schneier, F. R., Johnson, J., Hornig, C. D., Liebowitz, M. R., & Weissman, M. M. (1992). Social phobia: Comorbidity and morbidity in an epidemiologic sample. Archives of General Psychiatry, 49, 282–288.

Schover, L. R., & Jensen, S. B. (1988). Sexuality and chronic illness: A comprehensive approach. New York: Guilford Press.

Schuckit, M. A. (1994). Low level response to alcohol as a predictor of future alcoholism. American Journal of Psychiatry, 151, 184–189.

Schwalberg, M. D., Barlow, D. H., Alger, S. A., & Howard, L. J. (1992). Comparison of bulimics, obese binge eaters, social phobics, and individuals with panic disorder on comorbidity across DSM-III-R anxiety disorders. Journal of Abnormal Psychology, 101, 675–681.

Schweizer, E., & Rickels, K. (1991). Pharmacotherapy of generalized anxiety disorder. In R. M. Rapee & D. H. Barlow (Eds.), Chronic anxiety: Generalized anxiety disorder and mixed anxiety-depression (pp. 172–186). New York: Guilford Press.

Segraves, K. B., & Segraves, R. T. (1991). Multiple-phase sexual dysfunction. Journal of Sex Education and Therapy, 17, 153–156.

Segraves, R. T. (1988). Drugs and desire. In S. R. Lieblum & R. C. Rosen (Eds.), Sexual desire disorders (pp. 313–347). New York: Guilford Press.

Seligman, M. E. P. (1975). Helplessness: On depression, development, and death. San Francisco: W.H. Freeman.

Shea, M. T., Elkin, I., Imber, S. D., Sotsky, S. M., Watkins, J. T., Collins, J. F., Pilkonis, P.A., Beckham, E., Glass, D. R., Dolan, R. T., & Parloff, M. B. (1992). Course of depressive symptoms over follow-up: Findings from the National Institute of Mental Health Treatment of Depression Collaborative Research Program. Archives of General Psychiatry, 49, 782–787.

Show, M. (1985). Practical problems of lithium maintenance treatment. Advances in Biochemical Psychopharmacology, 40, 131–138.

Silverstone, T. (1985). Dopamine in manic depressive illness: A pharmacological synthesis. Journal of Affective Disorders, 8, 225–231.

Skinner, B. F. (1971). Beyond freedom and dignity. New York: Knopf.

Smalley, S. L. (1991). Genetic influences in autism. Psychiatric Clinics of North America, 14, 125–139.

Sobell, M. B., & Sobell, L. C. (1978). Behavioral treatment of alcohol problems. New York: Plenum Press.

Soloff, P. H., George, A., Nathan, R. S., Schulz, P. M., Cornelius, J. R., Herring, J., & Perel, J. M. (1989). Amitriptyline versus haloperidol in borderlines: Final outcomes and predictors of response. Journal of Clinical Psychopharmacology, 9, 238–246.

Southwick, S. M., Krystal, J. H., Johnson, D. R., & Charney, D. S. (1992). Neurobiology of posttraumatic stress disorder. In A. Tasman & M. B. Riba (Eds.), Review of psychiatry (Vol. 11, pp. 347–367). Washington, DC: American Psychiatric Press.

Spector, I. P., & Carey, M. P. (1990). Incidence and prevalence of the sexual dysfunctions: A critical review of the literature. Archives of Sexual Behavior, 19, 389–408.

Spiegel, D., & Cardena, E. (1991). Disintegrated experience: The dissociative disorders revisited. Journal of Abnormal Psychology, 100, 366–378.

Stanley, M. A., Borden, J. W., Bell, G. E., & Wagner, A. L. (1994). Nonclinical hair pulling: Phenomenology and related psychopathology. Journal of Anxiety Disorders, 8, 119–130.

Stanley, M. A., Borden, J. W., Mouton, S. G., & Breckenridge, J. K. (1995). Nonclinical hair-pulling: Affective correlates and comparison with clinical samples. Behaviour Research and Therapy, 33, 179–186.

Steffenburg, S., Gillberg, C., Hellgren, L., Andersson, L., Gillberg, I. C., Jakobsson, G., & Bohman, M. (1989). A twin study of autism in Denmark, Finland, Iceland, Norway, and Sweden. Journal of Child Psychology and Psychiatry, 30, 405–416.

Stevenson, J., & Meares, R. (1992). An outcome study of psychotherapy for patients with borderline personality disorder. American Journal of Psychiatry, 149, 358–362.

Stone, M. H. (1986). Borderline personality disorder. In A. M. Cooper, A. J. Frances, & M. H. Sacks (Eds.), The personality disorders and neuroses (pp. 203–217). New York: Basic Books.

Stone, M. H. (1989). The course of borderline personality disorder. In A. Tasman, R. E. Hales, & A. J. Frances (Eds.), Annual review of psychiatry (Vol. 8, pp. 103–122). Washington, DC: American Psychiatric Press.

Stone, M. H., Stone, D. K., & Hurt, S. W. (1987). Natural history of borderline patients treated by intensive hospitalization. Psychiatric Clinics of North America, 10, 185–206.

Straus, M. A., & Gelles, R. J. (1986). Societal change and change in family violence from 1975-1985 as revealed by two national surveys. Journal of Marriage and the Family, 48, 465–479.

Straus, M. A., & Gelles, R. J. (1990). Physical violence in American families. New Brunswick, NJ: Transaction.

Straus, M. A., Gelles, R., & Steinmetz, S. (1980). Behind closed doors: Violence in the American family. New York: Doubleday.

Striegel-Moore, R. H., Silberstein, L. R., & Rodin, J. (1986). Toward an understanding of risk factors for bulimia. American Psychologist, 41, 246–263.

Strober, M., & Humphrey, L. L. (1987). Familial contributions to the etiology and course of anorexia nervosa and bulimia. Journal of Consulting and Clinical Psychology, 55, 654–659.

Strober, M., Freeman, R., & Rigali, J. (1990). The pharmacotherapy of depressive illness in adolescence: I. An open trial of imipramine. Psychopharmacological Bulletin, 26, 80–84.

Strube, M. J. (1988). The decision to leave an abusive relationship: Empirical evidence and theoretical issues. Psychological Bulletin, 104, 236–250.

Swedo, S. E., Leonard, H. L., Rapoport, J. L., Lenane, M. C., Goldberger, E. L., & Cheslow, C. L. (1989). A double-blind comparison of clomipramine and desipramine in the treatment of trichotillomania (hair pulling). New England Journal of Medicine, 321, 497–501.

Sweeney, P. D., Anderson, K., & Bailey, S. (1986). Attributional style in depression: A meta-analytic review. Journal of Personality and Social Psychology, 50, 974–991.

Taylor, M. A., & Abrams, R. (1981). Early and late onset bipolar illness. Archives of General Psychiatry, 38, 58–61.

Telch, C. F., & Agras, W. S. (1993). The effects of a very low calorie diet on binge eating. Behavior Therapy, 24, 177–193.

Tellegen, A., Lykken, D. T., Bouchard, T. J., Wilcox, K. J., Segal, N. L., & Rich, S. (1988). Personality similarity in twins reared apart and together. Journal of Personality and Social Psychology, 54, 1031–1039.

Tinbergen, N., & Tinbergen, E. A. (1972). Early childhood autism: A ethological approach. Berlin: Paul Parey.

Tollefson, G. D. (1993). Major depression. In D. L. Dunner (Ed.), Current psychiatric therapy. Philadelphia: W. B. Saunders.

Torgersen, S. (1983). Genetic factors in anxiety disorders. Archives of General Psychiatry, 40, 1085–1089.

Torgersen, S. (1990). Genetics of anxiety and its clinical implications. In G. D. Burrows, M. Roth, & R. Noyes (Eds.), Handbook of anxiety (Vol. 3): The neurobiology of anxiety. Amsterdam: Elsevier.

True, W. R., Rice, J., Eisen, S. A., Heath, A. C., Goldberg, J., Lyons, M. J., & Nowak, J. (1993). A twin study of genetic and environmental contributions to liability for posttraumatic stress symptoms. Archives of General Psychiatry, 50, 257–264.

Tsai, L. Y., & Ghaziuddin, M. (1992). Biomedical research in autism. In D. E. Berkell (Ed.), Autism: Identification, education, and treatment (pp. 53–74). Hillsdale, NJ: Lawrence Erlbaum.

Tucker, L., Bauer, S. F., Wagner, S., Harlam, D., & Sher, I. (1987). Long-term hospital treatment of borderline patients: A descriptive outcome study. American Journal of Psychiatry, 144, 1443–1448.

Tyrer, P. (1989). Classification of neurosis. New York: Wiley.

Tyrer, P., & Owen, R. (1984). Anxiety in primary care: Is short-term drug treatment appropriate? Journal of Psychiatric Research, 18, 73–79.

U.S. Department of Health and Human Services (1990). Seventh annual report to the U.S. Congress on alcohol and health from the Secretary of Health and Human Services. Rockville, MD: National Institute on Alcohol Abuse and Alcoholism.

Van Hasselt, V. B., Morrison, R. L., & Bellack, A. S. (1985). Alcohol use in wife abusers and their spouses. Addictive Behaviors, 10, 127–135.

Ventura, J., Nuechterlein, K. H., Lukoff, D., & Hardesty, J. P. (1989). A prospective study of stressful life events and schizophrenia relapse. Journal of Abnormal Psychology, 98, 407–411.

Veronen, L. J., & Kilpatrick, D. G. (1983). Stress management for rape victims. In D. Meichenbaum & M. E. Jaremko (Eds.), Stress reduction and prevention (pp. 341–374). New York: Plenum Press.

Vivian, D., & Heyman, R. E. (1996). Is there a place for conjoint treatment of couple violence? In Session: Psychotherapy in Practice, 2, 25–48.

Volkmar, F. R., Szatmari, P., & Sparrow, S. S. (1993). Sex differences in pervasive developmental disorders. Journal of Autism and Developmental Disorders, 23, 579–591.

Wagner, A. W., & Linehan, M. M. (1994). Relationship between childhood sexual abuse and topography of parasuicide among women with borderline personality disorder. Journal of Personality Disorders, 8, 1–9.

Walker, L. E. A. (1989). Psychology and violence against women. American Psychologist, 44, 695–702.

Walsh, B. T. (1991). Fluoxetine treatment of bulimia nervosa. Journal of Psychosomatic Research, 35, 471–475.

Walsh, B. T., Hadigan, C. M., Devlin, M. J., Gladis, M., & Roose, S. P. (1991). Long-term outcome of antidepressant treatment of bulimia nervosa. Archives of General Psychiatry, 148, 1206–1212.

Waterhouse, L., Wing, L., & Fein, D. (1989). Re-evaluating the syndrome of autism in light of empirical research. In G. Dawson (Ed.), Autism: Nature, diagnosis, and treatment (pp. 263–281). New York: Guilford Press.

Wehr, T. A., Goodwin, F. K., Wirz-Justice, A., Breitmeier, J., & Craig, C. (1982). Forty-eight-hour sleep-wake cycles in manic-depressive illness: Naturalistic observations and sleep-deprivation experiments. Archives of General Psychiatry, 39, 559–565.

Weiden, P. J., Dixon, L., Frances, A., Appelbaum, P., Haas, G., & Rapkin, B. (1991). In C. A. Tamminga & S. C. Schultz (Eds.), Advances in neuropsychiatry and pharmacology, Vol 1: Schizophrenia research (pp. 285–296). New York: Raven Press.

Weissman, M. M., Bruce, M. L., Leaf, P. J., Florio, L. P., & Holzer, C. (1991). Affective disorders. In L. N. Robins & D. A. Regier (Eds.), Psychiatric disorders of America: The epidemiologic catchment area study (pp. 53–80). New York: Free Press.

Widiger, T. A., & Frances, A. J. (1989). Epidemiology, diagnosis, and comorbidity of borderline personality disorder. In A. Tasman, R. E. Hales, & A. J. Frances (Eds.), Annual review of psychiatry (Vol. 8). Washington, DC: American Psychiatric Press.

Widiger, T. A., & Rogers, J. H. (1989). Prevalence and comorbidity of personality disorders. Psychiatry Annual, 19, 132.

Widiger, T. A., & Weissman, M. M. (1991). Epidemiology of borderline personality disorder. Hospital and Community Psychiatry, 42, 1015–1021.

Wincze, J. P., & Carey, M. P. (1991). Sexual dysfunction: A guide for assessment and treatment. New York: Guilford Press.

Winokur, G., Coryell, W., Endicott, J., & Akiskal, H. (1993). Further distinctions between manic-depressive illness (bipolar disorder) and primary depressive disorder (unipolar depression). American Journal of Psychiatry, 150, 1176–1181.

Winokur, G., Pfohl, B., & Tsuang, M. (1987). A 40-year follow-up of hebephrenic-catatonic schizophrenia. In N. Miller & G. Cohen (Eds.), Schizophrenia and aging (pp. 52–60). New York: Guilford Press.

Wiseman, C. V., Gray, J. J., Mosimann, J. E., & Ahrens, A. H. (1992). Cultural expectations of thinness in women: An update. International Journal of Eating Disorders, 11, 85–89.

Witherington, R. (1988). Suction device therapy in the management of erectile impotence. Urologic Clinics of North America, 15, 123–128.

Wittchen, H. -U., Zhao, S., Kessler, R. C., & Eaves, W. W. (1994). DSM-III-R generalized anxiety disorder in the National Comorbidity Survey. Archives of General Psychiatry, 51, 355–364.

Zanarini, M., Gunderson, J., Marino, M., Schwartz, E., & Frankenburg, F. (1988). DSM-III disorders in the families of borderline outpatients. Journal of Personality Disorders, 2, 292–302.

Zubin, J., & Spring, B. J. (1977). Vulnerability: A new view of schizophrenia. Journal of Abnormal Psychology, 86, 103–126.

Zubin, J., Steinhauer, S. R., & Condray, R. (1992). Vulnerability to relapse in schizophrenia. British Journal of Psychiatry, 161, 13–18.

Name Index

Lewisohn, P.M., 139
Liberman, R.P., 247
Liebowitz, M.R., 16, 42, 43, 49, 51
Liepman, M.J., 188
Linehan, M.M., 228, 229, 234, 235
Links, P.S., 227, 234
Linton, M.A., 67
Lord, S., 227
Loseke, D.R., 101
Lovaas, O.I., 263
Lukoff, D., 241
Lykken, D.T., 213

Mackenzie, T.B., 277, 278
Magdol, L., 102, 103
Maiuro, R.D., 102
Maletzky, B.M., 204, 205
Malone, J., 102
Mann, A.H., 166
Mannuzza, S., 42
Manov, G., 58
Marder, S.R., 247
Margolin, G., 102, 103
Marin, D.B., 234
Marino, M., 227
Markman, H.J., 103
Marks, I.M., 86, 87
Marlatt, G.A., 215, 222, 276
Marshall, W.L., 196, 204
Marstellar, F.A., 140
Marten, P.A., 6
Martin, N.G., 132
Masters, W.H., 182, 188, 189
Mattick, R., 50, 87
Mavissakalian, M., 76, 197
McAdoo, W.G., 254
McCahill, T.W., 68
McCall, C., 203
McCarthy, P.R., 86
McChesney, C.M., 6
McCreery, J.M., 220
McCullough, B.C., 102
McEvoy, M.A., 67
McGuffin, P., 149
McKay, J.R., 222
McLellan, T., 222

McLeod, D.R., 6, 16
McLeod, J.D., 135
Meares, R., 234
Meisler, A.W., 183
Mellman, T.A., 58
Meltzer, H.Y., 241
Mercier, M.A., 158
Merikangas, K.R., 132
Metalsky, G.I., 133
Meyer, L.C., 68
Mezzacappa, E., 228
Michelson, L., 76
Miller, I.W., 158
Miller, N.S., 180
Miller, W.R., 222
Mitchell, J.E., 172, 277, 278
Mittelman, M., 203
Monck, E.M., 242
Monroe, S.M., 135
Monti, P.M., 222
Moras, K., 34, 49, 76
Moreau, D., 135, 142
Morgenstern, H., 243
Morin, C., 196
Morris, R., 278
Morrison, R.L., 102
Mosimann, J.E., 165
Mouton, S.G., 271
Mrazek, F.J., 203
Muehlenhard, C.A., 67
Mueller, T.I., 157
Mueser, K.T., 247
Mufson, L., 135, 142
Mukherjee, S., 158
Muller-Oerlinghausen, B., 157
Murdock, T.B., 68-69
Murphy, C.M., 102, 221
Murphy, D.L., 86
Murrell, S.A., 15
Muser-Causemann, B., 157

Nasrallah, A., 156
Nathan, P.E., 221-222
Neale, M.C., 6, 24, 132, 148, 212
Neidig, P.H., 96
Newlin, D.B., 212

Subject Index

AA. *See* Alcoholics Anonymous
Abnormal electrical activity in brain, dissociative symptoms and, 125
Abnormal psychology
  adolescent social phobia, 37–52
  alcohol dependence, 207–223
  autistic disorder, 249–264
  bipolar disorder, 143–159
  borderline personality disorder, 224–235
  bulimia nervosa, 160–174
  dissociative identity disorder, 105–126
  domestic violence, 89–104
  generalized anxiety disorder, 1–18
  major depression, 127–142
  male erectile disorder, 175–190
  multiple personality disorder, 105–126
  obsessive-compulsive disorder, 71–88
  panic disorder with agoraphobia, 19–36
  paraphilia, 191–206
  pedophilia, 191–206
  physical abuse of adult, 89–104
  posttraumatic stress disorder, 53–70
  schizophrenia, 236–248
  sexual disorder, 191–206
  sexual dysfunction, 175–190
  trichotillomania, 265–280
Abuse
  alcohol, versus alcohol dependence, 211

domestic violence and. *See* Domestic violence
  physical. *See* Physical abuse
  sexual, dissociative identity disorder and, 113
Active phase of schizophrenia, 246
ADHD. *See* Attention deficit hyperactivity disorder
Adhering to certain rules and sequences, obsessive-compulsive disorder and, 76
Adolescent social phobia, 37–52
  case formulation using integrative model, 41–44
  clinical history, 39–40
  course of treatment and treatment outcome, 44–49
  DSM-IV diagnosis, 40–41
  treatment goals and planning, 43–44
Adult, physical abuse of. *See* Domestic violence
Aggressiveness, psychological, domestic violence and, 102
Agoraphobia, panic disorder with. *See* Panic disorder with agoraphobia
Alarm
  false. *See* False alarm
  learned, panic disorder with agoraphobia and, 26
Alcohol, panic disorder with agoraphobia and, 22, 23–24, 34

324

Panic disorder with agoraphobia (PDA) (continued)
clinical history, 21–23
course of treatment and treatment outcome, 29–33
DSM-IV diagnosis, 23–24
treatment goals and planning, 26–29
Papaverine, male erectile disorder and, 188
Paranoid type of schizophrenia, 239
Paraphilia, 191–206
Parasuicidal acts, borderline personality disorder and, 229, 234
Pathological gambling, trichotillomania and, 269
PDA. *See* Panic disorder with agoraphobia
Pedophilia, 191–206
case formulation using integrative model, 194–197
clinical history, 192–193
course of treatment and treatment outcome, 197–203
definition of, 193–194
DSM-IV diagnosis, 193–194
treatment goals and planning, 196–197
Penile implants, male erectile disorder and, 188
Penile vacuum device, male erectile disorder and, 189
Perphenazine (Trilafon), schizophrenia and, 243, 244, 247
Persecutory delusions, bipolar disorder, 153
Personality disorder, borderline. *See* Borderline personality disorder
Pervasive developmental disorders, 252
Phenelzine, adolescent social phobia and, 51
Phobia, adolescent social. *See* Adolescent social phobia
Physical abuse
of adult. *See* Domestic violence
dissociative identity disorder and, 113
Placebo
depression and, 140
generalized anxiety disorder and, 16, 17

Pleasuring, nongenital, male erectile disorder and, 183
Posttraumatic stress disorder (PTSD), 53–70
alcohol dependence and, 215, 219–220
bulimia nervosa and, 170
case formulation using integrative model, 57–60
clinical history, 54–55
course of treatment and treatment outcome, 61–67
dissociative identity disorder and, 108, 115, 125
DSM-IV diagnosis, 56–57
treatment goals and planning, 60
Prediction testing, panic disorder with agoraphobia and, 32
Premature ejaculation, 188
Pressured speech, bipolar disorder and, 153
Probability overestimation
generalized anxiety disorder and, 9, 12
panic disorder with agoraphobia and, 30
Prodromal phase of schizophrenia, 246
Prozac. *See* Fluoxetine
Psychoactive drugs, autistic disorder and, 263
Psychological aggressiveness, domestic violence and, 102
Psychology, abnormal. *See* Abnormal psychology
Psychology Service of the Veterans Administration Medical Center, 207
Psychotherapy, interpersonal, depression and, 135–138, 140–141
PTSD. *See* Posttraumatic stress disorder
Pyromania, trichotillomania and, 269

Rape, posttraumatic stress disorder and, 53–70
Reinforcement, austistic disorder and, 256
Relapse, alcohol dependence and, 215
Relaxation
applied, panic disorder with agoraphobia and, 35
cue-controlled, 83

Stable attributional style, depression and, 133
Stress, generalized anxiety disorder and, 3
Stress disorder, posttraumatic. *See* Posttraumatic stress disorder
Stress inoculation training (SIT), posttraumatic stress disorder and, 68–69
Substance use disorders, domestic violence and, 102

Tangentiality, schizophrenia and, 239
Tantrums, austistic disorder and, 256
Tardive dyskinesia, 243
Target weight, bulimia nervosa and, 170
Temporal lobe epilepsy, dissociative symptoms and, 125
Tension, worry and, 7
Testing, prediction, panic disorder with agoraphobia and, 32
Testosterone, male erectile disorder and, 180
Therapist-assisted format of situational exposure, panic disorder with agoraphobia and, 27, 28
Thinking
 catastrophic. *See* Catastrophic thinking
 dysfunctional, depression and, 134
Thoughts, automatic, adolescent social phobia and, 45
Three-systems analysis, adolescent social phobia and, 45
Time-out, domestic violence and, 96
Tolerance, alcohol dependence and, 211, 214
Tourette's syndrome, obsessive-compulsive disorder and, 86
Trance, hypnotic, dissociative identity disorder and, 114–115
Tranquilizers
 borderline personality disorder and, 234
 minor, generalized anxiety disorder and, 16
Trichotillomania, 265–280
 case formulation using integrative model, 269–271
 clinical history, 265–268

course of treatment and treatment outcome, 272–277
DSM-IV diagnosis, 269
treatment goals and planning, 271
Tricyclic antidepressants
 adolescent social phobia and, 51
 bipolar disorder and, 152
 borderline personality disorder and, 234
 bulimia nervosa and, 173
 depression and, 140, 141
 male erectile disorder and, 180
Trilafon. *See* Perphenazine
Twins. *See* Dizygotic twins; Monozygotic twins

Uncontrollable worry, generalized anxiety disorder and, 1–18
Undifferentiated type of schizophrenia, 239–240
Unexpected panic attacks, panic disorder with agoraphobia and, 24–25

Vacuum device therapy, male erectile disorder and, 189
Valium. *See* Diazepam
Valproates, bipolar disorder and, 158
VAMC. *See* Veterans Administration Medical Center
V-Code conditions, domestic violence and, 94–95
Veterans Administration Medical Center (VAMC), 207, 211, 214, 215, 219
Violence, domestic. *See* Domestic violence
Vitamin B6, autistic disorder and, 263
Voyeurism, 193
Vulnerability
 biological, adolescent social phobia and, 41
 panic disorder with agoraphobia and, 25

Weight, target, bulimia nervosa and, 170
Withdrawal, alcohol dependence and, 211, 214
Withdrawal delirium, alcohol dependence and, 214

334 · Subject Index

Worry
    autonomic arousal and, 7
    generalized anxiety disorder and, 1–18
    tension and, 7
Worry behavior prevention, generalized
    anxiety disorder and, 8–9, 12–13,
    14
Worry control
    daily record of, 11, 13

    generalized anxiety disorder and,
    8–9
Worry exposure, generalized anxiety dis-
    order and, 8–9

Xanax. *See* Alprazolam